...*and forgive them their debts*

Lending, Foreclosure and Redemption

From Bronze Age Finance to the Jubilee Year

by

Michael Hudson

ISLET-Verlag
Dresden 2018

Michael Hudson

… and forgive them their debts: Lending, Foreclosure and Redemption from Bronze Age Finance to the Jubilee Year

© 2018
© Michael Hudson
© ISLET-Verlag Dresden

Schriftsatz: Cornelia Wunsch
Cover design: Miguel Guerra, 7robots.com
ISBN 13: 9783981826029

To Carl Lamberg-Karlovsky
my mentor at Harvard's
Peabody Museum
since 1984

Acknowledgements

For over thirty years I have discussed the ideas in this book with Carl Lamberg-Karlovsky at Harvard's Peabody Museum. Together, we organized the series of five ISLET-ISCANEE colloquia that form the basis for the economic history of the Bronze Age Near East that forms the core of this book. Cornelia Wunsch has constantly drawn my attention to the relevant literature and helped me avoid anachronistic interpretations. She has played the major editorial role as publisher of this book and the ISLET colloquia.

Steven Garfinkle has focused my attention on the role of entrepreneurial trade and credit in its symbiosis with the palatial economy. Marc Van De Mieroop has given steady advice and perspective over the decades, and Baruch Levine was an early guide and co-editor regarding Judaic economic history. All these readers have been helpful in alerting me to the relevant bibliography.

David Graeber has been helpful in emphasizing the anthropological setting for how debt has evolved and the diverse ways of treating debtors who are unable to pay. Charles Goodhart has helped emphasize the relevance of the history of debt jubilees to today's financial crisis. Dirk Bezemer also has co-written articles with me drawing this linkage and applying it to modern economic theory and statistics.

Lynn Yost has provided editorial help with early drafts of this book, and Ashley Dayman has proofread the manuscript and found many improvements.

My web manager, Karl Fitzgerald, has hosted ongoing radio discussions on my interpretation of ancient Near Eastern history. Early versions of some of this work also have appeared on Naked Capitalism and Counterpunch.

Throughout the decades it has taken me to complete this book, my wife Grace has been a constant supporter and provided many types of help. I could not have completed it without her love and encouragement.

TABLE OF CONTENTS

The Rise and Fall of Jubilee Debt Cancellations and Clean Slates

The idea of annulling debts nowadays seems so unthinkable that most economists and many theologians doubt whether the Jubilee Year could have been applied in practice, and indeed on a regular basis. A widespread impression is that the Mosaic debt jubilee was a utopian ideal. However, Assyriologists have traced it to a long tradition of Near Eastern proclamations. That tradition is documented as soon as written inscriptions have been found – in Sumer, starting in the mid-third millennium BC.

Instead of causing economic crises, these debt jubilees preserved stability in nearly all Near Eastern societies. Economic polarization, bondage and collapse occurred when such clean slates stopped being proclaimed.

What were Debt Jubilees?

Debt jubilees occurred on a regular basis in the ancient Near East from 2500 BC in Sumer to 1600 BC in Babylonia and its neighbors, and then in Assyria in the first millennium BC. It was normal for new rulers to proclaim these edicts upon taking the throne, in the aftermath of war, or upon the building or renovating a temple. Judaism took the practice out of the hands of kings and placed it at the center of Mosaic Law.[1]

By Babylonian times these debt amnesties contained the three elements that Judaism later adopted in its Jubilee Year of Leviticus 25. The first element was to cancel agrarian debts owed by the citizenry at large. Mercantile debts among businessmen were left in place.

A second element of these debt amnesties was to liberate bondservants – the debtor's wife, daughters or sons who had been pledged to creditors. They were allowed to return freely to the debtor's home. Slave girls that had been pledged for debt also were returned to the debtors' households. Royal debt jubilees thus freed society from debt bondage, but did not liberate chattel slaves.

A third element of these debt jubilees (subsequently adopted into Mosaic law) was to return the land or crop rights that debtors had pledged to creditors. This enabled families to resume their self-support on the land and pay taxes, serve in the military, and provide corvée labor on public works.

Commercial "silver" debts among traders and other entrepreneurs were not subject to these debt jubilees. Rulers recognized that productive business loans provide resources for the borrower to pay back with interest, in contrast to consumer debt. This was the contrast that medieval Schoolmen later would draw between interest and usury.

---

[1] For more detailed discussion see *Debt and Economic Renewal in the Ancient Near East*, Hudson and Van De Mieroop, eds., 2002.

Most non-business debts were owed to the palace or its temples for taxes, rents and fees, along with beer to the public ale houses. Rulers initially were cancelling debts owed mainly to themselves and their officials. This was not a utopian act, but was quite practical from the vantage point of restoring economic and military stability. Recognizing that a backlog of debts had accrued that could not be paid out of current production, rulers gave priority to preserving an economy in which citizens could provide for their basic needs on their own land while paying taxes, performing their corvée labor duties and serving in the army.

Most personal debts were not the result of actual loans, but were accruals of unpaid agrarian fees, taxes and kindred obligations to royal collectors or temple officials. Rulers were aware that these debts tended to build up beyond the system's ability to pay. That is why they cancelled "barley" debts in times of crop failure, and typically in the aftermath of war. Even in the normal course of economic life, social balance required writing off debt arrears to the palace, temples or other creditors so as to maintain a free population of families able to provide for their own basic needs.

As interest-bearing credit became privatized throughout the Near Eastern economies, personal debts owed to local headmen, merchants and creditors also were cancelled. Failure to write down agrarian debts would have enabled officials and, in due course, private creditors, merchants or local headmen to keep debtors in bondage and their land's crop surplus for themselves. Crops paid to creditors were not available to be paid to the palace or other civic authorities as taxes, while labor obliged to work off debts to creditors was not available to provide corvée service or serve in the army. Creditor claims thus set the wealthiest and most ambitious families on a collision course with the palace, along the lines that later occurred in classical Greece and Rome. In addition to preserving economic solvency for the population, rulers thus found debt cancellation to be a way to prevent a financial oligarchy from emerging to rival the policy aims of kings.

Cancelling debts owed to wealthy local headmen limited their ability to amass power for themselves. Private creditors therefore sought to evade these debt jubilees. But surviving legal records show that royal proclamations were, indeed, enforced. Through Hammurabi's dynasty these "*andurārum* acts" became increasingly detailed so as to close loopholes and prevent ploys that creditors tried to use to gain control of labor, land and its crop surplus.

Social purpose of Debt Jubilees

The common policy denominator spanning Bronze Age Mesopotamia and the Byzantine Empire in the 9th and 10th centuries was the conflict between rulers acting to restore land to smallholders so as to maintain royal tax revenue and a land-tenured military force, and powerful families seeking to deny its usufruct to the palace. Rulers sought to check the economic power of wealthy creditors, military leaders or local administrators from concentrating land in their own hands and taking the crop surplus for themselves at the expense of the tax collector.

By clearing the slate of personal agrarian debts that had built up during the crop year, these royal proclamations preserved a land-tenured citizenry free from bondage. The effect was to restore balance and sustain economic growth by preventing widespread insolvency.

Babylonian scribes were taught the basic mathematical principle of compound interest, whereby the volume of debt increases exponentially, much faster than the rural economy's ability to pay.[2] That is the basic dynamic of debt: to accrue and intrude increasingly into the economy, absorbing the surplus and transferring land and even the personal liberty of debtors to creditors.

Debt jubilees were designed to make such losses of liberty only temporary. The Mosaic injunction (Leviticus 25), "Proclaim liberty throughout the land," is inscribed on America's Liberty Bell. That is a translation of Hebrew *deror*, the debt Jubilee, cognate to Akkadian *andurārum*. The liberty in question originally was from debt peonage.

To insist that all debts must be paid, regardless of whether this may bankrupt debtors and strip away their land and means of livelihood, stands at odds with the many centuries of Near Eastern clean slates. Their success stands at odds with the assumption that creditor interests should take priority over those of the indebted economy at large.

In sum, the economic aim of debt jubilees was to restore solvency to the population as a whole. Many royal proclamations also freed businesses from various taxes and tariff duties, but the main objective was political and ideological. It was to create a fair and equitable society.

This ethic was not egalitarian as such. It merely aimed to provide citizens with the basic minimum standard needed to be self-sustaining. Wealth accumulation was permitted and even applauded, as long as it did not disrupt the normal functioning of society at large.

How well did Debt Jubilees succeed?

Creditors sought to avoid these laws, but Babylonian legal records show that the debt cancellations of Hammurabi's dynasty and those of his neighbors were enforced. These proclamations enabled society to avert military defeat by preserving a land-tenured citizenry as the source of military fighters, corvée labor and the tax base. The Bronze Age Near East thus avoided the economic polarization between creditors and debtors that ended up imposing bondage on most of classical antiquity.

In the 7th-century BC, Greek populist leaders called tyrants (at that time with no original pejorative meaning) paved the way for the economic takeoff of Sparta, Corinth and Aegina by cancelling debts and redistributing the lands monopolized by their cities' aristocracies. In Athens, Solon's banning of debt bondage and clearing the land of debts in 594 BC avoided the land redistributions to the rich and powerful that much of the population had feared.

---

[2] For a repertory of how writers have shown the impossibility of compound interest being paid, starting with Babylonian scribal training texts in mathematics, see Hudson 2014, Chapter 4: "The All-Devouring 'Magic of Compound Interest.'"

So popular was the demand for a debt jubilee that the 4ᵗʰ-century BC Greek general Aeneas Tacticus advised attackers of cities to draw the population over to their side by cancelling debts, and for defenders to hold onto the loyalty of their population by making the same offer. Cities that refrained from cancelling debts were conquered, or fell into widespread bondage, slavery and serfdom.

That ultimately is what happened in Rome. Its historians describe how disenfranchising indebted citizens led to the hiring of mercenaries (often debtors expropriated from their family homestead) as wealthy creditors concentrated land in their own hands, along with law-making power and control of state religion. What, instead, threatened the security of widely-held property and ultimately led to collapse was the financial oligarchy's ending of the power of rulers to restore liberty from bondage and to save debtors from being deprived of land tenure on a widespread scale.

Plutarch's lives of Sparta's kings Agis and Cleomenes shows a problem of cancelling mortgage debts other than those owed by owner-occupants. A land speculator had bought property on credit, and hoped to have his debts annulled along with those of smallholders who were supposed to be the nominal beneficiaries. One can well imagine cancelling today's mortgage debts of investors who have bought their real estate on credit, with the loan to be paid out of the rent. Instead of the bankers or the tax collector receiving the rental value, the landlords would be by far the greatest windfall gainers. Plutarch's narrative shows that if all property debts were cancelled, it would be necessary to adjust the tax system to collect the appropriate rental value of such properties in the tax base, in order to prevent a windfall gain. Otherwise, absentee owners would gain instead of the actual occupants and users of the economy's debt financed real estate.

Why did debt Jubilees fall into disuse?

Throughout history a constant political dynamic has been maneuvering by creditors to overthrow royal power capable of enforcing debt amnesties and reversing foreclosures on homes and subsistence land. The creditors' objective is to replace the customary right of citizens to self-support by its opposite principle: the right of creditors to foreclose on the property and means of livelihood pledged as collateral (or to buy it at distress prices), and to make these transfers irreversible. The smallholders' security of property is replaced by the sanctity of debt instead of its periodic cancellation.

Archaic restorations of order ended when the forfeiture or forced sale of self-support land no longer could be reversed. When creditors and absentee landlords gained the upper political hand, reducing the economic status for much of the population to one of debt dependency and serfdom, classical antiquity's oligarchies used their economic gains, military power or bureaucratic position to buy up the land of smallholders, as well as public land such as Rome's *ager publicus*.[3]

---

[3] Toynbee 1965 as well as Livy's *History of Rome*, emphasize the monopolization of Rome's land, above all by creditors and political insiders disenfranchising smallholders.

Violence played a major political role, almost entirely by creditors. Having overthrown kings and populist tyrants, oligarchies accused advocates of debtor interests of being "tyrants" (in Greece) or seeking kingship (as the Gracchi brothers and Julius Caesar were accused of in Rome). Sparta's kings Agis and Cleomenes were killed for trying to cancel debts and reversing the monopolization of land in the 3rd century BC. Neighboring oligarchies called on Rome to overthrow Sparta's reformer-kings.[4]

The creditor-sponsored counter-revolution against democracy led to economic polarization, fiscal crisis, and ultimately to being conquered – first the Western Roman Empire and then Byzantium. Livy, Plutarch and other Roman historians blamed Rome's decline on creditors using fraud, force and political assassination to impoverish and disenfranchise the population. Barbarians had always stood at the gates, but only as societies weakened internally were their invasions successful.

Today's mainstream political and economic theories deny a positive role for government policy to constrain the large-scale concentration of wealth. Attempting to explain the history of inequality since the Stone Age, for instance, Stanford historian Walter Scheidel's 2017 book *The Great Leveler* downplays the ability of State policy to reduce such inequality substantially without natural disasters wiping out wealth at the top. He recognizes that the inherent tendency of history is for the wealthy to win out and make society increasingly unequal. This argument also has been made by Thomas Piketty and based largely on the inheritance of great fortunes (the same argument made by his countryman Saint-Simon two centuries earlier). But the only "solutions" to inequality that Scheidel finds at work are the four "great levelers": warfare, violent revolution, lethal pandemics or state collapse. He does not acknowledge progressive tax policy, limitations on inherited wealth, debt writeoffs or a replacement of debt with equity as means of preventing or reversing the concentration of wealth in the absence of an external crisis.

The Book of Revelation forecast these four plagues as punishment for the greed and inequity into which the Roman Empire was falling. By Late Roman times there seemed no alternative to the Dark Age that was descending. Recovery of a more equitable past seemed politically hopeless, and so was idealized as occurring only by divine intervention at the end of history. Yet for thousands of years, economic polarization was reversed by cancelling debts and restoring land tenure to smallholders who cultivated the land, fought in the army, paid taxes and/or performed corvée labor duties. That also would be Byzantine policy to avoid polarization from the 7th through 10th centuries, echoing Babylonia's royal proclamation of clean slates.

Within Judaism, rabbinical orthodoxy attributed to Hillel developed the prosbul clause by which debtors waived their right to have their debts cancelled in the Jubilee Year. Hillel claimed that if the Jubilee Year were maintained, creditors would not lend to needy debtors – as if most debts were the result of loans, not arrears to Roman tax collectors and other unpaid bills. Opposing this pro-creditor argument, Jesus announced in his inaugural sermon that he had come to proclaim the Jubilee Year of the Lord cited by Isaiah, whose scroll he unrolled. His congregation is reported to have reacted with fury. (Luke 4 tells the story). Like other populist leaders of his day, Jesus was accused of seeking kingship to enforce his program on creditors.

---

[4] Plutarch's *Lives of the Noble Greeks and Romans* tells these stories in dramatic form.

Subsequent Christianity gave the ideal of a debt amnesty an otherworldly eschatological meaning as debt cancellation became politically impossible under the Roman Empire's military enforcement of creditor privileges. Falling into debt subjected Greeks and Romans to bondage without much hope of recovering their liberty. They no longer could look forward to the prospect of debt amnesties such as had annulled personal debts in Sumer, Babylonia and their neighboring realms, liberating citizens who had fallen into bondage or pledged and lost their land tenure rights to foreclosing creditors.

The result was destructive. The only debts that Emperor Hadrian annulled were Rome's tax records, which he burned in 119 AD – tax debts owed to the palace, not debts to the creditor oligarchy that had gained control of Rome's land.

A rising proportion of Greeks and Romans lost their liberty irreversibly. The great political cry throughout antiquity was for debt cancellation and land redistribution. But it was achieved in such classical times only rarely, as when Greece's 7th-century BC tyrants overthrew their cities' aristocracies who had monopolized the land and were subjecting the citizenry to debt dependency. The word "tyrant" later became a term of invective, as if liberating Greek populations from bondage to a narrow hereditary ethnic aristocracy was not a precondition for establishing democracy and economic freedom.

A study of the long sweep of history reveals a universal principle to be at work: The burden of debt tends to expand in an agrarian society to the point where it exceeds the ability of debtors to pay. That has been the major cause of economic polarization from antiquity to modern times. The basic principle that should guide economic policy is recognition that debts which can't be paid, won't be. The great political question is, how won't they be paid?

There are two ways not to pay debts. Our economic mainstream still believes that all debts must be paid, leaving them on the books to continue accruing interest and fees – and to let creditors foreclose when they do not receive the scheduled interest and amortization payment.

This is what the U.S. President Obama did after the 2008 crisis. Homeowners, credit-card customers and other debtors had to start paying down the debts they had run up. About 10 million families lost their homes to foreclosure. Leaving the debt overhead in place meant stifling and polarizing the economy by transferring property from debtors to creditors.

Today's legal system is based on the Roman Empire's legal philosophy upholding the sanctity of debt, not its cancellation. Instead of protecting debtors from losing their property and status, the main concern is with saving creditors from loss, as if this is a prerequisite for economic stability and growth. Moral blame is placed on debtors, as if their arrears are a personal choice rather than stemming from economic strains that compel them to run into debt simply to survive.

Something has to give when debts cannot be paid on a widespread basis. The volume of debt tends to increase exponentially, to the point where it causes a crisis. If debts are not written down, they will expand and become a lever for creditors to pry away land and income from the indebted economy at large. That is why debt cancellations to save rural economies from insolvency were deemed sacred from Sumer and Babylonia through the Bible.

Archaic Economies versus Modern Preconceptions

Our epoch is strangely selective when it comes to distinguishing between what is plausibly historical and believable in the Bible, and what seems merely mythic or utopian. Fundamentalist Christians show their faith that God created the earth in six days (on Sunday, October 23, 4004 BC according to Archbishop James Ussher in 1650) by building museums with dioramas showing humans cavorting alongside dinosaurs. While deeming this literal reading of Genesis to be historical, they ignore the Biblical narrative describing the centuries-long struggle between debtors and creditors. The economic laws of Moses and the Prophets, which Jesus announced his intention to revive and fulfill, are brushed aside as anachronistic artifacts, not the moral center of the Old and New Testaments, the Jewish and Christian bibles. The Jubilee Year (Leviticus 25) is the "good news" that Jesus – in his first reported sermon (Luke 4) – announced that he had come to proclaim.

Today the idea of annulling debts seems so unthinkable that not only economists but also many theologians doubt whether the Jubilee Year could have been applied regularly in practice. The widespread impression is that this Mosaic Law was a product of utopian idealism. But Assyriologists have traced it to a long tradition of royal debt cancellations from Sumer in the third millennium BC and Babylonia (2000–1600 BC) down through first-millennium Assyria. This book summarizes this long Near Eastern tradition and how it provided the model for the Jubilee Year.

Hammurabi's Babylonian laws became instantly famous when they were discovered in 1901 and translated the next year. Less familiar is the fact that nearly each member of his dynasty inaugurated his rule by proclaiming a debt amnesty – *andurārum*, the source of Hebrew cognate *deror*, the Jubilee Year, which has the same root as its Babylonian model. Personal agrarian debts were cancelled, although commercial "silver" debts were left intact. Bondservants pledged to creditors were returned to the debtor's family. And land or crop rights pledged to creditors or sold under distress conditions were returned to their customary holders.

These rules are so far at odds with the creditor-oriented ideology of our times that the instinctive response is to deny that they could have worked. For starters, why would creditors be willing lend if they thought that a debt annulment or Jubilee Year was coming? Wouldn't the economy be disrupted when credit dried up?

This criticism is anachronistic, because most agrarian debts did not stem from actual loans. They mounted up as unpaid bills, starting with fees and taxes owed to the palace. Early economies operated on credit, not cash on the barrelhead. Much like modern drinkers running up a bar tab, Babylonians ran up debts to alewives. Their bills were put on the tab, to be paid on the threshing floor at harvest time.[1] It was out of these crop payments that pub keepers (literally public agents) paid what they owed to the palace or temple for their consignments of beer. Other personal debts were owed out of the harvest to palace collectors for irrigation water, seeds and other inputs needed during the time gap from planting to harvesting. Palaces and

---

[1] See below, Ch. 17, for Ammisaduqa's 1646 BC edict, §17 regarding debts to tavernesses.

temples or their officials were the main early creditors, advancing agricultural inputs and various consumer goods.[2]

When harvests failed as a result of drought, flood or pests, there was not enough crop surplus to pay agrarian debts. In such cases rulers cancelled debts owed above all to themselves and their officials, and increasingly to private creditors as well. The palace had little interest in seeing these creditors force debtors into bondage. Rulers needed a free population to field an army and provide corvée labor to build city walls and temples and dig irrigation ditches.

This principle of keeping debts in line with the ability to pay and forgiving them under extenuating circumstances also governed commercial shipping loans. From Hammurabi's laws down to those of Rome, such mercantile debts were annulled in cases of shipwreck or piracy, and for overland caravans that were robbed.

Another modern objection to the practicality of debt cancellations concerns property rights. If land is periodically returned to its customary family holders, how can it be bought and sold? The answer is that self-support land (unlike townhouses) was not supposed to be sold as a market commodity. Security of land tenure was part of the quid pro quo obliging holders to serve in the military and perform corvée labor.[3] If wealthy creditors were permitted to "join house to house and lay field to field … until there is no more room and you alone are left in the land" (Isaiah 5.8) while reducing debtors to bondage, who would be left to build infrastructure and fight to defend against the ever-present aggressors?

These public needs took priority over the acquisitive ambitions of creditors. Cancelling debts did not disrupt economic activity, nor did it violate the idea of good economic order. By saving debtors from falling into servitude to a financial oligarchy, such amnesties preserved the liberty of citizens and their subsistence land rights. These acts were a precondition for maintaining economic stability. Indeed, proclaiming amnesty to restore the body politic – like periodically returning exiles from cities of refuge – was common to Native American as well as Biblical practice. The logic seems universal.

It was customary for Near Eastern rulers to proclaim amar-gi or *mīšarum* upon taking the throne for their first full year, and also on the occasions when droughts or floods prevented crop debts from being paid. Cancelling debts and restoring land rights reasserted royal authority over creditors engaging in usury to obtain the labor of

---

[2] See Wunsch 2002: 249: "Sources from private archives reveal several reasons why people got into debt." Citing fourteen types of debt for the Neo-Babylonian period (7th to 5th century BC), Wunsch finds that the most common recorded loans were "issued to small farmers, mainly consumption loans in the wake of crop failures and with regard to agricultural advances of seed grain and draft animals that had to be repaid in kind. Another typical reason for running into debt was to pay dues and taxes, including military obligations that were linked to certain holdings, and fees for access to irrigation and maintenance of the infrastructure. When the harvest was not sufficient to enable these obligations to be paid on time, debts mounted up." What are not found is borrowing to pay dowries, such as plague modern India's rural economy.

[3] As late as Rome landholdings of each size bore an obligation to serve and outfit oneself in a specific military rank, from infantry to cavalry and charioteers. See Steinkeller and Hudson, eds., 2015.

debtors at the expense of the palace. The practice goes back to Sumerian amar-gi attested by Lagash's ruler Enmetena c. 2400 BC. Down to nearly 1600 BC in Babylonia, the texts of Clean Slate *mīšarum* proclamations grew increasingly detailed to prevent creditors from developing loopholes. Cancellations of payment arrears and other debts to the palace, temples and their collectors or local creditors are found throughout the ancient Near East, in the Assyrian trade colonies in what is now Turkey, to first-millennium Assyria and the Jewish lands.

As credit became more widely privatized, usury became the major lever to pry away land and crop rights, and to reduce labor to irreversible bondage. The process culminated with classical antiquity's oligarchies replacing "divine kingship" with creditor-oriented rules. To resist widespread bondage and expropriation of debtors, Judaism placed debt cancellation at the core of Mosaic Law.

***

My own professional training is as an economist. During the 1960s and 1970s I wrote articles and books warning that Third World debts could not be paid – or those of the United States for that matter.[4] I came to this conclusion working as Chase Manhattan's balance-of-payments analyst in the mid-1960s. It was apparent that the U.S. and other governments could pay their debts only by borrowing from foreign creditors– adding the interest charges onto the debt, so that the amount owed grew at an exponential rate. This was "the magic of compound interest." Over time it makes any economy's overall volume of debts unpayably high.

In the late 1970s I wrote a series of papers for the United Nations Institute for Training and Development (UNITAR) warning that Third World economies could not pay their foreign debts and that a break was imminent. It came in 1982 when Mexico announced it could not pay, triggering the Latin American "debt bomb," leading to the Brady Plan to write down debts. The capstone of the UNITAR project was a 1980 meeting in Mexico hosted by its former president, Luis Echeverria, who had helped draft the text for the New International Economic Order (NIEO).[5] An angry fight broke out over my insistence that Latin American debtors would soon have to default.

The pro-creditor U.S. rapporteur for the meeting gave a travesty of my position in his summation. When I stood up and announced that I was pulling out my colleagues in response to this censorship, I was followed out of the hall by Russian and Third World delegates. In the aftermath, Italian banks financially backing the UNITAR project said that they would withdraw funding if there was any suggestion that sovereign debts could not be paid. The idea was deemed unthinkable – or so creditor lobbyists wanted the world to believe. But most banks knew quite well that global lending would end in default.

[4] Hudson 1968; 1969; 1972; 1992.
[5] I described this in Hudson 1981.

This experience drove home to me how controversial the idea of debt writedowns was. I set about compiling a history of how societies through the ages had felt obliged to write down their debts, and the political tensions this involved.

It took me about a year to sketch the history of debt back to classical Greece and Rome. Livy, Diodorus and Plutarch described how Roman creditors waged a century-long Social War (133–29 BC) turning democracy into oligarchy. But among modern historians, Arnold Toynbee is almost alone in emphasizing the role of debt in concentrating Roman wealth and property ownership.

By the time Roman creditors won, the Pharisee Rabbi Hillel had innovated the *prosbul* clause in debt contracts, whereby debtors waived their right to have their debts annulled in the Jubilee Year. This is the kind of stratagem that today's banks use in the "small print" of their contracts obliging users to waive their rights to the courts and instead submit to arbitration by bank-friendly referees in case of dispute over credit cards, bank loans or general bank malfeasance. Creditors had tried to use similar clauses already in the Old Babylonian era, but these were deemed illegal under more pro-debtor royal law.

In researching the historical background of the Jubilee Year, I found occasional references to debt cancellations going back to Sumer in the third millennium BC. The material was widely scattered through the literature, because no history of Near Eastern economic institutions and enterprise had been written.[6] Most history depicts our civilization as starting in Greece and Rome, not in the preceding thousands of years when the techniques of commercial enterprise, finance and accounting were developed. So I began to search through the journal literature and relatively few books on Sumer and Babylonia. "Debt" rarely appeared in the indexes. It was buried in the discussion of other topics.[7]

Not being able to read cuneiform, I was obliged to rely on translations – and was struck by how radically the versions in each language differed when it came to the terms used for royal proclamations. The American Noah Kramer translated the Sumerian amar-gi in texts of the third-millennium Lagash ruler Urukagina as a "tax reduction." In 1980 he even urged incoming President Ronald Reagan to emulate this policy, as if Urukagina were a proto-Republican.[8] The British Assyriologist Wilfred Lambert explained to me that *andurārum* meant "free trade" – typical of English policy since it abolished its Corn Laws in 1846. Looking at the Assyrian trade, Mogens Larsen of Denmark agreed with this reading.[9] The German

---

[6] The absence of an economic history of the Near Eastern genesis of Western civilization's economic enterprise has now been rectified by Landes, Mokyr and Baumol, eds. 2010, which includes my overview of "Entrepreneurs: From the Near Eastern Takeoff to the Roman Collapse" (pp. 8–39).

[7] That continues to be the case today. The massive four-volume 2,966-page compendium on *Civilizations of the Ancient Near East* (Jack Sasson *et alia* 1995) contains only six references to debts and loans.

Fritz Kraus saw the royal edicts of Hammurabi's dynasty as what they certainly were: debt cancellations. But I found the most enlightening reading to be that of the French Assyriologist Dominique Charpin: "restoration of order."

All these translators knew that the basic root of Sumerian amar-gi is "mother" (ama), as in "mother condition." This was an idealized original state of economic balance with no personal or agrarian debt arrears or debt bondage (but with slavery for captured prisoners and others, to be sure).[10]

Even before reading Charpin's books and articles, it was obvious that what was needed to understand the meaning of royal inscriptions was more than just linguistics. It was necessary to reconstruct the overall worldview and indeed, social cosmology at work. In 1984, after three years of research, I showed my findings to my friend Alex Marshack, an Ice Age archaeologist associated with Harvard's Peabody Museum, the university's anthropology department. He passed on my summary to its director, Carl Lamberg-Karlovsky, who invited me up for a weekend to discuss it. The upshot was an invitation to become a Research Fellow at Peabody in Babylonian economic archaeology. For the next decade we discussed the Bronze Age economy and structures out of which interest-bearing debt is first documented.

I presented my first academic paper on the ancient Near East in 1990, tracing how interest was developed in Mesopotamia, most likely initially to finance foreign trade, and how Syrian and Levantine traders brought the practice to the Mediterranean lands only around the 8th century BC.[11] In Greece and Rome, however, charging interest was not accompanied by debt cancellations. Charging interest was brought from the Near East and transplanted in a new context of chieftains and clan leaders who used interest-bearing usury to reduce populations to a state of dependency, creating oligarchies that soon were overthrown from Sparta to Corinth, until Solon's debt reforms in Athens in 594 BC. Classical antiquity's "takeoff" thus adopted Near Eastern economic practices in an increasingly oligarchic context. Tension between creditors and debtors led to ongoing political and economic turmoil.

Widespread misinterpretation of Neolithic and Bronze Age society

My long view meant that interest-bearing debt did not evolve "anthropologically" out of tribal practices of the early Greeks, Romans or other Europeans, as was claimed by Mauss in *The Gift* (1925). The Near Eastern Bronze Age was the formative era of Western civilization's economic institutions. But there is still a tendency to isolate Near Eastern development from that of classical antiquity.

Market-oriented financial historians have woven origin myths about allegedly primitive individuals lending cows in return for some of their calves as a bonus, or

---

[8] Kramer 1981.
[9] See below, Chapter 14.
[10] See below, Chapters 16 and 18. Charpin's readings were published after the others, starting in 1986.
[11] Hudson 1992.

loans of new tools for a share of the added output they produce. These anachronistic fables depict our Stone Age ancestors as following modern individualistic logic. Thorstein Veblen poked fun already a century ago at such descriptions based on a "simple scheme of economic life ... to throw into the foreground, in a highly unreal perspective, those features which lend themselves to interpretation in terms of the normalised competitive system."[12] According to such presumptions, the temples and palaces of Sumer and Babylonia (and by extension, modern public institutions) could not play a productive role, but were only a burdensome overhead.

Such armchair preconceptions are based on how modern castaways on a desert island would organize life. If these individuals found themselves stranded back in the Bronze Age, they probably would have done to Mesopotamia what neoliberals have done to post-Soviet countries and the Eurozone. Privatizers, bankers and other grandees would lord it over a dependent labor force, leading to emigration such as the past decade has seen from Latvia, Ukraine and Greece (about 20 percent of working-age adults in each case). It was to avoid such flight that ancient rulers sought to maintain their populations intact with basic means of self-support, free from creditor claims and willing to fight for their communities and to provide corvée labor to build up their infrastructure.

These early societies were not egalitarian. Wealth was concentrated at the top of the social pyramid, largely via temples and palaces acting ostensibly on behalf of the citizenry. But the more one looks at archaic societies, the clearer it becomes that there is no single "natural" way to organize them. That perception has led Assyriologists and Near Eastern archaeologists to avoid much interaction with the economics discipline, both the individualistic school and "temple state" or Oriental Despotism ideologues. And economists for their part likewise shy away from discussing the ancient Near East, because its institutions are so at odds with modern theories and assumptions about how economies are supposed to work.

To explain how debt originated – and what kinds of debts were cancelled regularly – it is necessary to discuss the social and anthropological context in which debt and credit, money and interest were innovated. The Bronze Age Near East was organized on principles so different from those of today that it seems unconnected to modern civilization. That is why most economists and social theorists prefer to pick up the historical thread with the more familiar Greece and Rome. There is a problem of cognitive dissonance and outright ideological rejection in dealing with the ancient Near East, precisely because its organizing principles and economic dynamics are so far at odds with those of today's mainstream economics and popular opinion. Most mainstream social science misses the point that the temples and palaces of the ancient Near East were the initial innovators of commercial enterprise and accounting, money and interest, standardized prices, weights and measures. As for anthropologists, their focus is more on tribal enclaves that have not developed into full-blown civilization.

---

[12] Veblen 1919 [1908]: 183 ff.

The International Scholars Conference on Ancient Near Eastern Economies (ISCANEE)

By 1993, I had written a draft of the present book, but it was not a propitious time to talk of debt cancellation. The financial bubble was just taking off, and seemed to promise a way for most people to get rich. One reader for a university press found it unthinkable that debts could have been annulled on a widespread level, and intimated that the Assyriological profession had always believed this.

That was almost the case in the 1980s. The most popular books on Sumer for the general audience were written by a politically conservative literary specialist, Samuel Kramer, who believed that if debts were indeed cancelled, it would only have been temporarily during a royal festival. Today's Assyriological mainstream have come to accept the idea that debts were annulled and financial clean slates proclaimed with more lasting effect again and again.

Part of this turnaround was catalyzed by a series of colloquia that I organized with the Peabody Museum to reconstruct the origins of modern economic practices, enterprise and finance. Our group brought together leading Assyriologists, Egypt-ologists and other specialists to describe the early evolution of debt, land tenure and the privatization of enterprise in their specific areas and time periods of expertise.

At the outset we envisioned three colloquia. Our first area of study, in 1994, was the structure of "mixed" economies and how the temples and palaces – the largest economic institutions of their day – assigned or leased trade and other enterprise to private merchants and operators and lead to the publication of *Privatization in the Ancient Near East and Classical Antiquity*.[13] Land was the most important asset to be privatized, and debt was the major lever prying land away from communal tenure. So our second colloquium, in 1996 at New York University, was on land tenure and the origins of urbanization and fiscal authority, published as *Urbanization in the Ancient Near East*.[14] By this time our group had gained some renown and we held a supplementary 1997 meeting on this same topic in Saint Petersburg at Russia's Oriental Institute, with attendees including scholars relatively unknown in the West.

The specialists that we assembled during what became five colloquia on the economic history of the ancient Near East will be cited often in the chapters that follow. Archaeologists included Karl Lamberg-Karlovsky, his Harvard Peabody Museum colleague Alex Marshack traced urban iconography back to seasonal Ice Age gathering points, and Giorgio Buccellati, the excavator of Urkesh in northern Syria. The Sumerologists included Dietz O. Edzard of Munich University and, also from Germany, Johannes Renger, a leading follower of Karl Polanyi. The Neo-Babylonian specialists were Michael Jursa of the University of Vienna and Cornelia Wunsch of SOAS and Berlin. From Russia's Institute of Oriental Studies in Saint Petersburg, our group had Muhammed Dandamayev and Nelli Kozyreva. From England were Eleanor Robson from Oxford and Karen Radner from the University of London. And from the United States were Marc Van De Mieroop of Columbia University,

---

[13] Hudson and Levine, eds., 1996.
[14] Hudson and Levine, eds., 1999.

Piotr Steinkeller of Harvard, Seth Richardson from the University of Chicago, Elizabeth Stone from SUNY Stony Brook, William Hallo of Yale, and Robert Englund from UCLA. For northern Mesopotamia our group included Alfonso Archi to deal with Ebla, and for upstream Nuzi, Carlo Zaccagnini from Naples and Maynard Maidman from the University of Toronto. For Bronze Age Mycenaean Greece we had Tom Palaima from the University of Texas and his colleague Dimitri Nakassis. Our group's Egyptologists were headed by Ogden Goelet of New York University, the archaeologist Mark Lehner of Harvard and Edward Bleiberg of the Brooklyn Museum of Art. From ancient Israel, Baruch Levine, and Michael Heltzer for the Syrian coast city of Ugarit.

Having established the role of debt in foreclosing on land rights and obtaining labor to work off personal debts, our third colloquium dealt with credit and Clean Slate proclamations. Held in 2000 at Columbia University, that conference provided the basic narrative of the present book, tracing the origin of commercial and personal agrarian debt, and the continuity of Clean Slates. Only personal agrarian barley debts were annulled, not commercial silver debts among merchants. And only subsistence land-holdings were returned to their customary holders, not townhouses and other wealth over and above the basic subsistence needs of citizens. So the aim was not equality as such, but the assurance of self-support land and production for the citizenry. The pertaining volume is *Debt and Economic Renewal in the Ancient Near East*.[15]

These three colloquia proved so successful that we decided to follow up by discussing the origins of money and accounting in 2002, at the British Museum, with the publication of *Creating Economic Order*.[16] This meeting established that money did not emerge out of individuals bartering goods to set prices. Administered initially as part of the accounting system developed in the temples and palaces of Sumer early in the third millennium BC, "money" was a price schedule to denominate payments of grain debts for sharecroppers on temple or palace lands, and for free citizens owing payments for water transport, draught animals, consumer goods such as beer or emergency borrowing, while silver debts were owed for long-distance trade with Cappadocia, Bahrain and the Iranian plateau.

In 2004 we held a fifth colloquium on labor in the ancient Near East and Mycenaean Greece, published as *Labor in the Ancient World* This survey returned to our earlier discussions of the evolution of land tenure as part of a quid pro quo by which landholders were obliged to provide corvée labor and serve in the military.[17] Looking back to the Neolithic, it became apparent that labor on the vast ceremonial centers originally had to be voluntary, not based on slave labor. From Mesopotamia's infrastructure to Egypt's pyramids, great feasts and drinking parties were held upon the completion of major building projects, making them part of a basic communalistic socializing experience.

That final volume of our colloquia was published in 2015, taking account of

---

[15] Hudson and Van De Mieroop, eds., 2002.
[16] Hudson and Wunsch, eds., 2004.
[17] Steinkeller and Hudson, eds., 2015.

Neolithic and Egyptian studies that were occurring rapidly as the field of prehistory was being rethought. Yet for the most part our research remained limited to Assyriologists, Egyptologists and other prehistorians.

By that time, widening recognition of the need for a debt writedown in the modern world led to a revival of interest in how societies through the ages have handled credit and debt. The most popular treatment of debt in its broad perspective was the anthropologist David Graeber's *Debt: The First 5,000 Years* (2011). We had corresponded over the years, and our collaboration has increased since publication of his work. The present book approaches debt from the perspective of early history and documentation from the ancient Near East.

What makes Western civilization "Western"?

Tension developed between the palace and local authorities and merchant-entrepreneurs seeking to pry away labor for themselves, by obliging it to work off debts. The rise and fall of society in Sumer's Ur III period, and in Babylonia's and Egypt's "Intermediate Periods," reflected the ebb and flow that has characterized all subsequent economies and is still shaping today's world: the conflict between social constraints on predatory finance, and the attempt by a rentier class to gain control. Today's era of collapsing central authority is strikingly like antiquity's "Intermediate Periods," marked by appropriation of land and public infrastructure, debt peonage and vast emigrations. These phenomena and the social tensions they cause seem timeless.

The origins of Western civilization are to be found in the way Bronze Age Sumer and Babylonia, Egypt and the Aegean broke down and gave way to their successors. In Greece, local Mycenaean palace managers disappear from records in 1200 BC, reappearing in the 8th century as *basilae*, concentrating land and hitherto palace wealth and authority in their own hands and that of their clans. The oligarchies that emerged as trade revived were overthrown in due course by populist "tyrants," or managed a softer landing as in Athens under Solon. Nonetheless, credit and land were held much more in private hands than in the Near East. That is what has created constant tension between creditors and the indebted citizenry.

What made classical antiquity "modern" – and in the minds of many historians, "Western" – was the privatization of credit, land ownership and political power without the more or less regular Clean Slates that had been traditional in the Near East. Pseudo-Aristotle's *Constitution of Athens* (XVI.2) reports that the 5th-century BC tyrant Peisistratus gained the support of many rural poor by paying off their debts himself. Cicero (*de Rep.* II. 21) likewise describes the legendary Roman king Servius as having strengthened his position by paying off the obligations of local debtors. Diodorus says much the same thing of Servius's predecessor Tarquin.[18] But in the end it was the large landowners and creditors who became wealthy enough to decide elections.

---

[18] Diodorus, VIII, frag. 13. See Ure 1922: 216 and 221 f.

The concept of private property permitting creditors to expropriate mortgage debtors that is widely accepted today, already throughout antiquity led to a cry for debt cancellation – as late as Kings Agis V and Cleomenes III in Sparta (late 3rd century BC) and Mithridates in his three wars against Rome (88 to 63 BC).

The absence of royal, religious or civic debt amnesties made classical Greece and Rome different from the Bronze Age Near East. Our own civilization inherited Rome's pro-creditor legal principles that helped the oligarchy impoverish its citizenry.

A legacy of financial instability

Babylonian scribal students were trained already c. 2000 BC in the mathematics of compound interest. Their school exercises asked them to calculate how long it took a debt at interest of $\frac{1}{60}$th per month to double. The answer is 60 months: five years. How long to quadruple? Ten years. How long to multiply 64 times? Thirty years. It must have been obvious that no economy can grow in keeping with this rate of increase.

Babylonian training exercises grasped that herds and production grow in S-curves, tapering off – while debts mount up, ever growing at interest. This tendency for debts to accrue faster than the economy can grow is missing from today's academic curriculum. Mainstream economic models assume that financial trends are self-correcting to restore balance. The reality is that debts growing at compound interest tend to polarize and impoverish economies, if not corrected from "outside" the economy. Sumerians, Babylonians and their Near Eastern neighbors recognized the need for this action.

Today's "free enterprise" model-builders deny that debt writeoffs are needed. Modern ideology endorses chronic indebtedness as normal, despite debt service drying up the internal market and forcing a widening range of debtors into financial dependency.

In all epochs a basic maxim applies: Debts that can't be paid won't be paid. What always is at issue is just *how* they won't be paid. If they are not written down, they will become a lever for creditors to pry away property and income from debtors – in practice, from the economy and community at large.

At the outset of recorded history, Bronze Age rulers relinquished fiscal claims and restored liberty from permanent debt. That prevented a creditor oligarchy from emerging to the extent that occurred in classical antiquity. Today's world is still living in the wake of the Roman Empire's creditor-oriented laws and the economic polarization that ensued.

The Major Themes of this Book

1. Charging interest on debts was innovated in a particular part of the world (Sumer, in southern Mesopotamia) some time in the Early Bronze Age, c. 3200–2500 BC. No trace of interest-bearing debt is found in pristine anthropological gift exchange, or even in the Linear B records of Mycenaean Greece 1600–1200 BC. The practice diffused westward to the Aegean and Mediterranean c. 750 BC.

2. A major task of Babylonian and other Mesopotamian rulers upon taking the throne was to restore economic balance by cancelling agrarian personal debts, liberating bondservants and reversing land forfeitures for citizens holding self-support land.

3. The easiest debts for rulers to remit were those owed to the palace, temples and their collectors or professional guilds. But by the end of the third millennium BC, wealthy traders and other creditors were engaging in rural usury as a sideline to their entrepreneurial activities. Enforcing collection of such debts owed to the palace, its bureaucracy and private lenders would have disenfranchised the land-tenured citizen infantry and lost the corvée labor service and military duties of debtors reduced to bondage.

4. Debt cancellations were not radical, nor were they "reforms." They were the traditional means to prevent widespread debt bondage and land foreclosures. Bronze Age rulers enabled economic relations to start afresh and in financial balance upon taking the throne and when needed in times of crop failure or economic distress. There was no faith in inherent automatic tendencies (what today is called "market equilibrium") to ensure economic growth. Rulers recognized that if they let debt arrears mount up, their societies would veer out of balance, creating an oligarchy that would impoverish the citizen-army and drive populations to flee the land.

5. Palace collectors and merchant entrepreneurs acted increasingly as creditors on their own account. A political tug of war ensued as nomadic tribesmen conquered southern Mesopotamia and took over temples and turned them into exploitative vehicles while trying to resist customary checks on the corrosive effects of debt.

6. Classical antiquity replaced the cyclical idea of time and social renewal with that of linear time. Economic polarization became irreversible, not merely temporary. Aristocracies overthrew rulers and ended the tradition of restoring liberty from debt bondage. This brought "modern" land ownership into being as debtors forfeited their land tenure rights or fell into bondage with little hope of recovering their free status.

7. Without Clean Slates, creditor oligarchies appropriated most of the land and reduced much of the population to bondage. Creditors translated their economic gains into political power, casting off the fiscal obligations that originally were attached to land tenure rights. The burden of debt and its mounting interest charges led to the foreclosure of land as the basic means of self-support and hence the loss of the debtor's liberty.

8. Livy, Plutarch and other Roman historians described classical antiquity as being destroyed mainly by creditors using interest-bearing debt to impoverish and disenfranchise the population. Barbarians always stood at the gates, but only as societies weakened internally were their invasions successful. The invasions that ended the fading Roman Empire were anticlimactic. In the end, the only debts that Emperor Hadrian could annul with his fiscal amnesty were Rome's tax records, which he burned in 119 AD – tax debts owed to the palace, not debts to the creditor oligarchy that had gained control of Rome's land.

9. Archaic traditions of restoring order, originally legally enforceable, were given an otherworldly eschatological meaning as the social order collapsed under the burden of debt. Losing hope for secular revival, antiquity felt itself to be living in the End Time.

10. The Qumran scroll 11QMelchezedek wove together Biblical texts concerning debt cancellations with apocalyptic texts about the Day of Judgment. Although many of Jesus' sermons used images and analogies associated with debt, the idea of redemption and forgiveness was spiritualized to the point where it lost its basis in fiscal and debt amnesties that had released debtors from bondage.

11. Byzantine rulers revived the Near Eastern practice of returning land tenure to smallholders, nullifying foreclosures, "gifts" and even outright purchases as constituting stealth takeovers by the wealthy. Takeovers via antichresis (taking the land as ostensibly temporary collateral to pay the interest due) also were annulled.

12. The common policy denominator spanning Bronze Age Mesopotamia and the Byzantine Empire was the conflict between central rulers acting to restore land to smallholders so as to maintain royal tax revenue and a land-tenured military force, and wealthy or powerful families seeking to concentrate land in their own hands, denying this usufruct to the palace. When royal power to preserve widespread land tenure waned under assertive oligarchies, the result was economic shrinkage and ultimate collapse.

Part I: OVERVIEW

1. A Babylonian Perspective on Liberty and Economic Order

Modern American society retains many iconographic references that can be traced back to ancient Babylonia. Our nation's two most familiar symbols of freedom, the Statue of Liberty and the Liberty Bell, recall vestiges of an ancient tradition that has been all but lost since imperial Roman times: liberty from bondage and from the threat of losing one's home, land and means of livelihood through debt.

To a visitor from Hammurabi's Babylon, the Statue of Liberty might evoke the royal iconography of the important ritual over which rulers presided: restoring liberty from debt. The earliest known reference to such a ritual appears in a legal text from the 18th century BC. A farmer claims that he does not have to pay a crop debt because the ruler, quite likely Hammurabi (who ruled for 42 years, 1792–1750 BC), has "raised high the Golden Torch" to signal the annulling of agrarian debts and related personal "barley" obligations.[19]

Unlike today's business cycle economists, Bronze Age societies had no faith in the spontaneous equilibrating forces of modern-style market mechanisms, nor did they believe that all debts should be paid. Their laws recognized that floods and droughts, military conflict or other causes prevented cultivators from harvesting enough to pay the debts they had run up during the crop year. Palaces and temples were the major creditors, and their guiding objective was to maintain a free citizenry to serve in the military and provide the seasonal corvée labor duties attached to land tenure. Instead of letting "the market" resolve matters in favor of foreclosing creditors, rulers saw that if cultivators had to work off their debts to private creditors, they would not be available to perform their public corvée work duties, not to mention fight in the army.

By liberating distressed individuals who had fallen into debt bondage, and returning to cultivators the lands they had forfeited for debt or sold under economic duress, these royal acts maintained a free peasantry willing to fight for its lands and work on public building projects and canals. Cuneiform references to such debt cancellations have been excavated in Lagash, Assur, Isin, Larsa, Babylon and other Near Eastern cities as far west as Asia Minor. By clearing away the buildup of personal debts, rulers saved society from the social chaos that would have resulted from personal insolvency, debt bondage and military defection.

The Babylonian ruler's ceremonial gesture of holding aloft a flame to signal *mīšarum*, clearing the slate of debts, seems to have marked the transition to a new reign by the new ruler upon the death of his predecessor after the period of mourning

---

[19] Finkelstein 1965: 233–246. Charpin 2000: 185 gives a bibliography for the symbolism of rulers "raising the golden torch for the land," and related expressions for annulling barley debts. To the north in Mari, he notes (1990a: 265), the Shamshi-Adad text ARM VIII 6: 17 ff.) refers to "The day when the governor raised (the torch)".

Figure 1:
Liberty Bell, Philadelphia, referring to Leviticus 25.

had ended. A loan contract from year 9 of Hammurabi's father, Sin-muballiṭ (1803 BC), specifies that the loan was "after the king raised high the golden torch," indicating that it was not subject to that northern ruler's *mīšarum* act.

"'I Am the Sun of Babylon' appears in the Prologue to Hammurabi's laws. Earlier, Shulgi proclaimed himself 'Sun of his land,' or 'faithful god, sun of his land.' Shu-ilishu of Isin called himself 'Sun of Sumer.'"[20] Casting themselves in the image of Babylonia's sun god of justice – Shamash, Illuminator of Darkness – rulers restored order and equity by cancelling back taxes, crop-rent arrears and other consumer debts.

A long imagery of social cosmology was at work extending down through the Hellenistic 2nd and 1st centuries BC. As Arnold Toynbee summarized this imagery, "the Sun stood for justice. The Sun distributes his light and warmth impartially. He bestows them on the poor just as generously as on the rich. They are blessings in which all living creatures alike have an equal share, and one human being cannot be deprived of them by another. All are at liberty to share in the Sun's gifts, so he stands, not only for justice, but for the liberty that justice demands." For Hellenistic Stoic philosophers this solar principle was Helios Eleutherios."[21] The Statue of Liberty's

[20] Charpin 2013: 65 and 72.
[21] Toynbee 1965: vol. II, p. 606, citing Bidez 1943.

base is inscribed with lines from Emma Lazarus's poem "The New Colossus": "Give me your tired, your poor, your huddled masses yearning to breathe free." This sentiment is kindred to Hammurabi's pledge in the epilogue to his famous laws, inscribed on imported diorite stone for all the public to see – and to be copied by scribal students for over a thousand years:

> ... that the strong might not oppress the weak,
> that justice might be dealt to the orphan and widow ...
> I write my precious words on my stele ...
> To give justice to the oppressed.[22]

Should our Babylonian visitor proceed to the Liberty Bell in Philadelphia, he would find further vestiges of the idea of absolution from debt bondage. The bell is inscribed with a quotation from Leviticus 25.10: "Proclaim liberty throughout all the land, and to all the inhabitants thereof." The full verse refers to freedom from debt bondage when it exhorts the Israelites to "hallow the fiftieth year, and proclaim liberty throughout all the land and to all the inhabitants thereof; it shall be a Jubilee unto you; and ye shall return every man unto his family" (and also every woman, child and house slave who had been pledged). Lands were restored to their traditional holders clear of debt encumbrances. Sounding the ram's horn on the Day of Atonement of this fiftieth year signaled the renewal of economic order and equity by undoing the corrosive effects of indebtedness that had built up since the last Jubilee.

The Hebrew word translated as "liberty" in the Leviticus text is *deror*. It is cognate to *andurārum* in Akkadian, a related Semitic language of early Babylonia. The root meaning of both words is to move freely like running water – in this case like bondservants liberated to rejoin their families. As early as 2400 BC the Sumerian term amargi signified the return to the mother. Similar terms existed in most Near Eastern languages of the period: níg-si-sá in Sumerian, *mīšarum* in the Akkadian language used in Babylonia, and *šudūtu* in Hurrian-speaking Nuzi upstream along the Euphrates.[23]

Until the 1970s translators construed these terms as meaning freedom in an abstract sense. The idea of creditors not being paid seemed so radical that academics doubted that debts could really have been cancelled without deranging social life, or perhaps triggering a political backlash by the well-to-do against rulers annulling their claims for payment.

What helped settle matters was the Rosetta stone. Nearly everyone knows that this trilingual Egyptian inscription provided the key for reading nd understanding hieroglyphics after it was dug up by Napoleon's troops in 1799. What is almost always

---

[22] William Hallo points out that the Neo-Assyrian rulers Sargon II (722–705) and Ashurbanipal (668–627) used similar language in their inscriptions, as did the Persian ruler Darius (550–486). See Hallo 1990: 205.

[23] Sumerian words such as amar-gi or níg.si.sá are not italicized. A non-serif typeface is used to set Sumerian words apart.

overlooked is what the stone reports. It was a debt amnesty by a young ruler from the Ptolemaic dynasty (a lineage founded by one of Alexander the Great's generals in 314 BC). The stone's inscription commemorates the cancellation of back taxes and other debts by the 13-year old Ptolemy V Epiphanes in 197 BC, evidently indoctrinated by Egypt's priesthood, into the ways of emulating former pharaohs.

In one language after another, initial doubts have been dispelled: The economic liberty referred to was an amnesty on arrears of back taxes and other personal debts. Rulers cancelled these arrears to liberate citizens and their family members pledged to creditors for debt, and to restore the customary land-tenure rights that had been forfeited to creditors. There can be no doubt that these edicts were implemented. Over the course of Hammurabi's Babylonian dynasty (1894–1600 BC) they grew into quite elaborate promulgations, capped by his great-great-grandson Ammisaduqa in 1646 BC.

Proclamation of these clean slates became so central a royal function that the phrase "to issue a "royal edict" (ṣimdat šarrim) usually referred specifically to a debt cancellation.[24] The act typically was commemorated in the year-name for the ruler's second year, reflecting what they had done in their initial year upon taking the throne. These texts have been excavated mainly from temple foundations, where Urukagina (2352–2342 BC) and Gudea of Lagash (c. 2150) buried them on the occasion of inaugurating temples or celebrating their coronation. In 1792 BC, Hammurabi's "second" year commemorated this initial coronation act, repeated when he celebrated his 30th anniversary on the throne in 1762 after defeating Rim-Sin of Larsa, as well as when he responded to economic or military pressures to cancel debts in 1780 and 1771 BC.

By the first millennium BC, however, kings had lost the power to overrule local aristocracies. Where they survived, they ruled on behalf of the wealthy. From Solomon and his son Rehoboam through Ahab and most subsequent rulers, the Bible depicts most Israelite kings as burdening the people with taxes, not freeing them from debts or palace demands. That is why the Biblical prophets shifted the moral center of lawgiving out of the hands of kings, making debt cancellation and land reform automatic and obligatory as a sacred covenant under Mosaic Law, handed down by the Lord.

Today's readers of the Bible tend to skim over the Covenant Code of Exodus, the septennial šemittah year of release in Deuteronomy and the Jubilee Year of Leviticus as if they were idealistic fine print. But to the Biblical compilers they formed the core of righteousness. Liberated from bondage to Egyptians (apparently designated as a mythic analogy to the oppressive Judean oligarchy), the Israelites are represented as holding their land in trust as the Lord's gift to support a free population, never again to be reduced to debt bondage and lose their land to foreclosing creditors, or to sell the land irrevocably under economic distress. "Land must not be sold in perpetuity, for the land belongs to me and you are only strangers

---

[24] Ellis 1972: 74–82.

and guests. You will allow a right of redemption on all your landed property, and restore it to its customary cultivators every fifty years" (Leviticus 25: 23–28).

The broad theme of this book is how the modern concept of economic liberty has stood the original meaning of liberty on its head. Today's pro-creditor "market principle" favoring financial claims by holding that all debts must be paid, reverses the archaic sanctity of releasing indentured debt pledges and property *from* debt bondage. The idea of linear progress, in the form of irreversible debt and property transfers, has replaced the Bronze Age tradition of cyclical renewal.

Central to any discussion of this inversion is the fact that Mesopotamia's palaces and temples were the major creditors at the beginning of recorded history. To enable them to perform their designated functions, communities endowed them with land and dependent labor. Neither temples nor palaces borrowed from private creditors (although their functionaries and entrepreneurs acting for them did). Nowhere in antiquity do we find governments becoming chronic debtors. Debts were owed to them, not by them.

Today's world is the opposite. When the U.S. Congress discusses ways to reduce the federal budget deficit, the most untouchable category of expenditures is payment to bondholders on the public debt. The same is true for Third World countries negotiating with banks and the International Monetary Fund – creating the recent debt-ridden austerity and economic collapse imposed on Greece.

A Babylonian would be more open than most modern economists to recognizing the corrosive impact of debt. There was no faith in "automatic" adjustment mechanisms guiding economies to be able to carry their debts. Economic balance had to be imposed from "above" the market Ancient history provides a series of case studies illustrating how annulling an overbearing debt overhead renewed economic growth and stability rather than disrupting it. From the Biblical prophets to Roman Stoic historians a central theme was the accusation that what tore their society apart was the failure to cancel debts.

The legacy of lawgivers proclaiming clean slates is commemorated at the entrance to the United States House of Representatives. Grouped around Moses in the center, with Hammurabi on his right, are "23 marble relief portraits of 'historical figures noted for their work in establishing the principles that underlie American law.'"[25] Hammurabi promulgated debt cancellations by royal edict (depicted as showing his cuneiform laws to the sun-god Shamash). But Moses – in the later Biblical epoch when kings no longer promoted widespread liberty – received his body of law directly from the Lord. The Jubilee Year and related laws were taken out of the hands of worldly rulers and placed at the center of Judaic religion.

Among these stone portraits of lawgivers is Lycurgus, whom Plutarch descibes as annulling Sparta's debts and even abolishing gold and silver money, replacing it with iron whose value was controlled by the state, not the wealthy. The other portrait from Greece is of Solon, who lay the groundwork for Athenian democracy by freeing the *hektemoroi* debt serfs and ending debt bondage in 594 BC.

---

[25] Van De Mieroop 2016: 143 f. discusses this.

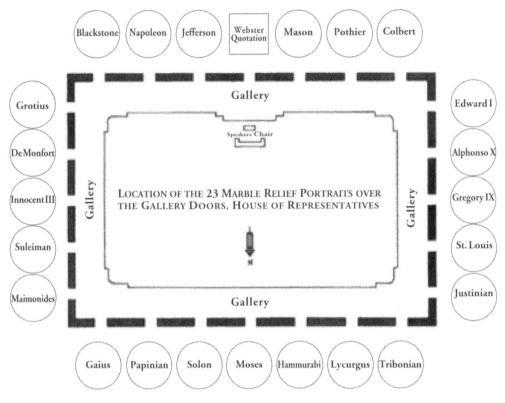

Figure 2. House of Representatives, location of the portraits of 23 lawgivers

The sponsorship of financial Clean Slates by these lawgivers is the opposite of the principles governing today's economies. According to modern economic orthodoxy, cancelling personal debts should have led to financial chaos instead of saving the economy from chaos. The reality is that Mesopotamia's takeoff could not have been sustained if its rulers had adopted today's sanctity of debt.

We are living in the kind of market economy that favors ambitious tycoons, corporate raiders and emperors of finance indulging in what classical philosophy called hubris. This term meant economic egotism and selfishness in ways that were injurious to others, above all the injurious and predatory greed of creditors against debtors. It was the role of goddesses from Mesopotamia to classical Greece to protect the weak and poor by punishing hubris. Today, on top of the Capitol is a Statue of Freedom. She is female, but the planners would have had no memory of the role that Nanshe of Lagash played, or even Nemesis in Greece. Like the ancient male gods of justice, from Hammurabi's Sun-God Shamash to the Mosaic Lord, these consorts have become a lost tradition. All that remains in the public mind are myths and images whose original meaning has been forgotten, because their tradition is alien to our modern ideology and the way that our major religions have evolved.

2. Jesus's First Sermon and the Tradition of Debt Amnesty

In the first reported sermon Jesus delivered upon returning to his native Nazareth (Luke 4:16ff.), he unrolled the scroll of Isaiah and announced his mission "to restore the Year of Our Lord." Until recently the meaning of this phrase was not recognized as referring specifically to the Jubilee Year. But breakthroughs in cuneiform research and a key Qumran scroll provide a direct link to that tradition. This linkage provides the basis for understanding how early Christianity emerged in an epoch so impoverished by debt and the threat of bondage that it was called the End Time.

Jesus was both more revolutionary and more conservative than was earlier recognized. He was politically revolutionary in threatening Judaic creditors, and behind them the Pharisees who had rationalized their rights against debtors. Luke 16:13–15 describes them as "loving money" and "sneering" at Jesus's message that "You cannot serve both God and Money/Mammon."[26] The leading rabbinical school in an age when creditor power was gaining dominance throughout the ancient world, the Pharisees followed the teachings of Hillel. Now credited as a founder of rabbinical Judaism, he sponsored the *prosbul* clause in which creditors obliged their clients to waive their rights to have their debts cancelled in the Jubilee Year.

Jesus's call for a Jubilee Year was conservative in resurrecting the economic ideal central to Mosaic Law: widespread annulment of personal debts. This ideal remains so alien to our modern way of thinking that his sermons are usually interpreted in an broad compassionate sense of urging personal charity toward one's own debtors and the poor in general. There is a reluctance to focus on the creditor oligarchy that Jesus (and many of his contemporary Romans) blamed for the epoch's deepening poverty..

The meaning of Biblical *deror* (and hence "the Year of Our Lord")

The recent discoveries start with the derivation of a Hebrew word that is a key to understanding pivotal passages in the Old and New Testaments. That word is *deror*, used in Leviticus to signal a debt cancellation in the Jubilee Year as described above. Translated on America's Liberty Bell as "Proclaim liberty throughout the land," *deror* refers specifically to cancelling debts, freeing bondservants and returning land to its cultivator-occupants who had lost it through debt foreclosure or economic duress.

That is the word's meaning in Jeremiah's narrative of King Zedekiah's promise to cancel the people's debts on the eve of war with Babylonia in 588 BC. Jeremiah, the king's counselor, interpreted the Babylonian King Nebuchadnezzar II's subsequent defeat of Judea as punishment by the Lord for Zedekiah's going back on his word and violating sacred law: "You did not release [your people from their debts], so I will release sword, pestilence and famine!" (Jeremiah: 17–22). By breaking the

---

[26] Lyndon Drake 2014: 233–244 citing Neusner 1971: 117–120 in support of the consensus "that the prosbul predates Jesus."

Figure 3: The Jesaiah scroll, the only complete scroll found in the caves of Qumran

Mosaic covenant with the Lord, Zedekiah's behavior condemned the land to destruction at the hands of Babylon. "He did evil in the eye of the Lord" (2 Kings 224: 19f. and Jeremiah 52: 2 f.).

Much as early Christianity made charitable debt forgiveness the test of one's personal purity of soul and admissibility to heaven, this narrative gave the *deror* proclamation key significance in deciding Israel's fate on the national plane – its salvation or damnation.

From Judaism to Christianity

Isaiah 61: 1–2 provides the bridge to the New Testament. Written by the prophet known as Third Isaiah c. 400 BC soon after the codification of the Priestly Laws of Leviticus in the wake of Nehemiah and Ezra, this remarkable passage reads:

> The spirit of the Sovereign Lord [Yahweh] is upon me, for the Lord has anointed me to preach good news [gospel] to the poor. He has sent me to bind up the broken-hearted, to proclaim liberty (*deror*) for the captives and release for the prisoners, to proclaim the Year of the Lord's favor and the day of vengeance of our God ...

Many of these phrases have become so familiar that they appear hackneyed today, but they were quite specific in their original setting. The word "gospel" means literally "good news." But apart from Isaiah 61 and its quotation by Jesus in his inaugural sermon (in Luke 4: 18 f. and Matthew 11: 6 // Luke 7: 23), the full phrase "good news to the poor" appears nowhere else in the Synoptic gospels. It refers to the deror tradition, the amnesty freeing citizens from bondage and restoring their means of self-support on the land in "the Year of the Lord's favor," the Jubilee Year. The Year's yobel trumpet is to be blown on Yom Kippur, the Day of Atonement signaling the restoration of worldly order, righteousness and equity. The yobel trumpet, a ram's horn blown on the tenth day of the seventh month, gave its name to the Jubilee.

By the first century BC the Isaiah 61 passage had come to play a prominent role in the Qumran archive. A scroll dating from 50 to 25 BC, known as 11QMelchizedek (11Q stands for Qumran cave number 11, where it was buried during Judea's war with Rome), weaves together the *deror* and related debt cancellation passages from Leviticus, Deuteronomy and Isaiah, combined with various psalms to elevate the Levitical image of restoring equity.

Discovered in 1956, the Qumran scroll highlights Isaiah 61 as the basis for projecting the idea of release to cover not only debts and loss of landownership, but all evil in the world – everything that an amnesty should set straight. The author(s) evidently searched through the Jewish Bible to find all its references to *deror*, and collated them in such a way as to describe the Day of Judgment as a grand release to end all releases. At the End of Time the Lord will return to earth to save his followers and smite those who have digressed from the path of righteousness.

The scrolls' authors were long thought to be Essenes, a sect whose members believed that they were living in the End Time, a cycle-ending Jubilee year conceived along the lines of renewal called for in the laws of Leviticus and Deuteronomy. But recently there is some support for the idea that the Qumram collection was the sacred library of the Jerusalem temple, stored for safe keeping during the Roman wars.[27] Whoever drafted these scrolls believed that it would take an apocalyptic new order, imposed from "above" the world of economic suffering, to replace wrongdoing and decadence with righteousness.

The Melchizedek scroll shows the key role played by Jubilee traditions in shaping Qumran and Christian hopes for how the End Time would be resolved. Yet even today, half a century since its discovery, this text still remains more an antiquarian curiosity than an explanatory link to the Near Eastern tradition and idea of economic righteousness in which Judaic law was grounded.

Describing Melchizedek as "a priest on high" (indeed, as founding the Judaic priesthood), Hebrews 7 explains why he is so important: He appeared to Abraham (Genesis 14) and blessed him after he rescued his nephew, Lot, and his caravan of goods from the towns of Sodom and Gomorrah.

In today's interpretation of the Sodom story the narrow focus on sexual license and other noneconomic behavior misses the symbolic association of sodomy with the unrighteous behavior of greed. From Roman Stoic history down through the medieval prosecution of the Knights Templar it was customary to depict major moneylenders as sodomists, as the ultimate expression of predatory behavior was usury. The word seems outdated today, but of all the vices condemned by the Biblical prophets, it was the sin against which they warned above all. (See Part IV below.)

Having rescued Lot, Melchizedek helped bring about the universal release of captives. His name comprises the Hebrew words for "king" and "justice" or "righteousness," alluding to the "king of righteousness."[28] That was the same title Mesopotamian rulers used when they proclaimed *andurārum*. The scroll (lines 2–6) identifies Melchizedek with Zadok the priest under King David.[29] Deemed to be the prototypical high priest in Psalm 110, he became a savior figure bringing about the release of the oppressed in the End Time.

[27] This view that the Dead Sea Scrolls originated at the library of the Jewish Temple in Jerusalem was first voiced in 1963, by Karl Heinrich Rengstorf of the University of Münster. Norman Golb (1995) believes that the manuscripts were heterogeneous. Among the alternative interpretations that have been suggested, Larry Schiffman believes that the Qumran manuscripts were mainly by followers of Zadok, hence, their focus on Melchizedek. See Magen and Peleg 2006, and Crawford and Wassen, eds., 2016.

[28] Kugel 1997: 151–162.

[29] For a discussion see Kobelski 1981. Also Roberts 2002: 264, 267.

The Dead Sea Scroll 11QMelchizedek
(based on Sanders 1973, apud J. T. Milik in JJA 23 [1972])

1. …
2. and what he said, In this year of Jubilee each of you will   Lev. 25:13
    return to his possession. That has the same meaning as
    what is written: This is
3. the manner of the Release. Let every creditor release that   Deut. 15:2
    which he lent to his neighbor; he shall not exact it of his
    neighbor or his brother for Release has been proclaimed
4. for God. And the Release will be proclaimed in the end of
    days concerning those taken captive, as He said: to proclaim   Isa. 61:1
    Liberty to the captives. This is its interpretation:
    God is going to declare
5. that they will become part of the sons of heaven and that they
    they will participate in the heritage of Melchizedek, for he
    is to assign them a part in the portion of Melchizedek who
6. is going to make them enter this lot and proclaim   Isa. 61:1
    Liberty for them while relieving them of the burden   Lev. 25:10
    of all their inequities. And this event will take place
7. in the first week (of years) of the jubilee following the
    nine jubilees. And the day of atonement is the end of   Lev. 25:9
    the end of the tenth jubilee
8. when atonement will be effected for all the sons of God and
    for men of the lot of Melchizedek, and a decree will be issued
    concerning them to provide recompense for them. Indeed,
9. it is the Period of the Year of Favor for Melchizedek   Isa. 61:2
    and he, by his force, will judge the holy ones of God
    by effecting (the sentences) of judgment. As it is written
10. concerning him in the Songs of David who said: God   Ps. 82:1
    stands in the divine assembly, in the midst of
    gods he will give judgment. And concerning him he said: Ps. 7:8–9
    Above the congregation of the peoples
11. in the heights, repent! God will judge the peoples.
    As for what he said: How long will you judge unjustly and   Ps. 82:2
    honor the face of the wicked? Selah.
12. Its meaning concerns Belial and the spirits of his lot, who have
    remained rebels, because they have turned away from the
    commandments of God to act in an impious manner.
13. And Melchizedek is going to execute the vengeance of the   Isa. 61:2
    judgments of God among men and he will rescue them from
    the hand of Belial and from the hand of all the spirits of his lot,
14. and all the gods of justice will come to his aid to contem-   Isa. 61:3
    plate the destruction of Belial: for the heights are the   Ps. 7:8
    support of the sons of God; and he (Meliki-sedeq) will mar-
    velously execute this

15. plan. It is the day of peace about which god said in the
    words of Isaiah, the prophet, who said: How beautiful   Isa. 52:7
16. upon the mountains are the feet of the herald who
    proclaims peace, who heralds good, who proclaims
    salvation, who says to Zion, your God has become king!
17. This is its interpretation: the mountains are the prophets,   Isa. 52:7
    whose words are the feet, which they prophesied
    to all those who heed God.
18. And the herald is the anointed of the spirit, of whom Daniel Isa. 61:1
    spoke: Until the event of the Anointed One, of a Prince,   Dan. 9:25
    seven weeks will pass. And He who proclaims peace,   Isa. 52:7
19. a good man who proclaims salvation, he it is who is inscribed
    with the (Anointed One in the Book of Life), about whom
    He said, To comfort all who mourn, to grant to all   Isa. 61:2–3
    who mourn in Zion.
20. to comfort those who mourn means: to instruct them   Isa. 61:2
    in all the periods of the world …
21. in truth to make …
22. …
23. she (the congregation?) will remain apart
    from Belial and she …
24. … by the judgments of God, as it is written about him:
    He who says to Zion, your God has become king. Zion is   Isa. 52:7
25. the congregation of all the sons of justice.
26. Melki-sedeq who will save them from the hand of Belial.
    As for what he said: You shall sound the horn loud in the land Lev. 25:9
    in the seventh month the tenth day of the month.

The words of Isaiah 61 woven into the Melchizedek text turn the Jubilee Year's period-icity into an End Time eschatological destiny. The text's linkages suggest why Jesus found that passage an appropriate focus for his career-defining sermon. Isaiah, the Qumran sect's Melchizedek priesthood and Jesus all proclaimed liberty (*deror*) for debt bondsmen and other captives of the world. Early Christianity would extend this idea to signify a release of the poor from suffering in general, overshadowing the original focus on debt.

It was in the footsteps of Melchizedek that Jesus appears to have walked.[30] Early Christian iconography depicts Jesus as sitting on the right hand of God as a priest "after the order of Melchizedek." The Epistle of the Hebrews 7 depicts him, like Melchizedek, as being "without father, without mother, without descent, having neither beginning nor end of days, nor end of life, but made like unto the Son of

---

[30] "Yahshua the Messiah came into the earth-plane to remove this priesthood and establish a new priesthood after the order of Melchizedek, where everyone that believes would receive direct access to Elohim without a priest (Hebrews 7:1, Timothy 2:5). In short, Yahshua the Messiah made the 'key of knowledge' available to the masses." (Wise, Abegg Jr. and Cook 1996).

Figure 4: 11QMelchizedek scroll

God." The bread and water that Melchizedek is reported to have given to Abraham was viewed as a precursor of Christ giving bread and wine for the Eucharist.[31]

Judaic religion already had taken such proclamations out of the hands of rulers (with whom they did not have a fortunate experience) and placed them in the hands of the high priest of Jerusalem. Jesus's "good news" sought to take sponsorship of *deror* out of the hands of the Judaic priesthood that had followed Hillel and the Pharisees in contrast to Mosaic Law.

Debt in the Biblical laws, historical narratives and parables

The story of Joseph advising Egypt's pharaoh how to obtain all the land for himself by getting the population into debt during the famine illustrates the typical cause of personal debt throughout the ancient world. The debt forgiveness laws of Exodus, Deuteronomy and Leviticus to counter incursions into economic liberty are sanctified by Moses leading the Exodus in protest against the pharaoh's oppression. Moses received the Law on Mount Sinai as part of the Lord's covenant with the Israelites enjoining them to show compassion toward debtors, and to remember that they all were once slaves and bondsmen in Egypt. The story of Job highlights righteousness toward debtors, and many other Biblical stories and parables are about how debt should be treated in a way that preserves an equitable society. But such stories usually are remembered today without the moral message perceived by their hearers in the 4th through 1st centuries BC.

Loyalty (and disloyalty) to the spirit of the Mosaic Law stands at the center of the narratives of the monarchies under David, his son – the heavy taxer Solomon – and Solomon's son Rehoboam, whose fiscal oppression split Israel away from Judah. Obedience to the debt laws underlay the good rule of Josiah supporting Deuteronomy's reforms, but Judah was destroyed under Zedekiah a generation later. Seeing many kings fail to defend the spirit of the law, the prophets denounced the avarice of creditors and land monopolizers, warning that social destruction would ensue from the failure to promote economic justice. By contrast, Nehemiah's narrative of re-settling Israel under Persian suzerainty centers on his abolition of debt bondage and cancellation of mortgages on the land.

The most worldly of the four gospel authors, Luke (6: 35), reports Jesus's admonition: "Lend, without expecting to be repaid." Jesus's Parable of the Unmerciful Servant (Matthew 18, discussed below in Chapter 22) made charitable debt forgiveness the paramount test of one's moral righteousness. It is the spirit of the Sermon on the Mount and the Beatitudes, and the criterion on which admittance to heaven would be based, reiterated in the Lord's Prayer.

---

[31] Kugel 1997: 155, citing Clement of Alexandria, *Miscellanies* 4161. Roberts 2002: 264 and 267 points out that the Qumran community associated the release laws with the "year of favour" in Isaiah 61 in eschatological expectations related specifically to Jesus's sermon reported in Luke 4.

But this core ethic of Biblical law is now all but ignored, indeed rejected by the pro-creditor temper of our times. Although the Torah (the Pentateuch) provides for periodic restoration of equity, Judaic society found itself confronted with the property-based spirit of Roman law overwhelming the ancient world. It was in response to this End Time that Christianity focused increasingly on forgiving sin in more non-economic dimensions. In today's world the Christian idea of redemption has been turned into an analogy for amnesty and salvation to heal suffering in general – almost everything except indebtedness.

The prototypical redemption was to liberate a human pledge from bondage. Where no relative or community body stepped forward to pay the creditor, Bronze Age rulers (and later the High Priest of Jerusalem) became redeemers liberating bondservants. That is how Handel's *Messiah* embodied the image of Christ, literally as Redeemer – by using the proceeds of its first performance (in Dublin in 1742) to redeem debtors from prison. Subsequent performances continued this tradition.

The occasion for royal proclamations restoring order was much like the New Year. It was the start of a new period, above all the inauguration of a king's new reign. The idea was to renew not only nature but also social balance in general. The common denominator is to restore amity and equity in a celebratory setting. Many societies have released lawbreakers on such occasions. Europeans and Asians, African and Native Americans have long used the New Year as an occasion to clean their homes, bring their extended families together and put their economic relations in order, especially by settling debts.

Figure 5: Autograph score of Händel's Messiah, part "Worthy is the Lamb that was slain."

3. Credit, Debt and Money: Their Social and Private Contexts

All archaic and surviving tribal communities studied by anthropologists have relied on credit and reciprocal gift exchange. Interpersonal debts such as wergild-type fines for inflicting personal injury, bride price and dowries were socially cohesive. Paid with customary baskets of goods or assets such as cattle or maidens (slave girls), they were pre-monetary (as Chapter 4 will trace). Gift exchange did not impose liabilities for non-payment. There is no indication of interest being charged, or of such reciprocity being beyond the normal means to sustain.

How then did such mutual aid, initially to help families survive, turn into rural usury reducing debtors to bondage and expropriating their self-support land as economies became wealthier?

The answer lies in how economies became wealthier. Mesopotamia's "managerial revolution" late in the fourth millennium BC saw a cluster of innovations, headed by written record keeping and cost accounting based on standardized weights and measures, 30-day administrative months, money and, at some point, the charging of interest. The aim was to mobilize crop rent to supply weaving and other workshops producing handicraft exports to exchange for silver, tin and other raw materials.

The resulting prosperity accrued mainly to the rulers and clan heads who managed the palace and temple bureaucracies and conducted foreign trade. Not until Roman times did economies grow rich enough to afford the luxury of reducing much of the population to debt bondage and replacing the citizen-army with landless mercenaries.

To understand why Mesopotamian rulers resisted that fate, it is necessary to explain how and why interest-bearing debt came into being, and how its changing political context – and privatization – ended up destroying the prosperity that it originally must have been designed to promote.

The explanation is to be found in the rising power of creditors seeking gains by making loans to cultivators and obliging them to work off their debts. Rural usury threatened to appropriate the crop surpluses otherwise owed to the palace, and diverted labor from performing its traditional corvée duties as well as fighting in the infantry. Reducing debtors to bondage threatened to drive labor to flee or defect, leaving such economies liable suffer flight and defection or to be conquered by less predatory ones.

When pastoral nomads conquered Babylonia, the new multiethnic chiefdoms had to hold the loyalty of their subjects. Otherwise, debtors would have fled or defected to rival leaders promising them more liberty and security of their land tenure.[32] Rulers proclaimed Clean Slates to maintain their royal power over local headmen, merchants and creditors in their own palace bureaucracy. "During times of a powerful state, *i.e.* Ur III, the state attempted to monopolize all property and

---

[32] Renger 1972: 167–182.

establish all production by state command; when the state was weak, *i.e.* Kassite Babylonia, property and production fell into the hands of private families and individuals."[33]

From chieftain households to temples

The role of chieftains in tribal communities is to act as their "face" in dealing with outsiders. Through the ages they have maintained their authority by being open-handed. A typical role of the chieftain's household is to absorb newcomers, fugitives and dependents. In Sumer such households expanded to include widows, orphans and the infirm who could not work the land. Many became handicraft workers in temple workshops, fed by crops produced on temple or palace land.

Early evidence for communities mobilizing free labor (mainly to build ceremonial structures) is found in the pre-pottery Neolithic c. 10,000 BC. Göbekli Tepe in southeastern Turkey created monumental carvings that required intensive stone working by men and women coming from far afield. The work must have been voluntary, because there was no way to force attendance – but such occasions were accompanied by feasting, drinking and socializing.[34] By the Bronze Age such public labor had become a compulsory corvée tax for work building city walls, temples and other infrastructure. Clan chiefs were responsible for allocating land in exchange for the holder providing such labor and fighting men.

All this required forward planning and provisioning. The growing responsibility of chiefs gave them a cosmological status in what Carl Lamberg-Karlovsky has called "a smooth transition from secular to sacred." The architectural design of Sumerian temples reflects that of the late Neolithic chieftain's house: "Somewhere in the Ubaid [c. 6500–3800 BC] there is a building at Eridu that looks like it could function as both a corporate household and a temple. A household shrine is put into a previous household – a powerful household. The individual who was before a patriarch is now also a religious leader."[35]

The fourth and third millennia BC saw chieftainship institutionalize itself in the form of palaces and temples under their control: "'family communes,' 'territorial communities,' 'council of elders,' and what Jacobsen (1943) referred to as 'primitive democracy' [were absorbed] into the powerful patronage of the temple economies and the 'houses' of the ruling elite."[36] Van Driel notes that "Uruk seal impressions of around 3000 BC depict a person who behaves like a prince in cult, war and hunt. This is not sufficient for a confident claim that temple and palace were separate institutions, with separate purposes, around 3000 BC. The prince has an obvious cultic role."[37]

---

[33] Lamberg-Karlovsky 1996: 97.
[34] This was common throughout the ancient Near East. See Steinkeller and Hudson 2015.
[35] Lamberg-Karlovsky 1999: 194 and 189.
[36] Lamberg-Karlovsky 1996: 83–84, citing Jacobsen 1943.
[37] Van Driel 1999: 26.

The Sumerian lugal (literally "big man") or "large householder" commanded the é-gal, "big house," the temple or city palace with "an increasing managerial bureaucracy … controlled by kin-related individuals" – clan heads, relatives of the chief, other large landholders and wealthy traders.[38] "To view the temple as a benign public utility, dedicated to the public interest, overlooks the struggle for power," concludes Lamberg-Karlovsky. "By the 25th–24th century the temple estates increasingly fell under the control of a specific ruler and his family, becoming de facto their private property."

Today's contrast between "public" and "private" therefore is anachronistic. Rulers such as Urukagina in the city-state of Lagash (one of the best-documented Sumerian city-states) found it in their interest to consolidate power by proclaiming amargi Clean Slates to restore liberty from debt and from the tendency of administrators in the palace and temple bureaucracy or professional guilds to act in predatory ways.

Anachronistic views of the Mesopotamian takeoff and its enterprise

When the wealth of Babylonian and Sumerian administrative and personal archives, royal proclamations and legal inscriptions began to be translated in the 1870s, the initial impulse was to idealize Mesopotamians as conducting their affairs much like modern European or American businessmen. But as thousands of more tablets and inscriptions from different places, periods and contexts have been translated, it is apparent that many of the wealthiest individuals occupied administrative positions in the royal bureaucracy or acted as its agents, often treating their office as their own personal domain. What seemed to be the public sphere was private, and what seemed to be private business had a public interface. Mogens Larsen points out that the most archaeological digs have naturally focused on excavating public buildings rather than on the smaller private houses. This bias of the archaeological evidence, in conjunction with royal inscriptions and palace and temple records, encouraged the "temple-state" view of a centrally administered economy.[38a] Subsequent excavation of private archives, above all from Assur in the early second millennium and Old Babylonian families have shown that "The assumption of conflict between these two spheres ["public" and "private"] is a modern construct," notes Steven Garfinkle. The ambiguity of modern categories to describe the dam-gàr/tamkārum "is brought out very clearly by the profusion of terms used (officials, commercial agents, employees of the administration, etc.), and in particular by the difference in emphasis that we find in the analyses offered."[39]

---

[38] Lamberg-Karlovsky in Hudson and Levine 1999: 170.

[38a] On this point see Larsen 2015: 102f.

[39] Garfinkle 2012: 150 and 3, citing Gledhill and Larsen 1982: 206. Garfinkle 2012: 152 adds: "Membership in a larger, often institutional household was always subsequent to membership in a local, often familial, household. … the primary source of identity in the Ur III period was not the association of the individual with the state, but rather his/her association with a smaller, local and familial household." He elaborates this point in Garfinkle 2004: 1 and 3n.

Marvin Powell describes the guiding principle of palace and temple officials to be self-interest, with wealth shared by their elites "only insofar as unavoidable custom and economic necessity demands."[40] David Graeber quips that although rulers depict themselves as shepherds "benevolently tending their flocks ... what do shepherds ultimately do with sheep? They kill and eat them, or sell them for money."[41]

But the palace and temples were not initially a "state" whose laws governed the entire economy. In the bifurcated "dual economies" of Sumer and Babylonia, rural areas governed themselves by clan-based oral common law, and the power to declare war seems to have belonged to the assemblies of land-tenured citizens ("sons of the city"). Corvée labor was initially communal, but became increasingly a palatial claim on landholders. And instead of levying taxes, the early palaces and temples were endowed with their own resources so that they could be self-supporting.[42] So they lacked the three centralized functions by which political theorists traditionally define a state: the power to tax, declare war, and set laws for society as a whole. The palaces and temples were set corporately apart, with their own land, herds and dependent labor force. But as these institutions were taken over by conquerors, mainly pastoral nomads, they levied taxes and extracted fees as tribute. Land, herds and workshops were managed increasingly on behalf of the palace.

The main strategy of traders and other entrepreneurs was to work via the palace and temples as customers for imports and as suppliers of consignments of textiles and other handicraft exports, or as managers of what today would be called public utilities such as boating or pubs (ale houses, traditionally supplied by temples in many societies). Johannes Renger finds that many economic activities in Ur III palaces and temples in the late third millennium "were handled by entrepreneurs for the household for which they acted (*Palastgeschäft*)."[43] It often is difficult to distinguish "between loans given by individuals or institutions since the contracts recording institutional loans often name as the creditor not the institution but the official responsible for granting the loan. Thus a whole archive is needed to recognize that a group of loan contracts are institutional loans." What formerly seemed instances of private creditors foreclosing on loans turn out to be officials or semi-officials acting on behalf of the palace to collect back taxes and fees, rents or other agrarian obligations in a "mixed" public/private economy.[44]

Assyriologists refer to Mesopotamia's temples and palaces simply as the "large institutions." These may seem public in the sense that a Chamber of Commerce in small-town America is nominally public while actually serving the town's leading businessmen and real estate developers. Like the local church and main bank, such institutions are controlled by the leading families.

To be sure, Sumer's "managerial class" built city walls and gates, storehouses and other infrastructure. Their scale and cost was beyond the scope of individual families. "The difference between the 'household' and the 'great household' indicates more

---

[40] Powell 1999: 18.
[41] Graeber 2011: 196.
[42] See Diakonoff 1982 (originally published 1967/68 in Russian) and 1991.
[43] Renger 1994: 197.
[44] Yoffee 1977: 6.

than a doubling of personnel managers and food production, and something beyond a tripling of industrial production and legal-commercial concerns."[45] Organizing this resource allocation required cost accounting. The essence of any accounting system is that someone is reporting to a superior. Accounting is a tool of control, so hierarchy, oversight and centralized authority went together.

Growing scale of the temple and palace economy leads to monetization

Merchants received sanctified protection as guests in most towns to which they travelled, and sealed their bargains by swearing oaths to the local god of justice and commerce, and to each other's appropriate gods if the transaction was among members of different communities. The smooth functioning of trade needed safekeeping for debt obligations and other contracts, as well as requiring standardized weights and measures for honest dealing. Much as temples safeguarded their communities' savings of grain and precious metals, their registries long served an archival function.

To achieve cost accounting, the large institutions issued weights and measures, including money as a formal unit to schedule and track the value of food, raw materials and other resources supplied to their workshops and labor force.[46] In addition to providing a standard of value to measure these transactions, money served the fiscal function of denominating temple and palace transactions with the economy at large. Credit extended for such payments involved much more than the loose formalities of gift exchange among individuals. It required money in order to standardize prices for settling these debts.

The origins of money thus are grounded in the enterprise and specialization of labor in the palaces and temples of Sumer and Babylonia. When Ur-Namma and Shulgi appealed to Nanna in the Ur III empire late in the third millennium, and when Hammurabi appealed to Shamash c. 1750 BC, these deities were gods not only of justice in the abstract, but specifically of commercial justice. The past half-century's analysis of palace and temple records show how money was called into being to serve its basic functions of (1) account keeping as a common denominator of prices, (2) a common means of payment for settling debts, above all those owed to the large institutions at the end of each harvesting or trade cycle, and (3) a vehicle for saving and measuring economic gains. These functions of money required standardized measures of volume and weight to quantify the commodities being supplied or purchased, or debts being paid. These standards, along with public regulation of honest measures and quality, were overseen by the temples.

Most arrangements adopted the legal formulae of loan contracts as their basic model, although no money advances were involved. For instance, if an owner of a date grove leased it out to sharecroppers, he might draw up a document stating that the

---

[45] Lamberg-Karlovsky 1996: 82.

[46] For a general review see Hudson and Wunsch, eds., 2004, esp. Englund 2004, tracing the early development of written accounts in Uruk toward the end of the 4th millennium BC. Graeber 2011: 52, emphasizes that "What we call 'money' isn't a 'thing' at all, it's a way of comparing things mathematically, as proportions."

tenant "owed" dates or their money-equivalent at harvest time. The obligation was recorded as a debt. "Because of its abstract nature and phraseology, by simply stating who owes whom how much," the obligation contract appears as payment due on a loan.[47]

Payment of such debts, or for products in general, is unworkable without accurate weighing and measuring. Biblical denunciations of merchants using false weights and measures – a light weight for lending, a heavy weight for repaying – find their antecedents already in Babylonia. Markets were located in the open spaces in front of the temples, which regulated official weights and measures to prevent fraud, much as did the classical Athenian *agoranomoi* (public market regulators) today's national bureaus of standards and related consumer protection agencies.

For payment in metals, standards of purity had to be created, and trusted. The problem was solved by refining silver and other metals in the temples.[48] Our word "money" derives from where Rome minted its coinage, the Temple of Juno Moneta ("warner," reportedly for its honking geese that warned Rome of an impending attack by the Gauls).

The great monetary challenge was to integrate the palatial and temple sectors with each other and with the rest of the economy. The palace was in charge of foreign trade to obtain metal, stone and other raw materials not available in Mesopotamia, and to produce or obtain luxury goods, working with networks of private traders and merchants. This trade was denominated in silver and other raw materials. Many handicraft exports were supplied by temple workshops, which provided basic "welfare" functions for the subsistence economy on the land by employing beside war captives and endowed personnel also widows and orphans, the weak and infirm. The palace supplied their imported materials and oversaw their accounts, which were kept in terms of grain, the basic monthly food supply.

The problem was how to keep income and expense accounts for these diverse commodity flows and employment. The solution was to designate grain and silver as the main monetary and debt-paying commodities – grain for the agrarian economy, and silver for the palatial economy that dominated foreign trade in its dealings with merchant entrepreneurs. This enabled balance sheets, monthly and annual statistics to be expressed in terms of a dual common denominator: silver and grain. A "quart" of barley was set as equal in value to a shekel of silver (8 grams), and this ratio was used to denominate fees and other payments owed to the large institutions.[49] Transactions typically were paid for at a single point of time – for grain debts, on the threshing floor when the harvest was in.

What was not required was formal coinage. Weighed pieces of silver were sufficient, often stamped by temples to attest to their degree of purity.

---

[47] Renger 1994: 200.

[48] I review these complexities in Hudson and Wunsch, eds., 2004: 303–329. See also Hudson 2004a and 2003: 39–76.

[49] Accounting and debt-paying prices also were administered for wool and other basic commodities. Powell (1999) points out the problems of weighing tiny amount that silver, but that rings or bracelets with standardized sections that could be easily broken off enabled it to be used in small individual trading.

Creating markets for commodities, and as a fiscal vehicle for tax debts

Graeber points out that the economic focus was extended from relations among people to "things," headed by commodities supplied by the large institutions, or to pay debts that mounted up to them during the crop year.[50] Monetizing the temple and palace sectors created the basis for market exchange. The effect might be called the "state theory" or "chartalist theory" of markets as well as of money.[51] Accounting in the large institutions valued commodities at standardized prices, and provided a basis for debts to be paid in a specific amount at a specific time – and, if late, at a specific interest charge. Most trade contracts involved the large institutions or their retinue. Payment was seasonal and in bulk.

Retail trade occurred among individuals in marketplaces near the city gates, but this initially was marginal – and mostly with the temples and palaces, purchasing handicrafts and paying for services from these large institutions, or selling surplus crops to support their labor force. However, official accounting and debt-settlement values used by the large institutions did not prevent market prices in the rest of the economy from varying. Crop prices were prone to vary in times of drought or crop failure. Trade occurred outside the city gates, and no doubt among individuals, so administered prices and market prices co-existed. Karl Polanyi's threefold distinction between gift exchange (reciprocity), administered prices and market prices set by shifting supply and demand thus should not be viewed as sequential stages but as usually being found together, in today's economies just as in Bronze Age Mesopotamia.

Land tenure

The archaic concept of property was ambivalent, above all for land. Mario Liverani emphasizes that "in the Bronze Age private property was owned by the family rather than by individual persons – as demonstrated by the restrictions in selling land outside the family. Personal ownership emerges in the temple/palace and in the family sectors, especially during the late Bronze Age, through processes of usucapion,"[52] that is, by coming to be socially accepted simply with the passage of time.

Archaic communities assigned land in exchange for labor duties and tax-like fees. Amorite chieftains assigned it on the condition that holders provide a stipulated military service and tribute. Hammurabi's laws were typical in prohibiting creditors from foreclosing on land assigned to chariot fighters. It was not altruism or abstract idealism that led rulers to protect self-support land and liberty from bondage for citizens, but their interest in keeping the land's labor services, fighting men and crop contributions for the palace. Clean Slate proclamations asserted royal priority for these services over that of merchants and other creditors. These royal checks were capped by Ammisaduqa's detailed 1646 BC Clean Slate, protecting the archaic principle that land rights came with the reciprocal obligation to supply corvée labor, crops or kindred taxes.

[50] Graeber 2011: 60, 85 and 55.
[51] For the discussion and bibliography on Chartalism see Knapp 1924 and Wray, ed., 2004.
[52] Liverani 2005: 50.

Such proclamations saved indebted cultivators from being subjected to bondage and losing their land rights as moneylending became a predatory means of obtaining labor to work off the debt, and ultimately to acquire the debtor's land. But royal authority to protect cultivators waned and flight from the land accelerated after the fall of Babylonia c. 1595 BC. By Roman times the "freedom" of moneylenders to break free from palace overrides involved a loss of liberty and land for a widening swath of the population, stripping the Late Roman Empire of money as it descended into barter for most of the population. So instead of the long-held speculation that markets and interest-bearing debt started with barter and then evolved into money and credit economies, we find the reverse sequence: an archaic credit economy creating money, catalyzed by the large institutions, ultimately collapsing into barter when bankrupted by debt overhead not kept in check.[53]

What Sumerian commercial enterprise bequeathed to antiquity

Charging interest is not a universal phenomenon that has existed since the origins of civilization. But that mythology has been bolstered by the tendency for historians to pick up their narrative relatively late, in classical Greece and Rome. Many anthropologists follow Marcel Mauss in speculating that gift exchange may have led to primitive interest as a kind of "one-upmanship" of the sort practiced by the Kwakiutl of the Canadian Pacific Northwest, taken as stand-ins for the Indo-European-speaking tribes that settled in Asia Minor, Greece, Italy and the rest of Europe, or even earlier in the Near East. Austrian economists following Anton Menger and the German laissez faire advocate Fritz Heichelheim have made up scenarios of Neolithic individuals lending out cattle or tools at primordial interest (Chapter 5).

To counter such speculations, Chapter 6 will describe the logic by which Sumerian palaces and temples developed interest-bearing debt some time in the 3rd millennia BC. Charging interest was how the palace took its share in the gains made from handicrafts consigned to merchants by its own workshops and those of the temples. Such mercantile debts were productive to the extent that traders were able to make a profit over and above the consignment price plus the interest charge that doubled the principal in five years.

Agrarian debts were another matter. They bore interest even when crops yielded less than the expected norm. Their interest rate was steep: one-third (specified in the laws of Ur-Namma in Ur III and later in those of Hammurabi). This rate apparently was based on the sharecropping ratio of one-third of the crop. However, royal Clean Slate proclamations distinguished between commercial and personal debt by cancelling only these "barley" debts. Commercial "silver" debts were left intact. Rulers drew an implicit distinction between what modern economists call productive and unproductive loans. Although antiquity's vocabulary did not distinguish interest from

---

[53] The "three-stage" theory from barter to commodity money to credit economies was popularized by Bruno Hildebrand in 1864. Graeber 2011: 394 points out: "The idea of an historical sequence from barter to money to credit actually seems to appear first in the lectures of an Italian banker named Bernardo Davanzati (1529–1606)."

usury, Hebrew *tarbīt* ("growth") and *nešek* ("bite") reflect the contrast between paying commercial interest out of mercantile gains and a "bite" taken by the creditor who "eats" the crop interest. This is essentially the distinction the Christian Church drew in the twelfth century by banning consumer usury while permitting bankers to charge an *agio* on currency dealings involving trade or payments for travel on the Crusades or gainful commercial purposes.

Rulers recognized that there always would be families that fell behind, and that new arrears would mount up after such debt cancellations. But they made no attempt to ban usury from starting all over again. Instead, royal edicts undid its most adverse effects, by repeatedly reversing debt bondage and absentee creditor ownership of the land. That policy was the cornerstone for preserving a self-supporting citizenry.

Classical antiquity privatizes credit and stops cancelling agrarian debts

Many historians consider the hallmark of Western civilization to be private property, enterprise and credit. Pro-Aryan historians follow free enterprise advocates in presenting classical antiquity as inaugurating a new continuum, starting c. 750 BC, after the Dark Age that followed the collapse of Aegean civilization c. 1200 BC.[54] The legacy of this first Dark Age was personal control of property and credit breaking free of royal overrides. Triggered by climate change and folk wanderings, this "intermediate" transition period of social upheaval saw warlords and clan heads replace Bronze Age monarchies, creating aristocratic senates that protected creditors from royal Clean Slates and other checks on predatory behavior.

The new Mediterranean states were not pristine formations. They adopted the techniques of economic enterprise, money and interest-bearing debt that Mesopotamia's palatial economies had innovated.[55] But the economic surplus that earlier had been squeezed out by palace rulers and temples was privatized in the hands of the new classical oligarchies. The leading families concentrated what had been self-support land, trade and industry into their own hands, reducing indebted smallholders to clientage or irreversible bondage. Societies polarized between debtors and creditors, clients and patrons, slaves and masters.

Tribal communities typically remove chiefs who are greedy and self-seeking. The 7th century BC indeed saw populist revolts overthrow aristocracies from Sparta to Corinth. But by the 3rd century BC, Sparta's kings Agis and Cleomenes (and Nabis) were killed or exiled for seeking to cancel debts. In Rome, a bloody century of civil warfare started with the Senate's murder of the Gracchi brothers and thousands of their supporters after 133 BC. Subsequent politicians who endorsed pro-debtor policies were killed in the conflict that followed, such as the praetor A. Sempronius Asellio in 89 BC by a gang of creditors. In Asia Minor the Mithridatic Wars saw

---

[54] For a review of racially prejudiced accounts see Bernal 1987; Gress 1998 and his article on the *Case Against Martin Bernal* 1989.

[55] I summarize the transmission, probably by Phoenician traders, in Hudson 1992: 128–143. I review how the large Sumerian institutions innovated most of the practices of economic enterprise in Hudson 2010: 8–39.

thousands of Roman *publicani* creditors and other Romans murdered in a broad uprising. Then came the coups of Sulla and other generals in Rome, the slave uprising led by Spartacus, and the assassination of Julius Caesar in 44 BC.

Figure 6:   Hadrian coin, depicting Hadrian himself or a lictor applying a torch to a heap of documents (stipulationes) symbolizing the debts being canceled. The burning occurred in Trajan's Forum, where Hadrian erected a monument inscribed "the first of all principes and the only one who, by remitting nine hundred million sestertii owed to the fiscus, provided security not merely for his present citizens but also for their descendants by this generosity."

Rome's imperial economy sank into stagnation and fiscal crisis as creditors became warlords holding dependents in clientage. In 119 AD, Emperor Hadrian issued a bronze *sestarius* coin showing him burning the tax records in Trajan's Forum, recognizing that these taxes were politically uncollectable. By the 4th century, Rome's taxing power was exhausted. Money was disappearing except among the very rich, who spent it mainly on imported luxuries. By the time the Goths invaded Italy, towns were being depopulated, headed by Rome itself. Debts disappeared simply through society-wide insolvency as economic life sank into subsistence production.

How the modern financial and legal system emerged from antiquity's debt crisis

Much as occurred in the earlier Dark Age after 1200 BC, Western civilization's post-Roman Dark Age led to a radically new economy. The Christian Church banned usury, and then banned debt bondage in the 5th century, along with chattel slavery, even for war prisoners – to be replaced with serfdom. To stop the demographic decline, slaves were freed from their sexually segregated barracks to marry and possess their own cottages. Under the patronage of local lords, these slaves-become-serfs held land under customary tenure, subject to payment of crop rent and labor service.

In the Eastern half of the Empire, Byzantine emperors made their economy resilient for many centuries by land reform protecting subsistence smallholders against creditors, and cancelling back taxes, the major category of personal debt. In Western Europe the papal Crusades in the 12th and 13th centuries looted enough silver and gold from Byzantium to revive commerce. The rising prosperity – and royal borrowing to finance wars – led the Church to lift its ban on interest charges.

Much as the temples had acted as Mesopotamia's major creditors, the Knights Templar and Hospitallers became the major creditors, followed by Italian bankers close to the papacy. Churchmen deemed it moral to charge interest on commercial loans to merchants, because such loans were productive and lenders shared in the risk.

Antiquity's commercial lending was almost exclusively for trade, not to finance new means of production. Our modern industrial epoch's distinguishing financial feature until recently has been to direct credit into tangible capital formation. However, the creditor-oriented spirit of Roman law has bequeathed a primacy to financial claims over all forms of property. What our era calls "security of property" is really an inexorability of creditor claims over the property of debtors pledged as collateral.[56] Reversing the Sumerian and Babylonian concept of liberty *from* creditors, modern property must be forfeited when debt service is not paid. Indebted governments and entire countries are being sacrificed on the altar of debt as global creditors privatize their land, natural resources and public monopolies.

The relevance of studying antiquity's financial destiny is to see how the initial safety valves it enacted were dismantled by creditor oligarchies that imposed debt-ridden austerity as credit and markets became increasingly privatized. Today's sanctity of debt reverses the Bronze Age idea of periodically renewing social order with Clean Slates. Even the happy feature of productive industrial credit is now being reversed by predatory lending, while centuries of more lenient personal bankruptcy laws now face a rollback of bankruptcy protection for debtors, most glaringly in the bank-sponsored U.S. bankruptcy "reform" of 2005. The ancient problem of usury is

---

[56] In *The Mystery of Capital* the Latin American banker Ferdinand De Soto (2000) proposed that customary occupiers of shacks or housing in slums or rural plots be assigned personal property rights that they can pledge for mortgage loans — and forfeit them in due course, so that gentrification can take place. The "wealth" to be created is that of creditors, not the impoverished debtors.

recurring on an economy-wide scale as our epoch limits bankruptcy to individual cases rather than with foresight and planning on a society-wide basis.

Creditors are doing what Bronze Age rulers sought to prevent: gaining wealth in ways that are impoverishing populations, stifling growth and prosperity under the weight of public, corporate and personal debt. The end result promises either to force a new round of public and private debt cancellations, or insolvencies imposing a new Dark Age marked by a flight of populations from economies that do not free themselves from debt.

A Chronology of Clean Slates and Debt Revolts in Antiquity
Mesopotamian Debt Cancellations, 2400–1600 BC[57]

The third-millennium Mesopotamian city of Lagash, in southeastern Sumer, is the best documented. Its ruler Enmetena (2404–2375) achieved suzerainty over southern Mesopotamia by defeating neighboring Umma and its allies. After his victory c. 2400 he inscribed the earliest known amar–gi law cancelling agrarian debts and obligations.

A half-century later Urukagina (2351–2342) reformed economic relations. Upon becoming war-leader (lugal) in his second year to defend Lagash against Umma, his "reform text" cancelled agrarian debts (2350).

During his reign Lagash and the rest of Sumer was conquered, first by Lugalzagesi of Umma and Uruk (2351–2327) and then by the northerner Sargon of Kish, who ruled Mesopotamia as a military overlord from the new capital he built at Akkad.

In the revival after the collapse of the Akkadian dynasty, the Lagash ruler Gudea restored broad trade relations between Sumer and Egypt, Ethiopia, Anatolia and the Taurus range, Dilmun (the island of Bahrain) and Elam. He has left many inscribed statues, and one of his cylinders contains the longest surviving Sumerian poem (1400 lines), commemorating his rebuilding of the city-temple and how he restored order by cancelling the land's debts at the festival celebrating this occasion c. 2130.

The Neo-Sumerian Third Dynasty of Ur (2112–2004 BC) was founded by Ur-Namma (2112–2095). After defeating Lagash and killing its ruler Namhani (Gudea's brother-in-law) in battle in 2112, Ur-Namma led a great extension of trade and installed provisional governors in Elam (Susa), Assur and Mari. He drew up an extensive body of legal rulings and cancelled debts with a níg-si-sá act c. 2100.

His son Shulgi (2094–2047) consolidated Sumerian domination over Mesopotamia. He inscribed the laws of his father and seems to have proclaimed his own debt cancellation.

In the city of Isin the ruler Ishbi-Irra (2017–1985) founded a dynasty comprising fifteen rulers in 223 years. Ishbi-Irra was an Amorite subordinate of Ur's last ruler, breaking away when related Amorite tribesmen and Elamites invaded the land. Many debt cancellations of the Isin rulers survive, starting with the níg-si-sá acts of the third Isin ruler, Iddin-Dagan (1974–1954) at the start of his reign c. 1974, and by his successor Ishme-Dagan (1953–1935), probably upon taking the throne in 1953.

Lipit-Ishtar (1934–1924) left a body of legal rulings that, like that of Ur-Namma c. 1923, led off with a níg-si-sá debt cancellation in 1934.

During his rule an Amorite dynasty in Larsa established itself with Elamite backing. Its first ruler was the Amorite chieftain Naplanum (2025–2005). The city became a dominant power a century later under Gungunum (1932–1906), who

---

[57] Chronology of the dynastic rulers from Brinkman in Oppenheim 1977, and of the early Lagash rulers from Oates 1979.

defeated Lipit-Ishtar of Isin. Larsa reached the peak of its influence a century later under two Elamite brothers, Warad-Sin (1834–1823) and Rim-Sin (1822–1763). Rim-Sin reasserted palace authority over the private sector, which had been growing steadily since the demise of Ur III's centralized economy. He "purified the foreheads" of the land's debt-servants c. 1800. After six decades of rule, in 1763, he was defeated by Hammurabi of Babylon.

In the city of Assur, Ilushuma and Erishum proclaim *andurārum* c. 1900, emulated in the 19th century BC by local leaders cancelling debts in the Cappadocian trade colony, Karum Kanesh. This act applied to tariff debts owed on trade, as well as to agrarian debts owed to the palace.

The Amorite dynasty of Babylon comprised eleven rulers in three hundred years (1894–1595). Benefiting from the city's upstream position, its dynasty was founded by Sumuabum (1894–1881), but the actual ruler in Babylon itself was Sumulael (1880–1845), who cancelled debts with a *mīšarum* act. The dynasty's fifth ruler, Sin-muballit (1812–1793) oversaw the first great assertion of Babylonian power. He declared *mīšarum* debt cancellations in 1812, 1803 and 1797. His son Hammurabi (1792–1750) headed an alliance that carried Babylon to the height of its power. He declared *mīšarum* acts in the year of his accession (1792) and in 1780, 1771 and 1762 after defeating Rim-Sin of Larsa.

Hammurabi's son Samsuiluna (1749–12) declared *mīšarum* to restore order upon taking the throne, and again in 1741. Abi-eshuh (1711–1684) likewise declared *mīšarum* upon taking the throne. Ammiditana (1683–1647) cancelled agrarian debts upon his succession, and again in 1662 and 1647. Ammisaduqa (1646–1626) declared *mīšarum* upon his accession, and again in 1636. His *mīšarum* act is the longest and most detailed of all such proclamations. It also is the last Babylonian act on record. In 1595 the city was raided by the Hittites, and then occupied for 370 years by the Kassites, a tribe from the Iranian highlands.

Rulers of many other cities of the Old Babylonian period (2000–1600) also proclaimed *mīšarum* acts. In Hana (near Mari on the Euphrates) the rulers Kastiliiash, Ammi-rabih and Sunuh-rammu cancelled debts. In Eshnunna, Abi-madar, Naram-Sin and Ipalpiel (or Dadusha) proclaimed *mīšarum*. In Der, Nidnusha used the term *mīšarum* to signify a debt cancellation.

Allusions to Debt Cancellations in Canaan/Israel/Judah, 1400–131 BC

Around 1400 BC Abdi-Ashirta lead *hapiru* attacks on Canaan's mountainous area, bidding for local support against the large landowners who have reached an accommodation with Egyptian puppet rulers. Many *hapiru* were uprooted fugitives from debt pressures in their native lands.

845–817: The prophet Elijah, followed by Amos and Hosea, identify the Jehovah religion with the ideal of protecting the poor from the increasingly powerful landed aristocracy. Israel's destruction is predicted if it fails to maintain social equity. Tribute-levying Assyria is represented as the Lord's tool of vengeance against the resented oligarchy.

740–700 (?): Isaiah preaches social justice. (The Biblical book of Isaiah took its present form only after the exile ended in 537.)

639–609: Josiah ascends the Judean throne. In the process of renovating the temple at Jerusalem, the Deuteronomy scroll is found and becomes the basis for Josiah's reforms. These are made in conjunction with the preachings of Jeremiah.

626–604: The prophet Jeremiah denounces usury, much as did his contemporary Greek "tyrant"-leaders in Corinth, Megara, and Sicyon.

597: When the Babylonian king Nebuchadnezzar prepares to attack Judah, Zedekiah frees the Jewish slaves, cancelling the debts which had bound them in servitude (Jeremiah 34:8–19, 2 Chronicles 32 and 2 Kings 25.)

432: Nehemiah leads the second "return from exile," resettling deported Jews in Judah. The land is returned to its former as well as existing families, freeing them from the debts owed to local creditors and landlords.

131: The Hasmonians liberate Israel from the yoke of debts and taxation marking the beginning of a new era under Simon the high priest. (I Maccab. 13–14.)

Egypt

663–609: Bocchoris/Psammeticus cancels consumer debts, freeing the debt-servants.

196: The 13-year old new Pharaoh Ptolemy V proclaims a fiscal debt amnesty, apparently recalling normal Egyptian pharaonic practice. Commemorated by the Rosetta Stone.

Debt Crises in Classical Antiquity, 650 BC–425 AD: Greece and Rome

650–580: Popular reformers ("tyrants") come to power in Corinth, Megara, Sicyon (under Cleisthenes) and other Greek cities, overthrowing landed aristocracies (often including their own relatives), redistributing their lands and cancelling the debts.

594: When Athens succumbs to a similar debt-polarization crisis, Solon is given powers to act as *archon* ("premier"). He cancels the debts, bans personal debt-servitude for Athenians and alien landownership, thereby preventing foreign creditors from foreclosing. He avoids the more drastic land redistributions carried out in other cities.

500–450: Rome's secessions of the plebs over the debt issue. Indebted Romans refuse to fight until their debts are cancelled and economic polarization mitigated.

450 (443?): Rome's XII Tables set interest rates at $8\frac{1}{3}$ % (= $\frac{1}{12}$th) per annum, but this tradition and its fourfold penalty was repeatedly violated by creditors, and had to be re-iterated (*e.g.* in 357). Meanwhile, the law permitted debt-servitude (the *nexum* institution).

367: After an impoverished thirty years, plebeian legislation permits debtors to count the interest as amortization payments from the balance that is owed paying off the balance in three years instead of all at once.

357: A public commission is appointed to lend Roman funds to save bankrupt debtors from slavery and loss of their lands (revived in the 217 Punic War emergency).

347: Rome's legal interest rate is cut in half, to 4⅙ % (= ¹⁄₂₄ᵗʰ) and a moratorium is declared on existing debts, which are to be paid off in four equal installments. To ameliorate matters further, the war tax and levy are lifted.

342: The plebeian tribune Lucius Genucius moves to ban outright the charging of interest.

326: After popular riots, Rome's Poetillian-Papirian laws ban *nexum* debt-servitude.

220–200: Sparta's kings Agis, Cleomenes and Nabis cancel the debts, seeking to return to the legendary Lycurgan golden age with its egalitarian ethic. The objective is to restore a free land-tenured peasant-army. But Sparta is defeated when oligarchic cities call in Roman aid.

204: After Rome defeats Carthage and levies huge reparations, wealthy contributors to the war effort in 216 demand repayment of what they had contributed, representing that their donations actually were loans. The money is to be paid in three installments.

200: With its treasury bare after paying two installments, Rome has only the public land to turn over, above all the rich Campagnia. Instead of being settled by war veterans as had been customary, this land is turned over to wealthy war-contributors in lieu of reimbursement. It is to be taxed at only a nominal rate. Beginning in 198, foreign slaves are imported en masse to cultivate the resulting latifundia.

193: The Sempronian law extends the XII Tables' 8⅓ % interest-rate ceiling to cover non-Romans within the expanding Republic as Greece and other regions are absorbed.

133: Attalos III of Pergamon bequeaths his kingdom to the Romans. In 129 it becomes a Roman province. Aristonicus, the local claimant, mobilizes the population against Rome, promising to cancel their debts and establish a "Kingdom of the Sun" (Heliopolis), a political ideal probably influenced by the Stoic philosopher Blossius. Rome defeats local armies by poisoning the water supply. After looting local temples, it burdens Asia Minor with huge reparations debts, paving the way for over half a century of warfare. Regular tribute starts in 126.

133–130: Rome's domestic Social War is fought largely over the debt issue. In 133 the brothers Tiberius and Gaius Gracchus sponsor land reform (in particular to limit the extent of large estates carved out of the public domain. They also sponsor a general financial reform, creating a class of *publicani* "knights" to act as creditors and financiers, so that senators will not perform this function. Tiberius Gracchus is murdered by oligarchic senators in 133, the first tribune to be killed. A decade later, in 123, his brother Gaius and his supporters were defeated when they occupied the Aventine, and Gaius had a slave kill him in 121.

111: The oligarchic Agrarian Law declares all occupied public domain to be the property of existing holders, thereby defeating plebeian hopes for land reform.

100: The tribune L. Apuleius, supported by the Consul Marius, sponsors a land-settlement reform, but the oligarchs oppose it, and repress a popular revolt.

89: The praetor Asellio is murdered for sponsoring restoration of the XII Tables law punishing creditors fourfold for charging excessive interest (over $8\frac{1}{3}$ %). In the ensuing riots, debtors agitate for "new account books," that is, a Clean Slate debt cancellation.

88: The Vespers of Ephesus: As many as 80,000 Romans are killed in Asia Minor in retaliation against Roman tax farming and moneylending. During 88–84 Mithridates of Pontus turns what had began as a local war in 92 into a region-wide war by Asia Minor against Rome.

86: The Valerian Law remits three-quarters of the debts of all Romans. Publican financiers and senators join forces in the face of their common fear that demagogues might bid for popular support by endorsing a general debt cancellation and land redistribution.

86–85: The Roman general Sulla sacks Asia Minor and imposes a huge tribute, forcing many cities and much of the population into debt to Italian bankers. This helps make Sulla the richest man in Rome in 83. His army takes over the city and he kills many of his opponents during his dictatorship of 82–79.

73–71: Slave revolt led by the Thracian war-captive Spartacus.

70: Rome declares a moratorium on Asia Minor's war tribute, which had multiplied six-fold from the 20,000 talents imposed by Sulla in 84 to 120,000 talents, despite the fact that Asia Minor already had paid 40,000 talents (not including the looted treasure of Asia Minor's temples). The local Roman general, Lucullus, sets a 12% interest rate and decrees that where interest payments have exceeded the original principal, the debt is to be considered paid. Debt service is limited to a quarter of the debtor's income.

63–62: Catiline and some three thousand supporters are killed in battle. A major plank of their program (which Cicero called a "conspiracy") was a cancellation of debts.

49: Caesar marches on Rome. In the turmoil he allows debtors to count their interest payments as repayments of their principal, and introduces Rome's first bankruptcy law. But this alleviates debt pressures only on the wealthy. His *cessio bonorum* saves them from having to sell off their property under distress conditions by letting them turn over real estate at pre-Civil War prices. To support collapsing land prices, Caesar also directs that two-thirds of all capital assets must be held in the form of Italian real estate. This is not much help to the landless and smallholding population at large. Demagogues such as Caelius (Rufus) and Milo are killed after leading a popular insurrection. In 47, Cneius Cornelius Dolabella likewise advocates cancellation of debts, and is killed for leading riots in the Forum. This is the final defeat for Rome's indebted poor. Henceforth, lending is concentrated mainly among the wealthy.

AD 33: A financial crisis results from emperors hoarding coinage in the imperial treasury, aggravated by private hoarding and a drain of bullion to the East (largely to purchase luxuries). Tiberius re-imposes the traditional 8⅓ % interest-rate ceiling, and Caesar's decree that two-thirds of all personal capital be invested in Italian real estate. This leads to widespread foreclosure on mortgages as lenders convert their financial claims into land. Tiberius decrees that debtors are obligated only to pay two-thirds of debts that are called due, but his measures nonetheless aggravate the general financial crisis.

AD 325: The Council of Nicea bans the practice of usury by members of the Christian priesthood.

AD 118: Hadrian burns the tax records.

AD 178: Marcus Aurelius emulates Hadrian's burning of the tax and debt records.

AD 425: Charging interest is banned for the lay population generally.

458: Emperor Majorian (457-461) issues Novel No. 2, proclaiming an amnesty for land-tax arrears. The aristocracy overthrew him.

578–582: Tiberius II Constantine remits a year's taxation (the major debts of the Byzantine era) to restore morale.

797–802: Byzantine Empress Irene remits tax debts, mainly to gain support against opponents who ultimately overthrew her).

934: Romanos I bars powerful *dynatoi* from acquiring village land, and reverses their acquisitions

947: Constantine VII strengthens the restoration of smallholdings to their original families, rendering acquisitions since the winter of 929 null and void, and bans the dynamo from acquiring them in the future.

959–963: Romanos II rules that any lands sold since Constantine took the throne in 945 are to be "restored without obligation to reimburse the buyers"

976: Basil II reinforces Romanos II's ruling. In his last year of rule, 1025, "he waived two years' worth of land and hearth taxes"

4. The Anthropology of Debt, from Gift Exchange to Wergild Fines

Anthropologists have documented how tribal communities create webs of gift exchange that bind families to each other, such as bride price owed to inlaws. Also prevalent are wergild-type compensation to heal breaches of the peace when injuries are inflicted, typically with collection procedures to ensure payment. The great question that prehistorians must answer is how such interpersonal debt practices, which originally must have been socially integrating, ended up reducing debtors to a state of dependency and bondage by classical antiquity.

The first imperative of low-surplus economies is to enable their members to survive. Failure to provide mutual aid threatens their viability. Economic surpluses come largely from collective efforts to exploit nature – the hunt or harvest – and also in battle. There is little leeway for disparities in income and wealth to develop, so self-seeking at the expense of others is discouraged. Instead of personal self-interest to amass fortunes at the expense of one's neighbors, peer pressure praises openhanded generosity and non-individualistic conspicuous consumption, headed by honoring ancestors (and hence their own and the community's roots) with great feasts and elaborate sacrifices.

Being needy was natural enough for many families, but one's clan and neighbors normally provided mutual aid. A reciprocating gift was appropriate at some point, but there was not yet a formal compulsion to do so – to say nothing of paying interest. Exploitation forcing families into dependency, especially to pledge land for debt and forfeit it to moneylenders irreversibly, became the norm only relatively late in history. A history of debt therefore must explain the transition from "anthropological" obligations to classical usury.

The reciprocity of gift exchange

In *Argonauts of the Western Pacific*, Bronislaw Malinowski points out that most Trobriand Islanders could be self-sufficient if they so desired, but use mutual obligations to promote social cohesion. "The whole tribal life is permeated by a constant give and take; ... every ceremony, every legal and customary act is done to the accompaniment of material gift and counter-gift." This cements friendly relations among clans and villages, pulling their members into mutual relationships with one another. "At harvest time all the roads are full of big parties of men carrying food, or returning with empty baskets." A man might travel far "to fill the yam house of a man who could do it quite well for himself, if it were not that he is under obligation to give all the harvest to his sister's husband!"[58]

---

[58] Malinowski 1922: 167, 174f.

These exchanges are more akin to good manners than to formal economic debts. And indeed, such reciprocity survives even among modern families and friends. Marcel Mauss, the father of French structuralist anthropology, called this "prestation" in *The Gift* (1925). A gift is not really a loan. It is part of a system of reciprocating presents and hospitality.

"Rather than being employed to acquire things," as David Graeber notes, gift exchange and similar reciprocity debts "are mainly used to rearrange relations between people. Above all, to arrange marriages and to settle disputes."[59] Delay in reciprocating such obligations is not usurious or socially divisive. "When reciprocity is delayed," another anthropologist explains, "as it is in the ceremonial kula trade of the Trobriand Islands … an umbrella of peace is created to enable ordinarily hostile people to engage in utilitarian trade while they wait for ceremonial gifts to be reciprocated the following year."[60]

How classical moneylending differs from gift exchange

In view of the stretched-out time element in reciprocity, Mauss concluded, "a gift necessarily implies the notion of credit,"[61] in the sense that a balance was due. He then made a jump directly to classical antiquity by suggesting that the customary reciprocation might express one-upmanship as a primordial form of "interest" and even "usury."[62] As an example he cited the *potlatch* feasts of the Kwakiutl in America's Pacific Northwest, whose tribal leaders indulged in a competitive destruction of copper sheets in great potlatch bonfires. They obtained these coppers by trading furs with the Hudson's Bay Company, so the practice was not pristine. The idea that Kwakiutl gift exchanges typically lead to return exchanges with a customary "over-plus" is by no means a form of productive investment in the modern economic sense of the term.

Andrew Strathern stretches matters along similar lines by writing that the *moka* gift exchange of New Guinea's highland men competing for prestige by outdoing each other in openhandedness "can be looked on simply as a means of investment making."[63] But the "investment vehicles" are luxury goods (decorative shells or coppers, roast pigs and so forth). Their destruction does not finance new means of production to increase the economic surplus. "Topping" a counterparty's gift is rarely a calculated percentage. Such examples are a far cry from commercial investment building up capital as in the ancient Near East. There was not even a formal legal compulsion to return a quid pro quo, to say nothing of paying interest.

Mauss acknowledged that the reciprocity dimension of gift exchange, cementing social ties by establishing obligations to return generosity at some future date,

[59] Graeber 2011: 60.
[60] MacCormack 1981: 161 f.
[61] Mauss 1967 [1925]: 35. Mauss even believed that failure to offer a counter-gift in the potlatch was sanctioned by debt slavery. For a critique of this view see Testart 1998.
[62] Mauss 1967 [1925]: 4, 24, 73, 85, 100, 108, *etc.*
[63] Strathern 1971: 219.

overshadows its commercial aspects. But his followers have taken reciprocity as a starting point to analyze the flowering of interest-bearing credit in classical antiquity.[64]

But Marshall Sahlins warns against viewing surviving hunter-gatherer enclaves as proxies for those of Europe and the Near East seven thousand years ago. "The anthropology of hunters is largely an anachronistic study of ex-savages … the paleolithic disenfranchised, occupying marginal haunts untypical of the mode of production." Herded onto reservations like Native Americans, these groups are no longer pristine, but are "barred from the better parts of the earth, first by agriculture, later by industrial economies."[65]

Mary Douglas likewise recognizes that although individuals in tribal communities often have entrepreneurial ability, they "are incapable of long-term accumulation of capital. They do not produce anything which will yield over a longer time than the life cycle of a pig. These are not systems of primitive capitalism, but merely primitive commerce."[66] The study of their prestation-type exchanges cannot explain Mesopotamia's commercial takeoff c. 3500 BC.

A major problem with seeking the roots of interest-bearing credit and money lending in gift prestation is the latter's ubiquity. "The exchange of gifts is an integral feature of all major ceremonies, such as marriages, funerals, alliances, peace treaties" – in short, almost all social intercourse.[67] When such reciprocity obligations are incurred among neighbors, friends and other peers, there is no legal necessity for repayment. The guest who fails to return hospitality or a gift may lose face, but there is no formal collection procedure. This polite reciprocity does not involve witnesses or contracts, sureties or the pledging of collateral. There is a long way to go before personal obligations lead to debt bondage or forfeiture of access to self-support land. The characteristic Indo-European terms for debt among peers have more to do with parity and mutuality (as in Latin *mutuum*, a non-interest-bearing loan) than with interest-bearing obligations.[68]

Being so important in so many diverse contexts throughout the world, the ethic of reciprocity is not helpful in explaining how lending at interest evolved in Bronze Age Mesopotamia, especially in connection with its early association with long-distance commerce, *e.g.* trade with outsiders rather than with fellow community members and peers. Surviving tribal enclaves lack the outward-reaching commercial dynamics that characterized Mesopotamia's palaces and temples in the third millennium BC.

Given the socially cohesive context for gift exchange, it is necessary to look elsewhere for the dynamics that led to usury. Debt terminology in many languages derives from fines for inflicting personal injury. These fines did not entail payment of interest,

---

[64] Gernet 1981 and Vernant 1983.
[65] Sahlins 1972: 8.
[66] Douglas 1967 [1965]: 126.
[67] Sundstrom 1974 [1965]: 86.
[68] The classical Greek *eranos* organizations created to raise money for well-born individuals also involved a reciprocity of equivalents among peers.

but they did bring into being proto-monetary means of settling obligations, as well as formal collection procedures that even included enslavement for non-payment of compensation debts for personal injury. But unlike Near Eastern money, the usual payments were in the form of capital assets such as cattle or servant girls.

Fine-debts for personal injury catalyze special-purpose proto-money

Money is a standardized means of payment. An analysis of Indo-European vocabulary indicates that the earliest payments were fines for personal injury. The English verb "pay" derives via French *payer* from Latin *pacare*: to pacify, appease, to make peace with. The idea is compensation and restitution – a subspecies of reciprocity.

Lacking public mediation to carry out judgment, retaliation against aggressive outbursts was left to the injured party or his family, *i.e.*, by taking vengeance. Such feuds evidently prompted development of a peaceful alternative: compensation payments to settle disputes rather than to let animosities erupt into vendettas. Making a restitution payment expiated one's offense.

Restitution was based on the injured party's social status – his worth or "man-price" (*wergild*). The Brehon laws of medieval Ireland (named after the local officials who served as arbitrators), for example, punished offenses by *eric* fines proportioned to the rank of the person slain or otherwise injured.[69] Anglo-Saxon law likewise fixed the *wergild* on a king's life at 30,000 *thrisma* coins, that of a prince at 15,000, a bishop or alderman at 8,000, a sheriff at 4,000, a thane or clergyman at 2,000, and a common churl at 266.[70]

Homer's *Iliad* (9.743) illustrates this principle. "A sire forgives the slaughter of his son: the blood-price being discharged, the murderer lives." The epic (18.497ff.) describes the portrayal on Achilles' shield of a dispute over whether a proffered *wergild* payment of two talents in gold was sufficient. It is in this spirit that Rome's XII Tables (VIII.2) specifies: "If a limb is injured, unless peace is made with him [*i.e.* with the injured party, by paying compensation], there shall be retaliation."

Accepting monetary payment was more for the weak than the strong. As a Greek proverb put matters: "Those who cannot, sue; those who can, take vengeance."[71] A larger payment was needed to dissuade high-status families from indulging in

---

[69] *Senchus Mor*, vol. I (*Ancient Laws of Ireland*, 1869). Dating back at least to 100 BC and originally part of an oral tradition, the earliest judgments are contained in the *Senchus Mor*, the Great Book of Irish law. Saint Patrick is said to have fixed their form in 430. They remained a living institution until nearly 1700.

[70] Murphy, ed., *The Works of Cornelius Tacitus* (1822, vol. V, 355), citing Blackstone 1765–1769, vol. IV, ch. 23 and Hume's *History of England*). Only as commercial trade with outsiders developed did debts come to be denominated in precious metals and coins.

[71] Payment is made in full when there is no desirability of leaving a balance outstanding. The Corsican phrase *Siamo pace* means "We are quits" as far as further conflict is concerned (Black-Michaud 1975: 84). Alternatively, if the offending party (or his relatives) cannot pay, he might become a debt bondsman to the injured party.

retaliation in kind. Families with social power did not have to accept pecuniary restitution – and were able to pay the assessed wergild or other fines rather than going into exile (*viz. Iliad* 9.632ff.: "The manslayer at a great price abideth in his own land").

Exacting monetary retribution for human life and personal injury has little to do with the trucking and bartering to which Adam Smith points as the foundation of economic relations. But such injury debts did help bring about proto-monetary means of settling them. This can be seen in the metonymy of classical Greek *timē*. At first the word connoted worth, esteem or valuation, and subsequently wealth or tax assessment – "the nominal value of which an Athenian citizen's property was rated for the purposes of taxation, his rate of assessment, rateable property" (Liddell and Scott, *Greek-English Lexicon*) – hence came the term timocracy, rule by property holders or other wealthy persons. As a legal term *timē* signified a penalty, such as the compensation due a victim.[72] The penalty could range from a monetary liability to exile or death of the offender.

Among the Hittites in the 2nd millennium BC, "if a member of the family commune was killed, it was the patriarch who, in the Hittite expression, was 'owner of the blood,' and received a compositio for the killed person."[73] The transition to "debt" is reflected in Jacob Black-Michaud's observation: "among the Bedouin – and in all other feuding societies in the Mediterranean and the Middle East – an original homicide is spoken of as a 'debt' and vengeance as a 'redemption of the debt': the mnemonics of vengeance may ... be better seen as statements of account."[74]

Tacitus describes the Germanic tribes of the 1st century AD as imposing such restitution debts, and they were enacted by the Gauls, Franks and Lombards, being called *wergeld* or *wirgild* ("man-price") in Anglo-Saxon usage, and *kinbote* by the Swedes. Henry Maine notes in his *Early History of Institutions*:

> Compensation in the Welsh laws is reckoned primarily in cattle and in the Irish ones in cattle or bondmaids (*cumhal*), with considerable use of precious metal in both. In the Germanic codes it is mainly in precious metal: gold shillings and *sceattas* in the oldest laws of Kent, shillings or denarii in those of the Franks, ounces of silver (*øre*) in those of Norway. In the Russian codes it is in silver and furs, graduated from marten down to squirrel.[75]

---

[72] The related verb *timoreo* meant to avenge or to help by way of redressing injuries. This Homeric usage of *timē* as associated with valuation referred to the assessment of "damages with a view to compensation, and so compensation, satisfaction, especially in money" (Liddell and Scott, *Greek English Lexicon*). The Athenian *timētes* was an official charged with appraising damages, penalties or taxes, similar to the Roman *censor* in charge of taking the census and rating the property of citizens.

[73] Diakonoff 1982: 39.

[74] Black-Michaud 1975: 84.

[75] Maine 1888: 273. He adds: "Their detail is remarkable ...– specific compensations for the loss of an arm, a hand, a forefinger, a nail, for a blow on the head so that the brain is visible and the bone projects ..."

Wergild-type fines have been found throughout the world as administered legal prices, including Mesopotamia, "whether payable in cattle or axe-blades, rings or pig-tusks, shell ornaments or mats," observes Philip Grierson. "The common standards were based on objects of some value which a householder might be expected to possess or which he could obtain from his kinsfolk."[76]

Debt terminology, and probably the earliest formal collection procedures, evidently first developed in the realm of common law governing compensation for personal injury, followed by obligations owed to the public sector. The penalty might include bondage to one's victim. Under Irish law a repeat offender "might be detained in his creditor's service till he had paid off the debt by work, or he might be handed over to the king and his officers with a similar end in view …"[77] This practice paved the way for later debt bondage to lenders.

Most Indo-European languages retain a legacy of associating guilt (for an offense or "sin") with the liability to make restitution by paying a fine. The following table traces the etymology of Indo-European terms associated with Sanskrit *skhal* (to stumble, which even today is a metaphor for sin). The English verbs *should* and *shall* (Anglo-Saxon *scyld*; Swedish *skuld/skull*; Danish *skyld*) derive from the Germanic root *skal*, meaning to owe, be in debt or to be liable.[78] In those societies where these verbs developed, to stumble, to stray from the straight path, obliged offenders to pay a fine. German *Schuld* can mean guilt or sin, and by extension, any debt or obligation.

These words indicate that pecuniary obligations originated as moral legal debts long before they came to be applied to market or lending transactions. The line of causation was from injuries and damages leading to compensation payments being owed. The dual sin/debt connotations of *Schuld* and its semantic cognates did not imply that individuals were reprehensible for needing to borrow. What was meant was that debts *inevitably entailed the obligation to pay*.

A related archaic social context of debt terminology was "tax obligation." Medieval Sweden used "sakir or saker mostly as meaning 'obliged to pay a fine' and only a few times in the sense of 'punishable, guilty.'"[79] The metonymy linking the idea of should or duty with debt is found in French *devoir*, and English "duty" still refers to a customs tax. Calling a fine or tax a "should" or "ought" reflected the liability originally attached to a person's obligation (*Schuld*, guilt or "sin") to compensate for having caused an

---

[76] Grierson 1978: 12ff.

[77] Bryant 1923: 344f. Falkenstein 1956: 84, 132ff.) describes a Sumerian Ur III perpetrator being absent and his family being enslaved in his place to compensate victims of murder and theft.

[78] Benveniste 1973: 153f. points out: "The [Gothic] noun skula 'debtor' … designates the one who 'owes' money, is liable to some obligation, possibly some punishment, from which comes: culpable or accursed of in a criminal manner, etc. (cf. German *schuldig*, 'guilty')."

[79] Springer 1970: 41ff. He adds: "We find in Old Norse the weak verb *saka* in the sense of 'to accuse, blame, harm, scathe,' as well as *sekja*, 'to sentence to a fine, penalize, punish,' and the nouns *sok* f. 'offense charged, accusation, suit (in court)' and *sekt* for 'guilt, penalty.'" Old Icelandic sagas use *sekr* "most frequently in the sense of 'outlawed.'" The relationship to "sacrifice" and "sacred" seems clear.

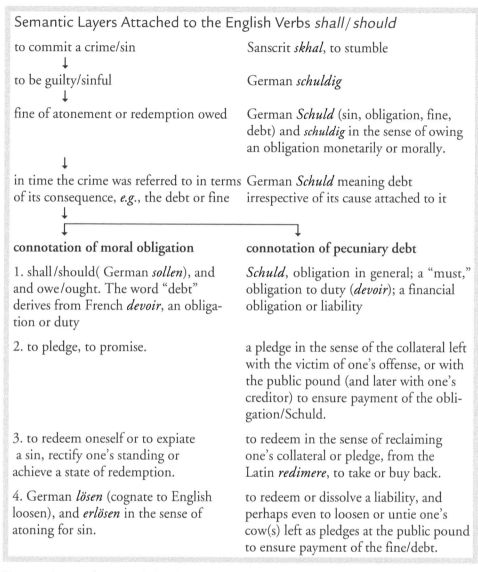

Semantic Layers Attached to the English Verbs *shall/should*

to commit a crime/sin ↓	Sanscrit *skhal*, to stumble
to be guilty/sinful ↓	German *schuldig*
fine of atonement or redemption owed ↓	German *Schuld* (sin, obligation, fine, debt) and *schuldig* in the sense of owing an obligation monetarily or morally.
in time the crime was referred to in terms of its consequence, *e.g.*, the debt or fine ↓	German *Schuld* meaning debt irrespective of its cause attached to it

connotation of moral obligation	**connotation of pecuniary debt**
1. shall/should(German *sollen*), and and owe/ought. The word "debt" derives from French *devoir*, an obligation or duty	*Schuld*, obligation in general; a "must," obligation to duty (*devoir*); a financial obligation or liability
2. to pledge, to promise.	a pledge in the sense of the collateral left with the victim of one's offense, or with the public pound (and later with one's creditor) to ensure payment of the obligation/Schuld.
3. to redeem oneself or to expiate a sin, rectify one's standing or achieve a state of redemption.	to redeem in the sense of reclaiming one's collateral or pledge, from the Latin *redimere*, to take or buy back.
4. German *lösen* (cognate to English loosen), and *erlösen* in the sense of atoning for sin.	to redeem or dissolve a liability, and perhaps even to loosen or untie one's cow(s) left as pledges at the public pound to ensure payment of the fine/debt.

Figure 7: Semantic layers attached to the English verbs shall/should

injury or owed the community.[80] Moral responsibility to pay originated with owing restitution or public responsibility.

Modern preconceptions tend to invert the relationship between debt and sin by stigmatizing debt. It is deemed morally wrong (if not technically sinful) not to pay what one owes. Yet today's debts are not owed for having committed offenses, but

---

[80] Klein 1971: 877, *q.v.* "shall." Aristophanes based the opening of *The Clouds* on the wordplay between Greek *chreos* (debt) and *chreon* (necessity).

mainly to financial creditors for loans, or to merchants for goods and services. Graeber illustrates how acceptance of the moral premise that all debts should be paid – under rules drawn up by creditors – leads debtors in today's world, including "anthropological" tribal communities, to willingly accept slavery, sexual exploitation and other degrading treatment.[81] It is the debtors who suffer injury, at the hands of creditors who now are victimizers, not victims as was the case when wergild claims arose from personal injury.

Debts called into being monetary means to pay them

A similar complex of ideas characterizes the terminology for money. German *Geld* is related to Gothic *gild,* "tax," but an early connection to the payment of fines is indicated by Old Icelandic *gjald,* "recompense, punishment, payment," as well as Old English *gield,* "substitute, indemnity, sacrifice."[82] The linkage here is between money Geld and "guilt" as well as guild. "In Gothic, gild translates as the Greek *phoros* 'tax.' … We are thus on three lines of development: first religious, the sacrifice, a payment made to the divinity, secondly economic, the fraternity of merchants, and thirdly legal, a compensation, a payment imposed in consequence of a crime, in order to redeem oneself. At the same time it is a means of reconciliation."[83]

The associations of *wergild*, marriage payments, duties and tax assessments predate money lending. In fact, they predate money. Debts (guilt) came first, and led to a need for money (*Geld*) as a standardized means of settlement. The origin of personal debt in the form of fines or tax accruals indicates that the earliest debtors were not borrowers in the sense of having obtained an advance of money. The prototypical debtors were offenders making restitution to their victims or to the community. The first recipients of such debt payments were not money lenders, but families who had suffered injury.

In his study of Indo-European words for exchange, Benveniste finds no archaic words for market payment as such. The Greek "expressions for 'purchase' and 'sale' are not separable from those of 'give' and 'take.'"[84] Mauss likewise notes that the Kwakiutl of North America make "no clear distinction between the meanings 'to give food,' 'to return food' and 'to take vengeance.'"[85] The vocabulary for commodity exchange and credit adopted words hitherto used for prior forms of legal obligations as the linguistic

---

[81] Graeber 2011: 334.

[82] Benveniste 1973: 8.

[83] Benveniste 1973: 57 and 61. See also http://www.etymonline.com/index.php?term=guilt &allowed_in_frame=0, and etymology of the word 'guilt', by 5ocietyx: https://5ocietyx. wordpress.com/ 2014/04/26/etymology-of-the-word-guilt/: "The suspicion that the word 'guilty' originates from '*gieldan*' meaning 'to pay a debt' makes sense even if the OED consider it inadmissable phonologically speaking. When the courts find a defendant guilty the next thing they do is make them 'pay their debt to society'."

[84] Benveniste 1973: 53 ff., 66.

[85] Mauss 1952: 105, citing Boas 1913–1914, glossary under *yenesa* and *yenka*. Mauss notes (p. 102): "it seems that even the words 'exchange' and 'sale' are lacking in the Kwakiutl language." Benveniste 1973: 53 ff. makes a similar observation with regard to classical Greek.

path of least resistance, appropriating pre-existing words to describe the evolving financial practice. The archaic words for payment, debt and the association with sin or civil infraction carried over, later to be applied to debtors paying usury.

Cattle as a denominator of debts, but not of commercial exchange or interest

As the prototypical archaic capital, producing calves, milk and draught power, cattle were the most important archaic form of wealth, and hence a common unit for fines, as well as for offerings at the communal festivals that marked the archaic calendar. A person's honor price reflected his wealth, measured most visibly in livestock. The word "pecuniary," meaning monetary or market-oriented, stems from Latin *pecus*, meaning livestock, either singly or in herds.[86] Also deriving from *pecus* is "fee," whence "feudal."

Although penalties typically were denominated in cattle, these assets almost never were items of gift exchange, and rarely of commerce. Anthropologists have found that tribal communities may exchange the fruits of their harvest or luxuries, but livestock, seed, tools or capital rarely are gifts. And although they were a standard of worth when used to pay fines, payments in cattle would have represented much larger sums than normal exchange called for.[87] But although not used for retail trade, cattle fines and public contributions helped pave the way for a pecuniary mentality, and hence in time for monetizing exchange and credit. Bernard Laum attributed the origins of Greek *oboloi* "spit money" to food contributions to archaic festivals, temples or public feasts.[88] Standardized contributions to these public festivals and other occasions developed, by extension, into other public gifts establishing one's status in the primitive community.

Debt collection procedures originally preserved economic viability

As the most archaic "prices," compensation payments for inflicting personal injury were denominated in the first literally pecuniary form of money: livestock. To compel payment, formal collection procedures were developed to impound a fine-debtor's assets, or to name someone to stand surety for the debt. In contrast to gift exchange,

[86] Benveniste 1973: 40 believes that the Indo-European root *peku* (< Latin *pecus*) originally referred to "personal chattels, movables in general," and only later, in classical antiquity, came to mean specifically livestock, then smaller livestock and sheep. "Similarly the English term cattle, French chaptel, goes back to Latin capitale 'principal property' ..." The Sanskrit word for cattle, *rupa*, gave its name to the Indian rupee coin. Some early ingot money from Asia Minor used in the Mycenaean period, was shaped in the form of cowhides, perhaps to indicate that the value of the metal content was commensurable with that of steers.

[87] Quiggen 1949.

[88] Laum 1924. The term for small coin, *obol*, derives from the spits or skewers (*oboloi*) on which meat was cooked and distributed. The **drachma** meant originally a "handful" of six obols. Theopompus (cited in Athenaeus VI. 231) noted that in archaic times the sacred precinct at Delphi "was adorned with bronze offerings which were not statues, but cauldrons and tripods made of bronze."

enforcement procedures presuppose an unfriendly breach, and hence are not associated with mutual prestation, bride price or other friendly obligations. But as noted above, they remain in the sphere of reciprocity exchange.

The usual practice was to distrain the offending party's assets. A debtor who lacked sufficient collateral might be obliged to provide a pawn – movable property such as cattle or a maidservant – or to make his extended family responsible for his obligations. A natural step was to name a well-established community member, perhaps a chieftain, to act as enforcer or to stand surety for the debtor – a natural role for chieftains taking on the function that temples, religion and civil courts later would serve.[89] Reflecting the fact that archaic communities lacked "any public enforcement of private engagements. … suretyship is an almost universal feature of early society."[90] It is found in Babylonia and Assyria, Israel, Greece and Rome, among the Germanic tribes, and in the recent experience of Japan, China and Indonesia.

Laws governing the distraint of a debtor's property are found in Irish, Teutonic, Hindu and other Indo-European speaking communities. The plaintiff/creditor might take the debtor's assets subject to proper rules of seizure after giving due notice. As Maine has described:

> The person assuming himself to be aggrieved seized the goods (which anciently were almost always the cattle) of the person whom he believed to have injured him or failed in duty towards him. He drove the beasts to a pound, an enclosed piece of land reserved for the purpose, and generally open to the sky. …
> [T]here is no more ancient institution in the country than the Village-Pound. It is far older than the King's Bench, and probably older than the kingdom. … The seizure of the cattle, the rescue and counterseizure, belong to the oldest practices of mankind.[91]

Collateral distrained in this way was called distress, putting the debtor in what subsequently have become spoken of as distressing circumstances. Most of Ireland's Senchus Mor dealt with distraint procedures, imposing heavy penalties for violating strict formalities. These often involved officials comparable to an English sheriff. The levying of distress "was available for the recovery both of tributes and of ordinary debts,"[92] as well as for "all sorts of mulcts, forfeitures, penalties, and fines, and for the satisfaction of every species of liability."[93]

---

[89] Until the modern era entire nations and their merchants could be held liable for judgments against their compatriots. British courts in the 17th and 18th centuries issued Letters of Marque permitting privateers to seize ships of countries owing such obligations. The captains of such privateering vessels (the privatization of debt collection) were not pirates but acted lawfully (at least according to the laws of their own countries). Like sheriffs and bailiffs, they were permitted to take a cut of the sums they recovered.

[90] Binchy 1970: 355–367.

[91] Maine 1888: 261 ff.

[92] Bryant 1923: 260.

[93] Ginnell 1894: 159.

The assets being distrained did not necessarily reflect the value of the debt outstanding, but were taken to pressure the debtor to pay. Babylonian documents from the time of Hammurabi "show that the 'distress' (Babylonian *nipûtum*) is something seized not in satisfaction of a debt but to ensure or compel the payment of it (*e.g.*, Code of Hammurabi §§ 114–115)."[94] The debtor either would acknowledge his creditor-distrainor's claim and pay the sum due, or would put up other security in place of what was seized.

Even in the case of fines – or penalty-debts against offenders and lawbreakers – the intention seems not to have been to impose such permanent distress on offenders as would deprive the social body of the wrongdoer's ability to meet his normal commitments, including serving in the army. For thousands of years, distraint procedures were not permitted to seriously disrupt economic life by depriving cultivators or craftsmen of adequate resources to maintain their self-support. Certain vital assets were declared exempt – plow oxen, the miller's grinding stone and the smith's anvil. In the laws of Hammurabi (§ 241) an ox is not to be distrained: "If a man seize an ox for debt, he shall pay 20 shekels (one-third mina) of silver." According to Job 24:3 it is iniquitous to "take the widow's ox for a pledge." Deuteronomy 24:6 commands that "No man shall take the nether or the upper millstone to pledge: for he taketh a man's life to pledge."[95] The 6th-century BC laws of Gortyn, on the island of Crete, exempt the peasant's plow, the warrior's armor and the woman's wool from being taken as pledges or seized for nonpayment of debts.[96] Wilhelm Roscher describes how "a very old Norman law provides that in actions for debt, execution should not issue against effects of the debtor which are indispensably necessary for him to maintain his position, such as the horses of a count or the armor of a knight. Magna Charta extended this provision so as to include the agricultural implements and cattle of the peasantry," for these were needed by cultivators as part of the vital agricultural foundation on which economic life rested.[97]

Maine points out that the principle of exempting essential capital assets from distraint "was not in its origin the least intended as a kindness to the owner. It was entailed by the very nature of the whole proceeding, since without the instruments of tillage or handicraft the debtor could never pay his debt."[98] Maintaining the viability of the community took priority over claims by individual creditors. That is why land tenure rights were long exempt from foreclosure in early low-surplus communities.

Only late in antiquity did debt foreclosure and clientage lead to permanent deprivation of the means of self-support and personal liberty on a large scale. Bronze Age Mesopotamian rulers limited creditor attempts to enserf debtors in order to keep

---

[94] Driver and Miles 1955: 65. Roth 1997 §§ 113 and 114. The ruling implies that creditors with a claim of grain or silver can distrain a member of the debtor's household.

[95] Schaeffer 1915: 137 ff.

[96] Halbherr 1897: 223.

[97] Roscher 1878 vol. I: 283. Even today, in fact, the state of Vermont allows debtors to keep one cow, two goats and three swarms of bees.

[98] Maine 1888: 262.

the debtors free enough to perform corvée labor duties and serve in the army. This broad aim of social survival is what makes Sumerian, Babylonian and other Near Eastern Clean Slates so striking as compared to classical Greek and Roman practice. But increasingly, royal fee collectors and moneylenders acted in economically aggressive ways. The rise of creditor oligarchies made the seizure of debtors' assets and irreversible bondage for their family members acceptable.

Collecting debts from borrowers who committed no offenses

Early debtors owing fines were not borrowers of money or individuals unable to pay public authorities, but offenders who owed restitution to their victims or to the community. The original seizure of collateral from debtors was to compel payment owed to the victims of crimes. The first recipients of these debt payments were the victims or families who had suffered injuries. These injured parties were, in effect, proto-creditors.

Even before moneylending gained momentum, *wergild*-type obligations could result in the fine-debtor's servitude.[99] § 54 of Hammurabi's laws ruled that an individual who could not make restitution for the economic injury he caused his neighbors (for instance, by not keeping his dike in proper repair) might be sold into bondage and his property sold to reimburse his neighbors. At that time – c. 1750 BC– the main personal debts stemmed from fees owed to palace collectors, and emergency borrowings.

At first such seizures were only temporary. Personal debts owed to the palace were forgiven by royal amnesties, but by classical antiquity most debts were owed to private creditors. They gained control of governments, and prevented debt write-downs. Non-payment of debts became subject to collection procedures imposed for breaking the peace. Such debts had begun as payments to expiate personal offenses, but these collection procedures came to be imposed on poor borrowers. Debt and foreclosure procedures became socially divisive, no longer supporting peaceful relations. Debt bondage threatened to turn debtors into fugitives or criminals by driving them to economic extremity or imprisoning them for debt, much as archaic offenders were exiled if they could not pay wergild fines.

Herodotus (I. 138) wrote that the Persians "consider telling lies more disgraceful than anything else, and, next to that, owing money. There are many reason for their horror of debt, but the chief is their conviction that a man who owes money is bound to tell lies." But of course, creditors were notorious throughout antiquity for using false weights and measures when lending money and collecting debts. From Babylon to Egypt, debts had to be written and documented in order to be legally collectable, evidently a response to creditors being likely to lie by either claiming that they had made a loan, or falsely claiming that they had not received a deposit or not been repaid.

---

[99] Falkenstein 1956, vol I: 84, 117 and 132 ff. describes Ur III families c. 2000 BC as being enslaved to compensate victims of murder and theft.

5. Creditors as Predators: The Anthropology of Usury

No problem has proved more vexing to economic historians than how interest-bearing debt originated. Anthropologists have found no indication of interest charged on gift exchange or restitution debts. Mauss's idea of the mutually destructive Kwakiutl one-upmanship – "topping" partners when reciprocating gifts – is too informal to be a fixed *a priori* rate of interest. In the 1st century of our era, Tacitus (*Germania* 26) noted that the Germans, whose debts were mainly for *wergild*-type fines, "were not acquainted with loans on interest."

There are many reasons why low-surplus tribal communities are unlikely to have charged interest. It was considered bad form to be so mercenary as to reinvest surpluses to generate further profits from one's compatriots. Individuals who did accumulate wealth were expected to act openhandedly and give away most of their gains. For communities self-sufficient in food and other basic necessities, economic exertion tapers off once subsistence needs are met.[100] When such communities do produce surpluses, it is to pay tribute, hire military support or trade with outsiders for jewelry, shells and other luxury or prestige articles, not to reinvest as capital. There is no universal tendency to accumulate capital by lending in a self-expanding process.[101]

Mycenaean Greek palace accounts (1600–1200 BC) have no indication of interest-bearing obligations to the palace or on commercial trade credit or agrarian loans. Interest appears in the Mediterranean lands only around the 8th century BC, evidently brought by Near Eastern traders. Later, lending among friends and peers tends to be interest free, as in the *eranos* loan clubs of well-to-do Athenian aristocrats.

The prominent role of cattle has led some economists to speculate that charging interest may have evolved in archaic pastoral economies. But the productive powers of cattle or other assets do not lend themselves to supporting an obligation for debtors to pay a stipulated monetary return accruing at specific calendrical intervals. Interest-bearing debt is distinct from "anthropological" exchange. Interest is a regular and periodic financial return, stipulated in advance and computed as a standard proportion of the debt principal.

The present chapter outlines how the innovation of charging interest mutated as it was transplanted into new contexts that lacked the checks and balances of Bronze Age Sumer, Babylonia and their neighbors.

A misleading theory of how usury began

Economists have speculated about how Neolithic populations some seven thousand years ago might have originated interest-bearing debts if their motivation were similar to those of modern society. This preconception conjures up a fictitious epoch of peas-

---

[100] Sahlins 1972.
[101] Polanyi, Arensberg and Pearson, eds. 1957.

ants borrowing cattle, seed grain or other assets to invest productively, paying some (perhaps half) of the resulting surplus to self-seeking lenders as interest. Depicting interest-bearing loans as invariably productive, this story appeals to pro-creditor ideologues – while overlooking the social disruption that universally has resulted from foreclosure and forfeiture of assets (and personal liberty) as debts mount up at interest.

The recorded experience of all known low-surplus communities indicates that peasants borrow only out of dire need, not to make gains. Already a century ago Eugen von Böhm-Bawerk refuted this "naïve productivity" theory of interest, pointing out that "on the lower stages of economical development there regularly appears a lively dislike to the taking of interest. Credit still has little place in production. Almost all loans are loans for consumption, and are, as a rule, loans to people in distress. The creditor is usually rich, the debtor poor; and the former appears in the hateful light of a man who squeezes something from the little of the poor, in the shape of interest, to add it to his own superfluous wealth." [102]

This did not deter the free-market Austrian-school Fritz Heichelheim from depicting lending as the mainspring of economic development. He speculated that individuals might have advanced loans to help borrowers make enough economic gains to pay their creditors. His pretentiously titled *Ancient Economic History, from the Paleolithic Age to the Migrations of the Germanic, Slavic and Arabic Nations* was revised and translated from German into English in 1958. Its introduction alleged that personal wealth seeking has been a natural and universal characteristic at least since the Stone Age.

According to Heichelheim, early "food-money" provided a basis for productive credit: producing crops with seeds borrowed from well-to-do individuals – without any involvement of communal or public agencies. Around 5000 BC, he suggests: "Dates, olives, figs, nuts, or seeds of grain were probably lent out … to serfs, poorer farmers, and dependents, to be sown and planted, and naturally an increased portion of the harvest had to be returned in kind." Naturally! In addition to fruits and seeds, "animals could be borrowed too for a fixed time limit, the loan being repaid according to a fixed percentage from the young animals born subsequently. … So here we have the first forms of money, that man could use as a capital for investment, in the narrower sense." [103]

Heichelheim grants that "emergency credits and friendly loans were yet more common than seed and animal loans at this time, and did not require interest. But even as relatively early as this, rich owners must have given out their surplus stocks regularly to poorer farmers and herdsmen, and gained interest in kind." Like modern bank lobbyists who rationalize high rates of interest as compensation for risk, he suggests that lenders "had to demand a higher return in view of the possible losses from bad harvests or animal diseases." Neolithic debtors thus are depicted as actuarial calculators, borrowing cows to make gains when more cattle were born than had to be paid as interest, while creditors practiced an agrarian arbitrage, adjusting their interest rates to compensate for risk (Heichelheim's "possible losses").

[102] Böhm-Bawerk 1890: 15.
[103] Heichelheim 1958, vol. I. (rev. ed., Leiden, 1958): 54 f.

Despite its purely speculative basis, Sidney Homer of the Wall Street investment bank Salomon Brothers popularized that argument in his *History of Interest Rates*. Hoping to show the virtues of credit (and by logical extension of modern banking), he grounded his argument on the premise that "cattle probably comprised the first true productive assets or capital of tribes and individuals." Pointing out that "Sumerians used the word mash for calves and for interest," he guessed that cattle or seed grain could indeed "be loaned out at interest ... and provided [their] own increment."[104] Might not such loans have been self-amortizing, rather than eating into the agrarian debtor's resources?

This interpretation, however, misses the metaphoric character of archaic terminology for interest. The Latin word is *foenus*, whose prefix *fe-* connotes the idea of fecundity and fertility, much as the Greek word for interest/usury, *tokos*, alludes to the "offspring" of capital, as did Sumerian máš, a young goat and hence "birth" or offspring. What was "born" was not an actual animal but a monthly mathematical "baby," $\frac{1}{60}$th (a shekel per mina) in Mesopotamia, an annual tenth in classical Greece, and a twelfth (an *uncia*, our modern troy ounce per pound) in Rome.[105]

Each region set its interest rate for ease of calculation in the local system of fractions – Mesopotamia's sexagesimal (60-based) system, the Greek decimal system or the Roman duodecimal (12-based) system. To Heichelheim this seeming decline in the official Bronze Age rate from the 20 percent ($\frac{1}{60}$th per month) in the 3rd and 2nd millennia to 10 percent in Egypt and classical Greece, to $\frac{1}{12}$th in Rome reflected the rising security of credit, meaning a declining riskiness of loans with the spread of pro-creditor and "private property" laws to make foreclosures permanent.

Failure of physical productivity or risk levels to explain early interest rates

Explanations of how interest rates are determined by productivity, profit rates and risk are irrelevant to antiquity's rural lending to consumers in arrears or in need. How much of a usufruct can livestock yield? Cattle may provide plowing services and milk, and give birth to calves. But with regard to antiquity's long-term decline in interest rates from the Bronze Age through classical antiquity, it hardly can be assumed that Sumerian livestock reproduced more rapidly than Greek livestock, or that the latter increased more quickly than those of Rome. Herds do not grow at 20 percent, to say nothing of the agrarian interest rate of 33⅓ percent per year. The Sumerians knew this, as demonstrated by a tablet showing the growth of a herd of cattle.[106] A debtor's cattle or seeds may multiply if weather conditions are normal and there is no military interruption, but such conditions rarely are maintained year after year. Herds may be raided or military attacks occur, and crops have failed more or less regularly ever since the Neolithic. But interest rates remained relatively stable in each region for extended periods of time.

---

[104] Homer 1963: 26.
[105] I explain this metaphoric terminology for interest accruals in Hudson 2000.
[106] Gelb 1967: 1–8, and more recently Nissen, Damorow and Englund 1993: 139 ff.

It would be futile to suggest a productivity or profit explanation for the rate of antichretic interest for the value of women – the servants or daughters of debtors, typically pledged to perform menial and sexual services in the creditor's household. Many Babylonian and Biblical laws are about this phenomenon.

Most personal loans are for consumption, not to make a profit

Aristotle (*Politics* 1256 f.) points out that loans of metallic money are by no means as productive as cows or seeds, which reproduce themselves. Metal is barren in these respects. That is the central problem of usury. Interest is demanded on the basis of loans whose proceeds are not invested productively, or at least not at sufficient profit to pay the return demanded by creditors.

If cattle really were lent out and calves paid as interest, such loans would be self-financing. But most agrarian debts "stemmed from need, above all to subsist until the next harvest, to pay taxes or interest on old debts, not from investment opportunities." [107] When loans are for consumption, borrowers can pay only by selling or forfeiting their assets. That leaves them "worse off at the end of the process than at the outset."

Economists tend to assume that all debts can be paid with mutual benefit to borrowers as well as creditors. Unproductive lending is treated as an anomaly, not the norm. But the economy-wide effect of usury is to enable creditors to draw society's wealth into their own hands. That is why most civil wars in antiquity were debt revolts. Borrowing was a losing proposition for most debtors.

Heichelheim and Homer were confused about just whose livestock were being transferred. They assumed that cattle were advanced to debtors, enabling them to pay the stipulated calf-interest or money payment. But this idea of lending out cattle is contrary to the spirit of pastoral communities throughout the ages. [108] What invariably has been the case is a pledging of livestock (as well as land and other productive resources) from debtors to creditors. Antichretic interest and agrarian usury was paid out of the needy cultivator's own stock, not out of profits from investing the loan proceeds.

Having few means to earn the money to pay the debts they took on, debtors usually ended up forfeiting their collateral and falling into debt bondage. That is what creditors really wanted: Not merely the interest as such, but the collateral – whatever economic assets debtors possessed, from their labor to their property, ending up with their lives.

---

[107] Renger 1972: 179.

[108] Lending cattle in exchange for interest or animals did spread among the Nuer pastoral herders in Sudan, but this is a late interaction with other non-pristine economies. When anthropologists find shepherds receiving a proportion of the sheep or calves born to the livestock given into their care, as in Basque and Mexican *partido* practice, this is not so much a loan phenomenon as what used to be called "wages of superintendence."

Paying interest out of the surplus provided by the debtor's own collateral

The original idea in taking collateral was to ensure payment of an obligation, starting with fines for personal injury or similar damages. Lending money to make a pecuniary gain led creditors to seek collateral that would provide an economic return. Borrowers had to sell their most valuable assets on a conditional basis, retaining the right to redeem their assets by paying off the loan. In the meantime, the creditors got the use value from the pledge. That is what economists call an antichretic loan, in which the collateral produces a usufruct ("use of the fruits") for the creditor.

Antichretic lending involving debt-pledges is well documented in modern tribal communities. "In central Africa," one anthropologist observes, "the charging of interest was a fairly recent phenomenon, except in the form of labor and produce of animate pawns exploited by the creditor." Under such antichretic loans, "[t]he value of the pawn's work was sometimes deducted from the debt to the extent of discharging it. In other instances it might be considered to constitute the interest on the loan. In some cases, when livestock was pawned, any offspring born during the loan period was kept by the creditor. On the other hand, the creditor's cost of maintaining the pawn might be charged to the debtor." [109]

Cattle have been the most typical assets pledged in early 20th-century Nigeria: "The primary surety ... was found in the chattel given as pledge. A loan would be for only half the value of the pledge – security in the amount of 200 per cent of the loan was called for as in standard American first mortgage practice. Interest consisted of the use of the article without responsibility for ordinary wear and tear. The borrower was forced to divest himself of the total productive capacity of the pledged resource." [110]

The essence of such antichretic lending is that while the loan typically is merely to enable the debtor to get by (or to pay taxes or tribute), *the debtor's own collateral produces a usufruct for the creditor.* The usufruct is not produced by capital that is *borrowed*, but by what is pledged! Inasmuch as borrowers are needy to begin with, this pledging of collateral makes loan repayment all the more difficult. "The interest might or might not be high percentage-wise. Yet it was devastating in its net effect. Add to this 'service charges' to the witnesses, the agent, and the creditor, which ate up the equivalent of two shillings to the pound, and you get the Ashanti proverb: 'A debtor's things go away in great heaps.'" [111]   Many debtors were unable to redeem their collateral, and creditors kept the pledges when debtors defaulted. Sometimes for the price of a relatively small loan, creditors were able to gain valuable assets. The practice culminated in debt bondage.

Antiquity's creditors initially wanted interest in the form of labor power. By the end of the 3rd millennium BC, borrowers are found pledging their labor service to creditors – one of the earliest stages in the evolution of wage labor. Piotr Steinkeller traces this practice to the Ur III period, influenced largely by private credit practices

---

[109] Sundstrom1974 [1965]: 34, 38.
[110] Hoebel 1968 [1964]: 230.
[111] Hoebel 1968 [1964]: 230.

from Northern Mesopotamia, "apparently the beginning of a long process by which debt-bondage arrangements were progressively more and more wide spread, becoming eventually a major economic and social problem."[112]

Steinkeller quotes Finley's description of how this process ended up in classical antiquity: "Why should a rich man lend … except to another rich man? The conventional answer is that he seeks profit through the interest he charges (at excessive rates, of course)." The reality, Finley found, was that "labour power and solidarity were historically prior to profit in the form of interest … debt was a deliberate device on the part of the creditor to obtain more dependent labour rather than a device for enrichment through interest."[113]

Likewise, Steinkeller quotes the historian Cornell's finding that the aim of moneylending in Rome and other archaic agrarian societies was precisely to create a state of bondage. The whole point of lending was precisely that "Impoverished peasants had no serious prospect of repaying, and no security other than their own persons … The purpose of the 'loan,' which was secured on the person of the debtor, was precisely to create a state of bondage."[114]

The idea of productive borrowing to finance profitable fixed capital investment was rare in antiquity, as it has been in all known tribal communities. Finley emphasized this point throughout his works (maybe to an extreme), most notably in *The Ancient Economy* (1973). The main example of productive commercial lending was investment in mercantile voyages, in which creditors shared in the risk.

If ancient communities had adopted Heichelheim's individualistic scenario, usury would have polarized them between creditors and debtors. They would have succumbed to civil warfare or lost their members through emigration or defection to rivals. It was to avoid such a fate that rulers canceled personal non-commercial debts. The alternative would have been to let creditors cannibalize societies. Only at the end of antiquity, in the Roman era, did "freedom" for creditors from palace overrides lead to a loss of liberty for much of population.

Today's world provides an idea of how archaic communities would have been torn apart by adopting debt relations without checks and balances. When modern financial practices are brought to tribal enclaves, chieftains register their clans' herds and lands (and subsoil mineral rights) in their own name, often selling these rights to foreigners—and keeping their payments abroad as privatizers did in the post-Soviet states after 1991. The privatizers send their children for schooling abroad, to take economics courses informing them that all this reflects the efficient workings of a free market.

Something similar occurred when Near Eastern credit practices were brought to the Aegean and Mediterranean lands in the first millennium BC. Privatizing credit in the hands of local chieftains led to chronic conflict. After 133 BC, Rome's Equestrian Knights, the *publicani*, obliged subject cities to borrow to pay tribute. Their exactions prompted the historian Livy (45.18.4) to comment: "Wherever there was

---

[112] Steinkeller 2002: 124.
[113] Finley 1981: 153 and 155 f., cited in Steinkeller 2002: 110 f.
[114] Cornell 1989: 282 f., quoted in Steinkeller 2002: 111 f.

a *publicanus*, there was no law and no freedom for the subjects." The creditor oligarchy class ended up destroying the Republic in the ensuing century of Social War.

Rome's pro-creditor legal philosophy survived in medieval Europe. Royal land and mines were pledged to bankers, *e.g.* Spain's silver mines to the Fuggers. Today, entire nations are so deeply indebted that they are subjected to financial austerity and asset stripping, all in the name of free markets as if this means equity and stability.

Archaic societies could not have impoverished debtors along these lines without collapsing. What saved them were social pressures that deterred chieftains from permitting palace collectors and other well-to-do individuals to get everybody they could (along with their property) into their grasp. Communities kept needy unfortunates from sinking into chronic dependency, because this would have lost labor that could hardly be spared.

These early "anthropological" norms of equity did not survive to save a large portion of late antiquity's population from losing its liberty and property to creditors. Agrarian usury became a deepening wedge between rich and poor, leading to forfeitures and distress sales that created private property as our modern world knows it. Our modern legal philosophy endorses the expropriation of debtors' property, not their security of property on terms that required creditors to absorb a loss when loans are too heavy to be paid.

The polarizing dynamics of agrarian usury, contrasted with productive credit

Throughout history, usury has been the most important force polarizing economies and leading to the monopolization of land. It absorbs the property and income of relatively poor people (and by imperial Roman times, that of the profligate aristocracy), without supplying the means for debtors to pay. Borrowers are in danger of losing whatever assets they have pledged, ending with their personal liberty and land tenure rights.

The historical riddle to be solved is how such a dynamic began. If interest did not begin by "anthropological" gift exchange or lending out cattle, grain or other means of production, how *did* it begin? Social ethics in low-surplus communities traditionally have deterred the well-to-do from impoverishing the poor. Something must have seemed fair and natural about the original idea of charging interest. It must have been part of a system aimed at promoting rather than eroding social survival. It must have been paid for purposes deemed socially necessary, and been charged to borrowers able to pay under normal circumstances.

To explain this development, the next chapter traces the great takeoff of interest as part of the complex of gain-seeking enterprise that emerged in Bronze Age Mesopotamia.

6. Origins of Mercantile Interest in Sumer's Palaces and Temples

A public entrepreneurial nexus of enterprise is not what archaeologists expected to find when they began unearthing Bronze Age administrative records a century ago. The main search was for religious texts, myths, wisdom literature or other cultural artifacts such as the Gilgamesh epic and the laws of Hammurabi. But the vast majority of cuneiform tablets are debt contracts and administrative accounts.

Reconstructing the context for these economic records and royal proclamations of "justice and equity" reveals the translator's preconceptions. Most translations reflect how the modern world works, as if this is the only way of doing things. Modern prejudices assume private enterprise and interest to be primordial. Today, it seems natural to pay interest on whatever is owed, except among family and friends.

Yet the idea of charging interest at a stipulated mathematical rate cannot have arisen simply because one day a rich person told his debtor, "Pay me interest on what you owe." It had to be invented, and introduced in a way that must have been compatible with traditions of fairness at the time. Charging interest must initially have played a productive economic and social role, not expected to become a dynamic impoverishing the population at large!

The explanation for why interest appeared where and when it did – in southern Mesopotamia some time in the third millennium BC – is to be found in the economic function it must have been intended to serve. For starters, charging interest always has involved different classes of creditors and debtors. As Chapter 4 has described, the tribal chieftainships familiar to anthropologists do not use loans to finance the means of production, or writing to track what is owed under gift exchange and fines. The relevant parties know what is owed, and no formal charges or penalties mount up for non-payment. Agriculture, handicrafts and social infrastructure are self-financed.

Interest-bearing debt is documented earliest in Mesopotamia. Chapter 3 has described the innovations of writing and record keeping, weights and measures, and royal proclamations administering prices to monetize payment of debts. It is hard to imagine interest being charged on an extensive and formal scale without written accounts. In central Anatolia interest-bearing debt appears as a transplant brought by Assyrian merchants c. 2000 BC to their trade colonies. The Hittite kingdom has left no documentation of interest, nor have the Linear B palace records of Mycenaean Greece or Crete (1600–1200 BC).

A social precondition for charging interest was an ethic endorsing the accrual of claims for payment as economically desirable. This ethic traditionally has involved official institutions – temples and palaces. The most characteristic early Mesopotamian debts were owed to their bureaucracies by households in the land-based community at large running up debts for various services. Some households were entrepreneurial and made gains as suppliers or agents of the temples and palace.

How the social values of tribal communities discourage enterprise

Most mutual-aid communities cannot afford individuals or even chieftains profiteering at the expense of their fellow members. Tribal chiefs are expected to be openhanded, and families gain status by sacrificing, contributing to communal feasting or sacred bodies, giving their surpluses away via gift exchange, burying them with their ancestors, or simply destroying them outright. The more egalitarian they are, the more sanctions against personal accumulations of wealth is found.[115] Modernist economic doctrine views such conspicuous consumption and even mutual aid as an unproductive dissipation of wealth. But this view that resources would best be invested to accumulate wealth most rapidly ignores the (mal)distributional effects of such gain-seeking.

As the community's "face" to outsiders, the chief typically is designated to trade on its behalf. This gives commerce a quasi-public character. But his gains normally must be justified by being used in socially acceptable ways. When his household accumulates wealth at the expense of too many other families, he may be overthrown. Revolts against inequality that impoverishes communities are a timeless phenomenon. So to become acceptable, the charging of interest needed public legitimacy. It hardly could have gained acceptance if it produced wide disparities in wealth and reduced large numbers of citizens to dependency – at least, not initially.

Temples of enterprise

Today's economic ideology rarely deems public agencies to have played a productive role in civilization's takeoff. Archaic surpluses are assumed to have been produced by individuals who lent out cattle, seeds or tools in exchange for interest to be paid out of their yield or output, which in due course came to be monetized.

This myth assumes that interest and mercantile profit are universal and timeless – while depicting palaces, temples and public regulations as drags on economic development, not catalysts for a takeoff. But Mesopotamia's large-scale organization involved entrepreneurs acting in association with the palaces and city-temples, simply because that is where the money and surpluses were concentrated. Merchants (dam-gàr in Sumerian, *tamkārum* in Babylonian) and officials or collectors in the palace or temple hierarchy built up fortunes in conjunction with that of the large institutions.

Temples were endowed to be self-supporting as corporately distinct institutions, supporting a dependent labor force with land and herds of animals set corporately apart from the community's family holdings. As major producers of export goods for palace merchants to exchange for raw materials, as well as leasers of land and infrastructure, temples developed financial practices much larger in scale than the interpersonal "anthropological" scale of chiefs or clan heads acting simply on their own account.

Temples were the centers where accounting practices were innovated above all because of their role in mobilizing labor. This required detailed forward planning to allocate materials, and that in turn requited detailed accounts. In contrast to the

---

[115] Smith 1976, vol. II, p. 310, cited in Kohl 1978: 463.

temples, the palace did not keep such accounts for its consignment of export goods to merchants, who apparently simply had to pay the palace its stipulated return, not document each transaction. The detailed temple accounts are largely responsible for the 20th century's "temple state" belief that temples must have run the whole economy.[116] But in fact the temples' workshop and related production accounts are so detailed and their distribution of food and other raw materials are so heavily documented (as compared to palatial trade) because they were reporting to the palace.

Dominated by palace and local elites, and later by the nomadic leaders who conquered southern Mesopotamia, temples served as public utilities along formalized "economic" lines. Royal inscriptions describe their wealth as serving the common good, with rhetoric that anticipates the euphemisms of politicians and bankers in today's world.

The temples' role as monetary centers stemmed from the fact that they were the main repositories for society's savings (grain and precious metals), and their oversight role in being charge of refining the precious metals. Silver and gold offerings were cast into sacred objects that could be melted down and minted in emergencies to purchase food, hire mercenaries or buy off attackers.[117] The city-temples' sacred status was supposed to protect their savings, stores of seeds for seasonal planting and tools from theft and attack.[118] The "grain goddess" Inanna was not simply a fertility or harvest deity, but was associated with storing food. Her emblem was two rolled-up mats that formed a doorway to her date storehouse. Grain storage facilities and repositories of the community's monetary savings remained a feature of temples through Greek antiquity, called the *thesaurus*.

The need for merchants and other commercial agents to manage trade

For hundreds of thousands of years the Euphrates, Tigris and their tributaries washed rich alluvial soil down from the surrounding mountains into the Sumerian land. The region was still largely arid in the late Neolithic and swamp-ridden in the far south, requiring heavy labor investment to manage water for irrigation and transport. The scarce resources required for agricultural production in this region were headed by

---

[116] Schrakamp 2013: 445–465, provides the most recent and balanced view of the relationship between the palace and temples. See the discussion in Chapter 9 below on Urukagina's "reforms." The vast literature on the role played by temples long viewed them more than the palace as being the central economic actors. For this "temple state" approach see Frankfort 1951; Falkenstein, 1974; Oppenheim 1957: 27–37, and 1972; Gelb 1965: 230–243, 1971: 137–154, and 1972: 1–21; Oates 1978: 457–485; Lipiński, ed., 1979, esp. Renger (pp. 249–256); Makkay 1983: 1–6; and Lundquist 1983: 205–219.

[117] See for instance Oppenheim 1949: 172–193. The Parthenon provided this function in classical Athens.

[118] Lewis Mumford emphasized the role of cities as "containers" in his contribution to the University of Chicago's colloquium on *City Invincible* (1960). Temples were the first such containers and storehouses. Falkenstein1954: 794 f. has pointed to the "enormously large surpluses accumulated in the [temple] storehouses."

labor, draft animals and tools to work the land. But the soil did not contain metal, stone or even grew hardwood – the materials necessary for tools and infrastructure. These materials, above all copper and tin, had to be obtained from far away.

This resource dependency made trade necessary on a scale far beyond the "anthropological"-type gift exchange found in self-sufficient tribal enclaves. Imported materials were supplied by a managerial class consisting mainly of entrepreneurs trading on their own, over and above supplying the large institutions as their major customers.

Southern Mesopotamia's city-temples took on the role that chieftains played in less bifurcated societies, in which outsiders seeking asylum were assigned to the chieftain's household. They housed war widows and orphans, the blind, crippled, infirm and elderly whose relatives could not afford to support them. As a result of infirmity, or loss of their husbands and fathers through warfare or disease, these dependents were set to work grinding flour, producing textiles and other handicrafts with a specialization of labor far above the family scale, as well as gardening and performing other tasks in an epoch when there was scant supply of wage labor. Modern jargon would describe this as turning welfare functions into "workfare" or "working for the dole."

Construction of early cities had created a communal spirit around the temples, enabling "much of the resources of these early cities [to be] organized for institutional benefit." That benefit included foreign trade to obtain raw materials from distant lands – trade that was left to travelling merchants. The result was a mixed economy in which "the efficient operation of the economy by the central administration was dependent on the existence of individual entrepreneurs."[119] A symbiosis developed between these institutions and the merchants to whom their administration consigned textiles, crops and other products. Palaces and temples were major actors in domestic agriculture and crafts, while private traders moved in more "market-like" parts of the economy.

Along these lines, Mario Liverani divides trade in these economies into two basic segments. The first of these concerns the relationship between the temple or palace and its trade agents; the second segment (or set of segments) is related to the merchants' activities once they left their home country and ventured into foreign lands; the final segment is related to the settling of accounts between merchants and central agencies at the end of the (yearly) process. The administered relationship, using fixed values and pursuing materials unavailable at home, was limited to the starting move and the closing move: trade agents got silver and/or processed materials (that is, mainly metals and textiles) from the central agency and had to bring back after six months or a year the equivalent in exotic products or raw materials. The economic balance between central agency and trade agents could not but be regulated by fixed exchange values. But the merchants' activity once they left the palace was completely different: they could freely trade, playing on the different prices of the various items in various countries, even using their money in financial activities (such as loans) in the time span at their disposal, and making the maximum possible personal profit.[120]

---

[119] Garfinkle 2004: 391 and 389.
[120] Liverani 2005: 53 f.

By the end of the third millennium, caravans financed by well-placed family members carried textiles, tin and other goods up the Euphrates to northern Mesopotamia and Asia Minor, and eastward across the Iranian plateau. Commercial credit to provision this trade was a byproduct of this bifurcation between palace and temple households and mercantile traders. The palace advanced goods produced in its own and temple workshops on terms that apparently doubled the original consignment value in five years (60 months, at interest of $\frac{1}{60}$th per month). Interest on these debts seems to have been paid by traders working for their own gains while supplying the large institutions with imports. Merchants paid the doubling of their commercial advance in five years, as long as they could make even larger trading profits for themselves. Their public obligations included import duties and tithe-like commissions in the form of offerings to the commerce deities. Their trade enjoyed official protection, and their contracts were sanctified by being sworn to the local gods of commerce.

The primary role of the large institutions in setting interest rates

Profit seeking and interest bearing debt were catalyzed was the fact that the overall gains were associated with the large institutions acting as public utilities. As Chapter 3 has described, temples took the lead in developing account keeping as a planning tool and reporting control, as well as weights and measures to rationalize production and administer the temples' distribution of commodities to their labor force.

Such measures are attested from 6000 BC. Although many variations are found before region-wide standardization developed, a common denominator was the 60-based (sexagesimal) counting system. This facilitated the distribution of food and key commodities on a monthly basis within the large institutions. A 360-day administrative calendar was created, divided into 12 equal 30-day months so that the same quantity could be distributed each month. The aim was to allocate food on a standardized basis, to be consumed twice each day – 60 units per month.

A "bushel" of grain was divided into 60ths, and the mina weight of silver contained 60 shekels. The interest rate of $\frac{1}{60}$th each month evidently was a derivative of this sexagesimal system. Charging interest in this way was the only way the temples could recover and make a gain on the foreign-trade value of their consignments. There is no evidence of detailed records for each trade the merchants made. All the temples or other consignors could know was the value of what they consigned.

There is some controversy over when this commercial rate of interest at $\frac{1}{60}$th per month (the decimal equivalent of 20 percent) was plugged into this sexagesimal system. Piotr Steinkeller finds no specific interest rates attested in the records of the third-millennium Early Dynastic period or the Akkadian occupation, or even in the Ur III period c. 2100 BC. He concludes that before this time the term máš "was still used only in its literal sense" of a young goat or kid, payable as a fee for the use of grazing lands or some other such public-sector obligation, not for monetary interest payable in silver.[121] However, Marc Van De Mieroop explains the lack of records of

---

[121] Steinkeller 1982: 140 f.

a specified interest rate by the fact that commercial trade investment contracts were denominated in silver and not documented even in the second millennium.[122] Evidently the debt tablets were destroyed when such contracts were settled between merchants and their consignors or investors.[123] To view interest as originating with payment in animals would leave a vacuum as to how commercial trade was organized in the form of advances to travelling merchants.

Any rate of interest implies a doubling time. An exponential doubling time for interest-bearing credit is different from the growth of herds or a rental fee. Such calculations have been made, and they are not exponential, but taper off.[124] The "1 shekel per mina" interest rate of $\frac{1}{60}$th each month suggests that the rate was easily plugged into the sexagesimal calendrical system of weights and measures. It was set by ease of calculation rather than reflecting profit rates or productivity, and remained remarkably stable century after century.

A similar grounding of the interest rate in the prevailing arithmetical system of weights and measures is found in subsequent regions for their local fractional system: $\frac{1}{10}$th in Egypt and Greece using the decimalized system, and $\frac{1}{12}$th in Rome, using a duodecimal system of 12 ounces per pound. Evidently this practice of setting the customary interest rate simply by mathematical ease of calculation was brought by Near Eastern traders to the Mediterranean lands after the 8th century BC.

Another ground for believing that the "original" interest rate referred to commercial silver loans rather than agrarian barley loans is suggested by the fact that the word "balance," as in balance sheet, originally meant "weighed out," evidently associated with silver balances falling due, while grain is measured in capacity units.[125]

Nullification of commercial silver debts when accidents prevented payment

What is remarkable from the modern standpoint is the early recognition that debts that couldn't be paid, wouldn't and shouldn't be paid. A basic archaic credit principle was that debts that could not be paid as a result of misfortune should be wiped off the books. § 103 of Hammurabi's laws states that if a caravan was robbed or a ship was lost at sea or raided by pirates, the debt did not have to be paid to commercial investors upon the trader swearing an oath.[126] This form of insurance made invest-

---

[122] See the "General Discussion" in Hudson and Van De Mieroop 2002: 338–341. See also Van De Mieroop 2005: 17–30.

[123] Crawford 1973: 232, contrasts the dearth of records for exports with the fact that the most important imports are well documented, including "all the basic raw materials for metal-working, stone-working, wood-working, and a thousand luxury goods such as precious stones, oils, essences, ivory, slaves and exotic animals."

[124] See Gelb 1967: 64–69.

[125] Powell 1999: 15: "Balances and their parts are treated in ten entities in the lexical series ḪAR-ra = ḫubullu (MSL 6, 60 f.; Powell 1971: 238–242.

[126] The numbering is that of modern translators. All references in this book to the laws of Hammurabi and other Mesopotamian rulers are from Roth 1997. Earlier translations cited this paragraph as § 98.

ment in commercial ventures a normally profitable entrepreneurial activity. A similar provision is found in Roman law nearly two thousand years later.

Under normal contracts, if an investor gave a trader money for a partnership, they would divide equally the profit or loss incurred. Hammurabi Law § 101 obliged traders failing to report a profit to repay the investor double the money that was borrowed, apparently on the assumption that they were being dishonest in understating their gain.

Royal *mīšarum* acts annulled debts burdening subsistence life on the land – crop debts that bore much higher interest rates than did commercial loans denominated in silver. Commercial obligations and investments were left intact by such acts. Nor did the periodic restoration of lands to their former owners apply to townhouses. Sales and debts attached to these urban properties and other commercial assets were left intact, because solvency and the means of subsistence were not threatened.

Diffusion of Near Eastern finance and commercial enterprise

Contrary to the modern prejudice viewing the public sector as antithetical to business enterprise, modern entrepreneurial practices, accounting and contractual terms, corporate business organization, annual reports and profit and loss statements find their genesis in Sumer's palaces and temples in the 3rd millennium BC. Their commerce and colonization spread interest bearing debt upstream (northwest) along the Euphrates to Syria, Phoenicia and Asia Minor, and eastward to the Iranian plateau and Indus valley.[127] In each region, private households adopted Near Eastern enterprise and credit practices.

This book focuses on debt amnesties for non-commercial debts – personal debts owed mainly by cultivators, denominated in grain or other crops or products. Commercial debts were different, reflecting the logic inherent in consigning long-distance trade to traveling merchants. Such commerce "was predominantly based on the family structure and the relationships between members of the extensive family," with sons or other relatives living in foreign trade outposts.[128] These families coordinated their dealing with each other via their own professional guilds. A wide variety of contractual arrangements were left to these traders as long as they remunerated their consigners as per agreement.

---

[127] Lamberg-Karlovsky 1996 discusses how Mesopotamia fit into a world economic system already in the 4th millennium BC. See also Kohl 1979: 55–85. For a general description of Sumerian and subsequent Babylonian foreign trade see Leemans 1950 and 1960. Lambert 1953: 37–69 and 105–120 shows that "textiles, grain, fish, beasts, oils, fats, wood, copper, tin, lead and silver were all regularly exported from Lagash in the third millennium," indicating an active re-export trade from the eastern to the western periphery. But mercantile contracts are lacking.

[128] Michel 2013: 47 f. describes the contractual details of this trade as they had evolved by the early 2nd millennium BC. See also Larsen 2015.

   Their practices came in due course to be extended to money-lending in general, including agricultural loans. Already by Ur III times (2112–2004 BC), the palace consigned management of its lands, herds, alehouses and other assets to entrepreneurs. This privatization became a major feature of the Middle Bronze Age, as later chapters will elaborate.

   Privatization of credit ultimately became a force sweeping aside the checks and balances that existed at the Mesopotamian outset. What is so striking is that the Sumerians innovated interest-bearing debt without letting it polarize society irreversibly. Babylonian rulers repeatedly annulled agrarian debt and reversed debt bondage and the forfeiture of land rights in order to prevent usury from depriving families of their liberty and basic means of self-support. But over the course of antiquity, agrarian usury led to extreme economic polarization, culminating with a creditor oligarchy winning decisively in Rome and reducing much of the population to bondage and ultimately to serfdom.

7. Rural Usury as a Lever to Privatize Land

Interest denominated in barley is attested from the mid-third millennium BC.[130] The usual term for barley debt was še.ur$_5$.ra. The element še means barley, in contrast to máš, used mainly for silver-interest on commercial loans. The word appears already in Enmetena's amar-gi clean slate c. 2400 BC in Lagash (described below in Chapter 9), and northern Mesopotamian records from Ebla c. 2400–2350 BC. One specialist in Ebla's records thinks that the interest rate most likely was 24 percent, but the typical interest rate in Old Babylonian times (after 2000 BC) was of one third of the principal.[131] That rate seems to have been based on the practice of leasing land to sharecroppers for a third of the crop, as if advancing a loan was like leasing land.

The basic debt formulae were standardized well before 2000 BC. Debt tablets stated the sum owed, the due date and the names of witnesses, along with the appropriate seals. Further stipulations might include guarantees by individuals who stood surety, the pledges involved, and the interest rate.

Crop debts were part of a different system from commercial trade advances. The motive for merchants taking on debt, denominated in silver, was to make a gain, paying back their silver loans out of prospective trade profits. Cultivators took on debt to meet their cost of production, typically denominated in barley. Fees mounted up for draught animals, water and consumption debts, to be paid "on the threshing floor" when the harvest was in.

Cultivators also borrowed out of need and for family matters. Debts to tax collectors or other creditors often accrued interest only if the fees or advances were not paid on time. But the time period often was less than a year, and lenders often took advantage of the debtor's distress and charged the equivalent of one third, one half or even more as a flat rate, regardless of how short the time period was.[132]

Just as commercial debts were forgiven if the merchant's ship sank, barley debts were forgiven if the harvest failed as a result of drought or flooding.[133] However, personal sickness, injury or other family disasters did not excuse debtors. Living on the margin of subsistence, their failure to pay fees or loans led eventually to bondage. By the second millennium BC the web of debt, which initially had bound archaic economies together by reciprocity relationships, had become a lever to obtain labor through servitude, and in time to pry away hitherto communally- or clan-allocated land rights.

---

[130] Steinkeller 1981.

[131] Archi 2002: 95 and 104.

[132] Van De Mieroop 1995: 357–364. Skaist 1994: 135 agrees that the interest was added onto the loan, without regard for the length of time involved. He bases his conclusion on the fact that many loan contracts are not dated, which would have been necessary in order to charge an annualized rate.

[133] See the discussion of Hammurabi's laws below, Ch. 16.

Alienation by debtors to creditors became the great catalyst for the emergence of private property in the modern sense of the term – land freely alienable by its holder. A key feature of such private property since classical antiquity has been the right of its holder to sell or otherwise dispose of it – starting with the right to pledge it as collateral for debt, and in due course to forfeit it to the creditor. Freedom for the creditor to foreclose represented a loss of the debtor's liberty, by depriving him and his family of their means of self-support.

The effect was to undercut the palace authority. The proliferation of rural usury after c. 2000 BC caused rising tension between rulers and local creditors over who would receive the labor services and crop usufruct of indebted cultivators: rulers, or creditors reducing debtors to bondage.

Creditors and property holders always have sought to break free of their fiscal and social obligations, while turning their debtors into clients and dependents. That is what makes Bronze Age economic history so relevant for today's world. Debt has remained the major fiscal and economic strain for the past four thousand years, causing a timeless and universal conflict of interest between the implicit aim of governments to preserve social resilience to help society survive and grow, and the privatized wealth of families looking out for their own interest, and rewriting laws to protect their land expropriations from being reversed while shifting the tax burden off themselves.

Today, advocates of this decentralized opposition to government authority depict themselves as calling for "free markets." Creditors, absentee landowners and privatizers have used their rising wealth and power to centralize lawmaking authority in their own hands and control the economy in predatory, extractive ways.

How debt bondage interfered with royal claims for corvée labor

From the Neolithic down through the Bronze Age, communities assigned land tenure to citizens as part of a reciprocity of obligations to supply corvée labor and serve in the military. The concept of property in land was subject to responsibility to the community's highest authority. Land belonged to its holders in return for work on public building projects and being subject to the draft. In Babylonia, *ilku* land was royal land leased out in return for military and labor services. It could not be alienated, nor could other royal land assigned to fighters. Corvée labor obligations are how communities built their infrastructure and ceremonial monuments. As Christopher Eyre describes Egyptian land tenure: "The man responsible for the tax was the 'owner' as far as the state was concerned."[134] Clan heads often were the intermediaries. Ogden Goelet elaborates: "Historically, the delegation of fiscal responsibility to the richest local residents has been normal in Egypt, as holders of liturgies in the Ptolemaic period, or as village headmen (*shaykh/umda*) in later periods. They were personally responsible for the flow of revenues to the 'lords of the land.'"[135]

---

[134] Eyre 2004: 174.
[135] Goelet 2015. This chapter's analysis of corvée labor, taxation and property closely follows that volume's papers on *Labor in the Ancient World*.

Landholding defined citizenship and voting rights. In classical Athens the largest landholders bore the duty of special public *leiturgoi* expenses. Rome's constitution weighted voting rights by the size of one's landholdings, defining "class" in terms of the land needed to outfit and support oneself at a given military rank. Down through Europe in the 19th century, voting was restricted to landholders. These privileges made land the most basic and prestigious form of wealth, and the great asset to be expropriated by making it part of the market, as if it were a commodity.

For many centuries most self-support land was conveyed from one generation to the next within clans. When families shrank in size, their cultivation rights might be transferred to more distant relatives, in-laws or neighbors, but sanctions were widespread against alienating such land to outsiders. Mesopotamia's few documented Early Bronze Age land sales were by communal or professional groupings selling their collective land to the palace or other corporate bodies, not to individuals.[136] But increasingly in the Babylonian epoch after c. 2000 BC, subsistence land rights were pledged to creditors outside the clan.

The tendency toward irreversible personal land transfers took centuries to develop. What initially was pledged was the crop usufruct, "use of the fruits." Sellers or testators remained on the land as long as they lived, even when relinquishing their crop rights. As long as the indebted family head was alive, creditors left him in place but took the crop usufruct, often at the expense of the royal share, normally one-third in Babylonia. Emile Szlechter found "no case of land appropriation by a family who retains possession and whose proprietor can dispose of it while living."[137] Land tenure rights might be redeemed by their relatives or returned to their original owners by royal edicts restoring the *status quo ante*. Otherwise, losing one's land had the effect of disenfranchising citizens.

Fictive "adoptions" to circumvent sanctions against alienating land to outsiders

Throughout history creditors have stretched the legal envelope to break "free" of communal traditions. The loophole enabling creditors to obtain self-support land had to fit into the tradition keeping it within customary tenure, by which land-use rights and the attached obligations passed to sons. The easiest opportunity to become interlopers occurred upon the debtor's death. To preserve the spirit of traditional law, creditors got themselves adopted as the debtor's number-one son.[138]

---

[136] Diakonoff 1982: 7–100, and Gelb, Steinkeller and Whiting 1989.

[137] Szlechter 1958: 121–136.

[138] I summarize how creditors gained possession of much of the citizenry's self-support land in "Reconstructing the Origins of Interest-Bearing Debt and the Logic of Clean Slates," in Hudson and Van De Mieroop, eds., 2002: 7–58, and also in **Hudson and** Levine 1999. Fincke 2010 reviews the literature and points out that direct land sales also were developing by c. 1800 BC.

Elizabeth Stone describes the ploy by which indebted Babylonian cultivators adopted their rich creditor as their son so as "to receive property through inheritance, while the adopter [the needy debtor] may receive an adoption payment. ... the text may describe the monthly and annual rations which are to be delivered by the adoptee to support his new father until his death." Or, the adopted son would pay off his adoptive father's debts in exchange for inheriting the property.[139] The creditor-son – who might be older than his debtor – thus nominally became part of the debtor's family while taking the land into his own family.[140] The debt tablet lists the witnesses and spells out the penalties for breaking the contract.

In addition to adopting their creditors as heirs, borrowers might arrange for their son to marry a daughter of the creditor/buyer. The effect was to concentrate land in the hands of an emerging oligarchy, breaking up the landholdings of poorer or shrinking patrilineal family lineages.

To borrow or fall into arrears was thus the first step toward losing one's land, and hence one's livelihood. One contract finds a cultivator named Ur-Lumma unable to support himself, yet he was "prevented by contemporary alienation restrictions from converting his property into cash through sale." The only way to sell his land to obtain cash and security in his old age was through the back door of adoption. He adopted the well-to-do Lu-Bau, son of a prominent temple official, "as his heir in exchange for support. The text includes an oath in which Ur-Lumma and his heirs foreswear all claims to Lu-Bau's new inheritance." That was the only way in which the creditor Lu-Bau could obtain good cropland. But as matters turned out, Lu-Bau died without issue. Ur-Lumma's natural sons pressed their traditional claims to inherit his land, and "thanks to the accident of Lu-Bau's childlessness, they regained control."[141]

The convoluted practices used by creditors helped make property more alienable, to the point where these roundabout charades were dropped.[142] Even when a nominal right of redemption of land remained, it rarely was exercised in practice. Once alienated, distressed families effectively lost their cultivation rights and typically became tenants on their own land. This led to their dependency, and often to flight

---

[139] Stone 1987: 24.

[140] Stone and Owen 1991: 2f.

[141] Stone and Owen 1991: 9f.

[142] Plutarch describes how radical such sidestepping of sons was in Sparta a thousand years later. (Not mentioning wealthy creditors, he used the melodramatic trope of a father disinheriting his son for being "ungrateful.") It seems that toward the end of Sparta's success in the Peloponnesian War against Athens and its allies (431–404 BC) or shortly thereafter, the "Law of Epitadeus" permitted *kleros* subsistence lands to be alienated in ways other than through inheritance. It was not necessary for the seller-debtor to go to the extreme of adopting his creditor. He could bequeath his estate simply in exchange for a money-gift, or for any other reason. Plutarch's source, the third-century Stoic Phylarchus, invents a personalized story in typically Stoic fashion, masking the obvious financial motivation. A father, spitefully wishing to disinherit an ungrateful son, established a fateful precedent that subsequently enabled impoverished family heads to bequeath their lands to creditors or other outside buyers. See Alexander Fuks 1984.

from their communities. The land that enabled the communal groupings to supply their quota of labor services was lost, obliging the community's remaining members to make up these duties if the palace was not to lose out when new outside owners avoided the customary obligations.

The contractual clause "sold at the full price"

Scarcely any real estate in antiquity was bought on credit, although sometimes a delayed final payment might be owed. Instead of speculators borrowing money to buy land and make a capital gain, land sales were not deemed valid unless "the full price" was paid. At first glance this might seem intended to save distressed sellers from being taken advantage of. But transferring land "at the full price" simply meant that all proper formalities were obeyed and properly witnessed by the affected relatives and neighbors of the seller parting with his homestead.[143] The proper ceremonial acts had to be performed, above all giving due notice so as to prevent subsequent disputes. In Sumerian times a formal meal with some exchange of presents would have been held to attest to the legitimacy of the land transfer. Earlier sale documents were turned over to the acquirers, so that interlopers would have no basis for asserting claims or redemption rights to the property.[144]

From Babylonia through Rome, wealthy individuals sought to convert the gains they had made by money-lending and commerce into land ownership, holding their property free and clear. The modern world has changed land acquisition to one where real estate is bought on credit – which is how modern home ownership has been extended to new buyers.[145]

Royal proclamations to save rural debtors from disenfranchisement

As subsistence land became alienable, its tenure became more precarious for small-holders. Credit became a lever to deprive its customary holders of their tenure rights. In Babylonia, absentee landowners turned to more labor-intensive cash crops such as dates, forcing cultivators off the land. Creating this disenfranchised debtor class threatened the community's self-support, especially where the new appropriators were able to avoid supplying the traditional corvée labor services. Such forfeitures undercut the army's troop strength, corvée harvest labor and canal maintenance on which the ruler's power and ultimately social survival was based.

---

[143] The documentary record is discussed in Wunsch 2002: 221–256.

[144] Ammisaduqa's clean slate edict proclaiming *mīšarum* c. 1648 BC required that creditors who had obtained claims to the cultivator's labor, crops or land were to break their sales or loan tablets and return the pledges or forfeitures they had taken, free and clear of any claims.

[145] Real estate mortgages represent about 70 percent of U.S. bank lending (and hence, debt), and have become the means of acquiring homes, not the first step toward losing them (at least until the junk-mortgage practices leading up to the 2008 crash). Mortgages account for more than half the value of U.S. residential real estate for most commercial investors and home-buyers. I explain the modern financialized dynamics of real estate and taxation in *The Bubble and Beyond* (2012) and *Killing the Host* (2015).

This dynamic gave rulers an interest in reversing land foreclosures. Coronations were the traditional occasion to declare amnesties. Debts also were canceled in periods of military conflict or major economic disruption. Such proclamations enabled the Near East to reduce and counteract the polarization that tore classical antiquity apart. In contrast to the modern world's safety valve of personal bankruptcy on a case-by-case basis, Mesopotamian rulers saw that debt problems were economy-wide. The paradigmatic agrarian debts were owed to the palace, but also to acquisitive local creditors, whose claims for payment rulers no doubt were happy to check, as this blocked a rival economic authority from emerging.

Figure 8:
Standard
of Ur,
War side.

Agrarian indebtedness became necessary simply to meet basic needs as cultivators were squeezed. Pledging land rights became the catalyst for private property to emerge in the modern sense of the term, freely alienable by its holder – and hence, "free" for creditors to foreclose on. Creditors wanted not only interest in the form of crops as the usus fructus, but outright ownership of the land. Toward this end they sought to make their financial claims immune from royal overrides and traditions of equity and personal liberty. Temple and palace wealth gave way to family fortunes and patron-client, creditor-debtor dependency. Land ownership became concentrated, turning citizens into debtors, renters and clients of large owners.

For half a millennium after the Babylonian empire fell c. 1600 BC, rising numbers of debt fugitives joined groups of seasonal laborers or became rootless bands serving as mercenaries and outlaws. A similar flight of debt refugees prompted the prophet Isaiah (ch. 5.8) to decry absentee owners who assembled vast estates by "joining field to field till no space is left and you live alone in the land." Seeing creditors gain control of politics and the law, the authors of Mosaic Law grounded the Jubilee Year in a sacred covenant. But the fact that by Roman times Hillel's Pharisees could establish the *prosbul* waiver as part of the rabbinical mainstream showed how great a problem irreversible forfeitures of land and personal liberty to creditors had become.

Concentration of land ownership and polarization between creditors and debtors is traditionally a formula for economic shrinkage and depopulation.

8. War, Debt and amar-gi in Sumer, 2400 BC

Much of our understanding of Sumer's economy in the mid-third millennium comes from the royal inscriptions and temple records of Lagash, the best-documented city-state up until Sargon's conquest c. 2300 BC. Located on the Tigris well situated for sea trade near what was then the mouth of the Persian Gulf, Lagash's territory was about 35 miles on each side – just over a thousand square miles.

Like other southern Mesopotamian cities, Lagash was centered on the temples of Inanna and Gatumdu. The city's sacred district, Girsu, housed the temple of its patron deities Ningirsu and Bau (sometimes read as Baba). Nearby was the town of Nigin, whose tutelary goddess was Nanshe. Thousands of clay tablets from these temples are ration lists, "prebend" income-in-kind for public officials, and related administrative accounts dealing with the receipt and disbursement of grain, oil and other resources. Other tablets list temple lands and their yields. Most royal records are short dedications of objects donated to the temples. Despite the fact that these institutions were major export producers, with the palace playing a dominant role, records are lacking concerning export and credit relations with merchants.

Almost all that is known of Sumer's political and social situation comes from royal year-names and the inscriptions that happen to have been excavated. The longest inscriptions deal with military and debt matters. These records reflect a three-way dynamic between the palaces and city-temples where the economic surplus was concentrated, and the citizenry at large. Documentation for early Sumerian debt relations comes primarily from royal inscriptions cancelling agrarian debts, starting with Enmetena's edict c. 2400 BC.

Like most royal inscriptions, Enmetena's amar-gi proclamation Enmetena's amar-gi proclamation following his military victory over Umma was inscribed on bricks in Girsu's city-temple. A narrative of the conflict with Umma and its failure to pay its tribute debt was publicly displayed on baked clay cones and plaques. Also inscribed in this manner were Urukagina's "reform" texts c. 2350 BC describing his economic policy in preparation for renewed war with Umma. Two centuries later, around 2150 BC, the ruler Gudea inscribed decorative clay cylinders and stone statues of himself with narratives of how he canceled debts at the festival celebrating his building of Lagash's temple to the goddess Gatumdu. These three edicts from Lagash form the primary examples of such proclamations.

The ceremonial character of these inscriptions associated with temple rituals shows that proclaiming amnesties, building temples and digging canals, were pious deeds expected of rulers responsible for maintaining social survival. That is why such edicts were proclaimed at the feast celebrating a new ruler's reign (Urukagina's edict), an important military victory (Enmetena's amar-gi proclamation) or dedication of a new temple (Gudea's debt cancellation). The ruler's fiscal forgiveness applied mainly to rural fees, crop rents and taxes owed to the temples and palace.

City-state rivalries and the rise of urban dynasties

Southern Mesopotamia's urbanization during the Early Dynastic half-millennium 2800 to 2300 BC has been attributed to cultivators gathering in walled cities, both to obtain access to water from the network of canals being dug by the urban centers and, increasingly, for populations to take refuge from the warfare that followed largely from water conflicts – and from foreign attempts to rob the riches they had accumulated. Fortified temple precincts protected their stores of seed and food, precious metals and other treasures from attacks by nomadic pastoral tribes from Sumer's periphery – Amorites from the northern pasture lands west of the Euphrates, Zagros mountaineers from the northeast, and from Susa on the Iranian plateau to the east.

Falling water levels along the Euphrates required digging more canals, culminating in far-flung networks expanded to facilitate barge transport. "Small settlements out in the countryside … almost ceased to exist … Settlements could only survive on a permanent basis if they lay on a watercourse that provided water throughout the year."[146] A rural exodus from the countryside helped cities build up their army and labor supply. They obtained metal to make their tools and arms mainly by exporting textiles produced in temple and palace handicraft workshops, and cereals.

By the middle of the third millennium "almost four-fifths of the population of the central flood plain was apparently crowded into large urban nuclei," headed by Uruk, Ur and Lagash in the south, and Kish in the north.[147] That was the densest urban concentration in Mesopotamian history. Uruk was so large that its dominance over Sumer is said to have lasted nearly a thousand years, c. 3500 to 2500 BC.

Nippur was a ceremonial and religious center for the various contiguous southern city-states, with its city-god Enlil heading the overall Sumerian pantheon. Royal inscriptions report local deities as receiving their authority from Enlil. But in the political and military sphere, shifting alliances blocked any major city-state from being dominant for long. Mainly at issue prior to the Amorite invasions was conflict between upstream and downstream users of water. Irrigation was the key to Sumer's soil fertility, and hence its population support capacity. In such conflicts "the cumulative advantage lies with those farther upstream" to the north – first Kish, later Akkad and finally Babylon.[148] Kish also was favorably situated on the overland route eastward to Iran and westward to Asia Minor, making it a major trade entrepot.

The first documented builders of the third millennium's military empires seem to have begun their careers as temple administrators. In the 27th century BC, Uruk's first dynasty-builder, Meskiaggasher, began as a temple en (sacred or war leader, also called ensí or lugal respectively), for he was called a son of Uruk's patron sun-god

---

[146] Nissen 1988: 129 f.

[147] Adams 1981: 244 and 138. See the urbanization chart in Chapter 17 below. However, "cities" were largely aggregations of villages.

[148] Adams 1981: 134, 234. The Sumerian King List refers to Kish's first ruler, Etana, as the "shepherd" who "stabilized the lands" in the period prior to 2700 when there is little sign of internecine warfare. Even after the city lost its preeminence to Uruk and Ur, Sumerian rulers called themselves "King of Kish" to connote suzerainty over the southern region.

Utu (= Anu) and ruled from Uruk's sacred Eanna district. He is said to have extended his realm by "entering the sea and ascending the mountains." His son Enmerkar is credited with building up the city of Uruk proper, integrating its sacred and secular districts.

In Lagash, Urnanshe founded a dynasty that ruled c. 2500–2350. (The dates for this period obviously are approximate, but are widely accepted by consensus.) His name suggests that he may have been sponsored by Nanshe, the city's patron goddess of justice. Probably he was a temple official like other contemporary énsis and even lugals. After his dynasty fell in 2365 BC, its first three successors – Enentarzi, Lugalanda and Urukagina – were selected by Girsu's temple administrators. Two centuries later, when Lagash re-emerged as an independent entity in the aftermath of Sargon's Akkadian dynasty, its most famous ruler, Gudea, focused his enterprise on rebuilding the city's temples.[149]

Reflecting the tradition of early Sumerian rulers as temple en officials, Babylonian kings depicted themselves as administrators first and foremost – builders of temples and later proclaimers of justice. Elizabeth van Buren found the characteristic iconography of kingship to be Ur-Nammu or Hammurabi facing Shamash or an analogous sun god, holding the symbols of royal authority – the (measuring) rod and "ring" representing the coiled surveying rope used to lay out temple precincts – literally ruling.[150] By extension, rulers regulated prices and credit terms in their public laws and proclamations.

Figure 9: Map of canals and irrigation systems to the west of the Euphrates, Old Babylonian

[149] For background see Schrakamp 2013.
[150] Van Buren 1949: 434–450.

Among Bronze Age rulers, only the pharaohs are depicted in a military posture, receiving tribute or holding captured foreigners by the hair, about to smite them with a mace. In upstream Mari c. 1750, Zimrilim had a mural painted for his palace to reflect his military prowess, but found the only visual source to be Egyptian iconography – one of the rare instances of its being adopted outside of Egypt. "Even in the great imperial days of the second millennium, the Elamite kings, strongly influenced by adjacent Babylonia, seem to have stressed the nonmilitary aspect of kingship in their artistic representations."

Lagash's water wars with Umma, and the ensuing tribute debts

By 2500 BC the water warfare between Lagash and Umma had become chronic. A neighboring ruler, Mesalim (probably from Kish in the north), was invited to mediate the conflict. He settled it in favor of Lagash, and a stone stele was erected to mark the boundary of the Gu'edena area ("watered territory"). But Umma twice waged war with Lagash over this land, finally winning it in a bitter four-year war under Lugalzagesi (2349–2345) whose victory helped prepare the way for Sargon of Akkad to conquer southern Mesopotamia.

Figure 10: Votiv plaque by Ur-Nanshe, ensí of Lagash. Louvre, Paris.

The Ur-Nanshe Dynasty of Lagash and Its Successors[151]

Ur-Nanshe (c. 2494–2465)	Promoted the temple of Nanshe. Defeated Umma and won independence from Kish
Akurgal (2465–2455)	During a relatively peaceful reign he relinquished some of the lands that his father had conquered.
Eanatum (2454–2425)	Reconsolidated Lagash's power and established a scribal school. Died in battle, and was succeeded by his brother
Enanatum (2424–2405)	Apparently had a long and relatively peaceful rule. When Umma attacked late in Enanatum's rule, Lagash's army was led to victory by his third son (and Eannatum's nephew),
Enmetena (2404–2365)	Defeated Umma and its allies. Achieving suzerainty over southern Mesopotamia, he inscribed the earliest known amar-gi proclamation canceling agrarian debts.

Sponsored by the Temples as "stewards" (énsi)

Enentarzi (2364–2359)	Had been chief administrator of the Ningirsu temple in Girsu.
Lugalanda (2358–2352)	Growing bureaucratic abuses as énsi (he never became lugal). Perhaps his ties to Uruk led the Girsu priesthood to replace him with:
Urukagina (2351–2342)	Reduced the predatory behavior of Sumerian political and economic bureaucracy, restoring nominal temple dominance. Became lugal in his second year to defend Lagash against Umma. His "reform text" cancelled agrarian debts.

Foreign Conquerors

Lugalzagesi (2351-2327)	First énsi of Umma and subsequently lugal of Uruk. Gained Uruk's throne c. 2355, about the time Urukagina became lugal of Girsu/Lagash. Conquered Lagash and the rest of Sumer, and even its neighboring regions before being overthrown by Sargon of Kish/Akkad. Early in his reign he warded off an Elamite threat from the northeast.

Figure 11: The Ur-Nanshe Dynasty of Lagash and Its Successors.

---

[151] These dates are intended more to indicate the relative lengths of each ruler's reign than to be an absolute chronology. However, they attribute suspiciously long reigns to early rulers. The dates from Enentarzi onward are internally firm, but Urnanshe may have begun has rule as late as 2450 BC. This would require his dates and those of his successors to be shortened somewhat. See also Bauer, Englund and Krebernik, eds., 1998.

Lagash's empire building began around 2500, when Ur-Nanshe (2494–2465) founded a dynasty in the aftermath of his city being sacked, probably by the Elamites. He seems not to have come from the ruling family, but to have been backed by the Nanshe temple. He rebuilt Lagash's ramparts and the walls around Girsu bordering the buffer zone with Umma. Stone reliefs from Girsu show him carrying a work-basket – part of a ritual in which Sumerian rulers took the lead in building temples – and drinking at the public ceremony, perhaps a New Year celebration when the new temple of Ningirsu likely was dedicated. He may have introduced the cult of Nanshe, a sister-goddess of Bau and daughter of the sky-god Anu. Some of his inscriptions state that he "had ships of Dilmun transport timber as tribute from foreign lands" to Lagash.[151a]

Few details are known concerning the reign of Urnanshe's son Akurgal (2465–2455), who built the Antasurra temple in the Guedena. He was succeeded by Urnanshe's grandson, Eanatum (2454–2425), a warrior prince who rose to dominate southern Mesopotamia. Umma's leader Gish took the opportunity of this distraction to invade the Guedena and destroy Mesalim's stele. Eannatum quickly defeated Umma's forces, but the peace he dictated c. 2440 was so one-sided that it sowed the seeds of further antagonism.

Figure 12: Stele of the vultures, detail

[151a] Frayne 2008, Ur-Nanshe E1.9.1., nos. 2 and 5. See also nos. 6A, 17, 22, 23 and 25. Unless otherwise noted I rely on this for most inscriptions from the Early Dynastic period. An earlier set of translations was edited by Cooper 1986, hereafter abbreviated as SARI, La 1.3 and 1.5.

Specifically, Lagash permitted Umma to farm the Gu'edena on the condition that it pay barley tribute to the Ningirsu temple, apparently 3,600 gur annually. The details were inscribed on the Stele of the Vultures, which Eanatum erected at the spot where Mesalim's stele had demarcated the boundary. (The limestone monument depicts vultures devouring the corpses of Umma's soldiers whom Eanatum had slain.) This obligation represents the earliest public debt on record, and it seems was subject to compound interest. The inscription also is the earliest historical narrative in cuneiform. But it does not explain who were to produce and pay the stipulated grain rent—presumably Umma's cultivators turning their crop over to the palace.

Nonpayment of tribute was normal in this period. Upstream Ebla is reported never to have paid the tribute assessed after it lost to Mari. Victors usually had to threaten renewed war to exact payment, and that is just what happened as Umma's arrears mounted up. Lagash administrators calculated that Umma's annual obligation of 3,600 gur had multiplied to the remarkable sum of 144,000 gur. Jerrold Cooper finds that most of this must have represented compound interest, for "one gur compounded annually at the 33 ⅓ or 50 percent rate common for grain loans and rent could grow to 8,640,000 gur (44,789,760,000 hl.) in 40–55 years, which could fit the chronology of these events very well."[152] The stele (xvi: 18–24) states that Umma's leader "swore to Eanatum: 'By the life of the god Enlil … I may exploit the field of the god Ningirsu as an (interest-bearing) loan.'"

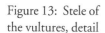
Figure 13: Stele of the vultures, detail

Having defeated Umma, Eanatum swept west to defeat Uruk and Ur, and claimed the title King of Kish. He established amity with Uruk by making it independent of Ur, and led an expedition to drive the Elamites out of southern Mesopotamia, along with their allies such as Mari upstream along the Euphrates. Uruk took the lead in defeating Kish, while remaining an ally of Lagash. Eanatum's son Enanatum enjoyed a peaceful rule for a number of decades.

---

[152] Cooper 1983: 56. See Frayne 2008, E1.9.3.1, and E1.9.5.1 ii 19–26. Also Lambert 1952: 52–77 and 198–216, esp. 203 f., and Kramer 1963: 55 ff.

Changing ecological conditions aggravated matters. The shifting Euphrates benefited Umma, enabling it to grow more rapidly. Umma cut off the southward flow of water to the Gu'edena, stopped its crop rent to Lagash and destroyed the stele inscribed with Eanatum's treaties, as well as the four chapels that he had erected to consecrate the boundary. Claiming the Antasura district as the new frontier, Umma's énsi Urluma attacked Lagash, aided by soldiers from Mari in the north.

Lagash's army was led by Eanatum's nephew, Enmetena, the Urnanshe dynasty's last ruler (2404–2375). One of his contingents defeated about sixty of Umma's best fighting men at a local canal. Umma's loss was not as serious as that of the preceding generation, but it fell under the domination of its own northern neighbor Zabalam, whose ruler Il proclaimed himself énsi of Umma, legitimizing his position by marrying off his son to Urluma's daughter.

Seeing that the warfare had weakened Lagash's army as well as that of Umma, Il renewed the conflict by cutting off Lagash's irrigation water from the Gu'edena and he stopped paying the stipulated grain rent. Once again the matter was submitted to a northern ruler for arbitration, and once again Lagash was awarded rights to the buffer territory. But the grain tribute ended and the issue of arrears was dropped. Lagash henceforth had to provide its own labor to farm the Guedena and maintain the canals to supply its irrigation needs.

To ward off future fighting, Enmetena concluded a treaty of brotherhood with Uruk. The remainder of his 30-year rule was spent in relative peace, building temples and sanctuaries as well as fortifications. His most ambitious project was to avoid future water struggles over the Gu'edena by digging a new canal flowing east to the Tigris.

Enmetena's proclamation of amar-gi, economic freedom from debt

Early in his reign Enmetena promulgated the earliest Sumerian debt cancellation on record, c. 2400. No doubt there were earlier amar-gi proclamations.[153] He instituted "liberty" for the "sons and daughters" of Lagash and some of its dependencies. "He cancelled obligations for Lagash. He restored child to mother, and mother to child. He canceled obligations regarding interest-bearing grain loans."[154] The term that Enmetena used for "obligations," še-ur₅-ra, no doubt included the principal, at that time mainly crop-rent and fees owed to public collectors, but not commercial claims.

In AD 1971, archaeologists unearthed the tablets recording this edict from the temple foundation in which it had been buried. The edict's sparse wording, like that of subsequent such proclamations, has created some controversy over just what amar-

---

[153] Lemche 1979: 16.
[154] Frayne, 1998, E1.9.5.4. iii 10 v 8. Confirmed by Lambert 1972: 2. Chapter 18 below discusses amar-gi and its related terms *andurārum* and *mīšarum*.

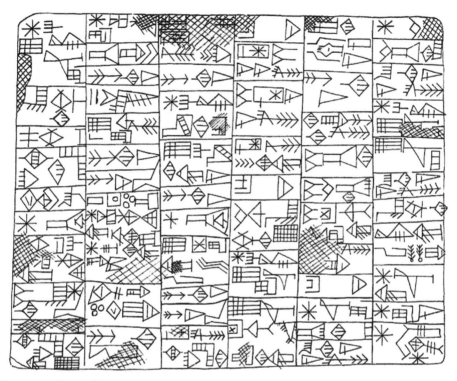

Figure 14: Text of Enmetena's amar-gi proclamation

gi meant. It consists of ama, "mother," and the verb gi, "to return," connoting a sense of "return to the mother [condition]," a release from the state of indebtedness. The term thus connoted liberty from debt bondage.[155]

Arrears for back payments and proto-taxes had accumulated against many citizens, no doubt aggravated by the long series of wars. The text's first translator, Maurice Lambert, interprets the situation as follows: "Vanquishing the foreign enemy, Enmetena gives to the poorest of his town a remission of their debts. Certain poor families have had to sell their children …; others have had to sell the mother. This is why, following his victory in the south, Enmetena 'restores the child to its mother, and returns the mother to her children.' He also (or rather, *thus*) annuls the interest due."[156]

Frayne notes that Enmetena's text then "cancelled obligations for the citizens of Uruk, Larsa and Pa-tibira," an action that would "normally follow a ruler's 'liberation'

[155] Discussing Ilushuma's *andurārum*, re "cleaning the copper or tablets," Diakonoff 1969 states: "It is a translation of Sumerian ama.r.gi, 'returning to mother,' *i.e.* 'to the original situation.' It does not mean liberation from some supreme authority, but cancelling of debts, duties and the like. Also 'cleaning' is a *terminus technicus* for 'release of payments.'"

[156] Lamber1972: 13. Rosengarten 1959: 134 comes up with a feminist reading, construing the term ama.gi as meaning to "mother" the people, as when Urukagina states: "Ningirsu had enjoined him to protect his people, to care for them as a mother." This misses the cosmological essence of restoring the *status quo ante*, as a cyclical return.

Figure 15: Enannatum

of a city," suggesting that Enmetena controlled them.[157] Enmetena's amar-gi edict seems to have "won the peace" by recognizing that it would be futile to ask populations to wage war under conditions that forced them into debt or threatened the sale of their widows or children as war slaves or debt servants.[158]

Not until classical antiquity was fighting allowed to impoverish populations in its wake. The wars fought by Rome's peasant army were notorious for leaving its soldiers and their families in debt, forfeiting their land to creditors. Some were resettled as coloni on the land of defeated territories, displacing *foreign* cultivators in a falling domino process.

But Enmetena's rule seems to have been one of increasing prosperity for Lagash. In the forefront of its industry were its weaving workshops, exporting textiles to Umma, Uruk, Adab and Nippur. Families in the communal sector sold wool and grain to the temples, and even a decade after Enmetena's rule, "The 'reform' texts of Urukagina presuppose the possession, even among poor people, of houses, gardens, farm animals and sheep."[159] But the palace and temple personnel sought to take the fruits of this prosperity increasingly for themselves.

[157] Frayne 2008 E1.9.5.4 v 4–8.
[158] Postgate 1992: 195 makes a speculative suggestion: "Perhaps the most striking feature of the edict is that persons freed and sent home by the ruler of Lagash come from neighboring city-states," formerly in bondage to Lagash creditors, not to those of their own cities. Frayne 2008: 229 notes that a similar amar-gi proclamation on a brick excavated in Girsu "apparently deals with events accompanying or preceding the ruler's inauguration; thus, in all likelihood, the inscription dates to a period very early in the reign, just as became the case with new Babylonian rulers taking the throne." That makes this brick (E.1.9.5.26 col. v 2–7) the earliest written example of amar-gi.
[159] Lambert 1966: 34 ff. See also Falkenstein 1974: 802.

9. Urukagina Proclaims amar-gi: 2350 BC

Enmetena's son, Enanatum II, ruled only briefly as a figurehead as the Urnanshe dynasty came to an end around 2365 BC. The Ningirsu hierarchy sponsored its temple manager (sanga), Enentarzi to become énsi (2364–2359), relegating Enanatum's son Lummatur to a secondary temple position.[160] Enentarzi's son Lugalanda (2358–2352) was followed by Urukagina (2351–2327), whose family seems to have been Bau temple officials. His "reform text" states simply that he was picked out of the crowd and appointed énsi without Lugalanda having died or suffered a military defeat.[161]

This episode has led to much speculation about the relative role of ens, énsis and sangas for Sumerian rulership in general. Uruk's ruler was called en, reflecting his role in the Inanna temple. In Lagash's neighbor Umma the ruler's title was sanga, evidently also the chief temple administrator. In Nicolas Postgate's reading, Urukagina's title of énsi reflects the rising dominance of palace rulers over temples, "not associated with the temple as such, but with the city-state of which the main temple is the ideological core. One is 'ENSI of Lagash' or 'of Adab,' not of a deity or of a temple."[162]

There does not seem to have been a coup. As énsi, Urukagina was in charge of the economy, largely via its temples, but evidently a conflict erupted between Lugalanda and the sanga, responsible for management of temple land and related economic functions.[163] Lugalanda continued to live in Lagash for several years, and his wife Baranamtara enjoyed a position of eminence. Maurice Lambert suggests that Lugalanda may have been considered too loyal to Uruk, whose throne had just been claimed by Lugalzagesi, énsi of Umma and soon to become Lagash's mortal enemy.[164] In any case, Urukagina became lugal four months after having been appointed énsi.

Domestically, the palace's takeover of temple property and the extortionate practices of its bureaucracy had led the population to clamor for reforms. That may explain Urukagina's name, which Dietz Edzard translates as "The State of Legitimate Laws," in the sense of "The Legitimate Lawgiver." Other versions include "The One who Make Laws Just in the City."[165]

---

[160] Parrot 1948: 130 f.
[161] Frayne 2008: Urukagina E1.9.9.2 iv 7–8 and E.1.9.9.1 viii 5–6, "selected from the myriad people."
[162] See Postgate 1995: 396.
[163] Charpin 1995: 809.
[164] Lambert 1966: 35 ff.
[165] Schrakamp 2015: 304–310 discusses the controversy over Urukagina's name and background. See also Frayne 2008: 245.

The Ningirsu temple officials designated the rulers, but the palace then absorbed Ningirsu's estates and herds. The wives of its énsis Enentarzi and Lugalanda were in charge of the Ba'u temple, while administrators representing their children were nominally in charge of the Shulshagana temple. Other relatives of the royal family took over public land. It seems that Lugalanda and his nubanda administrator Eniggal squeezed an economic surplus out of the temple labor force by lowering ration levels, and obliged members of each profession to pay the palace a share of what they charged for basic services to the population at large. This led the temple bureaucracy and professions to sharply increase their fees and requisite offerings for performing marriages, divorces and burials, measuring, shearing and other functions.[166] "Revenues from farming and fishing rights, tithes of shepherds and gardeners were precisely calculated according to their value."[167] The beneficiaries were the administrators, their wives, inspectors, overseers, traders, horse masters, herdsmen and even singers linked to the royal court.

Palace domination of the temples

"The palace was always a centre of religion," summarizes Walther Sallaberger. "The king acted for his land and his people before the gods."[168] Although grounding their legitimacy in temple sanctification of their rule, palace rulers controlled temple property and production, long-distance commerce and hence the flow of silver and strategic materials, as well as luxury goods such as perfumes.[169] Sales, credit and other transactions within this palatial sphere of the economy were based on silver. In Girsu, the Ba'u temple "did not actively control the politically important treasuries."[170] In neighboring Umma, numerous branches of the economy converted their primary goods annually "into tiny sums of silver, which were collected by the province and then delivered to the state in the form of donations to a religious festival." The palace mobilized silver to invest in foreign trade and entrust to merchants to obtain more silver, raw materials and provide luxuries, Sallaberger found. "Merchants were essential for the distribution of these goods over wide distances," conducting their business on the basis of silver loans and payments. Purchasing prestige textiles, other handicrafts and surplus crops was the main way in which the palace spent silver into the economy at large.

Rulers legitimized their status and wealth by donating silver and other prestige items to the temples, which served as the city's storehouse and treasury. In the early centuries of Sumerian development when most families survived on the borderline of subsistence, the city-temple provided basic welfare services and mutual aid. It functioned largely on the basis of barley and crop production to support its dependents

---

[166] Lambert 1960: 1–26 and 1961: 427–438. The palace had its own herds, and a monopoly on shearing white sheep.
[167] Rosengarten 1960: 82 ff.
[168] Sallaberger 2007: 269.
[169] Schrakamp 2013: 459 and 445.
[170] Sallaberger 2013: 244 and 226.

and workshops, managing fields and orchards, fishing and pasturage. The palace was supposed to build, repair and endow temples, not drain revenue from them. However, the excavation of tablets primarily from the Bau temple area led early Assyriologists to assume that the city-state of Lagash (and other Sumerian cities) and even its palace were dominated by their temples. In that reading, Urukagina's elevation to ruler would appear to be a temple assertion on behalf of the citizenry against the overly acquisitive palace.

By Urukagina's time the palace was draining temple income for itself.[171] This would become even more the case under Sargon and subsequent overlords, but for the time being it was resisted as unfair. Urukagina's elevation and inauguration of his rule with a "reform" text has inspired a long debate over whether the temples had lost control to the palace and sought to regain authority, or whether the temples had been in control all along. Kazuya Maekawa, for instance, has suggested that Urukagina's inaugural proclamation aimed at completing the process of sanctifying royal authority by acting on behalf of the oppressed people who had become indebted to the temple and palace bureaucracy.[172]

Urukagina's reform text c. 2350 BC

One of Urukagina's first acts was to compose a long text, commemorated in his "second year" inaugural inscription, detailing the grabbing that had proliferated under Lugalanda's rule. Copies exist in several variants, which were publicly displayed on clay cones and an oval plaque. Since French archaeologists discovered the first of these inscriptions in 1897, their language has confronted translators with interpretive problems. Many terms are idiomatic abbreviations for procedures whose details must be inferred from their context. What is clear is that burdens were being lifted by rolling back the charges of palace officials and cancelling the agrarian debts that had been built up.

The text starts by describing how palace officials appropriated temple oxen and asses, grain and fruits, as well as requisitioning labor. Urukagina "restored the custom of former times" so that temple property and that of the citizenry at large no longer would be subject to such takings. Royal properties were turned over to the Ningirsu temple administrators, and the queen's palace and its fields were re-assigned to the Ba'u temple, although it remained under the direction of Urukagina's wife Shasha and was administered by the nubanda Eniggal, as had been the case under Enentarzi and Lugalanda. The houses and fields of the royal children were returned to the Shulshagana and Igalim temples.[173]

---

171 Schrakamp 2013: 452.
172 Maekawa 1973–1974: 77–144.
173 Frayne 2008: Urukagina E1.8.8.1 vii 7–13 and ix 7–31. See Diakonoff 1958: 5 f., Lambert, 1956: 170, 179 and Kramer 1963: 318. Rosengarten 1960: 353 ff. asserts that the palace administration may simply have been installed in Girsu's temple, while the queen's quarters and offices remained in the Ba'u temple, so the practical impact is not clear.

Officials had invaded family gardens to take crops and livestock by force for payments owed for their services, or perhaps for loans, and even invaded houses belonging
to temple administrators and individual citizens at will. "If a poor man had an
interest-accruing loan for his fish tank, (his creditor) could take away its fish (simply
by) uttering a (simple) 'O Sun god' complaint." There is no indication that moneylenders were involved besides temple or palace officials, or that the latter actually had
to get a court order, much less place the asset in a public pound for the matter to be
settled fairly. Urukagina's reform ruled that these creditor-claimants "cannot take
away his fish" or buy them without the owner's agreement and permission.[174]

The administrators no longer plunder the orchards of the poor. When a fine ass is
born to a shub-lugal, and his foreman says to him, "I want to buy (it) from you"; whether
he lets him buy it from him and says to him, 'Pay me the price I want!" or whether
he does not let him buy (it) from him, the foreman must not strike at him in anger.[175]

That seems to be what Urukagina meant when he stated that prior
to his reforms officials "seized," "foreclosed upon" or "had in charge for
his own benefit" boats, sheep, fish-
eries and other professional property.
His reform also rescued citizens from
selling their houses to avaricious officials. Henceforth, owners could name
their own price, and if the prospective buyer would not meet it, the sale
could not be forced by bullying.

It may be too much to believe
that "the bureaucracy ceased operations," as Cooper reads these passages,
or that henceforth there would be no
more maškim collectors throughout
the land.[176] But Urukagina evidently
changed their modus operandi so that
they no longer were so predatory.

Figure 16: Clay cone of the
Urukagina reform text, Louvre
(Paris)

---

[174] Frayne 2008: **Urukagina** E1.9.9.3 ii 10–14 and 6′–9′ (SARI La 9.3.).
[175] Frayne 2008: **Urukagina** E1.9.9.1 xi 17–19 (SARI La 9.1). For a speculative reconstruction
from over half a century ago of how creditors operated, see Stephens 1955: 132f.
[176] Rosengarten 1959: 136, says simply, "No one speaks any more of the mashkim." Diakonoff
1958: 14 refers to "abolition of the mashkim-di."

Fees for marriages and divorces had become onerous. Under Lugalanda and perhaps Enentarzi, priests had charged a silver shekel for officiating in addition to five shekels going to the palace. To bring them back within popular reach, Urukagina decreed that these ceremonies be performed gratis. Burial fees were reduced from seven pitchers of beer and 420 loaves of bread to just three pitchers and 80 loaves "to furnish the essential meal for the singers and servants of the cult."[177]

Workshop rations had been cut back, forcing artisans, apprentices and blind laborers (slaves?) to beg for food. Urukagina guaranteed that specific amounts of bread, beer and other food would be provided to members of the Girsu and Lagash craft guilds, the blind and other workers. He also increased by nearly two-thirds the number of individuals entitled to receive these rations.

Cancelling debts and freeing bondservants

Under Enmetena, debts had stemmed largely from warfare and were canceled upon victory. But now, in peacetime, many citizens were forced into debt to self-dealing officials. Most dam-gàr collectors (fiscal agents) were not lending out their own money, but simply were owed fees or payments; or perhaps they lent out money they had collected and were holding to pay the palace and temples. They charged interest and, when they could, seized the assets of debtors.[178] One man had to sell his son to Enentarzi, "the first instance recorded of the mortgage or sale of one's own children; three slaves are bought from three different persons by Baranamtara, wife to Lugalanda."[179]

A Sumerian proverb indicates that debtors were members of the community who might soon recover their strength: "Do not drive away a debtor, that man may turn hostile against you."[180] But most proverbs tell of increasing misfortune resulting from usury. "A poor man worries about what he has borrowed" (i.e., "Money borrowed is soon sorrowed"); "The poor man has no power"; "Helplessness is the widow's lot"; and "What is snatched out of his mouth must pay his debts." And for landholders who had run so deeply into debt that they were unable to perform the harvest: "I am in debt over my improved real estate, so that I cannot cultivate the fields assigned to me,"[181] evidently because he fell into bondage to his creditor. Of a compassionate creditor, or a man who became rich without eating into another person's resources: "He did not take it out of the mouth of a poor man."

Debts had grown oppressive as arrears mounted under Lugalanda, and many families ran the danger of forfeiting their means of livelihood. Urukagina's reform text ends by stating that he "cleared and canceled obligations for those indentured families," and the clay plaque version of this text records that "Debt servitude for theft has been abolished."[182]

---

[177] Frayne 2008: Urukagina E1.9.9.1 vi 4–12, 17–24 and ix 26–32. See Rosengarten 1959: 141 and 149.
[178] Foster, oral presentation 1995.
[179] Struve 1969: 35.
[180] Alster 1974: 58.
[181] Gordon 1968: 2.19, 2.27, 2.30–31, 2.33, and 2.159.
[182] SARI: La 9.3 and p. 77, n6.

One version of the reform text stipulates: "As for women of former times – a man (could) take two of them; but for women of today – indemnity payments (for debt?) have been removed (and the practice has been abolished)."[183] This seems to refer to women pledged to creditors as debt servants, and hence belonging to two men: her husband and the creditor, "so that she had for all practical purposes, marital obligations to two men."[184] Henceforth women pledged for debt were to owe sexual services only to their husbands, not to the creditor. "Far from suggesting polyandry in ancient Sumer, this reform would have abolished the possibility of a woman distrained for debt being liable to sexual exploitation by a creditor."[185]

Urukagina concluded his reforms by "establishing their freedom" for citizens of Lagash living in debt," as well as an amnesty for lawbreakers. He made "a binding oral agreement with the god Ningirsu that he would never subjugate the orphan or widow to the powerful," evidently for payment.[186] As early as 1905, François Thureau-Dangin got to the heart of the matter in the earliest translation of the text. He pointed out that Sumer's term for "justice" meant specifically that officials and wealthy individuals ("the powerful") would have no legal claim for debt foreclosure against widows or orphans, that is, to oblige women or children to be turned over to creditors to work off the family's debts.[187]

Urukagina's debt amnesty is the first known amnesty alluding to protecting widows and orphans, although it was implied in Enmetena's amar-gi proclamation.

Sumerian amar-gi as an ideological Rorschach test for translators

Urukagina's text concludes with a statement that when he "received the kingship from Girsu, he instituted ama(r).gi," the word used by Enmetena.[188] Many Assyriologists have rendered this term as "liberty" or "freedom" in the abstract. Yet Thureau-Dangin recognized already in 1905 that the term was akin to Akkadian *andurārum* and *mišarum* used by Babylonian rulers canceling debts.[189]

Diakonoff has elaborated the meaning of amar-gi: "the word *andurārum* ... is a translation of Sumerian ama-r-gi 'returning to mother,' that is, 'to the original situation.' It does not mean liberation from some supreme authority but the canceling

[183] Frayne 2008: E1.9.9.3 iii 20–24′, parentheses in original.

[184] SARI: La 9.3, translation by Cooper pp. 77f., fn8.

[185] Foster 1995: 170, 174.

[186] Frayne 2008: Urukagina E1.9.9.1 xii 13–22 and 23–28.

[187] Thureau-Dangin 1905: 86f. Lambert 1956: 183, reads the reform text's closing section as saying that Urukagina "cleansed the dwellings of the residents of Lagash from usury (she.har.ra), engrossing (of grain), famine, theft, attacks, and he instituted liberty (ama[r].gi) for them." The word "cleansed" connotes a Clean Slate. Later usage suggests that the clay debt tablets were broken.

[188] Frayne 2008: Urukagina E1.9.9.1 xii 13–22 and E1.9.9.2 vii 4'–5'. Lambert 1956: 183n, and SARI: La 9.2.

[189] Thureau-Dangin 1905: 86f. Barton 1929 translated it as "release," but did not specify just what was released. Lambert 1956: 183. Father Deimel 1930: 9 suggested translating amar-gi rather vaguely as "security."

of debts, duties, and the like. Also, 'cleaning' is a *terminus technicus* for 'release from payments.'[190] Dominique Charpin concurs. The word for "mother," ama, should be thought of as "point of origin," the original "mother status."[191]

The significance of this interpretation of a return to the origin is that slaves were not freed, but were returned to their former owners. "Royal proclamations did not liberate captives such as women from the Zagros mountains bought from slave dealers, whose children were made family property but pledged as debt pawns. ... for a slave born of a slave mother, amargi meant a return to the master in whose house he or she was born."[192] This restored families intact with their servants, along with assets taken by creditors and fiscal collectors.

The question inevitably arises as to how effective Urukagina's reforms were. Kramer wrote glibly that they "were soon 'gone with the wind.' Like many another reformer, he seemed to have come 'too late' with 'too little.'"[193] This quip is unfair. Urukagina did not seek a utopian reconstitution of the social order. In granting amnesty to debtors who had forfeited property or the liberty of their family members, his reforms were part of what one might think of as the archaic financial cycle. It would not have been practical for Enmetena, Urukagina or any other ruler of the epoch to stop debt from building up again, because credit was essential to enable individuals to balance income and outgoings. What was important was to reverse the economic and social distortions this created.

The excavated Bronze Age policy inscriptions are a shadow of a social cosmology whose features must have been so well known that no one thought to explain the logic or write a manual of how amar-gi and its cognate policies worked. No alternative mode of economic organization existed to argue: "Let the market work and don't reverse progress. Let creditors foreclose and transfer property from weak hands to strong, from the poor to the wealthy so as to accumulate even larger surpluses." The archaic worldview was just the opposite. But it seemed so natural that there was no need to defend clean slates.

The response taken by Enmetena, Urukagina and their successors to rising personal debt was realistic in not banning interest but letting the process resume until it once again reached the point where it became destabilizing – and then putting the economy back in order. Inevitably, debt pressures grow into new crises, as they do in today's world. All that can practically be done in such circumstances (not only in the Bronze Age, of course, but today as well) is to wipe out debts that can't be paid and let the financial process resume, until it again goes too far.

---

[190] Diakonoff 1991: 234.
[191] Charpin 1987: 39. In his 1956 article, Lambert emphasized that it "does not designate 'liberty' in the sense that we use the word today. It is necessary to understand, in a manner more prosaic and specific, 'exemption from taxes.'" Only in 1972 did he discover Enmetena's amar.gi inscription banning usury as part and parcel of declaring "liberty" for Lagash.
[192] Charpin 1987: 39.
[193] Kramer 1959 [1956]: 49.

The timing of amar-gi and subsequent clean slates

There is no inscription saying that on such-and-such a date Enmetena, Urukagina or Gudea proclaimed amar–gi or *mīšarum*. Presumably everyone knew that they were announced, most notably when authority passed to a new ruler. The "second year" of most rulers was named for these proclamations, as each year-name reflected the major royal achievement of the preceding year. No doubt there was a formal ceremony to mark the transition to a new ruler. But when these acts were proclaimed in the middle of reigns, as often occurred in Babylonian times, there may well have been a regular ceremonial occasion to do so.

Throughout antiquity most such "renewal" ceremonies followed a ceremonial pattern similar to the New Year festival. Hendrik Versnel, a Dutch historian of classical antiquity's myth and ritual, has noted how Mesopotamia's New Year festival followed a ceremonial structure that was adopted for rituals as distant as the Roman military triumph.[194]

The common denominator is the re-ordering of social balance. Throughout Asia the New Year is an occasion for settling debts – by paying what one owes to be sure, not annulling them. For many governments and corporations, the fiscal year for summing up economic accounts dates from the spring. That was the time of Babylonia's New Year festival, at the start of Nisan. Coronations or annual enthronement ceremonies were similar "social renewal" occasions for the proclamations of Enmetena, Urukagina, Gudea, Shulgi, Hammurabi and other Mesopotamian rulers.

This counters Kramer's belief that the Clean Slate was limited to only a short Saturnalia. When rulers proclaimed amar-gi and *andurārum* from debts, it was not merely a short-run suspension of collections during the festival. They wiped out crop debts as part of a general amnesty that included freeing prisoners, not merely postponed payment. The same principle remained the case down through classical antiquity, as when Egypt's Rosetta stone commemorated freeing the population from back taxes, or much later, the Roman Emperor Hadrian annulling debts owed to the Roman state.

[194] Versnel 1970.

10. Sargon's Akkadian Empire and Its Collapse, 2300–2100 BC

Urukagina's reforms helped secure the loyalty of Lagash's fighting men under threat from Umma and Uruk. Meanwhile, Umma's énsi Lugalzagesi had acquired the throne of Uruk in 2351 BC. Perhaps he offered Umma's copious supply of water to alleviate the shortages that Adams noted for the Uruk region – water that had enabled Umma to increase its arable land area and population for a century, largely at Uruk's expense.[195]

Ending Lagash's alliance with Uruk, Lugalzagesi revived the conflict over the Gu'edena boundary land by diverting its water yet again. This confronted Lagash with the dilemma of "whether to accept his sovereignty, give up the contested territories, and pay indemnities without discussion; or to resist, preparing for war with Umma and, inasmuch as Lugalzagesi had become king of Uruk, with that city too."[196] As lugal, Urukagina chose war, evidently with the consent of the temples.

Lagash's army was hardly a match for the combined forces of Umma and Uruk. It was vulnerable to upstream attacks diverting its water and cutting off its trade with northern Mesopotamia. After war broke out, normal trade relations were maintained only with Dilmun in the Persian Gulf to the south, Susa to the east and Der in the northeast.

Urukagina went to Umma in his third year to try to negotiate a truce, but Lugalzagesi mounted a surprise attack on the canal that supplied Lagash with water from the Guedena, and destroyed many sanctuaries throughout the countryside while seizing half of Lagash's territory, from the Gu'edena to Girsu.[197] A lamentation text relates how "the leader of Umma set fire to the Ekibira. He set fire to the Antasur and bundled off its precious metals and lapis lazuli. He plundered the palace of Tirash, he plundered the Abzubanda" and other sacred places in Lagash, including temples and shrines to the gods Enlil, Utu, Inanna, Nanshe, Dumuzi-Abzu, Nindar, Ninmah and others. "In the fields of Ningirsu, whichever were cultivated, he destroyed the barley."[198]

These losses obliged Urukagina to cut back the rations he had increased at the start of his rule. Men were called into the army from the temples and weaving workshops. Their place was taken by women and "old ones," joined by about 60 "slaves (newly?) bought."[199] But the size of Lagash's weaving establishments was nearly doubled, apparently to produce goods to trade for raw materials.

---

[195] Adams 1981: 160, and Nissen1988: 129–132.
[196] Lambert 1966: 34.
[197] Westenholz 1975.
[198] Frayne 2008: **Urukagina** E1.9.9.5, i 1–11 and vii 7–9. See also Cooper, SARI: La 9.5.
[199] Lambert 1961.

Records of temple herds and offerings disappear in Urukagina's fourth year. The next year austerity intensified, and sheep and cattle disappear from the documentation. Another major attack came in Urukagina's sixth year, by which time the temple stores were empty and their cattle and sheep had to be let out to forage (although weaving employment still increased). After Urukagina's sixth year, "documents are unknown. ... [T]he scribes have been redirected to other tasks and services." All that has survived from the war's closing months are lists of refugees, missing persons and requisitions of pack animals, "lists of ruins and deaths with cruel precision and pitiless dryness. From a city in full expansion Lagash begins to shrink to the level of an insignificant town."[200]

Lugalzagesi subjugated nearly all of southern Mesopotamia by conquering Ur, Larsa, Nippur and Kish, but "did not attempt to consolidate it into a unified state," observes Diakonoff. "Although he defeated Kish, he did not destroy the Kish lugals, and having defeated Lagash, he was not able to remove Urukagina from power."[201] Yet he dreamed of creating a far-flung empire by moving westward to the Mediterranean and other regions beyond Mesopotamia's historic sphere of influence. In doing this he stretched his forces thin. Sumer had been at peace for two generations under Uruk's nominal but weak suzerainty. By conquering Kish and other northern cities, Lugalzagesi triggered a response that led to the region's militarization behind Sargon, former cupbearer to Kish's ruler Ur-Zababa.

Sargon's conquest of southern Mesopotamia

Historians have not learned just how or when Sargon attained the throne. The legends about his humble origins (the Sumerian Kings List states that his father was a gardener) stem from later times, when he was called Sargon the Ancient, probably referring to his 55-year reign, c. 2334–2279.[202] His royal name, *Šarru-kīn* ("Sargon"), means "The King is Legitimate" (in the sense of insisting on his legitimacy after his takeover) or "The King is Just," a rhetoric reminiscent of Urukagina.

Having conquered Mari in the north (probably in alliance with Ebla and Nagar), Sargon found the south weakened by Lugalzagesi's region-wide fighting. Using a mobile fighting technique with arrows and spears to outmaneuver his opponents' infantry phalanges weighed down by heavy shields and lances, Sargon attacked Uruk and defeated Lugalzagesi's "League of Fifty Ensis." Lugalzagesi mounted a last stand, but was beaten by Sargon and brought in neck stocks to the gate of Enlil to end his 25-years reign (c. 2351–2327).[203]

---

[200] Lambert 1966. Maekawa 1973–74: 77–144, believes that it was Lagash's need for a war mobilization that led Urukagina to take the temples under royal control and appropriate basic production, not simply a desire to reverse the inequities described in his reform text.

[201] Cooper and Heimpel 1983: 67–82.

[202] Diakonoff 1991: 84 finds no reason to doubt this tradition.

[203] Sallaberger 2007: 148, Kramer 1963: 324–60, and Diakonoff 1991: 84 ff.

For the first time on record Sumer was nominally unified. The King List later depicted the land as always having been integrated under a single ruler, with dominance shifting for military reasons, not because of favoritism of the gods.[204] That is what made Sargon's reign different from that of the preceding ens and énsis whose authority nominally was based on their relationship with the temples. There is no hint of a reform or amar–gi proclamation during his rule to alleviate his demands for tribute. He appointed "sons of Agade" as énsis of the southern cities, installing military garrisons to back their authority. Soldiers apparently were given land of their own, at the expense of former inhabitants. The result was many revolts throughout southern Mesopotamia.

Acting as overlord, Sargon took over temple estates in each southern city. He appointed his daughter Enheduanna high priestess to the moon-god Nanna at Ur, and to a similar position at Uruk. His grandson Naram-Sin did the same thing.[205] Instead of ruling at least nominally on behalf of the city-god that originally meant overseeing mutual aid, he took the title "strong god of Agade," deifying himself instead of ruling on behalf of the city's patron deity. Sacrifices and what became taxes were henceforth to the palace, not to the gods, because military rulers took over that role.[206]

For the remainder of Babylonian history, temples would be taken under direct palace control. Making no pretense of gverning on behalf of the local economy, the Akkadian dynasty was brutally extractive, turning the economic functions of temples and local governing institutions against their communities.

There is no record of any cancellation of debts, because attempts to protect or restore economic balance would have reduced the flow of tribute to Akkad. Ensis and their city priesthoods "ceased to be independent rulers by right of succession and became merely governors, who were appointed and removed by the king and who were moved from one economic center to another." Other officials and commanders likewise were shifted from town to town to ensure that they served Akkad's interests rather than developing a stake in promoting local development.[207] "Sargon and his successors kept at their court the representatives of the remaining aristocratic family lineages, especially the ruling ones; their status was part dignitary, part hostage."[208]

In cultural as well as economic life, individualism was concentrated at the top of society. History's earliest known author of a poem is Sargon's daughter Enheduanna. In art, "the place of a superhuman, impersonal image of a god or a priest was replaced by images exhibiting a powerful individuality."[209] Privatization of wealth occurred from the top down – what Leo Oppenheim called "feudalism from above," characterized by personal appropriation of public wealth and bureaucratic position.[210] A large standing army was created, overseen by a burdensome imperial bureaucracy headed by military commanders. Opportunities for personal achievement narrowed for most of the population. Only a small proportion of commoners "got promoted in the army or the administration, or … were connected with trade."[211]

---

[204] See Marchesi 2010: 234.
[205] Nissen 1988: 172.
[206] See Postgate 1995: 400 f.
[207] Tyumanev 1959: 81.

[208] Diakonoff 1991: 86.
[209] Diakonoff 1991: 86.
[210] Oppenheim 1957: 33.
[211] Diakonoff 1991: 192 f.

Although the Akkadians did not promote local prosperity, their extension of trade spread Sumerian entrepreneurial practices as far northwest as Cappadocia in central Anatolia. This seems to be the period when the northern Mesopotamian practice of assigning the palace's administrative and commercial functions to private traders spread throughout the southern region.[212] Sargon's trade missions are described as obtaining silver from Asia Minor's Taurus Mountains, and cedar wood from Lebanon and Syria. Sea trade with the Indus valley seems to have reached a peak, and Sargonic texts describe ships docking at Akkad from Dilmun, Meluccha (on the coast of India) and Magan/Oman.[213] This commercialization to squeeze out trading profits foreshadowed the centralized Ur III period and, to a lesser degree, the Isin, Larsa and Old Babylonian periods of the Middle Bronze Age, 2100–1600 BC.

Figure 17: Head of an Akkadian ruler

The Akkadian Dynasty[214]

Sargon of Akkad (2334–2279)	Reigned for 56 years, including the years before he defeated Lugalzaggesi. Reputed to be a former cup-bearer to Ur-Zababa of Kish, he founded the Akkadian Dynasty and united Sumer and Akkad into a single empire.
Rimush (2278–2270)	Sargon's younger son. Fought and reconquered Ur, Umma, Adab, Lagash, Der and Elam. Reigned 8 years. Was killed in a palace revolt.
Manishtushu (2269–2255)	Brother of Rimush, also a warrior prince who died in a palace revolt, reigned for 14 years
Naram-Sin (2254–2218)	Reigned for 37 years. Raised Akkad to its most extensive imperium and had himself worshipped as a god as King of the Four Quarters.
Shar-kali-sharri (2217–2193)	Ruled for 25 years over a shrinking kingdom as the Gutians invaded.

Figure 18: The Akkadian dynasty

[212] Gelb1952: xiii.
[213] Muhly 1973: 315ff., 222.
[214] Source: Brinkman 1977: 335 f.

Repression of resistance in the south had begun under Lugalzagesi, but Sargon and his sons engaged in unprecedented brutality. His son Rimush devastated Ur, Umma, Lagash, Der and Elam, and "many larger cities dwindle or are abandoned outright"[215] as the Sargonic rulers deported prisoners from recalcitrant cities whose rebellions were suppressed.[216] Lagash barely recovered from the devastation inflicted by Lugalzagesi, and built few monuments during the Akkadian period. Umma tried to make a stand against Sargon, but shrank "from over 400 hectares to somewhere between 200 and 40 hectares, while the substantial city of Umm-el-Aqarib to the south of it … was totally abandoned."[217]

Gutian Domination of Sumer: c. 2220–2120

The Gutians, a tribe from the Zagros mountains in Iran, brought social and economic anarchy to Sumer. Four kings ruled in the first three years of their domination. An attempted resurgence led by a Fourth Dynasty of Uruk (five kings in thirty years) succumbed to the Gutians, ruled by 21 kings in 91 years. Increasingly, the Gutians seem to have ruled Sumer via Lagash énsis.

After Rimush and his brother Manishtushu were killed in palace revolts, Sargon's grandson Naram-Sin (2254–2218) called himself King of the Four Quarters (of the world) and was the first ruler to use the divinity-title (a star-shaped dingir) as part of his name. By deifying himself, Naram-Sin became the "god of Akkad," much like the Roman emperors declaring themselves divine. Inasmuch as the city-deity invariably held land, workshops and other property, Naram-Sin "claimed title to the land" of Akkad and all the regions it controlled. His assertion of personal godhood over temple property threatened local priesthoods and overruled the power of local interests.[218]

Under Naram-Sin the Akkadian empire attained its furthest boundaries. Northern Mesopotamia was relatively calm, but the south disintegrated "into ever smaller units toward the end, until finally a situation had been created that corresponded, at least externally, to that in the Early Dynastic III period (2600–2350): a fairly large number of independent political units assembled around some of the centers known from the earlier period."[219] Naram-Sin's son, Sharkalisharri, defended his realm against the invading Gutians (who were joined by the Elamites and incursions of Amorites from the west), but his few victories were merely holding operations. His successors were of no political importance beyond Akkad's immediate boundaries. Its hour was over.

Descent of the Gutians into Mesopotamia, and the First Interregnum

Akkad represents history's first real empire and despotic state. But despite being weakened by two centuries of fighting, Sumer's population mounted local uprisings while the Gutian invaders were pressing into the turmoil. The epic called *The Curse of Akkad* (and sometimes *The Ekur Avenged*) states that Enlil, whose temple at the old

[215] Jacobsen 1981: xiv.
[216] Foster 1982.
[217] Parrot 1948: 142.

[218] Nissen 1988: 172.
[219] Nissen 1988: 184f.

religious center at Nippur was looted by Naram-Sin, picked the Gutian mountain tribes as his instrument of revenge. They are the only people described with hatred, even by comparison with the Akkadians, stereotyped as the classic "subhuman barbarian." [220]

Pointing out that the Gutians did not extend their authority much beyond the eastern region of Adab, Nissen views The Ekur Avenged and subsequent epics, along with the Sumerian King List, as exaggerating their role. [221] After sacking Sumer's cities, they were unable to run the urban administrative systems. The epic says that Sumer's "canal-boat towpaths grew nothing but weeds," and that Akkad's "chariot roads grew nothing but the 'wailing plant'; moreover, on its canal boat towpaths and landings no human being walks because of the wild goats, vermin, snakes and mountain scorpions." [222] Their brigandage blocked the overland trade that Sargon had developed to the north and to Asia Minor.

Sumer's Early Dynastic Period rivalry among the leading cities did not suffer the kind of warlordship brought by the Akkadian and Gutian military satrapies. The Sumerian King List asks plaintively, "Who was king? Who was not king?" as it enumerates 21 Gutian rulers in the span of 91 years. Their decentralization helped break Akkad's military looting and tribute taking, but economic life fell to a lower level than was the case under Akkad. Local dynasties developed during the half-century or so when the interregnum was deepest between the fall of Akkad and the rise of Ur.

Little is heard of debt relationships in the Akkadian period and its "Gutian" aftermath. Proclamations of liberty from debt and rural usury would have involved amnesties from the tribute demanded by Akkad. Meanwhile, trade and administrative enterprise were assigned to families acting in a quasi-official capacity. This set the stage for new vested interests to emerge over the next few centuries with increasing wealth and local power of their own over the next few centuries.

When economic life was reconstructed under the dynasties of Ur III, Larsa, Isin and Babylon, it was characterized by an entrepreneurial mercantile class that used its surplus wealth to engage in rural usury and, increasingly, to seek absentee landownership. Urukagina's amar-gi act had aimed mainly at reversing palatial and temple fees and payments that had led to indebtedness. It had not been necessary to address the loss of crop and land rights, and debt bondage had not reached nearly the extent that made it necessary for Ur III rulers and their Babylonian successors to deal with these problems. The economic transition brought about by these post-Sargonic trends appears already in the experience of Lagash leading up to the "neo-Sumerian" Ur III period.

---

[220] Hallo 2005: 149. He notes that the Gutians retreated to the East, but may have come from the northwest. Not even their linguistic affiliation is known.

[221] Nissen, *Early History* (1988), pp. 174f. and 186.

[222] Kramer, *The Sumerians* (1963), pp. 64f.

11. Lagash's Revival Under Gudea, and his Debt Cancellation, 2130 BC

It is only from Lagash that sufficient records survive to describe Mesopotamian society between the fall of Akkad and the beginning of the Ur III period c. 2100 BC. Thanks to the city's eastern location close to the Zagros Mountains, and possibly the willingness of its énsis to work with the Gutians in collecting tribute, Lagash enjoyed a renaissance for about half a century as its merchants re-established trade from the Taurus Mountains to Elam and Dilmun.[223]

Ur-Ba'u and his successor énsis of Lagash's "Second Dynasty"[224]	
Ur-Ba'u	Began the rebuilding of Lagash's major temples and other institutions.
Gudea	Son-in-law of Ur-Ba'u, restored trade relations between Sumer and Egypt, Ethiopia, Anatolia and the Taurus, Dilmun and Elam.
Ur-Ningirsu II and Ur-ayabba	Gudea's sons, ruled less than a decade.
Ur-Mama	Son-in-law of Ur-Ba'u, ruled quite briefly.
Nammahani	A third son-in-law of Ur-Ba'u. Probably also served as énsi of Umma as well as Lagash. He continued the policy of co-operating with the Gutians. He was killed by Ur-Nammu in 2112 BC.

Figure 19: Ur-Ba'u and his successors

A ruling dynasty was founded by Ur-Bau. Like Sargon and Naram-Sin, he dominated Ur by installing his daughter as high priestess of its Nanna temple. He also began to rebuild Lagash's temples and sanctuaries, although the major achievements along these lines were left to his son-in-law Gudea. The latter was "thought to have been the son of a priestess who represented a goddess in the 'sacred marriage' rite with a priest,"[225] evidently an auspicious ceremonial conception.

---

[223] Falkenstein 1966: 46–54, and Gudea's Statue A:xv. 15ff., and xvi.1ff.

[224] Source: Brinkman 1977: 335f. Lagash's "Second" dynasty has not been definitively dated. All Lagash rulers were expurgated from the Sumerian King List, redacted (apparently from an earlier Akkadian version) in the ensuing Ur III period largely for propaganda purposes.

[225] Diakonoff 1991: 91. Edzard 1997: 15 notes: Ur-Bau was "the father of Gudea's wife, Nin-alla. Another daughter of his, Nin-hedu, married Nammahani, Gudea's fifth successor. A third daughter of Ur-Bau, whose name is not preserved, dedicated a statuette to Ur-GAR."

The longest surviving Sumerian poem (Cylinders A and B, 1400 lines) commemorates Gudea's rebuilding of the temple of Gatumdug, c. 2130. Other inscriptions describe how he rebuilt the Ningirsu temple. "There is hardly any other group of inscriptions by a ruler as saturated with the ideology of the 'temple city' as Gudea's," observes Nissen. In contrast to the centralized Akkadian asset stripping, "the sixteen year names handed down to us from his reign report exclusively on the building of temples, the appointment of specific priests, or the production of emblems of gods."[226]

Nineteen statues of Gudea (Statues A to S) have been found. Seven are of diorite, a prized material for making monumental objects reflecting its rarity in view of the difficulty of transporting it from Magan to Mesopotamia. In addition to the lengthy inscriptions on these statues, Gudea's Cylinders A and B are of baked clay. These publicly displayed inscriptions describe his dream in which the goddess Nanshe instructed him to build the temples.

Like subsequent legal texts, Statue B has a prologue and epilogue calling down curses on anyone who would deface it, alter its judgments or substitute someone else's name for that of its original inscriber. It recalls Urukagina's amar–gi text in promising to protect orphans and widows against the rich and powerful, and by proclaiming a debt cancellation: "Within the boundaries of Lagash no one took an accused person to the place of oath-taking, and no debt collector (lú.har.ra or lú-ur₅-ra) entered anyone's house"[227] evidently referring to governors, supervisors, overseers and corvée levy supervisors (iv:13–19). The implication is that under normal conditions "the accused were frequently dragged to take an oath; creditors could enter the house of debtors at will."[228]

Gudea's texts describe a seven-day New Year temple dedication ritual and public banquet.[229] As with Urukagina's proclamation, their terseness has obliged Assyriologists to infer just what is meant. Gudea used the Sumerian terms níg-gi-na and níg-si-sá, but not amar-gi. Following the ordinances of Nanshe and Ningirsu, Gudea "paid attention to the justice [níg-gi-gina] ordained by Nanshe and Ningirsu; I did not expose the orphan to the wealthy person, nor did I expose the widow to the influential one."[230] Jacobsen and Edzard in read Cylinder B (xvii.18– xviii.9) and Statue B (vii.29) to state that Gudea "remitted debts."

For more than a generation, Assyriologists debated the extent to which Gudea's actions affected economic life after the ritual and banquet ended. Kramer viewed the inscriptions as ceremonial poetic texts of a literary or spiritual genre, describing an

---

[226] Nissen 1988: 187.

[227] Statue B, lines v: 5–11. Unless otherwise indicated, translations are from Edzard 1997. The term lú.har.ra seems to mean "obligations man" or "collector," from the terms lú (man) and har (loan or accrued debt). See for instance the next-to-last paragraph of Urukagina's reform text (Lambert 1956: 193).

[228] Kramer 1963: 137 ff.

[229] Sauren 1975: 95–103.

[230] Edzard 1997: E3/1.1.7StB, vii.38–43, and Jacobsen 1987: 440. The phrase that Edzard translates as "washed all hands," Jacobsen interprets as "granted pardons."

idealized ritual behavior adopted only during the festival itself. He granted that Gudea canceled personal debts, but viewed his festival as only a ceremonial interlude, a "rare occasion [on which] the citizens had to be on extra good behavior" in which "No one was lashed by the whip or hit by the goad, no mother would beat her child."[231] But such activity must have resumed later as the economy returned to the normal state of affairs in which "the orphan and the widow were at the mercy of the rich and powerful."

Figure 20:
Gudea with the temple
plan on his lap (Statue B).

On this ground he doubted that the debt moratorium was more than a temporary suspension (a kind of Saturnalia, an inversion of normal order). Being an inversion, it could only be realized in the form of a temporary ritualistic release of frustration in the face of economic inequality. That is indeed how the Roman Saturnalia and their

[231] Gudea, Statue B iv.10–12, in Edzard 1997: 32 (E3/1.1.7StB), and Kramer 1971: 5. See also Cylinder A, xiii: 3–9.

Greek counterparts were conducted.[232] But if Gudea's use of níg-gina and níg-si-sá [justice and equity] was like earlier Sumerian and subsequent Babylonian usage, the inversion of the indebtedness and disorder into which Sumerian society had fallen was a longer-lasting release from chaos – at least until debt imbalances built up to the point where they had to be canceled again.

Most Assyriologists now view Gudea as indeed freeing bondservants and canceling debts for Sumerian society at large, not merely for the duration of the New Year festival. But no doubt mothers did strike their children. The single lasting effect would have been liberation from debt. Equity would have been restored by canceling the arrears and obligations owed by the population, as they had been under Enmetena's and Urukagina's amar-gi acts, and later would be by Babylonia's frequent *mīšarum* acts. Edzard translates of the relevant passages on Gudea's Cylinder B (xvii.17–viii.11)as:

> He had debts remitted and he granted pardons.
> When his master had entered his House,
> for seven days the slave woman was allowed to be equal to her mistress,
> the slave was allowed to walk side by side with his master. ...
> He paid attention to justice [níg-gina] (ordained) [By Nanshe] and Ni[ngursu];
> He did not expose the orphan [to the wealthy person]
> nor did he expose the widow to the [influential] one. ...
> Days of justice [níg-si-sá] had risen for him,
> and he set (his) foot on the neck of evil and complaint.[233]

Jacobsen's translation is similar, except for rendering the last two lines (xviii 10–11) as:

> A grand period of equity had dawned for him, and he set foot on the neck of evil ones and malcontents; like the sun god from the horizon he came out unto the city.

This sounds like an underlying equality of status was established by freeing the economy from personal debt. Widows and orphans were liberated from being bondservants for their creditors because the financial claims that held them in servitude were canceled. Having reversed the most immediate and oppressive consequences of economic inequality by annulling the personal debts to local officials, overseers and other creditors, Gudea would have put the Sumerian economy back "in order" so that the New Year could begin in balance.

As noted above in chapters 2 and 9, in today's world it is typical throughout Asia for families to celebrate the New Year by going about paying off their debts, cleaning their houses and putting their affairs in order. In third-millennium Sumer, paying debts was increasingly beyond the ability of many families. Sumer's solution was to periodically cancel those debts at sacred festivals. Our modern world has reversed matters by sanctifying the payment of debts, not their cancellation.

---

[232] For a discussion of such festivals see Bourboulis 1964.
[233] Cylinder B, xvii.17–21, xviii.4–11, in Edzard 1997: 98.

12. Trade, Enterprise and Debt in Ur III: 2111–2004 BC

The revolt against the Gutians and Elam did not originate in Lagash, but was aimed largely against it. Perhaps that city had reached a modus vivendi with the easterners once Akkad was out of the way. Its nemesis was Ur's governor Ur-Namma, who broke away from Uruk's ruler Utuhegal in 2112 BC. Driving out the Gutians and Elamites, he built up sufficient power to attack Lagash, capturing and killing its ensi Namhani (Gudea's brother-in-law). Absorbing Lagash into Ur's domain and levying grain tribute, Ur-Namma put in place a dynasty that would govern Sumer for a century.

Few details are known of his rule apart from what is reflected in his date formulae and inscriptions. He installed his daughter as en priestess-administrator over Ur's city-temple of Nanna, which controlled trade with Dilmun (Bahrain) and Magan on the Iranian shore.[234] After seventeen years of rule, in 2095, Ur-Namma died in battle fighting the Gutians. His son Shulgi's 47-year rule extended Ur's sphere of control to Elam and the Zagros region to the east, and Assur in the north. In the tradition of Naram-Sin of Akkad he arranged to be deified in a sacred marriage with Ur's high priestess.

Two centuries of invasions from the north (Akkad) and east (Elamites and Gutians) exacting tribute had undercut local self-reliance. Military chiefs, local protégés and "big men" (lú.gal) had appropriated temple estates and other property for themselves. But the palace destroyed local independence even more than had been the case under the Akkadian conquest three centuries earlier. "It is the ruler of Ur who fulfills the obligations previously incumbent upon the local village prince [ensi]," summarizes Kraus. Extending palace authority over the temples, Ur-Namma and Shulgi "instituted a new State cult" and transformed the village-states "into administrative districts," partly by building a hundred and twenty new temples, administered by palace appointees.[235] Powell describes the general spirit as dominated "more by fear of punishment than economic self-interest."[236] Diakonoff describes the resulting political despotism as

> absolute, while the role of the local organs of self-government (including the community courts of justice) was reduced to a minimum. The 'nomes' ceased being traditional self-governing states and became administrative districts headed by royal officials whose title 'ensi' was now a mere sound. ... All royal land was cultivated by gangs of laborers denoted by the general term gurush, 'able-bodied men,' working the whole year round and receiving nothing but meager rations in kind. ... Both the gurush and the slave-women were cruelly exploited, and

---

[234] Oppenheim 1954.
[235] Kraus 1954: 525f.
[236] Powell 1999: 5.

their mortality was so high that a natural reproduction of all this labor force is hardly conceivable.[237]

Privatization of trade and agriculture

The Ur III century is the best documented in Sumerian history, mainly by palace archives but also those of the rising class of managers to whom the palace delegated authority as revenue collectors. The leading enterprise was the foreign trade that the Akkadians had built up, enabling merchants to make profits by exchanging palace consignments of handicrafts for raw materials and luxury goods. Although "much of the copper trade was financed by the state sector," writes Steven Garfinkle, on the basis of examining private mercantile archives, "the actual organization of the copper trade remained the prerogative of individual entrepreneurs."[238]

Domestically, Shulgi extended the Akkadian practice of delegating management of "a considerable increase in the area of the royal land" to "control personnel" wielding quasi-feudal authority over families that had lost their own land tenure in local

---

The Ur III Dynasty

Five rulers in 108 years (2112–2004)

Ur-Namma (2112–2095)	An usurper who is reported to have broken away from Utuhegal. He greatly extended foreign trade and installed client governors in Elam (Susa), Assur, Mari and other outlying regions. He drew up an extensive body of legal rulings, and cancelled debts with a nıg-sı-sá act. He reigned for 18 years.
Shulgi (2094–2047)	He reigned for 48 years. Extended Sumerian domination over Elam and the Zagros to the east, and to the edge of the Subarian lands in the north, peopled by Hurrian-speakers.
Amar-Su'en (2046–2038)	He reigned for 9 years.
Shu-Sin (2037–2029)	Built an extensive but ineffective wall in an attempt to block nomadic Amorite invasions from the northwest (Syria). Reigned for 9 years.
Ibbi-Sin (2028–2004)	Ruled for 25 years. Was defeated by the Amorites and Elamites, and finally was confined to Ur itself. He was captured when Elam conquered Ur and took him into custody, where he died.

Figure 21: The Ur III dynasty

---

[237] Diakonoff 1969: 195 f. See also Diakonoff 1971: 19, in which Diakonoff called Ur III "one of the worst totalitarian regimes known to history," a police state run "by a despotic bureaucratic machinery under whose supervision the gurush worked incessantly from sunrise to sunset, without holidays or feast days, receiving scanty rations, with a resulting high mortality rate. ... This system was extended not only to agriculture but also to handicrafts."

[238] Garfinkle 2012: 119.

communities.[239] Land managers, herding overseers and other economic functionaries owed the palace a stipulated return, but could keep whatever they could extract above this level.

Despite declining crop yields, the palace raised sharecropping rents to one-third of the harvest (compared to one-eighth or one-seventh in Lagash in Urukagina's time).[240] Arrears increased and many families fell into a state of clientage. Many parents had to sell their children to keep them alive, and "impoverished families, mainly widows together with their children and slaves placed themselves – presumably as clients – at the disposal of a temple household," or were donated to the temples by families that no longer could afford the cost of their upkeep.[241]

Pre-Sargonic personal debts had been owed mainly to collectors and functionaries in the palace or temple bureaucracies. But by the end of the third millennium BC, personal debt to moneylenders was becoming problematic as traders and entrepreneurial managers lent out some of the money they made. Their increasingly active role in the economy marked "the beginning of a long process by which debt-bondage arrangements were progressively more and more widespread, becoming eventually a major economic and social problem."[242]

As noted in Chapter 7, rural labor was scarce, largely because of the heavy corvée demands made by the palace. The major way for prosperous landowners or officials to obtain labor was to get it into debt and make it work off the interest. Barley loans were made not only to needy cultivators, but also to palace managers seeking to meet their quota of payments. In such cases the aim was simply to obtain interest, not labor. For example, the shepherd or herd manager SI.A-a advanced a barley loan of 23 gur (6900 liters).[243] The borrowers were military officials and provincial authorities, who evidently needed to obtain labor or the barley itself to meet their quotas to the Ur III palace.

These private mercantile archives analyzed by Garfinkle show that much money-lending was entrepreneurial and commercial, not usurious. "There were no apparent social or economic disincentives to money-lending. Indeed, the nature of the Ur III state made this activity attractive and, in some cases, necessary."[244] This was largely because, "by the end of the third millennium BCE, the crown had acquired control over many of the institutional estates of the various temples. The administration of these institutional holdings was still dependent throughout this period on the presence of entrepreneurs and craftsmen who were the heads of individual non-institutional households."[245] Foreign trade in particular was outsourced.

---

[239] Diakonoff 1982: 67 and 70.

[240] Falkenstein 1954: 793 and 791, and Adams 1981.

[241] Gelb 1972: 8–11. He adds: "The practice of giving human beings to the temple is a form of exposure. Strictly speaking, exposure involves getting rid of children, as well as of women, old people, and other unwanted individuals, by casting them off so that they may die or be killed by wild animals."

[242] Steinkeller 2002: 124.   [244] Garfinkle 2004a: 25.

[243] Garfinkle 2012: 9 and 138.   [245] Garfinkle 2004b: 394.

Entrepreneurs borrowing to make gains had long been the case with foreign trade. Borrowing from individual creditors now spread to other economic spheres as palace functions were privatized. "The non-institutional archives from the Ur III period indicate that the borrowers were frequently members of the highest echelons of their society – not subsistence farmers."[246] Research over the past two decades has shown that there is no contradiction between Ur III's political autocracy and this outsourcing and privatization of its extractive palatial economy. Dercksen summarizes the result of this new research: "The trader (DAM.GAR, *tamkārum*) under the Third Dynasty of Ur has long been regarded as a commercial agent in the service of a palace or temple, both institutions supposedly possessing a commercial monopoly. More recently, he is seen rather as a private entrepreneur who could also trade on behalf of the central administration, similar to the Old Assyrian and Old Babylonian *tamkārum*." These individuals formed a heterogeneous social group "ranging from those fully employed by an institution to those that were largely active privately."[247]

Garfinkle emphasizes that "Moneylending was not the sole province of merchants nor was it their chief occupation. The merchants of the Ur III period were primarily engaged in the business of exchange. ... merchants worked closely with the state but were not its employees. The chief function of merchants in this period was as facilitators of exchange, not as creditor."[248] But their moneylending became increasingly problematic from the vantage point of rulers seeking to maintain their own control over rural labor and crop surpluses.

What Ur-Namma's laws meant by níg-si-sá

The laws are usually ascribed to Ur-Namma although their first translator, Samuel Kramer, thought the laws were the work of Shulgi, which is now doubted.[249] Frayne points out that the laws contain parallels to Ur-Namma's hymns but not those of Shulgi, and Ur-Namma's name appears at least three times while Shulgi's does not appear at all.[250]

The laws have survived only on tablet fragments copied at a Babylonian scribal school around the reign of Hammurabi. The style of the hymnic prologue places these laws in the tradition of royal proclamations from Enmetena, Urukagina and Gudea in Lagash down to Lipit-Ishtar of Isin c. 1930 and Hammurabi's dynasty. Like Urukagina's appeal to Ningirsu and Hammurabi's appeal to Shamash, gods of

---

[246] Garfinkle 2004a: 7. Garfinkle cites a chief shepherd who advanced credit to numerous military officials.

[247] Dercksen, ed., 1999: Introduction, p. 2.

[248] Garfinkle 2012: 35n.

[249] Kramer 1983: 453–456. Kramer translated the laws in 1954; Finkelstein did his translation in 1969.

[250] The law tablets were excavated in Nippur at the beginning of the 20th century, but the Istanbul Museum classified them as just another school text and they were not translated until 1952. Frayne 1997: 43–45 discusses the background. My quotations are from Roth 1995. See also more recently Civil 2011: 221–286.

economic justice and commerce, the prologue states that these rulings reflect the principles of justice and equity sponsored by Ur's city-deity Nanna. "I established nig.sisa [justice in the land]." (Roth A iii:113.) The close of his prologue confirms this promise: "I established justice in the land" (Roth A iv:170; Frayne's translation is identical).

Not all the rulings can be translated fully, but like Urukagina the ruler promises relief to citizens whose animals and other property have been taken by avaricious headmen or chief herdsmen (Roth A ii:87–92 and A iii:114–24). After promising to liberate the population from seizures of property, the ruler promises to protect the poor from the rich, standardize weights and measures, and set fines for various crimes or infractions. There is no specific mention of freeing bondservants or returning lands that had been forfeited or sold under duress, but the ruler claims (A iv 162–168): "I did not deliver the orphan to the rich. I did not deliver the widow to the mighty. I did not deliver the man with but one shekel to the man with one mina (*i.e.*, 60 shekels). I did not deliver the man with but one sheep to the man with one ox."

The text echoes Urukagina's and Gudea's wording for cancelling debts. But like these earlier texts, translators are left to make their own rendition of what is being promulgated. Key legal terms remain so ambiguous that "literal translations of the texts, which are highly idiomatic and make use of a complex technical terminology" leave readers with "a new, equally unintelligible text."[251]

Kramer's early version sounds much like how Urukagina (in his reading) described officials as acting under Lugalanda: The ruler "removed the 'chiselers' and the grafters, or, as the code itself describes them, the 'grabbers' of the citizens' oxen, sheep and donkeys." Just how the "grabbing" was done is not spelled out, but evidently it was for payments due for palace charges or services.

Was this against the law? There is nothing in the literal text about grafters. Was the problem corrupt officials, or the buildup of debts owed to them – and behind them, to the palace? The officials appear to have been supervisors responsible for collecting taxes or related fees, such as guild heads responsible for paying what their underlings owed.[252]

Kramer admits that he is merely guessing that Ur-Namma "did away" with the duties of these various officials. He adds that the term may have meant "reformed," or "made just again," not necessarily clearing the slate.[253]

The Ur III laws also standardized fines for specific infractions. If a man failed to keep his portion of a dike in proper repair and thereby flooded the field of another man, "he shall measure out (for him) three gur of barley per iku of field." This apparently approximated the normal yield that would have been lost. For crimes: one mina for breaking someone's bone in a fight, two-thirds of a mina (40 shekels) for cutting off his nose with a knife, but only ten shekels for cutting off his foot. This

---

[251] Larsen 1976: 22.
[252] Mendelsohn 1940: 68–70.
[253] Kramer 1954: 411; 1956: 195; 1983 and 1963: 84. Moscati 1960: 26 follows Kramer in referring to "dishonest officials, *e.g.* 'the profiteers on the citizens' oxen, sheep and asses.'"

latter rule corresponds to §45 of the laws of Eshnunna as well as to Hittite laws, reflecting the common background for most Bronze Age Near Eastern legal inscriptions.

Most important, these laws set the interest rate for barley loans at one third of
the principal, and at the decimalized equivalent of 20 percent for silver loans:

> § m: If a man [gives another man] 300 silas of grain as an interest-bearing loan,
> its interest rate per annum is [100 silas in grain (= 33%)].
> § n: If a man [gives] another man 10 shekels of silver as an interest-bearing loan,
> its interest rate per annum is [2 shekels in silver (= 20%)].[254]

The parallels between these proclamations and those of Urukagina suggest a
customary forgiveness of back taxes and associated personal debts, which evidently
had grown oppressive. Most were owed to palace collectors or functionaries. If
cancelling these obligations occurred while Ur-Namma was making war on Lagash,
most such debts probably would have been owed to Lagash officials or those in the
Gutian or Elamite tribute-taking administration.

So we are brought back to what was meant by pledging to "establish níg.si.sá
("justice") and níg-gi-na ("truth") in the land." These words recall Urukagina's and
Gudea's texts, and foreshadow the prologue to Lipit-Ishtar's laws in Isin, as well as
those of Hammurabi, who rendered these two Sumerian terms in Babylonian as
mīšarum and kittum respectively. (See below, Chapter 16).

Steinkeller does not think that the Ur III laws went so far as to actually liberate
bondservants, as would be the case in the subsequent Old Babylonian period (2000–
1600 BC) "when debt-bondage became a way of life for a significant portion of the
whole population." Rural usury had not yet become so serious a problem that Ur-
Namma or Shulgi felt a "need to promulgate state-sponsored debt-cancellations (or
at least we have no firm evidence for them)."[255] Steinkeller attributes the rising problem of indebtedness to moneylending and the dominance of "northern" economic
traditions" with the incursion of Amorites and other northerners. "In northern Babylonia as far south as Nippur, "the evidence of private money-lending is very clear."
The northern socio-economic system "was dominated by the palace economy and
showed a marked presence of private economic activity, especially as far as the
ownership of arable land is concerned."[256]

Members of most mercantile families and other entrepreneurs inherited their
positions. Over the course of Ur III, William Hallo reports, "the post of chief administrator of the temple of Inanna at Nippur was the preserve of a single family, passing
from father to son over at least four generations, beginning with Ur-Me-me,"[257] from
one of Nippur's most prestigious families. Another branch included successive governors of the city. Richard Zettler's dissertation on the Inanna temple at Nippur finds
that "the family archive of the chief administrator is mixed in with records of the

[254] Roth 1997: 38.
[255] Steinkeller 2002: 124.
[256] Steinkeller 2002: 125
[257] Hallo 1972: 87–95.

Figure 22:
Ur-Namma Law Code

temple operations." Relatives of the temple's chief administrator "had sufficient authority to seal doors both in the administrative sector of the temple and in its
residential quarter. They could conclude contracts on behalf of the temple and at
least on occasion act for the chief administrator."[258]

[258] Zettler 1984: 441 and 461.

The private archives analyzed by Garfinkle show that despite the fact that Ur III was centrally planned and autocratic, it relied upon local entrepreneurs not only for foreign trade but also to act as managers of herds, agricultural resources and other functions. Garfinkle notes that "the largest creditor archive is that of SI.A-a, a chief shepherd. … His debtors included members of the military hierarchy, such as ugula-geštas, as well as prominent officials of the temple estates." [259]

This delegation of economic authority to self-seeking individuals lay the groundwork for such enterprise to spread over the next few centuries – the Middle Bronze Age and the Old Babylonian period. When Ur III's "statewide economic direction disappeared, the local entrepreneurs continued to serve as facilitators of exchange and commerce at a regional level." [260]

In fact, it seems to have been precisely the extractive demands of the Ur III palace that led to the organization of economic activities to squeeze out a surplus. What Garfinkle has found for Ur III seems to have characterized the Middle Bronze Age as a whole: "The texts show that management of the provincial estates was left in local hands," with private credit needed to provide flexibility – for instance, loans to enable officials to meet their quotas in time of lower crop yields.

To be sure, the gains were limited to the palace bureaucracy, generals and local leaders largely associated with it. As they built up fortunes of their own, they lent out some of their money, and also sought prestige by acquiring land. Orchards and other property was salable, but agricultural self-support land was protected by rulers as providing the basis for their corvée labor and the armed forces. The large customers for loans from Ur III onward thus would have been managers and entrepreneurial borrowers, but rural usury was becoming more prevalent and hence problematic for rulers. As a result, "the edicts of debt remission, *mīšaru*, that characterized the Old Babylonian period were a far greater intrusion into the operation of entrepreneurs and money-lenders than anything attested in the Ur III period." [261]

---

[259] Garfinkle 2004a: 26.
[260] Garfinkle 2012: 140.
[261] Garfinkle 2012: 147.

13. Isin Rulers replace Ur III and Proclaim níg-si-sá: 2017–1861 BC

Ur-Namma's dynasty had reached the peak of its power during Shulgi's half-century reign, 2094–2047 BC, extending Ur's domination eastward to Elam and the Zagros area, and north to the edge of the Subarean lands. Emulating Naram-Sin, Shulgi styled himself King of the Four Quarters and had himself deified. But the reign of his son Shu-Sin saw the first recorded incursions by nomadic Amorites ("Westerners"). They were related to the Semitic-speaking pastoral nomads who had been filtering into Sumer from the Upper Euphrates region since before 4000 BC. Most had been absorbed in the same way as other immigrants, paying taxes and submitting to military draft in exchange for land tenure. But around 2030–2000 they came in more tightly knit tribal groups, taking over northern towns such as Mari.

Trying to keep them out, Shu-Sin built a long fortified wall, called the Martu ("Western") wall, commemorated in his 4th and 5th year-names. What seems to have been an earlier version was built "already twenty-three years earlier" by Shulgi in northern Babylonia in the region where the Euphrates and the Tigris approach each other. The Amorite influx "contributed substantially to the fall of Ur. Literary texts characterise the Mardu as non-urban inhabitants of the steppe who are 'ignorant of grain.'"[262] But the new version of the wall seems to have functioned merely as a demarcation line, aimed more against pastoral herding of sheep than as a military defense. The Amorites breached it in 2022, the sixth year of the rule of Shu-Sin's successor, Ibbi-Sin.[263] Simultaneously, the Elamites besieged Ur, suggesting a common plan of action with Amorite leaders.

Ibbi-Sin did what beleaguered cities would do throughout antiquity (Athens during the Peloponnesian Wars in the 5th century BC, and Rome near the end of the Punic Wars in 205 BC): Drawing "on the temple treasuries in order to alleviate his city's needs,"[264] he delegated an official, Ishbi-Irra, to buy large amounts of barley at harvest time from upstream towns along the Euphrates at two gur per shekel, half the official price for paying debts. But the price soon doubled to the usual one gur per shekel, obliging Ishbi-Irra to spend 20 silver talents on 144,000 gur.

Diakonoff points out that there would have been no need to purchase such large volumes of barley if all land belonged to the palace, because it could simply have been taken. The crops must have come from non-royal land, and evidently the palace was not in a position to requisition it or even to fix its price.[265] Most self-support land presumably was held by local communities, whose members sold some of their surplus to the palace, as did cultivators who held temple and palace land on a sharecropping basis.[266]

Ishbi-Irra asked for six hundred boats to ship half the load of barley to Ur. But the Elamite occupation cut off Ur before the harvest could reach it, while Amorites poured into Sumer with little resistance. Retreating into the walled cities for protection,

---

[262] Sallaberger 2007: 444 f.

[263] The details are given by Kramer 1963: 68 f., and Jacobsen 1953.

[264] Jacobsen 1953: 41.

[265] Diakonoff 1971.

[266] See for instance Ellis 1976.

cultivators were unable to prepare the ground for the next season's crop, or perhaps even to finish the current harvest. That caused a drastic food shortage for Ur's urban population.

Ishbi-Irra stockpiled grain at the upstream town of Isin, which he made his own power base. Ensis of other cities stopped sending their bala tax contributions to Ur, and the city succumbed to hunger as grain prices rose to sixty times normal during the next two years, exceeding even the price of fish: A shekel would purchase 12½ sila of fresh fish but only 5 sila of barley. Oil stood at 2½ sila per shekel, just twice the price of barley. Villages defected to Ishbi-Irra, who maintained the loyalty of his fellow Ur III administrators by reconfirming the énsis appointed by Ibbi-Sin – who managed to maintain his own rule over Ur for 24 years.[267] But in the 24th year of his rule, after 18 years of fighting, Elam invaded Ur and carried him off to Susa, where he died in captivity.

Little procedural change occurred under the formerly subordinate official Ishbi-Irra. "The administrative texts of Isin follow precisely the forms and formulae of the bureaucrats of Ur III,"[268] as no other model was at hand to administer the region's complex economy. Ishbi-Irra also restored many of Ur's monuments, and even retrieved the statue of Nanna from Elam, whose soldiers had taken it when they captured Ibbi-Sin.

When Elam backed a client Amorite dynasty to rule Larsa, to the east of Ur, Ishbi-Irra reconquered Ur and established Isin's suzerainty from the Persian Gulf as far north as the sacred capital of Nippur. His Isin dynasty dominated the south for nearly a century (about as long as Ur III had ruled), from 2017 through Lipit-Ishtar's death in 1924 BC. But in contrast to Ur III's centralized control, most towns remained relatively independent. Many local dynasties managed to outlast the century of Ur's rule, but on a smaller scale, with no kingdom able to create an empire of its own.

Lipit-Ishtar's laws and the fall of the Isin dynasty

Debt problems became more pressing in the Isin-Larsa aftermath (2000–1800) as southern Mesopotamia reverted to a looser federation of city-states. Neither this period nor the rest of the Old Babylonian epoch restored the centralization of Ur III. Merchants and entrepreneurs played a growing economic role, and lent out as usury some of the money they made. Rulers responded to the ensuing rise in indebtedness by reasserting palace control over trade and enterprise, and protecting the indebted population from bondage to creditors and forfeiture of their self-support land at the expense of palace demands for corvée labor and army service.

The first surviving records of Isin's debt cancellations are those of its third ruler, Iddin-Dagan (1974–1954) and his successor Ishme-Dagan (1953–1935). As in Ur III, they used the term níg.si.sá. Ishme-Dagan's debt annulment appears to have coincided with a military campaign mounted just prior to his coronation. In addition to being a customary act of rulers upon taking the throne, this no doubt helped

[267] Diakonoff 1971. The Lamentation over the Downfall of Ur describes cultivators running from the fields.
[268] Edzard 1967: 162 f.

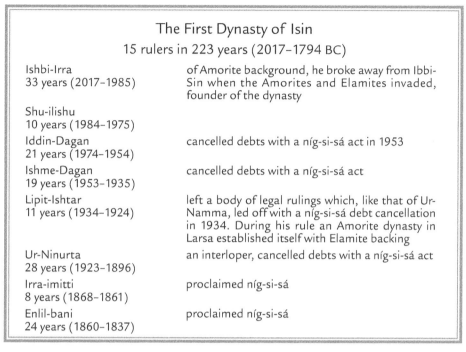

The First Dynasty of Isin

15 rulers in 223 years (2017–1794 BC)

Ishbi-Irra 33 years (2017–1985)	of Amorite background, he broke away from Ibbi-Sin when the Amorites and Elamites invaded, founder of the dynasty
Shu-ilishu 10 years (1984–1975)	
Iddin-Dagan 21 years (1974–1954)	cancelled debts with a níg-si-sá act in 1953
Ishme-Dagan 19 years (1953–1935)	cancelled debts with a níg-si-sá act
Lipit-Ishtar 11 years (1934–1924)	left a body of legal rulings, which, like that of Ur-Namma, led off with a níg-si-sá debt cancellation in 1934. During his rule an Amorite dynasty in Larsa established itself with Elamite backing
Ur-Ninurta 28 years (1923–1896)	an interloper, cancelled debts with a níg-si-sá act
Irra-imitti 8 years (1868–1861)	proclaimed níg-si-sá
Enlil-bani 24 years (1860–1837)	proclaimed níg-si-sá

Figure 23: Chronology of rulers of the First Isin dynasty.

protect his land-tenured citizen-infantry from the encroachments of tax officials and usurers at a time when Assur seems to have attacked at least as far south as Babylon.

Three years after Ishme-Dagan's son Lipit-Ishtar took the throne in 1934 BC, the ambitious fifth ruler of Larsa's dynasty, Gungunum (1932–1906), came to power and set out to conquer southern Mesopotamia. To prepare for the coming fight, Lipit-Ishtar cancelled agrarian debts throughout Isin's sphere. The problem of back tax debts evidently remained serious. Although he needed to ensure continuity of his revenue, sitting by and letting families forfeit their liberty and land rights would have led to defections from Isin. So, like other members of his dynasty, Lipit-Ishtar declared a general tax forgiveness and debt annulment. "When a year-date of Lipit-Ishtar announces that he 'decreed justice,'" notes Edzard, it is to be understood as cancelling debts by a nig.sisa act, not compiling civil laws.[269] The term he used for his debt release was the earlier Sumerian amar–gi.

The laws of Lipit-Ishtar have survived in scribal excerpts from schools where the inscription remained part of the period's belles lettres. University of Pennsylvania archaeologists dug up the first of these copies in the 1890s in Nippur, even before the laws of Ur-Namma and Hammurabi were found, but the tablet lay unidentified until Samuel Kramer discovered it in 1947 while searching through the museum's inventory at the University Museum in Philadelphia.[270]

[269] Edzard 1957: 68f. and 83.

[270] Other copies of Lipit-Ishtar's laws have come from Kish and Sippar. The laws were translated by Steele in 1948; Kramer (1955). See also Kraus 1984: 19f. I use the translation in Roth 1997.

As was normal for rulers from Urukagina to Hammurabi, a prologue announces that the source of Lipit-Ishtar's laws is divine, and that his purpose is "to establish justice (níg-si-sá) in the land, to eliminate cries for justice, to eradicate enmity and armed violence, to bring well-being to the lands of Sumer and Akkad" (i 20–37). He "established justice [níg-si-sá] in the lands of Sumer and Akkad," and "restored order" (amar-gi₄)" to "liberate the sons and daughters of Nippur, Ur, Isin and the rest of Sumer and Akkad "who were subjugated [by the yoke(?)]," that is, debt bondage (ii 1–15).

Lipit-Ishtar gave landholders three years to pay their taxes (§18):

> "If the master or mistress of an estate defaults on the taxes due from the estate and an outsider assumes the taxes, he [the master] will not be evicted for three years; (but after three years of defaulting on the taxes) the man who has assumed the tax burden shall take possession of the estate and the (original) master of the estate will not make any claims." [271]

Wealthy officials or others could pay the taxes due on the defaulter's land and gain it for themselves after three years.

This ruling brought back the essential characteristic of land tenure. Cultivation rights were granted on the condition of tax payments, in the form of corvée labor and army service as well as crops or money. But in this case the effect was to increase the process of property concentration. New absentee owners either obliged the tenants to perform the corvée duties, or hired replacements.

Lipit-Ishtar's epilogue following these laws returns to his guiding claim: "I made right [níg-gi-na] and truth shine forth, and I brought well-being to the lands of Sumer and Akkad" (xxi 5–17), and erected this stela "when I established justice [níg-si-sá] in the lands of Sumer and Akkad" (xxi 36–40). [272]

But Isin was losing influence. Lipit-Ishtar was followed by an outsider, Ur-Ninurta (1923–1896), who also proclaimed níg-si-sá, as did Irra-Imitti (1868–1861), Enlil-Bani (1860–1837) and probably other Isin rulers. [273] Isin's role as a successor to Ur III ended when Gunganum became ruler of Larsa in 1932 BC. By the end of his reign in 1906 he had conquered most of the south, with Ur changing hands frequently between Isin and Larsa. A period of general dissolution descended on southern Mesopotamia, which was becoming "an economic and political backwater

---

[271] Roth 1997: 29. Korošec 1971: 278, observes that §§ 30 f. of Hammurabi's subsequent laws likewise had a three-year rule regarding the performance of *ilku* "fief" duties on Babylonian land. Edzard 1967: 169 notes that "private ownership of [agricultural] land was probably still regarded as a deviation from the norm" of collective or public proprietorship. "The section of his [Lipit-Ishtar's] laws dealing with real property does not mention agricultural land."

[272] Roth 1997: 33 f., Laws of Lipit-Ishtar.

[273] Kraus 1984: 27 ff. See also Edzard 1957: 83 and 1967: 167 ff.

[274] Muhly 1973: 325.

14. Diffusion of Trade and Finance Via Assyrian Merchants, 2000–1790 BC

Sumerians founded the upstream trading post of Assur between 2500 and 2400 BC, about a century before Sargon built Akkad. Built on a cliff overlooking the Tigris, it was favorably situated on the east-west caravan trade route – east via Der to Susa and Iran's Diyala plain, and on to Afghanistan for tin, to bring back and trade west via Syria up to Asia Minor. Larsen describes Assur as a self-governing community of merchants in a great trading center and port [karum] for traders and craftsmen.[275]

Sumerian towns were basically agrarian along with stock raising, but every city "had a harbor or at least a quay... always on the outskirts of the cities, since commerce and all the things associated with trade had to be kept at a distance. Boats landed there, bringing provisions and goods from other cities and countries, and local traders had their warehouses there."[276] Parallels might be the island of Dilmun (Bahrain) in the Persian Gulf for sea trade with the Indus, or the island of Ischia for Near Eastern trade with Etruscan Italy in the 8th century BC, or the island of Hong Kong for European trade with China.

Sargon's dynasty shifted southern Mesopotamia's trade center to Akkad in order to keep commerce in its own hands. Ur III's rulers made Assur the seat of a military governorship, but after the fall of Ur III, Assyrian merchants became relatively free of foreign control as economic and political relations became more decentralized. This enabled Assur's merchants to restore their commerce providing tin and copper from the Iranian plateau to southern Mesopotamian towns to make weapons and tools, in exchange for luxury textiles and handicrafts sold to Asia Minor. Assur planted trade outposts in Anatolia after about 1900 BC to obtain silver as well as gold, which it sold to Elam for tin. Apparently as a result of this latter trade, gold became the main denominator of Assyrian trading investments, in contrast to southern Mesopotamia's emphasis on silver.

Much of the documentation for this trade comes from Kanesh in central Anatolia. Located directly north of the Mediterranean's eastern coast, it is the largest Assyrian outpost yet excavated. About three hundred Assyrians lived there for three generations during the 19th century BC, leaving over 22,000 letters, contracts, accounts and court records documenting their trade as "private entrepreneurs, working on their own account and at their own risk."[277]

[275] Larsen 1976: 27, 32, 85, 109 and 236, and 2015: 96. He finds a parallel with medieval Genoa. Assur was built just above where the Little Zab branches east, along the Zagros range's northwestern extension.

[276] Larsen, 2015: 148–149.

[277] Edzard 1964: 196–197; Larsen 2015: 223 estimates that "fifty to one hundred wealthy families in Assur were directly involved in joint-stock partnerships at any given time during the main period of the trade."

These business letters and other records document only the private side of this trade. No Assyrian temple records have been found, but the city-temple of Ishtar may have been the initial financier of this trade. One study has found that "down to and including the Ur III Dynasty the merchant class was indeed partly in the direct employ of the institutions." The merchants' "status seems to have given them entitlement to purchase the individual concessions to palace staples, but in the Ur III period and probably earlier it is clear that when they receive silver and copper they are being paid to undertake a commission, not being issued with a commodity for disposal on the open market, so that the initiative comes from the institution."[278] Another study of this period describes Assyrian traders as receiving their "stock of trade from the temple, in fact, from the officials in charge of the various specialized storehouses or the temple of Nanna in Ur."[279] In turn, "the temples not only received many valuable votive gifts and offered storage facilities, they also were in some way commercially involved."[280]

Most likely, the temple advanced capital and shared in the earnings from trade in an arrangement that enabled merchants to gain a profit for themselves after compensating the temple. Veenhof describes their *ikribu* gifts to their temples as reflecting the fact that "the merchandise or the silver belonged to a temple, and to all appearances had been entrusted to a trader, either simply as a commercial loan, or by means of a *commenda* partnership, or by way of investment in an enterprise." In view of the large sums of *ikribu* that merchants paid to their temples, "up to 10 and 15 minas of silver and several hundred pieces of expensive textile, the word cannot only refer to goods/money dedicated to a temple or deity, presumably to ensure the success of a trading operation. It also seems unlikely that *ikribu* (only) refers to shipments of silver or merchandise (part of) the *profits* of which had been vowed to a temple."[281]

By the time Assyriologists can pick up the record, the financing was private. Travelling merchants acted as agent for a wealthy *ummeānum*, usually well placed in the temple hierarchy. Most merchants belonged to the investor's extended family, and set out for Kanesh or some other commercial colony to join other merchants associated with the local temple-sponsored guild to sell raw wool (up to two tons in a single negotiation), clothes and rugs, tin, hides and fleeces.

The woolen trade was sufficiently large-scale for a fine of 11⅓ pounds of gold to be levied on smugglers. Silver and copper were imported by Assur in quantities as large as fifteen tons.[282] This trade developed in the hands of private families, but its revenue "benefited the whole Assur population: the king and his family, the high dignitaries, priests and temples and also the city-state. In fact, Assur's city hall raised many taxes from caravans leaving or arriving in the city."[283] The implication is that this trade was not duty free, but a major source of tariff revenue.

---

[278] Postgate 1992: 220.

[279] Oppenheim 1954: 14.

[280] Veenhof 1972: 113f.

[281] Veenhof 1972: 113f.

[282] The second largest copper shipment on record is five tons. On this trade see Larsen 1976: 92, Muhly 1973: 282 and Lewy 1958b: 99.

[283] Cécile Michel 2013: 48.

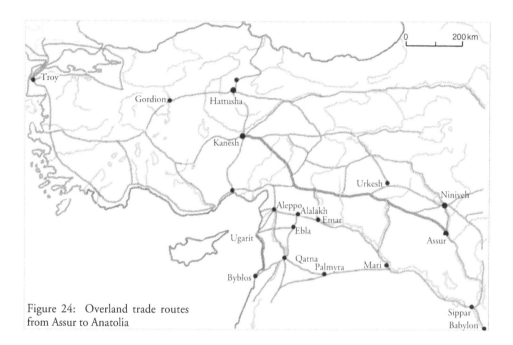

Figure 24: Overland trade routes from Assur to Anatolia

The typical commercial investment contract was for 16 minas of silver (equal to 2 minas of gold), with twice this amount to be returned in five years – the equivalent of the one shekel per mina monthly that also is found in neighboring Eshnunna and in the laws of Hammurabi for commercial loans. Gains above this interest charge were split between the silent-partner investor and the traveling merchant, although some agreements let the Assyrian trader "eat" (that is, use for himself) one third, perhaps representing his living and other expenses.[284]

Further anthropomorphizing this trade, silver lying around uninvested or not lent out was called "hungry" for profit-making opportunities. Loan contracts "died" or were killed when paid off or cancelled. To sustain its life cycle, "silver had to be in perpetual motion: converted into merchandise, which were exported, sold for silver, carried back and again converted into merchandise."[285]

Commercial and personal debts in Kanesh

Most Assyrian debts took the form of trade credit, but failed ventures might lead to bondage to Anatolians. Members of the *karum* Kanesh are found redeeming their countrymen. One merchant paid 1½ pounds of silver to an Anatolian to redeem a family – which then was obliged to reimburse the Assyrian, who took them into his own house as bondservants until such time as they might pay him back.[286]

---

[284] Larsen 1976: 94ff. and 229–230; Bogaert 1966: pp. 81 and 127; Leemans 1950: 31 and 99.
[285] Michel 2013: 50, citing Veenhof.
[286] Larsen 2015: 77–78.

Tablets found in the houses occupied by Anatolians show them to have been usurers and slave dealers. Many Anatolians "suffered from heavy economic and social pressures caused mainly by debt," at interest rates which rapidly made these debts quite onerous.[287] A Turkish Assyriologist, Kemal Balkan, reports that while the usual interest rate among Assyrian traders in Kanesh was 30 per cent, Anatolian borrowers had to pay twice this rate, with interest premiums occasionally rising to 120 or even 180 per cent. But their family members were not automatically enslaved if the signer of a debt note defaulted. Creditors therefore obliged wives and children to sign the family head's debt note, so that they all could be reduced to bondage in case of non-payment. "Often one reads in Cappadocian tablets that, because of debt, an Anatolian not only mortgaged his property, but also was compelled to pledge one of the members of his family, or even that a whole family was obliged to 'enter the house' of their creditor until the outstanding debt was paid."[288]

Anatolian rulers might proclaim a *hubullam masā'um*, literally "a washing away of the debt." Another term was "to kill the tablet," or "(by breaking) to make a loan contract invalid."[289] A number of loan documents show creditors trying to avoid having their loans subject to such cancellations. One creditor specifies: "If they should wash away debt (in the country), still they will not wash away their [the specific party's] debt." Assur's trade treaty with Kanesh's rulers specified that their edicts canceling debts and liberating bondservants would not apply to debts owed to Assyrians.[290]

In Assur itself a prominent merchant was chosen annually to serve as Year Eponym, overseeing legal disputes and in effect standing surety to ensure that mercantile debts were settled properly. When the head of a household died, his debts were inherited by his children, who might have to sell their property to pay his creditors. Several letters show Year Eponyms confiscating houses and impounding slaves and slave girls as security for such debts, because they "were personally responsible for the credit extended to debtors. ... On the occasion of the death of a debtor, his heirs would immediately be ordered to regulate the debts outstanding to the authorities in Assur ... and it was then the obligation of the previous eponym, during whose term of office the debt had been allowed, to see to it that the money was paid."[291]

Assur's trade strategy and *andurārum* proclamations

Two Assyrian rulers from the 20th century BC have left *andurarum* proclamations. Ilushuma and his successor Erishum. (fn Their dates are not clear. Ilushuma is said to have ruled for an unknown number of years before either 1973 or 1905 BC, and Erishum either from 1905-1866 BC or, as Larsen believes, earlier, from 1972 to1933 BC.) A temple building inscription of Ilushuma reads: "I freed the Akkadians and

[287] Larsen 1976: 105 and Orlin 1970: 179.
[288] Balkan 1974: 30.
[289] Balkan 1974: 33.
[290] Larsen 2015: 78.
[291] Larsen 2015: 120 and 128–129.

their sons (from forced labor) and cleared (literally 'washed') them of their (obligation to pay) copper (as tax)." The Chicago Assyriological Dictionary (E 321a) translates the key passage: "I proclaimed remission of debts (*addurarum*) for them from the edge of the swamps and Ur, also Nippur, Awal, and Kismar, the Der of Ishtaran as far (north) as the city of Assur."[292]

The term "wash" was used in Kanesh for cancelling debts, and Hammurabi used it in this way in his *andurarum* acts two hundred years later. So "washing the copper" may mean either a debt cancellation or more specifically, relinquishing a royal tariff on copper and perhaps other products. The word "copper" seems a strange word to use for either of these kinds of obligation. Although some commercial debts were denominated in copper (more often in tin, in which some fines also were denominated), most were denominated in silver.

An early translator interpreted "copper" here as being metal that was traded in general, which would mean that Ilushuma was proclaiming free trade in goods ("copper") by exempting them from tariffs or other commercial duties.[293] Larsen likewise considers Ilushuma's proclamation to be a free trade policy to attract traders from Babylonia, selling textiles to Assur's commercial networks for trade with Anatolia. "We know from the Old Assyrian texts that 'washed copper' and 'good quality copper' were identical concepts." Hence, he suggests, a royal trade monopoly was being ended, abolishing old tariff duties and taxes, and that "it is probable that it is connected with the international trade in which copper was one of the most important items."[294]

At issue is whether agrarian debts were included as part of a general remission. Most inscriptions using such language were debt cancellations, especially when justice is mentioned. Choosing a sacred temple-building inscription seems more appropriate for a general debt amnesty than just to proclaim such free trade – although it seems that the new city-temples built by Ilushuma played a major role in Assur's foreign trade.

We thus have two proposed solutions to the meaning of *andurārum* as used by Assyrians: on the one hand, freeing trade in copper and perhaps other commodities from royal tariffs; on the other hand, a broad debt cancellation. Both meanings may be true. A "free trade" act freeing merchants from tariff duties would relinquish a specific category of tax debt, but that is just one type of debt. Postgate has warned against the free-trade interpretation, but adds that Ilushuma "did more than revoke personal enslavement for debt."[295]

The next Assyrian debt cancellation on record, that of Erishum, was not limited to copper but emphasized a comprehensive list of imported commodities: "I pro-

---

[292] Grayson 1972: 7. Kraus 1984: 103 translates this building inscription: "I have established the freedom (*andurārum*) of the Akkadians and their children. I have washed their copper. From … and further to Ur and Nippur, Awal and Kismar, Der to the city of Assur, I have established freedom (*andurārum*)."

[293] Lewy 1958: 99. He suggests that copper and tin were "controlled materials" because of their strategic military character. I think this is anachronistic. Larsen shows that the key was simply Assur's enforcement of its commercial trade monopoly.

[294] Larsen 1976: 74ff, and 2015: 97.

[295] Postgate1992: 196.

claimed a remission of debts payable in silver, gold, copper, tin, barley, wool, down to chaff."[296] That would seem to cover tariffs owed for all the commodities being traded. The "chaff" or wheat obligations might refer to the small personal debts that were the focus of royal amnesties in the south.

The term used by both Ilushuma and Erishum was *addurārum* (= *andurārum*). The longest discussion of what it meant in Assur is by Larsen, citing four possible interpretations.[297] The basic meaning is "freedom of movement." The Chicago Assyriological Dictionary translates the verb *dararum* as "to become free (of a task), to move freely, to run off." In the south this referred to freeing debt pledges to return home.[298] But Larsen and most others focus on the freedom of goods to move across borders.

A second meaning of *andurārum*, Larsen notes, may connote political "liberation from oppression." This seems anachronistic for the Middle Bronze Age. To be sure, Helmut Schmoekel noted that already in the Bronze Age, "one described ... the conquest of foreign states as constituting their 'freeing.'"[299] But Hallo pointed out that as far as *andurārum* and its Babylonian cognates are concerned, "freedom" typically took the form of canceling personal debts, with "a kind of amnesty for debt-slaves."[300]

Larsen rejects this third (and to me the most reasonable) interpretation, on the ground that Ilushuma applied it as far south as Ur and the swamplands. Ilushuma had no authority to annul taxes owed to foreign rulers, but was able to annul trade tariffs due *from* their subjects to his own palace.

Suggesting that debts owed by Nippur and Ur merchants were meant, Larsen's fourth and preferred reading is "exemption from taxes," specifically the commercial trade levies cited by Lewy, von Soden and other Assyriologists. Freedom of movement in this case would be that of importing and exporting goods without having to pay tariffs. However, Larsen criticized Lewy for viewing Erishum as having "initiated, or at least perfected, the first experiment of free enterprise on a large scale.'"[301] Although he endorses Lewy's suggestion that *andurārum* denotes freedom of movement, he believes that it was connected with a tightly regulated Assyrian trade monopoly that Er-

---

[296] Grayson 1972: 7 translates this proclamation: "I have established the 'freedom' (*andurārum*) of silver, gold, copper, tin, barley and wool to the border." Kraus 1984: 103 admits he is not clear as to the purpose of this act. Diakonoff 1991: 234 concludes: "It is more probable that the 'liberation of the Akkadians and their sons' means release from some duties, for example, customs duties. ... In other words, the 'sons of the Akkadians' were citizens of Akkadian towns acting as trading agents or representatives of their respective trading societies on all the main trade routes, especially the south road to Lower Mesopotamia and the eastern route over the Zagros Mountains, and were admitted by Ilushuma to duty-free trade."

[297] Larsen 1976: 63ff.

[298] Diakonoff 1991: 234 points out that the idea recalls Sumerian *amargi* connoting the freedom of bondservants to return to their mothers and families.

[299] Schmoekel 1957: 74.

[300] Hallo 1958: 307n.

[301] Larsen 1976: 79.

ishum relinquished "for all the commodities mentioned in his text."[302] This left Assur's commerce to be "dominated by the free flow of private capital," leading to the great period of colonization that seems to have begun a generation or two later for Kanesh and other trading *karum*s in Asia Minor.

At issue is how many kinds of debts were meant. Obligations owed to the palace and temples would include personal debts and back taxes, along with import duties and other public fees. Certainly the major meaning of *andurārum* that survived into first-millennium BC Assyria was the free movement of bondservants regaining their freedom.[303] The debts being cancelled in royal *andurārum* proclamations by Babylonian times were personal agrarian debts, not commercial ones.

The Chicago Assyriological Dictionary translates *andurārum* as "1) 'remission of (commercial) debts'; 2) 'manumission (of private slaves)'; and 3) 'cancelling of services (illegally imposed on free persons).'" But the only kind of debts *not* cancelled by such edicts in the south's *mīšarum* and *andurārum* edicts (discussed in the next chapter) were commercial debts. Business investments were left intact, and the longer and more detailed *mīšarum* acts specifically excluded obligations to the Assyrians.

The freeing of "slaves" in the second translation actually must refer to debt pledges, not chattel slaves, so the term "manumission" is inappropriate. As for the CAD's third reading of *andurārum*, there seems little ground for thinking that the services being abolished were imposed illegally. We thus are confronted once again with the ideological prejudice that biases the translation and interpretation of Bronze Age economic terms.

The archaeological context for Assur's *andurārum* inscriptions

Assyrian rulers left three types of inscription: commemorations of their building enterprises on bricks, door sockets or other parts of the structures being dedicated; the dedication of objects (mainly to temples); and labels. These inscriptions typically were associated with the celebrations that seem to have been the occasion for new rulers taking the throne or dedicating new temples.

Renger criticizes Larsen for focusing too narrowly on "the Old Assyrian traders who clearly represent an exceptional case,"[304] neglecting Babylonian practice. The *andurārum* proclamations of Ilushuma and Erishum are appended at the end of building inscriptions for the Assur temple and placed in temple foundations – a context similar to Gudea's Lagash inscriptions and many kindred Sumerian proclamations. The inauguration of a new temple wing or other major sacred construction was a typical occasion for proclaiming a fiscal and financial clean slate. Assyrian rulers would have been unique in using this sanctified context to inscribe an exclusively commercial amnesty for import duties – indeed, permanently in Larsen's view.

[302] Larsen 1976: 75.

[303] Postgate 1973: texts 10 and 248, and 1974: text 132.

[304] Renger 1994: 164 and 173.

One of Ilushuma's *andurārum* proclamations is inscribed on a stone object as part of a lock, with holes for metal bars to go through.[305] The inscription begins: "Ilushuma, vice-regent, beloved of the god Assur and the goddess Ishtar ... built the temple for the goddess Ishtar, his mistress, for his life. He established the freedom (*a.du.ra.ar*) of the Akkadians." Another such inscription on several bricks, presumably from the Assur temple, describes the facade and new wall for the temple Ilushuma built, and the bricks he made for the wall. Ilushuma then adds the lines 49–65 noted above: "I established the freedom (*a-du-ra-ar*) of the Akkadians and their children. I purified their copper. I established their freedom from the border of the marshes and Ur and Nippur, Awal, and Kismar, Der of the god Ishtaran, as far as the city (Assur)."

Like these *andurārum* texts of Ilushuma, those of Erishum commemorate temple building. One version is found on two clay tablets from Kanesh in the archives of an Assyrian merchant. Lines 26ff. name the Seven Judges of the Step Gate, giving an idea of the social restructuring associated with Erishum's building activity: *Misharum* ('Justice'), *Ishme-karab* ('He Heard the Prayer'), *Sheraggu* ('Get Out, Criminal!'), *Ulli-misharum* ('He Extolled Justice'), *Assur-hablam* ('Watch over the Downtrodden!'), *Pushu-ken* ('His Speech is Upright'), and *Ishmelum* ('God has Heard'). The inscription concludes with the words "I, Erishum, vice-regent of Assur ... May (justice) [*misharum*] be established in my city." The word *mīšarum* alludes to debt cancellations in the royal inscriptions of Isin, Larsa and Babylonia.

Inasmuch as Assur's courts convened at the Step Gate, Grayson wonders whether Erishum's text may have been read out loud "on the occasion of the swearing-in of the judges of Kanesh."[306] This would seem to confirm the existence of a royal amnesty, which presumably would have extended to palace levies on trade by merchants in Kanesh in view of the fact that this is where the copy was found.

The other copy of Erishum's inscription is found on a door socket from Assur and describes building the temple wall: "When I started the work, my city being under my command, I made silver, gold, copper, tin, barley, and wool tax-exempt as well as payment of bran and straw (tax)." The implication is that this was considered a sacred act of kingship appropriate for rulers to cite in inscriptions commemorating their temple building.

Were personal debts to the palace other than import duties cancelled? Ilushuma ordered the clay debt tablets and tax tablets "washed," dissolved in water in the same spirit that other rulers boasted that they "broke" the debt tablets of their subjects. This reading would place Assyria's *andurārum* proclamations in the tradition of Sumerian amargi and Babylonian *mīšarum* decrees found in the south.

That is the view of Lewy. In the same year that he published his free-trade interpretation of Assur's Kanesh relations, he wrote an article on Biblical *deror* legislation in light of these Assyrian discoveries, suggesting two thousand years of continuity. Starting in Sumer, he describes the tradition moving upstream via Assur and Nuzi, angling northwest to the shores of the Mediterranean, upward into Asia Minor

---

[305] Grayson 1987: 15.
[306] Grayson 1987: 19.

(Kanesh, etc.) and down through Phoenicia and Canaan. These Sumerian, Assyrian and Babylonian examples confirm that the Old Testament debt cancellations and releases of bondservants were actually implemented, at least originally. "Numerous savants did not hesitate to accompany their conclusions as to the date of the final redaction of those legislative passages [in Leviticus and Ezekiel] with critical remarks about the 'unrealistic' or 'artificial' character of the relevant laws and the 'late origin' of the ideas underlying them," Lewy writes. "Yet such skepticism proves hypercritical if one determines the basic meaning of the Akkadian terms *duraru* and *anduraru*" as meaning "to move about," "be at large" or "to be free."[307]

Mesopotamian *andurārum* and Biblical *deror* are associated specifically with debts and debt bondage, with no hint of free trade or even commercial debts or tariffs. Offering a political consideration that may have added a special dimension to Assur's *andurārum* proclamations, Larsen suggests that Erishum's motive for granting duty-free trade was to gain the support of his city's merchant class, as well as to attract traders from Babylonia to feed into Assur's commercial networks to the west.[308] Also, proclaiming *andurarum* might well have benefited the Year Eponyms by freeing them from liability for the unpaid mercantile debts that were mounting up in Assur's trade colonies.

However, *andurarum* amnesties were proclaimed on special occasions, not as an ongoing systemic reform. My own view is that tariff duties resumed after *andurarum* was proclaimed. Taxes began to be paid once again as the major source of Assur's public revenue, and both personal and commercial debts also began to accrue once more. What seems to have been unique about Assur's *andurārum* proclamations is that wealthy traders as well as agrarian debtors were the main beneficiaries.

Assyrian monopolistic commercial policy

Larsen notes that it was normal for Bronze Age realms to establish trade monopolies. Emar and Ebla monopolized trade in the towns of the Amorite steppe. Assyrians had to seal their shipments of tin and textiles on the way to the Hahum transit point on the way to Anatolia further north, paying a specified tariff (or compensating local rulers if trade was interrupted).[309]

Just as Emar and Ebla established trade monopolies in their own region, Assur did so for its Anatolian trade. Assur's commercial strategy cannot be characterized as free trade. A draft of a treaty with an unknown small kingdom includes an oath: "You must not let Akkadians come here. If they do travel to your country, you must give them to us so we may kill them." An Assyrian king's letter to the Kanesh colony specified that "In accordance with the words of the stela no Assyrian at all may sell gold to an Akkadian, an Amorite or a Subarean. He who sells any will not live." The motive may have been to control the supply of gold for trade with Iran and further east.[310]

---

[307] Lewy 1958. See also along these lines Weinfeld 1982: 490–519.
[308] Larsen 2015: 96–97, 104 and 146–147.
[309] Larsen 2015: 117 and 24.
[310] Larsen 2015: 117 and 249.

Anatolians were only hired in subordinate positions, and "no Anatolian was allowed access to the overland trade with Assur; even the lucrative trade in copper and wool within the borders of Anatolia was in the hands of the Assyrians." Local rulers had to secure roads and were responsible for catching thieves and murderers They also had to "agree not to covet or seize houses, fields, gardens or slaves belonging to Assyrians … and to accept that the Assyrians were not obliged to perform corvée, forced labor on royal projects, duties that were otherwise normally tied to landholding." And if the king issued an edict ordering the manumission of slaves, this would not apply to slaves [Larsen means bondservants] belonging to Assyrians."[311]

But Assur soon lost its commercial prominence to Shamshi-Adad (1809–1776 BC), who conquered it along with much of the surrounding region, establishing his own capital at Shubat-Enlil in Syria. Southern Mesopotamia was becoming decentralized under a series of rival dynasties in Isin, Larsa and Babylon. In Anatolia a far-reaching break occurred, "for the world of the early Hittite kingdom that ensued retained next to nothing of the Assyrian traditions."[312]

[311] Larsen 2015: 154 and 78.
[312] Larsen 2015: 98 and 79.

15. Privatizing Mesopotamia's Intermediate Period: 2000–1600 BC

The Middle Bronze Age – the half-millennium from 2100 to 1600 BC – is one of civilization's most important transition periods. What gave it the quality of middle-ness was the dissolving of palace and temple control after Ur III broke down. Decen-tralization and privatization of enterprise and credit followed in the wake of invasions and social dislocations that enabled warlords to seize temple and palace estates and workshops. This phenomenon was akin to Boris Yeltsin's "Family" of grabitizers and "Red directors" picking up the pieces after the Soviet Union collapsed in 1991.

Early palaces and temples in Sumer's and Babylonia's mixed economies managed herds and fields, built infrastructure and ceremonial architecture, and provided aid for the needy. The late third millennium saw palace and temple regimes administered increasingly by the family and retainers of tribal leaders using their positions as rent extraction opportunities under Sargon's Akkadian dynasty, and then by chieftains or warlords from mountain areas (Gutians and Kassites), the Eastern Iranian plateau (Elamites) and the northwest (Amorites).

Business archives from this transition period show well-to-do individuals, mer-chants, administrators and entrepreneurs acting on their own account within the palace and temple bureaucracies. Local headmen and administrators were allowed broad leeway for gain-seeking as the economy became privatized.

Nomadic incursions by Amorites took over southern towns in a way much like Sargon's earlier conquests. Upstream towns along the Euphrates were swelled by immigration as Mesopotamia's economic and demographic center shifted northward. Describing "the process of the transformation from an urban civilization before Sargon to the nomadic culture of the Amorites," Sallaberger writes that: "The general process of the disappearance of urban centres in Upper Mesopotamia in the late Third Millennium suggests an ethnogenesis of Amorite nomads."[313]

A succession of Sumerian and Babylonian rulers bid for the support of Amorite chieftains and local clan heads by making military and economic alliances. The path of least resistance was to turn over temple properties to local headmen. Administration of Nippur's Inanna temple was relinquished to Amorite leaders ("Westerners") c. 2000 BC, apparently to deter them from raiding southern Mesopotamia. Similar privatizations occurred in Ur and Babylon.[314] Temple crop rents, offices and income

---

[313] Sallaberger 2007: 450. He adds (p. 445 f.): "If we apply the wide meaning for Mardu which is suggested by the literary texts, Mardu/Amorite came to mean also 'nomad' in Babylonia and it apparently applied also to persons of a recent nomadic past." The effect was far-reaching: "the descendants of the earlier urban agriculturalists of Upper Mesopotamia who changed to nomadic life and became 'Amorites' themselves," adopting their language along with their customs.

[314] Stone 1987, Zettler 1992, and Charpin 1986.

rights (prebends) became hereditary, divisible among the heirs and transferable after about 1800 BC. Within a few centuries these rights evolved into a veritable market of shares being subdivided, bought and sold.

Rulers leased out tracts of land for administrators to sublease to sharecroppers, and undertook trade ventures with merchants. Privatizing such enterprise led to more balances to be settled among the economy's various sectors. Widespread slave dealing is attested by the Isin-Larsa period in the 19th century BC, while a *nouveau riche* sector emerged in a symbiosis with the palace, including palace and temple agents, agricultural and property managers, *tamkārum* entrepreneurs, and unmarried *nadītum* heiresses cloistered in the Shamash temple in Sippar and other temples to invest their inheritances. They owned property and lent silver and grain on their own account.[315]

Property rights as an independent dynamic

Modern free-market ideology tends to think of land as existing in a primordial original state of nature, free and clear of a fiscal burden or other responsibilities and regulations. Taxes are viewed as intrusive. But viewing property simply as a "pure" asset without liability, is the reverse of how land tenure historically evolved. In an epoch when everyone was subordinate to a higher authority, land was part of a chain of social responsibility, defined above all by the fiscal liability of its holder. First came the obligation, from which its holders managed to break free only later.

Republican Presidential candidate Mitt Romney told voters in 2011 that "corporations are people."[316] In terms of rights, today's corporations enjoy precedence over those of human people. That is perhaps the most radical change of today's economic morality over that of Bronze Age Mesopotamia, where property in land and other assets was deemed to be an extension of their personal holders. As an extension of the person, property was subject to the hierarchies of status and responsibility to higher authorities, going all the way up to the ruler. Emile Szlechter notes that long before a general word for property emerged, there was a term for proprietor: "although the expressions LUGAL (in Sumerian) and *bēlum* (in Akkadian) are habitually translated as proprietor, one does not find in the Sumerian and Akkadian vocabulary a term which designates 'property' in the abstract sense of law of property."[317] The closest the Middle Bronze Age came was "domain of the lord." The basic concept was interpersonal – and patriarchal, as was land tenure.

Instead of individualism as our epoch understands the term, the Middle Bronze Age subordinated status from the bottom of the economic pyramid to the top. There were rival towns and personalities, but not competing ideologies to inspire a debate over economic principles. No record of popular walkouts is found such as Rome suffered with the withdrawal of the plebs on the eve of its Republic in the 5th century BC. "One finds mention, here and there, of 'peasant revolts,'" Jean Bottéro writes, "but these appear to have been provoked by terrible catastrophes such as famine, and are

---

[315] Leemans 1950: 117f. and Harris 1975.
[316] Rucker 2011; see also https://www.youtube.com/watch?v=E2h8ujX6T0A.
[317] Szlechter 1958: 121. See also Cardascia 1959: 19–32.

directed against an individual such as a king, not against an institution. In reality, the old inhabitants of Mesopotamia appear to have been devoid of any revolutionary spirit," as there was no idea of an alternative way to organize society. Populations "viewed the gods as having decreed an immutable order of things. They thus fatalistically accepted their state of social dependency, with all its consequences."[318]

The allegedly lacking revolutionary spirit, though, is reflected in the myth of Atrahasis. Attested on copies from the time of Ammisaduqa but based on earlier sources, it describes the world of the gods before mankind existed: Lower gods had to perform all the hard work for the maintenance of the higher-ranking gods:

> When the gods, instead of man did the work, bore the load …
> The god's load was too great, the work too hard, the trouble too much…
> They counted years of drudgery ,… and forty years, too much! …
> forced labor they bore night and day. They were complaining, denouncing …
> "Now them, call for battle "…
> They set fire to their tools, they put fire to their spaces,
> and flame to their workbaskets. Off they went, one and all,
> to the gate of the warrior Enlil's abode.[319]

Enki, the god of wisdom, contrived a solution: He suggested that humans be created to bear the workload thereafter.

The implication is that the idea of walkouts was not alien to the Mesopotamians. Given the biased nature of our sources for the political history surprise, we do not hear of any reports of such occurrence by the living population.

Economic entropy and indebtedness

Urbanization had peaked around 2600 BC, and continued to decline throughout the second millennium, as did Mesopotamia's population. The reasons are still being debated, but climate change seems to have played a role. Soil fertility fell to a third of pre-Sargonic levels. Some archaeologists attribute this to irrigation leaving salt from the rivers in the soil and forcing a shift from wheat to barley.[320] In any case, more labor was required to de-silt the canals, and large areas were abandoned to the desert. Meanwhile, the Indus civilization crumbled toward the end of the third millennium, cutting off Mesopotamia's eastern trade and its supply of many raw materials, prompting the Ur III economy to turn as far west as Asia Minor.

Indebtedness intensified from the Isin and Larsa periods through the Old Babylonian period as a combination of warfare and falling crop yields left many people unable to pay fees and taxes. Their debts to creditors – and the diversion of corvée labor to private debt bondage – threatened to weaken the palace's ability to requisition labor and collect fees, as local officials kept the crop surpluses and labor service for themselves as interest on their own lending.

[318] Jean Bottéro 1961: 163.
[319] Foster 2005.
[320] Jacobsen and Adams 1958: 1252 ff., and Adams 1981. Powell 1985: 7–38 disagrees.

The historian of commerce W. F. Leemans describes how "the *tamkarum* [merchant] was the obvious person to assume the function of giver of credit ... [as] a money-lender."[321] The returns to commercial investment were divided in a variety of ways ranging from pure interest to equity partnerships. "The invention of contract formulae for various forms of private economic transactions (sale, loan, tenure, sale-marriage, etc.) allowed for the transformation from state to private enterprise, and for the development of capitalistic economic patterns."[322]

Amorite takeover of the temples

An archive from 19th-century BC Uruk "shows the ruler making use of temple property normally and not by necessity, partly to invest it in trade ventures, partly to furnish the needs of the palace," notes Edzard. "It is significant that a large inventory of the possessions of the Nanaya temple of Uruk was kept in the palace. ... An Old Babylonian omen does indeed denounce such encroachments, predicting that 'the king will take property of the house of the gods to the palace; but Shamash [the sun god, guardian of law and right] will see it.'"[323] Elizabeth Stone finds that business was conducted increasingly in the private apartments of temple administrators, and that "a few offices had associated prebend fields" in Nippur, which "entitled the owner to a share of the sacrifice." By the Isin-Larsa period these revenues "had become a kind of private property which could have been passed on to the heirs of the owner."[324]

A financial market in *rentier* shares

Temple offices produced an earmarked usufruct or revenue in return for services to the temple, which was subdivided as it came to be bequeathed to new generations of family members. The earliest contracts with regard to these temple offices "record the control of whole or half offices," notes Stone, "suggesting that these offices had either only been in the family for a short period of time or that they were neither heritable nor divisible before the time of the first contracts." Stone concludes that "the offices became heritable and divisible at the time they were given to these families," whose possession of substantial agricultural land suggests a rural power base.[325]

When Nippur was attacked, most likely by Amorites from the northwest, the *Lamentation over the Destruction of Nippur* describes how "active warfare penetrated the city itself" during the reign of Ishme-Dagan (1953–1935). What may have stopped the fighting, Stone suggests, was the decision by his father, Iddin-Dagan (1974–1954), to buy off "the leaders of these rural, tribal groups. ... To stem future rebellion, the king moved them into the city, provided them with a large area of urban real estate, and co-opted the leaders with gifts of real estate and temple offices.

[321] Leemans 1950: 11 and 47.
[322] Landsberger 1974: v.
[323] Edzard 1967: 216.
[324] Stone 1987: 17f.
[325] Stone 1987: 21.

Like the British during the mandate period, they brought the tribal leaders into the cities where they could be controlled,"[326] giving them temple positions and the prebend revenues traditionally attached to them.[327] This is what happened in medieval English monasteries in the 13th century AD, when the papal court appointed Italians to local prebend-paying offices, as described vividly by Mathew Paris in his *Chronicles*.[328]

One result was to separate administrative functions from the prebend income earmarked to support temple officials. This was not unlike what Adolph Berle and Gardner Means described in the 1930s as representing the "new capitalism" of our own epoch, divorcing ownership from management duties.[329] Whereas only a single ugula (head administrator) received income from the Inanna temple in the Ur III period, "by Old Babylonian times, when up to one hundred may have shared a single office, the ownership of an office can have had little to do with the bureaucratic activities implied by the title."[330] It is hard to imagine that each individual who received temple income actually had to carry out the associated duties for just a few days. Their income rights were split from the office as such, and became alienable as long as a qualified individual could be hired to perform the designated service in return for part of the prebend income.

The upshot was that instead of building up wealth by their own enterprise, inheritors of these sinecures were passive recipients of temple income. The rural "troublemakers" simply collected the temple revenues traditionally allocated to support administrators.[331] Based on a similar study of Ur's temple personnel in Hammurabi's dynasty, Charpin concludes (as did Stone) that the subdivision of temple prebend incomes must have begun late in the Ur III period. After 180 to 200 years so many successive bequeathings and partitions of these prebends had occurred that some holders received only a few days' income per year. Typical revenue subdivisions appearing in the cuneiform records are 15 days ($\frac{1}{24}$[th] of the 360-day administrative Mesopotamian year), $7\frac{1}{2}$ days ($\frac{1}{48}$[th]), 5 days ($\frac{1}{72}$[nd]), $3\frac{2}{3}$[rd] days, and just $1\frac{2}{3}$ days per year. The number depends on how many heirs were left by successive generations of each branch of the original family. "The result, after a century and a half of successive divisions, is an extreme parcellisation of prebends: When we see an individual owning five days of service a year in the Nanna temple, we may conclude that this theoretically signifies that the income is divided among 71 other persons for that year." In effect, temples were reorganized "as a kind of joint–stock company whose shares have passed into the hands of the town notables."[332]

The sale of temple offices would continue down to Christian times from Mesopotamia to Asia Minor, and ownership of temple usufruct flows came to be marketable. After about 1800 BC temple offices "carried none of the alienation restrictions which applied to the more traditional kinds of property, *i.e.*, fields and houses."[333]

---

[326] Stone 1987: 72 ff. and 124.
[327] Charpin 1986: 62.
[328] Vaughan 1984.
[329] Berle and Means 1932.

[330] Stone 1987: 19.
[331] Stone 1987: 22.
[332] Charpin 1986: 260 ff.
[333] Stone 1987: 18 and 25.

Sale of these positions was not restricted to one's kinsmen. A *rentier* class of temple prebend-holders thus came into being – history's first attested absentee owners and "coupon clippers." Some owned prebend shares in more than one temple. One man appears to have held prebends in Ur's temples of Nanna, Ninlil and Gula. In the early 18th century BC during Rim-Sin's rule, a person paid 15 shekels of silver to purchase the office of anointer, brewer and chef for the temple of the healing-god Damu in Larsa for just a lunar half-month.[334] Such investment in temple incomes– and indeed, their marketability – introduced a *rentier* aspect to many public-sector functions.

This privatization and indeed, financialization of trade and professional life was the major economic novelty of the Middle Bronze Age. It was associated with the influx of nomadic groups that took over southern Mesopotamian towns.

Tensions between local headmen and the palace

Although allied to the palace in loose feudal-type arrangements, palace collectors, local chieftains, officials, merchants and "big-men" were an ever-present threat to break free as autonomous powers in times of weakening central authority. Local headmen in villages or areas where royal control weakened sought to resist centralized royal power. Modern historians will recognize this dynamic as erupting when England's barons rose to oppose King John, producing the Magna Carta to limit royal authority– and keep the land tribute quantified in the Domesday Book for themselves as privatized land rent. But in Mesopotamia there never was any such declaration of principles or ideology opposing the palace's power or its right to proclaim clean slates. There was, however, a constant maneuvering to find loopholes and simply to resist implementation of such proclamations.

Bronze Age Mesopotamia was no golden age, and rulers did not try to recover one when they proclaimed amar-gi and *mīšarum*. They simply sought to restore the status quo ante, the traditional state of affairs. Debt amnesties and liberty from bondage were means to build up the army, provide crop surpluses and corvée labor to the large institutions, and import luxury goods. What in time became the most corrosive form of exploitation – rural usury – thus was constrained by the need to field armies with free citizens. Villagers had some choice as to whether to side with the palace or to free themselves from overly predatory rule and its bureaucracy by defecting to the ever-present rival nomads.

This constraint on palace levies was required by all but the Akkadian rulers to preserve a self-supporting land-tenured citizen army. That was the main worldly motive for Babylonian rulers to continue the Sumerian practice of debt amnesties – to limit the avarice of an administrative bureaucracy acting selfishly to draw as much labor and enterprise as possible under its own patronage. When rulers canceled debts owed to royal collectors, managers of royal monopolies, and local headmen and merchants while deterring predatory behavior, this proclamation of justice and equity was as self-serving as it was an altruistic continuation of traditional social and religious

[334]Pritchard, ed., 1958 [1955], vol. II, p. 73.

values. Rulers were not seeking an idealized egalitarian society, but simply to restore their authority over the Middle Bronze Age's increasingly privatized economy.

How wide a sphere did royal debt amnesties affect?

It remains an open question as to how far royal proclamations had the ability to annul debts owed outside of the palace and temple sphere, in towns and villages away from the royal palace. Debts owed to sandal makers, smiths, weavers or other craftsmen in the village economy don't appear in the archives, so we can't confirm that these claims were enforced by royal clean slates. Hammurabi's legal prescriptions relate most obviously to the palace sector, its dependents, and debts owed to the palace retinue. But the dependence of Babylonian rulers on local headmen led to a constant tension when it came to enforcing royal proclamations. The palace sought to tighten its control by appointing officials such as the *wakil tamkārī* in charge of *tamkārum* merchants.

The nomadic takeover of Southern Mesopotamia

The Amorite leader Shamshi-Adad (1813–1781) conquered Assur, Mari and neighboring cities along the middle Euphrates early in the 19th century BC. He appointed one of his sons, Ishme-Dagan, to rule Assur and transferred the tin trade to Mari, upstream along the Euphrates, from where his father had come. Assur's commercial role declined. By the late second millennium, when Assyria revived as a military power at the onset of the Iron Age, the region had been transformed by centuries of northern Mesopotamia's legacy of tribal nomadism.

Meanwhile, the Cappadocian region fell to the Hittites, who sacked Assur's Kanesh colony. Assur rebuilt it and maintained a downsized trade with Asia Minor, but the ongoing warfare in northwest Mesopotamia interrupted what had been three generations of flourishing commerce. Also cut off what was the Melucchan commerce via Dilmun as the Indus Valley's Harappan civilization collapsed and gave way to Indo-European speakers.

Besides Shamshi-Adad, other Amorite leaders established themselves at Kish, Larsa, Der, Uruk and the relatively new upstream town of Babylon. While these disruptions sapped southern Mesopotamia's commercial prosperity, its internecine warfare made rising demands on resources, impairing the region's agricultural economy by over-farming. Many towns fell to the region's historical antagonists, Elam in the east and Amorites in the west.

Larsa's period of dominance, 1932–1763 BC

Located in the center of Sumer's south, Larsa increased its sway over southern Mesopotamia after c. 1932 BC. Its ruler Gungunum expanded his city's influence over the Elamite east, conquering Anshan and even Susa. His successor Abisare lost Ur to Isin in the final year of his rule, but Sumuel (1894–1866) extended Larsa's suzerainty as far north as Nippur. Still, Larsa never really became a region-wide power, mainly because it came into conflict with Babylon, which also was widening its sphere of influence. Babylon's ruler Sumulael (1880–1845) annexed Sippar and Kish, but found expansion further northward blocked by Eshnunna. For about two centuries Larsa, Babylon and Eshnunna jockeyed for position.

The distinguishing feature of this post-Isin period was the growth of private wealth outside of the palace and temples. Already in the early 19th century BC, c. 1875–1850, a more independent type of merchant was emerging in Kish and elsewhere in the north. In Larsa, large private estates were created in the mercantile quarter. Wealth was becoming independent of public control as the palace and temples were never as strong in Larsa as in other Mesopotamian towns.[335] Two brothers, Warad-Sin (1834-1823) and Rim-Sin (1822–1763), replaced Gungunum's dynasty with Elamite backing. Mercantile activities reached a peak during the early decades of their rule.

Family archives show large investors such as Balmunamḫe, Idin-Amurrum and Ubar-Shamash buying many houses and other real estate, grain stores, and possessing numerous slaves. Leemans finds "no evidence that these *tamkaru* had any relation to the palace. ... They seem to have been entirely independent merchants."[336]

It was natural for these entrepreneurs to engage in rural usury as a sideline. Commercial credit played a productive role in foreign trade, agricultural production and subleasing basic services. Whereas earlier barley debts were run up mainly in the form of rural usury to pay for palace or temple services – and were owed to creditors in the form of labor service to work off the interest – this Middle Bronze Age period saw the sphere of grain loans expand on a much larger scale.

Traditionally, small rural debtors who could not pay had been taken into the house of their creditors (including the temples), where they were treated more or less as family dependents. But Larsa's large-scale credit activity removed them from a personal family or institutional relationship with their creditors. Debt bondage was becoming commercialized as creditors hired out their bondservants to employers in need of labor.[337]

Most texts in the much-studied archive of Balmunamḫe, for instance, involve slaves and bondservants. Some sold themselves for debts, others were sold by their parents or owners because poverty prevented their support. "Almost all of the self-sales take place in the last three months of the year, thus in the winter when the supplies are low and the people are most likely in debt," finds Van De Mieroop. Labor by debt pledges was needed mainly in the fall, when fields were plowed and sown and dates were harvested, and in the spring and the summer months when crops were harvested. But "the winter months do not require a large number of laborers ... Balmunamḫe had thus no use for many of his slaves. Moreover, the price of grain was higher in that season, thus the maintenance of the slaves was more expensive." So to save the cost of providing food, clothes and supervision, Balmunamḫe might relinquish them to their own household (or those of other people) in the agricultural "off months" when their labor was not required.[338]

---

[335] See for instance Diakonoff 1971: 19–22.
[336] Leemans 1950: 113 and 106 and Kraus's review, and Edzard 1967: 169 and 190 f.
[337] Struve 1969: 54, Matouš 1956, and Klengel 1973.
[338] Van De Mieroop 1987: 11 and 23f.

The Larsa Dynasty
14 rulers in 262 years (2025–1763 BC)

Naplanum 20 years (2025–2005)	an Ur III Amorite living near Ur, benefitted from Elamite backing
...	
Gungunum 27 years (1932–1906)	defeated Lipit-Ishtar of Isin and established Larsa as an imperial power
...	
Warad-Sin 12 years (1834–1823)	Larsa reached the peak of its influence
Rim-Sin 60 years (1822–1763)	reasserted palace authority over the private sector, which had grown since the demise of Ur III, by "purifying the foreheads" of debt-servants, liberating them from dependency on local creditors. He was defeated by Hammurabi of Babylon in 1763

Figure 25: Chronology of rulers of the Larsa dynasty

A similar entrepreneurial maneuvering characterizes Balmunamḫe's real estate transactions. He bought "mainly large plots whose prices were low," and sought to consolidate large blocks of orchard land, presumably to shift to more profitable, capital-intensive crops. Balmunamḫe compensated the owners (often a group of relatives) in either land or silver, and also in "grain, wool and cloth, oil, and once a sheep."[339]

Rim-Sin's debt cancellations

A showdown came in the second half of Rim-Sin's 60-year reign (1822–1763). Like other rulers, he seems to have recognized that if he permitted usury and debt bondage to persist, much of the population would lose its land and be unable to provide corvée labor service or fight in the army. Despite the rising monetary wealth in private hands, the Middle Bronze Age was still far from being ripe for oligarchies to break anywhere near as free of palace control as occurred in classical Greece and Rome.

Unlike his contemporary rulers of Isin and Babylon, Rim-Sin did not refer to níg-si-sá proclamations in his year-names, but numerous references in the period's legal contracts have led Kraus to conclude that he cancelled debts on at least three occasions. One of his acts was to "purify the foreheads of the land."[340] This evidently meant freeing bondservants, because debt pledges taken into bondage typically were marked on their forehead to set them apart from freemen – and, as a collateral sign

---

[339] Van De Mieroop 1987: 13 f. and 24.
[340] Kraus 1984: 31 ff.

going back to Sumerian times, wore their hair short to leave such markings exposed.[341] In his 26th year Rim-Sin dug the "Liberty Canal" (íd níg-si-sá), likely to have commemorated a níg-si-sá proclamation. A coronation hymn commemorates "Rim-Sin, king of abundance, who walks majestically beside princes and who has the gods Kittum and Misharum as his aides."

In his 30th year, the midpoint of his long rule, Rim-Sin was at the height of his glory. Having conquered Isin and also ruling Nippur, Ur, Uruk and Eridu, he called himself "King of Sumer and Akkad," and even had himself worshipped as a god. "It seems that he utilized his glory to effect social reforms," concludes Leemans, "strengthening his own position at the same time." Having accomplished notable feats of arms, Rim-Sin had to rely on Larsa's rural population to do most of the fighting to counter the danger threatened by Hammurabi in the north. Also needed were "warriors from abroad, from the surrounding deserts, who had to be attracted by agreeable conditions." That seems to be why Rim-Sin moved to break the influence of powerful creditors "and to favor his soldiers, for example, by means of the loan of fields, upon which taxes were levied when the soldiers were not on active service."[342]

Rim-Sin limited the autonomy of private merchants by subordinating them to a palace-appointed "chief of merchants" (wakil tamkārī). "Records setting forth the division of the inheritance of Balmunamhe are not extant, but from the fact that his sons, unlike their father, do not appear to have been wealthy and influential people, it may be concluded that his wealth had disappeared."[343]

Rim-Sin was doing in Larsa what Hammurabi and other rulers were doing in Amorite-influenced Mesopotamia around this time. Archives from Sippar indicate the general situation: a proliferation of wuklū tumkūrī overseeing trade activities. Shamshi-Adad introduced this palace oversight to Assur.[344] Rulers concentrated control of trade in the palace, especially for basic materials such as wool and foodstuffs. "Prominent and wealthy tamkārū were no longer found during Hammurabi's reign," concludes Leemans,[345] and only a few major merchants are documented later.

After Hammurabi defeated his erstwhile ally Rim-Sin in 1764/1763, he proclaimed a mīšarum debt cancellation that Van De Mieroop describes as applying only to Larsa, not to Babylon itself. The result was that "some of the Larsa entrepreneurs whose careers we know about went out of business. Hammurabi clearly wanted to start out with a clean slate in Larsa."[346] For the next generation the history of Mesopotamia would be shaped by his empire building.

---

[341] On Rim-Sin's measures see Charpin 1980: 273f. and 133f.
[342] Leemans 1950: 122.
[343] Leemans 1950: 117.
[344] Larsen 1976: 220f.
[345] Leemans 1950: 122.
[346] Van De Mieroop 2005: 38.

16. Hammurabi's Laws and *mīšarum* Edicts: 1792–1750 BC

In contrast to Ur III's centralized control, Hammurabi extended his military alliances throughout southern Mesopotamia by delegating autonomy to his fellow Amorite chieftains and other local leaders. Norman Yoffee describes these men as coming "from mid- to upper-level elites of the community who had certain connections to resources embedded in local organizations that the crown wished to mobilize."[347] They were "able to establish their offices as hereditary positions and to profit from tax-farming at the crown's expense"[348] as well as that of the citizenry at large. They also were the major creditors. Diakonoff notes that "the majority of usurers consisted of priests, governmental commercial agents (*tamkāru*) and members of the king's own royal administration, *i.e,*. the main support of his power."[349]

Falling soil fertility, overcrowding of the land, and the uprooting and imperial taxation of local populations led to widespread inability to pay taxes, crop rents and other obligations to these headmen, creditors and palace officials. Hammurabi's laws and clean slate proclamations tried to protect indebted community members and tenants on royal lands from being reduced to bondage, so that their labor would remain available for corvée work and military service, and their crop surpluses paid to the palace.

His laws are the period's longest and best known inscription. But they were not binding law as our epoch understands the term.[350] The land-tenured citizens had their own long-standing customary law of injury debts and similar communal rules.[351] What called for new formulations was the community's interaction with the extensive palatial economy, especially debts owed to its bureaucracy and protection of soldiers from the most adverse consequences of debt. But these laws were not an all-encom-

---

[347] Yoffee 1979: 13.

[348] Yoffee 1977: 148.

[349] Diakonoff 1959: 199. This led Hammurabi to "often rule against his overzealous administrators in the face of long-standing rights of an injured party," he adds, but "his policy could not help stopping halfway."

[350] Korošec 1971: 281 describes Middle Bronze Age laws generally as having only a "provisional character." Van De Mieroop concurs with Finkelstein's 1961 view of Hammurabi's laws as guidelines being predominantly literary in spirit.

[351] Diakonoff 1982: 24 and 29: "Cases for which standard decisions were satisfactorily provided for by customary law (simple murder, theft from an awilum, sorcery, irrigation, *etc.*) were not included in the written law collections." Likewise, the practice of rulers issuing "instructions to officials, known from the Hittite kingdom and also from Egypt, touch[ed] very seldom upon everyday socio-economic life outside of the big organizations. … laws regulating the security of private property of the community members (even of slaveholders!), irrigation problems, problems of taxation and obligatory labor service (except for royal servants), relations between members of the community and the community itself – all this is absent from the Laws of Hammurabi."

The Amorite First Dynasty of Babylon
11 rulers in 300 years (1894–1595 BC)

Samuabum 14 years (1894–1881)	an Amorite Bedouin chief who never actually resided in Babylon, but sponsored Sumula'el
Sumula'el 36 years (1880–1845)	the actual founder of the Babylonian dynasty. He built the great wall around Babylon and its palace, and cancelled debts by proclaiming *mīšarum*
Sabium 14 years, 1844–1831).	
Apil-Sin 18 years (1830–1813)	
Sin-muballit 20 years (1812–1793)	was responsible for extending Babylon's influence after the death of Shamshi-Adad of Mari. He annexed Kish, Sippar, Marad and other small kingdoms, and declared *mīšarum* in 1812, 1803 and 1797
Hammurabi 43 years (1792–1750)	headed an alliance that carried Babylon to the height of its power. He proclaimed *mīšarum* in the year of his accession (1792) and in 1780, 1771 and (at least for Larsa) in 1762 after defeating his erstwhile ally Rim-Sin of Larsa in 1763. He had his laws inscribed on a stele, independently from his *mīšarum* acts
Samsuiluna 38 years (1749–1712)	proclaimed *mīšarum* upon taking the throne in 1749, and again in 1741, "raising the golden torch for the land" as his father had done
Abi-eshuh 28 years (1711–1684)	proclaimed *mīšarum* upon taking the throne in 1711
Ammiditana 37 years (1683–1647)	cancelled debts upon his accession in 1683, and again in 1662 and 1647
Ammisaduqa 21 years (1646–1626)	proclaimed *mīšarum* upon his accession in 1646, and again in 1636. His *mīšarum* act is the longest and most detailed of the Mesopotamian rulers
Samsuditana 31 years (1625–1595)	eleventh and last ruler of the Amorite dynasty, saw his city raided by the Hittites and then occupied by the Kassites from the Iranian highlands who would rule it for 370 years

Rulers of other cities also proclaimed *mīšarum* during the Old Babylonian period: in Hana (near Mari on the Euphrates) the rulers Kastiliiash, Ammi-ribih and Sunuh-rammu; and in Eshnunna, Abi-madar, Naram-Sin and Ipalpiel (or Dadusha)

Figure 26: Chronology of rulers of the first dynasty from Babylon

passing code.[352] Hammurabi's truly binding edicts were his proclamations of economic order cancelling agrarian arrears and debts. Like most Babylonian rulers, he started his reign by proclaiming a financial clean slate – *mīšarum*. It was these edicts that saved land tenure for Babylonia's indebted soldier-citizenry from passing into the hands of creditors on more than a temporary basis.

Retaining the loyalty of Babylonia's cultivators by proclaiming *mīšarum*

Located upstream from the major southern cities, Babylon was only of minor importance until Hammurabi's father Sin-muballit inherited its throne in 1812. His forebear Sumula'el, of Amorite descent, was the actual founder of Hammurabi's dynasty. He is the first documented ruler to use the phrase "breaking the tablets" as a synonym for cancelling debts by a *mīšarum* act at the start of his rule in 1880, and the term later was used by Samsuiluna, as well as in Eshnunna.[353]

The ritual phrase "breaking the tablets" annulled the debt records on which agrarian obligations were inscribed. For instance, when one creditor tried to collect the amount nominally due on a debt tablet predating one of Hammurabi's *mīšarum* acts, the debtor sued and won on the ground that the edict nullified the earlier debt tablet. The judges symbolically broke a clod of earth in lieu of the tablet, so that the latter should be considered void if the creditor ever again tried to collect. "Astounding as it must appear to our normally skeptical eyes," concludes Finkelstein, instead of the *mīša= rum* institution being "a pious but futile gesture," the fact is that "at the promulgation of the *mīšarum* formal commissions were established to review real-estate sales."[354]

Raising the sacred torch of "justice and righteousness" apparently symbolized the sun-god of justice Shamash, patron deity of wise rulers. The underlying idea was a cosmology in which sun gods of justice endorsed rulers as their earthly administrators. Babylonia's sun god was Shamash, from whom Hammurabi is depicted as receiving his laws. Shamash had two children, *kittu* and *mīšaru*, "Right" and "Justice."[355] He was patron of the New Year festival, the solar holiday *par excellence* which in my view was the most likely occasion for at least Gudea's proclamations of justice and order.

---

[352] There are many omissions. "Whatever the laws are, they are not a code in the modern sense of the term," concludes Miles (Driver and Miles 1952: 48).

Hammurabi's laws were part of a common tradition of royal rulings, although more extensive than others. A few decades earlier the ruler Bilalama of Eshnunna (about 70 miles northeast of Babylon) announced about sixty laws, "three quarters of which were reproduced more or less directly in the Laws of Hammurabi" (Speiser 1967: 9), suggesting "that there was a common customary law throughout the Fertile Crescent." See Bottéro 1992 for a general discussion.

[353] Edzard 1957: 68, 125 and 165 f. Trial documents of the period also refer to rulers "breaking the tablets," *i.e.*, annulling debts. Landsberger 1939: 231 points out that when Sumula'el used the phrase "breaking the tablets" he "meant not only the debt obligations, but also the sale (forced sale?) and hence turning over children for adoption." See Kraus 1958: 196–208 and 224–232, esp. 230 n. 52. See also Finkelstein 1965. Also important is Bottéro 1961: 150.

[354] Finkelstein 1965: 244 ff.

[355] Speiser 1967: 313–323, discusses their mutual relations. Elam and other regions had similar deities, as did the Neo-Babylonians a millennium later.

Finding northern expansion blocked by Assur and Mari, both ruled by Shamshi-Adad, Sin-muballit turned his attention south. After conquering Larsa and Ur he took on Isin and Eshnunna, gaining popular support by proclaiming *mīšarum*. The word stems from the Semitic root ʾšr. Its Akkadian form *ešēru* is the equivalent of Sumerian si-sá, making níg-si-sá and *mīšarum* the terms to cancel debts from Ur III through Isin and Babylon. The word's first documented use in Akkadian to signify a debt cancellation is by Nidnusha of Der, up the Euphrates from Mesopotamia. In Eshnunna, east of the Tigris, *mīšarum* was proclaimed by Abi-madar, Naram-Sin and by Ipalpiel II at the beginning of his rule. In Hana (a city-state that emerged late in the Old Babylonian period) Kastiliashu, Ammi-rabih and Sunuh-rammu decreed *mīšarum*.[356] Six consecutive rulers of Hammurabi's dynasty cancelled debts during a 166-year period, from the fifth ruler (Hammurabi's father, Sin-muballit) in 1812 through Ammisaduqa (Hammurabi's great-great-grandson) in 1636.

The terms *kittum* and *mīšarum* typically are found together. Ephraim Speiser describes how *kittum* represents "an immutable aspect of cosmic order ... that which is firm, established, true" on the highest and most abstract level, while *mīšarum* means "equity, justice" in the sense of timely policies to meet specific civil dislocations. ... The independent function of a ruler, whether divine or human, is confined to *mîšarum*, that is, just and equitable implementation."[357] Along similar lines, Bottéro elaborates:

> *Kittu*, by its basic meaning (*kânu: to establish firmly*) evokes something firm, immobile, and is best understood as that which derives its solidity from its conformity to the law ... *Mesharu*, derived from *eshēru* (*to go straight, in the right way; to be in order*) contains a more dynamic element; one can understand it ... as a state or as an activity. As a state it reflects the *good order* of each thing in its place and according to its ways. ... A particular use of the same word is understood as the *repair* and *restoration* of the activities of a society ... usually at least in the beginning of a reign, by 'abolishing the debts' of the working part of the population, whose precarious conditions made them increasingly dependent upon the rich elite. Thus the *mesharu* was an exercise in equity by the king par excellence, and indicated an 'act of grace' and a 'moratorium on debts.'[358]

[356] Kraus (1958: 230–232, nos. 49–52 and 54–57). If Eshnunna's *mīšarum* act was not by Ipalpielit was by Dadusha near the end of his reign. A coronation-year proclamation seems more likely.

[357] Speiser 1953: 874. Finkelstein 1961: 104 describes the same difference in shading between *mīšarum* and *andurārum* (and by extension its Sumerian antecedent amar-gi): "It would seem that *mīšarum* is the more general term, while *andurārum* was a more specific word for 'release' or 'return' of persons held in bondage for debt or real estate so held. In this sense an *andurārum* can form part of a *mīšarum*-act."

[358] Jean Bottéro 1992: 182. Along similar lines Charpin 2003: 150, states: "The maintenance of public order, such as when a borrower is required to repay his creditor according to the terms of their agreement, is covered by *kittum*, whereas *mîšarum* concerns the restoration of balance in society, such as when someone burdened with debt is given a measure of relief. This is the kind of justice embodied in the proclamation of a *mîšarum* on the occasion of a new king acceding to the throne."

By restoring presumably timeless norms of justice, these edicts were not "reforms." "In fact," Charpin emphasizes, "the ideology underlying these measures of justice is opposed to reformism. It proceeds from a desire *to return to the origin*, considered to be the social equilibrium point to be restored. The Babylonians did not imagine the social ideal as a future to be achieved, but as a past state of affairs to be recovered and renewed. It was like re-establishing the observance of rules in their 'original purity.'"[359]

Early in this century Mesopotamia's debt cancellations were understood to be like Solon's *seisachtheia* of 594 BC freeing Athenian citizens from debt bondage. But Near Eastern royal proclamations were grounded in a different social-philosophical context from Greek reforms aiming to replace landed creditor aristocracies with democracy. The demands of the Greek and Roman populace for debt cancellation can rightly be called revolutionary, but Sumerian and Babylonian demands were based on a conservative tradition grounded in rituals of renewing the calendrical cosmos and its periodicities in good order. The Mesopotamian idea of reform had "no notion of what we would call social progress. Instead, the measures the king instituted under his *mīšarum* were measures to bring back the original order. The rules of the game had not been changed, but everyone had been dealt a new hand of cards. So it should not be a matter of surprise to us that these measures had to be regularly repeated." The policy worked for many centuries in Babylonia, for "there is no suggestion that any subsequent announcement of an edict of grace indicated that an earlier one had been ineffectively applied."[360]

The increasing frequency of *mīšarum* acts reflected the need to reverse the loss of personal liberty and self-support land as economies became more commercialized, privatized, and polarized, while the population on the land became poorer. The spirit is reflected in a prophesy that the sun god Anu "commands Enlil to promulgate a mīšarum act … its message is by means of fire … the dispersed will be gathered … the righteous will be established."[361] Individuals pledged for debt who had lost their liberty would be reunited with their families, and tenure on their customary land would be restored to debtors who had relinquished their crop rights under financial duress. These debtors were to be freed from whatever back taxes and other barley obligations had accumulated.

mīšarum proclamations were central to Babylon's military campaigns. Releasing families of the soldier-cultivators from debt bondage and restoring their land rights gave them a stake in the society whose boundaries they were fighting to extend. Sin-muballit consolidated popular support by repeating his inaugural *mīšarum* act of 1812 in 1803 and 1797. When Hammurabi succeeded his father in 1792, his first political act was a *mīšarum* edict, memorialized in his date formula. He seems to have annulled debts again in 1780, 1771 and (at least for Larsa after he conquered it) in 1762. As was the case with his father, each *mīšarum* act seems to have accompanied

---

[359] Charpin 1990: 24. He adds: "'Social progress' is a notion totally absent in the *mīšarum* edicts."
[360] Charpin 2003: 151.
[361] Biggs 1967.

a conquest. The first such proclamation occurred on the eve of his initial incursion east of the Tigris; the final one, in 1762, followed his defeat of Rim-Sin. "Hammurabi did not simply annex the realm of Larsa," states Charpin; "he took his place as the successor of Rim-Sin" and did what he would have done in such circumstances, proclaiming *mīšarum*.[362]

The scope of Hammurabi's laws

Hammurabi inscribed his laws late in his reign, probably in 1754 BC, for their prologue lists his conquests and public achievements down through his 1761 victory over Rim-Sin.[363] That dating would explain why these laws were not commemorated by a separate date formula, but simply were an extension of his "proclaiming justice." As noted above, the only royal declarations that were legally binding were the *mīšarum* debt cancellations.

Discovered in 1902, Hammurabi's laws have come down in numerous forms, having been copied by Babylonian scribes for over a thousand years. Their most famous public example, now in the Louvre, is inscribed in bands circling a black diorite stone eight feet high. Its top quarter shows Shamash with solar flames emanating from his shoulders, seated on his throne or "mountain," holding in his right hand the attributes of power: the ruling rod and the coiled measuring ("ruling") cord. Hammurabi faces him to receive either these symbols of rule, or the laws themselves (interpretations vary). The very top of the stele is broken, but reportedly "the sun-symbol once stood in the damaged spot above the god's crown."[364] The prologue seems to confirm this symbolism of the sun god of justice, saying of Hammurabi, "May Shamash make his scepter long."

The spirit of rulers governing in the name of their local sun god is indicated by a Babylonian hymn praising Shamash as "illuminator of the heavens" and "dispeller of darkness." He also was the patron-god of commerce, at that time a profession closely interfacing with the palace and temple sectors:

> You save from the storm the merchant carrying his capital …
> You give the unscrupulous judge experience of fetters. …
> As for him who declines a present, but nevertheless takes the part of the weak,
> It is pleasing to Shamash, and he will prolong his life. …
> If [the merchant] demanded repayment before the agreed date, there will be
>   guilt upon him. His heir will not assume control of his property,
> Nor will his brothers take over his estate.
> The honest merchant who weighs out loans (of barley) by the maximum
>   standard, thus multiplying kindness.
> It is pleasing to Shamash and he will prolong his life.[356]

---

[362] Charpin 2000: 188.
[363] Van De Mieroop 2005: 100.
[364] Gadd 1948: 90.
[365] "Hymn to Shamash," lines 97–104 and 115–19, in Lambert 1967: 131–133.

This spirit is typical of Mesopotamia. In Susa's marketplace, Attahashu erected a "stele of righteousness" c. 1800 BC, containing an official price index for grain and other commodities under the aegis of Elam's sun-god Nahhunte, "creator of the day," with the inscription: "Whoever does not take a just price, may Nahhunte cause him to be taken." Later texts mention "great tables" with grain prices. "The majority of Elamite trials took place in the temple grove of the sun-god Nahhunte. In complement to Inshushinak, invoked by ordinary people as 'Father of the weak,' the lawgiver Nahhunte is the Elamite god of the execution of the law, and he in particular was responsible for trade; he established a rate of interest, standardized weights, and embarked on capitalist negotiations with mortal businessmen in commercial partnership."[366]

As patron god of commerce as well as Hammurabi's rule, Shamash was assigned oversight of fair weights and measures, the official standards of which were kept in the Shamash temple in Babylon. Punishment for cheating applied above all to moneylenders and other creditors, and corrupt judges. As Shamash's earthly executor, Hammurabi stipulated that merchants who lent grain or money by a small weight but demanded repayment by a larger one forfeited whatever they had lent (gap §x, sometimes read as §§

[366] See Hinz 1972: 94, 106 and 145, and his reproduction of the stele, akin to that of Hammurabi.

Figure 27: Stele with the Laws of Hammurapi.

94–95). Ale women found guilty of using crooked weights and measures were to be cast into the water (§ 108).[367]

The epilogue to Hammurabi's laws states his guiding philosophy of justice:[368]

> … that the mighty might not wrong the weak, to provide just ways for the waif
>   and the widow … and to provide just ways for the wronged (xlvii: 59–78);
> Let any wronged man who has a lawsuit come before the statue of me, the king
>   of justice (*šar mīšarim*), and let him have my inscribed stela read aloud to
>   him … and let my stela reveal the (result of the) lawsuit for him (xlviii: 3–15).

Hammurabi's laws (and similar promulgations by earlier rulers) enabled debts denominated in silver to be paid in grain at a ratio of 1 shekel of silver equal to 1 *kur* of grain. This applied specifically to debts owed by the community to the temples and palace as prices were free to fluctuate in the quay areas outside the city gates.

The importance of record keeping as a check on abuses

Along with oversight of standardized weights and measures, record keeping played an important role in maintaining the role of law. Temple and palace property was recorded in registers kept in the palace at Babylon or in the temples, available for inspection, and the spreading reliance on written contracts reflects the spread of temple and palace practices to society at large. Public records blocked creditors from using arbitrary power, by showing who held the land and under what tenure conditions. This ensured "regular payment of the full amount of tax due to the king or temple" from the holders of cultivation rights, while protecting both the palace and tenants from creditors taking the crop. For instance, a Babylonian named Lalum wrote to Hammurabi that a creditor "hath laid claim to a certain land which Lalum had held from days of old" and took the crop although the land was not his. Palace records confirmed Lalum's title, and the creditor was "condemned to lose the money which he advanced on the crop." [369]

Officials or merchants could be put to death as thieves for buying or taking on deposit silver or gold, slaves, animals or anything else from a man's minor son or unemancipated slave without witnesses and a contract, because this was theft (§ 7). No doubt the violator was first given the opportunity to pay the appropriate fine.

---

[367] Alcoholic beverages typically were sold by women in what seems to have been a public profession. Their payment claims on their customers were substantial enough to be annulled by *mīšarum* acts.

[368] All citations from Hammurabi's laws are from Roth 199: 133f. For a kindred translation see Pritchard, ed., 1969 vol. III: 178.

[369] King 1900 vol. III: 24. Hammurabi's laws pertaining to trade were like those governing agrarian debt. Merchants had to keep detailed records specifying all amounts lent, the dates of the transactions and payments made, as well as prices for the goods bought and sold. In Sippar and other centers of Shamash worship these records normally were filed in the temple of Shamash. When traders realized a profit, they were obliged to record it and calculate the return owed to the investor. See § 100 and Driver and Miles 1952: 186–192 for a general discussion.

Figure 28:
Hammurapi before the sun god
Shamash. Top of the stela of the
Laws of Hammurapi.

Individuals who turned over personal property for safekeeping without a properly witnessed contract had no recourse, but if a contract and witnesses disproved a safekeeper's denial that he was given items, "he shall give twofold that which he denied" (§ 124). Safekeepers who lost a depositor's assets by burglary or negligence were liable (§ 125), apparently to prevent them from falsely claiming that they had been robbed or in some other way lost the deposit. Rulings §§ 120–126 deal with such stratagems.

To prevent dishonesty, properly witnessed written records were needed to settle commercial disagreements. Hammurabi ruled that merchants who falsely denied borrowing from an investor had to pay triple damages (§ 106) if shown by witnesses to be lying, an idea that has survived into the modern world. On the other hand, if a trading agent was entrusted with goods by a merchant and then returns them or pays the merchant, but the latter falsely denies having received them – and can be shown to be lying by witnesses – the merchant must pay the trader six-fold damages (§ 107).

§ 128 of Hammurabi's laws stip-ulates that "if a man (*awīlum*) marries a wife, but does not draw up a formal contract for her, that woman is not a wife." To protect the wife's rights, Hammurabi states that she "should have her husband agree by binding contract that no creditor of her husband shall seize her (for his debts)" (§ 151). By the same logic, "if that man has a debt incurred before marrying that woman, his creditors will not seize his wife," and likewise the husband could not be distrained for a debt against her. However, § 152 specifies that "if a debt should be incurred by them after that woman entered the man's house, both of them shall satisfy the merchant [*tamkārum*]."

Physical punishment for lawbreakers too poor to pay

Near Eastern customary law, like that of Europe, punished offenders either by levying fines or permitting vengeance to be carried out by family members under the rules of feud justice. Surviving records of Babylonian lawsuits show that the retaliatory principle of *talion* – an eye for an eye, a tooth for a tooth – was used only as a last recourse, if the guilty party lacked the resources or family members able to pay *wergild*-type reparations for inflicting injury. Members of the non-palatial sector normally paid compensation. The laws of Ur-Namma (§§ 17–18) and those of Bilalama in Eshnunna (§§ 42–48) prescribed monetary payments for bodily injury.[370]

By Babylonian times most palace dependents lived near subsistence levels, with few if any relatives to pay the stipulated fines for them. The economic position of tenants on palace land hardly could be further reduced. The workableness of *wergild-type* fines presupposed a population whose members had just enough resources so that fines were an effective deterrent to committing crimes, while most injured parties were in a position to accept this payment as satisfactory compensation or presumably might negotiate as an alternative to indulging in feud vengeance. When § 8 of Hammurabi's laws stipulates that the palace is to receive thirtyfold restitution for the theft of public property (three times as high as that received by a personal victim) or else the death penalty is to be imposed, the latter is apparently meant as a deterrent, a maximum last resort for exemplary punishment only applying to incorrigible thieves who lacked the means to pay.[371]

---

[370] Lambert 1967: 12 f. Money payment provided an alternative to feud vengeance only when it was mutually acceptable, usually in cases where the injured party was poor.

[371] Some debate remains over whether the *talion* principle was based on archaic customary law of pastoral nomads or even more broadly, or developed relatively late as a response to deepening poverty. Endorsing Stanley Diamond's anthropological finding that the punishments of death and mutilation normally evolve later than fines, Lambert 1979: 313, finds "no evidence that the lex talionis was ever enforced under the First Dynasty of Babylon, and it belongs to those portions of the Code which have exemplary rather than practical application." Finkelstein 1981: 41, n. 6, likewise finds that "No extant texts record persons being put to death for theft. ... There is more reason for believing that convicted thieves were reduced to slavery ... [which] ensured some measure of compensation to the victim of the theft, who could either retain the thief as his own slave or could have him sold to another buyer and receive the proceeds of the sale." He concludes that "the punishment of Mesopotamian offenders for wrongs against property [was not] nearly as severe as the law corpora suggest." They seem to have been maximum punishments rather than normal rules of judgment.

Growing palace power over the temples and landed communities

One result of the increasing palace power was the diminution of temples as major protagonists of economic life.[372] Their workshops, herds and lands were shifted to the palace (or were obtained by the palace and *rentier* outsiders), especially in the northern towns taken over by nomadic tribal leaders. Instead of lending mainly to merchants as in the Sumerian period, temple lending became smaller-scale. "More than 90 per cent of the barley loans consist of small loans, 5 GUR of barley or less. About the same percentage of silver loans involves loans of three shekels or less," notes Rivkah Harris, citing loans to invalids and to poor Babylonian debtors to purchase their liberty from bondage.[373]

§ 32 of Hammurabi's laws reflects the strained financial condition of temples. It stipulates the responsibility of travelling merchants to redeem Babylonian soldiers captured and sold into slavery in foreign towns where merchants found themselves doing business. Upon being returned to his native city the ransomed war prisoner was supposed to repay the merchant – but not by borrowing against his own field, orchard or house, because land tenure was part of a *quid pro quo* in which cultivators owed the palace rental or tax payments, military and labor services. If the soldier was unable to reimburse the merchant, the local temple was to provide the funds. If it lacked the money, the palace would pay the ransom.

In addition to benefiting from royal gifts of land and prisoners and receiving "a more or less regular income from offerings and tithes," the temples took a share of the profits earned by the celibate *nadītu* women domiciled within their precincts. Elizabeth Stone describes these heiresses as being removed from the marriage market to keep their family property intact, so that inheritance could pass to their brothers.[374]

The rate of interest on silver and barley debts

To guard against creditors appropriating the crops or land of debtors at arbitrary and unfair prices, gap § t (sometimes read as § 96) specified that any citizen who owed barley or silver to a *tamkārum* merchant could repay the loan in goods of equivalent value, *e.g.* in grain, sesame or some other basic commodity "in accordance with the

---

[372] Kraus 1964: 535.

[373] Harris 1960: 131. She adds that "the temples situated in cities outside of Babylonia proper were in no way more favorably inclined or more magnanimous to their debtors than private persons. In one Mari temple loan (ARM 8 31), for example, the Shamash temple takes the debtor's wife as pawn for the loan. Furthermore, the temples in the Diyala region charged the same interest rates on their loans as did private persona." In Tutub, a man sold himself into slavery to the Shamash temple's *enum*-priest to redeem his father from debt bondage to the temple.

[374] Stone1987: 18 f. and 24. The *nadītum* "maintained very close economic ties with their brothers. The property which they received was at least partly controlled by these brothers, yet the *nadītum* was always recorded as the sole owner at times of property transfer. However, most of the economic transactions of the *nadītum*s were with fellow *nadītum*s, women who were drawn from other lineages." Control could be transferred among lineages via these *nadītum*s, enabling wealthy branches of families to obtain property from poorer branches seeking to avoid debt bondage or forfeiture of their land rights to outsiders.

ratio [to silver] fixed by the ruler" (referring to §51).[375]   §1 of Eshnunna's earlier laws likewise obliged creditors to accept barley in payment for loans denominated in silver, at the official rate of 300 silas of barley for 1 shekel of silver.

Also like Eshnunna's laws §§20–21, Hammurabi set the rate of interest for barley debts at one-third, but only the traditional one-fifth (20 per cent) for silver (gap §t), and enforced this ruling by saying that creditors would forfeit their claim if they tried to charge more (gap §u). Although these details were effaced on Hammurabi's surviving public stele, they have been filled in from scribal copies on clay tablets. Calling a debt a "silver" debt did not mean that actual silver had to be paid, but only that the interest rate was 20 percent. This ruling would have been important for agricultural entrepreneurs or herd managers who borrowed from the well-to-do. If their creditors wanted silver, they would have to convert their barley at low market prices for grain at harvest time when crops were plentiful.

This bimonetary standard had no problem of "bad money driving out good," and there was no fiat money (a currency without intrinsic value). Babylonia did not have a problem with the large institutions accepting grain payments in place of silver. Grain prices varied seasonally in the open market, but payments to these institutions were contractual and set in advance at what today would be called forward hedging. The aim was to enable cultivators who owed fees, taxes and other debts expressed in silver to make payment in barley or a few other key commodities without having to sell these commodities for silver, taking the risk of prices varying. Although prices outside of the large institutions might fluctuate in response to supply and demand, deliveries to their collectors would have been stabilized, minimizing risk.

The effect was to enable less grain be used to pay debts denominated in silver. Along with §§48–50, these rulings "are all meant to give a weak debtor (a small farmer or tenant) some legal protection and help," and are "'given teeth' by stipulating that if [the creditor] takes more he will forfeit 'everything he gave,' that is, his original claim." [376]   Creditors who charged compound interest (by adding the interest charge to the debt principal), or who collected part of the loan but did not write a new contract crediting the debtor with his payment, had to repay twice the value of whatever they had received (gap §w, sometimes read as §93).[377]

Essential assets such as oxen could not be taken as pledges (§241), because they were necessary means of production to produce crops, as well as to enable the debtor to pay taxes or work his way out of debt. Creditors who distrained such assets were fined one-third of a mina of silver, the same amount as for killing a man or wrongfully seizing a person as a pledge (§114).

---

[375] This ruling corresponds to §20 of the slightly earlier Eshnunna laws, whose kinship with those of Hammurapi is discussed by Diakonoff 1991: 114.

[376] Veenhof 2010: 286f.

[377] See Driver and Miles 1952: 176f. and Leemans 1950: 15. Babylonian school texts contain many scribal exercises computing maš.máš, compound interest. Other rates also were officially set: Grain storage charges were ⅟₆₀th annually (§121). The laws of Eshnunna open with a schedule of regulated prices, mainly for paying debts.

Enforcement of Hammurabi's laws in practice

What cannot be ascertained from Sumer through Babylonia and later Near Eastern economies is how far royal decrees were obeyed or enforced. Like his contemporary lawgiving rulers, Hammurabi heard many cases, or at least appeals of judgments, directly. Suits were pleaded by the parties involved, without recourse to professional lawyers.[378] However, access to the ruler would have been limited by the need to go through local officials or assemblies, whose ranks often included the abusive parties. Unlike the moral standards of our time, it was acceptable for public collectors to behave like loan sharks, and the temples themselves "took part in usurious activities, alongside of the bigger royal officials and especially of the trading and tax-collecting agents (the *tamkāru*) and the rich buyers-up of craftsmen's produce, the *ummiānu* (mostly craftsmen themselves); even the terms *tamkārum* and *ummiānum* got in some contexts the connotation 'usurer, creditor.'"[379]

Commenting on one attested reliance on Hammurabi's laws – a contract from Ur in 1744 BC containing a clause providing that in case of breach of contract the cultivator would be treated "according to the wording of the stele" – Edzard cites the general doubt that this ruling "was universally followed, or that it was valid for any length of time."[380] In light of these administrative complexities, Finkelstein judged that Hammurabi's laws functioned mainly as a moral model "of a literary genre ... addressed primarily to posterity, especially to future kings. ... Public condemnations, even in the guise of legal rules, do not constitute 'law' any more than do modern 'resolutions' by legislators or other 'sovereign bodies.'"[381]

Yet Hammurabi's rule oversaw the subordination of private fortunes to the palace, and blocked the land from being transferred to creditors. This prevented the formation of large family estates, which disappear from the record during the course of his long reign. Evidently his *mīšarum* acts played a major role in this, along with tightening palace oversight of mercantile activity.

---

[378] Lawyers became a distinct profession only in classical antiquity. In Athens, most legal advocates were rhetoricians presenting the plaintiff's case before public juries.

[379] Diakonoff 1982: 82, referring especially to the §§ 88–90, measures against usury.

[380] Edzard 1967: 221.

[381] Finkelstein 1961: 101 f. Van De Mieroop agrees (2005: 107).

17. Freeing the Land and its Cultivators from Predatory Creditors

The most troublesome fiscal problem facing Hammurabi was creditors (including officials) seizing the crops of debtors and refusing to pay the scheduled sharecropping rent and other fees or taxes due, claiming that this part of the harvest belonged to them rather than the palace. Hammurabi's laws aimed to ban the practice of creditors aggressively taking crops from their debtors, to prevent the sale of land held by his fighting force, and to limit the practice of reducing debtors to bondage.

To support his army, Hammurabi turned hitherto clan-tenured land throughout the south into inalienable royal property, and leased it to soldiers and cultivators who could not alienate it for debt. In return, they were levied taxes (*biltum* and *ilkum*). "The king had granted them the possession of a plot of land to which was attached an obligation to perform military service. Someone granted an *ilkum* field was allowed to keep all that he produced from that land in return for making himself available for specified duties, whether military or civil."[382] Despite alienating such land, sellers still had to provide the palace with labor services and military obligations. This practice enabled foreclosing creditors and other *de facto* appropriators to escape liability. (This same problem would reappear in the Byzantine period in the 10th century AD, as discussed in Chapters 27 and 28 below.)

Letting creditors reduce cultivators to bondage and take their crops would have deprived the palace of this usufruct. To prevent the forfeiture of cultivation rights from depriving the palace of the taxes, rents or public service obligations associated with *biltum* and *ilkum* land, Hammurabi's laws permitted debtors to pledge the usufruct of their fields only temporarily. But these could not be permanently lost (§ 48). The forfeiture of such land was supposed to last only until the next *mīšarum* decree. However, landholders could lose their rights if they failed to cultivate (or pay taxes on) land they had leased. In such cases the land reverted to its palace, temple or absentee acquirer, along with liability for the usufruct it normally would produce, based on rates yielded by neighboring plots (§§ 43 f.).

The Babylonian epoch thus was far from developing the idea of private property in cropland. Bronze Age land tenure had too many public obligations attached to it to be deemed private in the modern sense of the ability to be freely sold or otherwise transferred without recovery rights, as in Roman and modern law. Szlechter finds "no case of land appropriation by a family who retains possession and whose proprietor can dispose of it while living."[383]

---

[382] Charpin 2003: 117. See also Yoffee 1977: 147 f. Van De Mieroop 2005: 96 f. notes that his Laws (§ 26, Roth 1997: 85–86) rule that if a soldier tries to hire a replacement to fight, he shall die. Whoever denounces him will take his property. Labor was hired mainly for harvesting work.

[383] Szlechter 1958: 135 f.

How the palace saved subsistence land from being privatized

Increasingly in the Old Babylonian period (2000–1600 BC), traders and other entrepreneurs sought to convert their financial wealth into land ownership, the most prestigious and productive investment in social status. But like other Bronze Age rulers, Hammurabi blocked the land's alienability because the alternative would have been for it to be transferred to a small class of wealthy individuals – at the palace's fiscal expense.

Accordingly, §37 of Hammurabi's laws invalidated any sale of rural fields, orchards or houses belonging to soldiers, commissaries or feudatories. The buyer's deed "shall be invalidated and he shall forfeit his silver [that is, whatever he has paid for the property]; the field, orchard or house shall revert to its owner." §38 even prohibited soldiers, commissaries or feudatory tenants from deeding their *ilkum* fields, orchards and houses to wives or daughters, or pledging them as collateral for any obligation. However, §39 permitted property that already had been bought for cash to be freely disposed of, on the ground that it *already* had passed out of the royal sphere.

Restrictions against alienating the land are a long tradition. Although pre-Sargonic records attest to land sales, "when the lease-fields become 'private property' they refer only to houses, orchards or fields whose area is relatively small."[384] The sellers are professional guilds, and the buyer invariably is the palace.[385] This is not the same as a free land market, especially as guilds had a public character as part of the temple or palace sectors.

Creditors tried to assert a clause in the loan contract binding both parties to not avail themselves of the protection afforded debtors and other sellers of the land by royal Clean Slates. Some contracts stated "that the money had been lent 'after the *andurārum*,' so that the debtor could not claim that he did not have to repay the loan because of the recent edict."[386] Hammurabi's insistence on the proper dating of contracts enabled debts to be rendered null and void in years when *mīšarum* was proclaimed, permitting debtors to reclaim their land.

Babylonian land-sale deeds often contained a closing clause stipulating that "the seller and his descendants promise never to attempt to claim the land, and if they do make the attempt a heavy fine is imposed."[387] A document from upstream Mari early in the 18th century BC under the rule of one of Hammurabi's contemporaries, Zimrilim, states bluntly "that a loan is not canceled in case an *andurārum* should be carried out: 'this money shall not be released if a liberation should take place.'"[388]

Similar contractual clauses are found in upstream Hana during the reign of Kash-tiliashu in the late 1700s BC (whose date formula indicates that he "established justice" at least twice). A general strategy was at work beyond just land redemption. One such clause contains "a brief reference to an oath pledging the contracting parties not to contest the

[384] Szlechter 1958: 133.

[385] Diakonoff 1982: 8–19, 36 ff. and 67 ff.

[386] Charpin 1990: 256. However, he adds (p. 263) that "this is a type of clause that only appears in the 'periphery' (Cappadocia, Mari, Terqa, Yamhad), never in southern Mesopotamia itself."

[387] San Nicolò 1974 [1922].

[388] Lemche 1979: 17.

validity of their agreement by raising claims against each other."[389] The complaining party seeking to recover his land is to have his head "smeared with hot asphalt." Lewy infers that it was considered necessary to insert this clause into the contract because "without such a statement, the landed property ... might have been liable to reversion to its former owner." Such clauses anticipated Rabbi Hillel's *prosbul*, formulated much later to weaken the force of the biblical Jubilee debt cancellations. These legalistic ploys helped make property more irreversibly alienable, and in time the charades were dropped. But the transition to permanent and unconditional transfer of land took many centuries to develop. As it did, the Biblical prophets denounced it as causing the fall of Judah and Israel to foreign powers, and in the case of Rome, Michael Rostovtzeff largely blamed it for the Empire's collapse.[390] But in the Old Babylonian period the process was just getting underway.

Limits on creditors aggressively taking crops

To avoid a fiscal shortfall, §§ 49–50 of Hammurabi's laws stipulate that only the owner of the field could harvest the grain or sesame, not a creditor. (gap § a, formerly read as § 66, makes the same stipulation for dates.) The debtor implicitly was to pay the rents or fees to the palace first, and to pay creditors only out of what was left over.[391] Creditors were not allowed even to accept a debtor's "invitation" to go onto his land and harvest his crop. If they tried to do this, they were to repay whatever they had taken and forfeit their entire claim. § 38 prohibited creditors from foreclosing on royal fiefland owing feudal obligations to the palace, apparently because such seizure would deprive the palace of its scheduled yield and service. If a creditor foreclosed on a field, orchard or house belonging to a soldier or feudatory as a result of a loan, or even if he paid the full price for the land, the debtor/seller could take back the field without having to pay any obligation to the creditor. § 41 of Hammurabi's laws blocked land held by a soldier or state tenant from being pledged as collateral. Such debtors were allowed to reclaim their fields, orchards or house "and also keep full legal possession of the compensatory payment which was given."

On the assumption that creditors tended to take more than their due when not strictly regulated, § 113 of Hammurabi's laws prohibited them from collecting grain debts on the threshing floor or from the granary without the owner's permission. In such cases the taker "shall return as much grain as he took; moreover, he shall forfeit whatever he originally gave as the loan."[392]

Creditors practicing such abuses were nothing new. Already in Urukagina's reform text we find reports of improper seizure. Laws §§ 23–24 of Eshnunna imposed harsh penalties for false distraint: A claimant who took someone's slave girl without valid reason had to give back two slave girls. If he took a *muškēnum*'s wife or child and caused their death, he himself might suffer capital punishment.

---

[380] Lewy 1958: .24 f.

[390] Rostovtzeff 1957.

[391] Roth 1997: 91. I use her translations of Hammurabi's laws throughout this discussion unless otherwise noted. This ruling would have applied even if (as typically was the case) these creditors were officials. See Driver and Miles 1952: 146, and King 1900: vol. III, 50 f. (Letter no. xxi).

[392] Roth 1997: 102.

Laws saving citizens from debt bondage

Creditors used deepening distress as an opportunity to organize debt bondage into a system of labor-for-hire. Many debtors contracted "to provide the creditor with a more or less considerable number of reapers for the harvest. Since the debtor must have been poor, they could only have been members of his own household or his community." [393] Debt pledges became a source of workshop and seasonal labor, or "article[d] as apprentices to craftsmen," with the income taken by the creditors who provided this servile labor.

Debt bondage had not yet reached serious proportions in pre-Sargonic times.[394] Most slaves were foreigners or war prisoners. Members of local communities without families usually became temple wards. Only in the first half of the 2nd millennium BC did bondage for debt become widespread, with creditors often mistreating the debt-pledges. It became normal Mesopotamian practice to pledge family members as security for back taxes, loans or other obligations, to sell them to gain the money to settle outstanding debts or, in troubled times, simply to ensure their physical survival.

Physical abuse was common. § 116 of Hammurabi's laws provides that if a debt servant dies as a result of being beaten or otherwise mistreated, the creditor's punishment must reflect the injured party's rank. If the deceased pledge was the debtor's son, the creditor's own son must be put to death. But if the pledge was a slave, the creditor must pay only one-third of a mina, and forfeit all claims on the debtor. However, § 115 stipulates that there is no basis for a claim if the pledge dies a natural death.

In patriarchal Babylonian society, wives, children and servants of debtors could be pledged to creditors or sold outright for new loans, but not for the spouse's pre-existing debts. A family head could be sold into bondage if he neglected his dike or irrigation canal and let a neighbor's crops be ruined by floods (§§ 53–54). If he lacked the means to replace the barley that was lost, he was to sell his property – and himself as well – to raise the money to pay restitution.

§ 117 stipulates that wives, daughters, sons or servants pledged to creditors were to go free after three years of working in the creditor's or purchaser's house. This law has given rise to considerable debate as to how strictly it was enforced.[395] Many historians believe that only the promulgation of *mišarum* could have freed most Babylonian debtors from bondage.

Why three years? One plausible explanation is that the pledge's labor service was counted as the interest due (*i.e.*, an antichretic loan in which the collateral produces the interest). At the going annual rate of grain-interest, one third, the debt principal would be worked off in three years, so the creditor would have received back the value of his original claim for payment.

Some creditors tried to hold onto pledges despite the fact that the debtor had paid off his obligation. No doubt some got away with this, particularly when debtors

[393] Diakonoff 1982: 42. He finds usury to be "the most potent factor in dissolution of kinship-economic ties," aggravated by the partition of inheritances into smallholdings.

[394] Diakonoff 1982: 96.

[395] A debt-bondservant was called a *nepûtum*, in contrast to an outright slave (*wardum*). Regular slaves were not freed by the laws of Hammurabi or anyone else. They could be redeemed or

did not know their rights, lost their case as a result of judicial favoritism or outright bribery, or feared creditor retaliation if they protested. On the assumption that some judges reversed earlier (presumably fair) decisions as a result of bribery, § 5 directed such judges to pay twelvefold damages for whatever their ruling would have been, and expelled them from the judicial assembly. On occasion Hammurabi confiscated the value of the bribes from guilty officials.

How Hammurabi's laws preserved economic balance

The guiding principle of Hammurabi's fiscal legislation was to avoid debt obligations in excess of the normal ability to pay, except in cases of negligence or where punishment was warranted. His laws recognized "acts of god" as disturbing normal relations, and restored the status quo ante by cancelling the debts that resulted – or at least had the interest charges waived. Cultivators unable to meet their obligations because their crops failed as a result of pests, or from storms or drought (attributed in § 48 to the storm god Adad) received a debt amnesty. Whoever leased an animal that died by an act of god was freed of all liability to its owner. A typical such amnesty occurred if the lamb, ox or ass was eaten by a lion or if an epidemic broke out (§ 266), while § 249 states: "If a man rents an ox, and a god strikes it down dead, the man who rented the ox shall swear an oath by the god and he shall be released" from liability. Travelling merchants who were robbed while on business were cleared of liability if they swore an oath that they were not responsible for the loss (§ 103).[396] This seems consistent with § 115, which freed creditors from liability for pledges who died of natural causes while in their custody.

Hammurabi's philosophy of deterrence regarding creditor abuses

Anti-government, pro-financial historians blame "the state" for being always a deadweight burden, imposing taxes and inefficient regulations that slow economic progress. That is the theory that underlies most economic textbooks today, and Nobel Economics Prizewinner Douglass North has notoriously elaborated it into a grand rightwing neoliberal theory of history.[397] In this modernizing spirit, Driver and Miles

> manumitted individually. Diakonoff 1982: 99 alleges: "a person liberated from debtor-slavery apparently could not start a normal household of a community member anew, but was absorbed into the royal economy." Finley 1983: 162) suspects that § 117 was not often enforced in practice. But neither does he believe that Ammisaduqa's *mīšarum* acts were "actually functioning law." He certainly is wrong regarding the latter. Hammurabi's law § 117 finds its counterpart in Ammisaduqa's edict § 21. Among the possible explanations for why surviving documents do not confirm practical applications of § 117 are: (1) it did not affect public finances as such; and (2) it was lived up to in practice and thus did not inspire lawsuits.

[396] On these rulings see Korošeć 1971: 278 ff. Noting that the subsequent Hittite laws (§ 75) also provide for the keeper of an entrusted animal to avoid liability by taking an oath that it "died by the hand of god," Korošeć adds that "The notion of *vis major*, overpowering circumstances, occurs first in the Uruk fragments" published by Clay.

[397] North 1985: 557–576, quoted approvingly by Silver 1995: 184.

opine that Hammurabi's penalties went too far in protecting needy cultivators from aggressive creditors and tax collectors.[398] These legal historians thought it unfair that a Babylonian creditor had to forfeit his entire claim merely because he tried wrongfully to extort more than the legal rate of interest. "This is hardly logical," they protest, "for he had no right to the illegal interest but had to be repaid his capital sum." Whereas today the only punishment would be to make such lawbreakers conform to the law, in Hammurabi's time they had to pay a price for being found guilty of such offenses. Koschaker likewise objects to the idea of letting debtors receive back their pledges without satisfying their debts to creditors found guilty of illegal practices.[399]

Such views miss the point of deterrent punishment, and that such punishment also provided restitution for injury. Payment of damages was to the injured parties rather than to the palace. Modern lawmakers have expressed the wish that our own legal system might aim more at restoring justice to the injured. New York State Attorney General Robert Abrams has accused our legal system of treating

> victims with indifference and disdain. ... Still preoccupied with punishing offenses against the 'sovereign' (in America, the state) in a crime-ridden, in-dustrialized society, criminal courts have ignored the victim's plight. Instead, victims are sent to civil courts to seek in private actions return of their pro-perty or damages. ... Such was not always the case. Restitution was insepa-rably linked with criminal punishment in many ancient cultures – among the Babylonians, Greeks, Romans, Germanic and Hebrew tribes. The Law of Moses, for example, required fourfold restitution for stolen sheep and fivefold for the more useful ox. Not until after the Middle Ages, when the emerging nation-state began to monopolize the institution of punishment, did the theory evolve that crime is an offense solely against the state, whose dignity alone should be vindicated by criminal punishment.[400]

Bronze Age rulers overrode the incipient creditor oligarchy centered mainly in their own bureaucracy, until fading palace power after 1600 BC eroded their ability to do so. By Greek and Roman antiquity, Judea and Israel, the poor and oppressed would demand in vain that their debts and back taxes be canceled, their family members returned from debt bondage, and their hereditary lands restored or new land provided. Seeking such liberty, populations occasionally shifted their loyalties to the attackers of their cities, or threatened civil war. But in the end, Greece and Rome, as well as rabbinical Judaism, shifted the legal balance strongly in favor of creditors.

---

[398] Driver and Miles 1952: 177.

[399] Koschaker 1917: 97f.

[400] Abrams 1984. The attorney general added: "Revival of restitution as a criminal sanction serves justice by repairing harm and providing a constructive way for offenders to pay their debts to society. Restitution also supports the rehabilitative aims of modern penology by encouraging the offender to acknowledge and assume responsibility for his act." Abrams hoped that "a renaissance may be in the wind. Several states now mandate victim restitution where feasible. ... Proceeds from the sale of forfeited property [of the criminal] must be distributed first to the victim as restitution or damages."

18. Samsuiluna's and Ammisaduqa's *mīšarum* Edicts, 1749 and 1646 BC

By the time Hammurabi defeated Larsa, he headed an alliance that had conquered Uruk, Isin and most of the south. Had he stopped here, he would have achieved an empire roughly equivalent to that of Ur III. But his attempt to cross the Tigris and conquer Elam proved fatal. No Mesopotamian empire builder had been able to hold Elamite territory for long, as counterattacks by the Elamites, Zagros mountain tribes and Amorites had repeatedly fragmented the region.

Yet Hammurabi pressed on, capturing Mari in 1757 BC, four years after defeating Rim-Sin. Three years later he took Eshnunna, but was unable to establish firm domination over it or other towns east of the Tigris. In the face of military attrition from these ventures, Hammurabi undertook a costly program of building walls around the Tigris and Euphrates region as far north as Sippar, recalling the "Maginot line" attempt by Shu-Sin of Ur three centuries earlier.

Hammurabi's son Samsuiluna takes the throne, 1749–1712 BC

Hammurabi lay dying in 1749, having ruled for 42 years. A letter from his son Samsuiluna to one of his subordinate officials tells how, upon taking control ("The king, my father, is sick and I sat myself on the throne in order to (govern) the country"), he found the land so burdened by debt that he remitted arrears due from many types of royal tenants. To strengthen the position of these debtors he "restored order (*mīšarum*) in the land," remitting their tax debts and directing that tablets recording non-commercial debts be broken. "In the land, nobody shall move against the 'house' of the soldier, the fisher, and other subjects." [401] His inaugural year accordingly was named "The year in which Samsuiluna established freedom (amar-gi) in Sumer and Akkad," using the Sumerian word from nearly six hundred years earlier. A contemporary letter reported that "The king promulgated a redress (*mīšarum*) for the land: he raised the golden torch for the land and ended the period of mourning for the land," [402] cancelling the agrarian debts that had accumulated since the last such *mīšarum* act.

---

[401] TCL 17 76, translation in Oppenheim 1967: 157 and Kraus 1984: 67. The letter is written to Etel-pi-Marduk in Larsa. Ellis 1976: 61n and 248 describes him as "a functionary within the agricultural hierarchy, in charge of ishshakkus," whom Lieberman 1989: 254 describes as "husbandmen." Evidently Hammurabi's *mīšarum* act, and those of Samsuiluna later, returned property "which Etelpi-Marduk had taken away from them." Lieberman points out that the wording of this letter explaining his actions "is clearly paralleled in the Edict which comes from his eighth year."

[402] Charpin 2013: 72.

Samsuiluna's letter explained that his action helped the "revenue-bringers" – local headmen and officials responsible for collecting stipulated amounts of crops or money owed to the palace by cultivators and public professionals. They were freed from liability for owing the palace for payments by individuals who could not pay.[403] To be sure, these officials often still tried to collect the peasantry's former obligations, keeping the take for themselves.

The fact that such heavy debts were run up did not mean that new loans had been made by officials and merchants, but simply that arrears and obligations were accruing without being paid. Most were tax arrears owed by impoverished families in the face of declining crop yields, military disruption and the exorbitant interest rates common for agrarian usury. A rising proportion of these debt claims was uncollectible except by stripping debtors of their means of livelihood on the land – and Samsuiluna had no interest in consigning these families to bondage or stripping away their land rights.

In an attempt to hold his alliance together and maintain a loyal fighting force, he proclaimed a new *mīšarum* act in his 8th year.[404] The date formulae for his 9th, 11th and 14th years indicate rebellions by cities seeking independence, while smaller towns defected to rival empire-builders. The walls of Ur, Uruk and Isin were dismantled by a military axis including Mari, Elam and Eshnunna, some Zagros mountain tribes and the Subarians north of Assur.[405]

Babylon's former rival, Larsa, asserted itself for the first time since Hammurabi defeated Rim-Sin in 1763. The latter's son, Rim-Sin II, captured Nippur and cities further south. "Within a year, Samsuiluna had successfully regained control, but the evidence suggests that this strife led … to a fatal destruction of the supply of irrigation water to the southern area. All of the southern cities were abandoned, while cities in central Babylonia, like Nippur and Isin, suffered considerably."[406] The costs entailed in this fighting sapped the region's strength, preparing the way for rebellion by local chieftains and the intrusion of a new force, the Kassites.

By 1720, Samsuiluna's 28th year of rule, the deteriorating military and economic situation enabled the Sealand "marsh peoples" from the far south (where the Euphrates spread out into the Persian Gulf) to conquer Babylonia as far north as Nippur, which "was abandoned, not to enjoy full urban renaissance until late in the Kassite period," concludes Stone. "Traditional restrictions on the sale of land outside of one's kin were loosened, and the poor members sold their land to whomsoever would buy it and left town."[407] Fields, other real estate and temple offices passed into the hands of officials with ready cash at "only a fraction of its previous value. Many of those who bought this property were the wealthy outsiders who had entered the property-owning group through adoption."

---

[403] See Ellis 1976: 27, and § 11 of Ammisaduqa's edict a century later.
[404] Hallo 1995: 82 thinks that this edict is the prototype for Ammisaduqa's later edict.
[405] Edzard 1967: 221f.
[406] Hinz 1972: 95f.
[407] Stone 1987: 27f.

Toward the end of Samsuiluna's reign "the temple office association apparently became the dominant group in the society, and even fields were being exchanged between unrelated office-holders."[408] Growing antagonism developed between wealthy and poorer branches of families, with the better off (usually those with temple offices) buying out the latter's land. They formed an aristocracy seeking to muster enough economic patronage to become rivals of the palace, accumulating property and becoming more or less independent of royal or communal controls.[409]

Assur, Mari and the southern Sealand swamp area broke away after Samsuiluna was defeated in 1743. Yet none of these revolts were over social policy disagreements, much less of anything like class warfare. Seth Richardson notes that for the Old Babylonian period (2000-1600), "more than five dozen rebellions (some successful) can be identified through state accounts alone (*i.e.*, through year-names and royal inscriptions)."[410] But these were rivalries *within* the existing system, not aiming to *change* the system. Revolts were not over how to re-structure a state, just to reject exploitative rulers, especially foreign occupiers. Debtors might flee the land, local rebellions try to throw off foreign control, and palace coups might be mounted, but economic policy as such was not at issue. Beyond the traditional ideas of proper royal practice proclaiming Clean Slates and protecting "the widow and the waif" there are no arguments over the virtues of public vs. private, no laws checking the conflict of interest of public officials such as are found in Rome's Justinian Code banning them from acquiring land or emoluments while in office. There are no known proposals or discussions of an alternative mode of organizing economic or social relations, only protests against the exploitation and misbehavior of overbearing rulers.

The Bronze Age political ideal, celebrated at New Year festivals and coronations, was that the tradition of royal proclamations of *mīšarum* and amar-gi could restore a primordial economic balance, less debt-ridden and with families able to support themselves on their cropland. Down through the Neo-Assyrian Empire in the first millennium, most revolts were power struggles, or local breakaways from empires.[411] The motivation was opportunistic. There is nothing like Plato's or Aristotle's contrast of different political constitutions, or today's economic ideology.

Ammisaduqa's *mīšarum* edict closes legalistic loopholes

How thoroughly were these edicts enforced? Assyriologists have confirmed that on some occasions they had a far-reaching effect, based on surviving legal records and judgments, above all from the reign of Ammisaduqa, whose first year-name reports that he "faithfully went forth like the Sun god Shamash for the sake of his country and instituted the redress (*mīšarum*) for his countless people."[412] His *mīšarum* act is the most elaborate on record (and the latest), spelling out much of what earlier

---

[408] Stone 1987: 18.
[409] Yoffee 1977: 12f.
[410] Richardson 2016: 33.
[411] See for instance Frahm 2016.
[412] Charpin 2013: 72.

proclamations left unspecified. Finkelstein, the first major translator of his act, translates this year-name as describing the king rising like the sun over his land to establish
"straight (correct) order" for his subjects.[413]

Finkelstein considered the Edict of Ammisaduqa from his inaugural year on the
throne in 1646 to be the most important Middle Bronze Age legal text, more important
even than Hammurabi's laws as far as the actual workings of society were concerned.[414] Providing a profile of Babylonia's financial, fiscal and land tenure arrangements in the 17th century BC, it is the only complete *mīšarum* act on record, as well
as being the last major document of the Amorite dynasty.

It had been sixteen years since Ammiditana proclaimed *mīšarum* in 1662. Ammisaduqa's edict annulled most agrarian debts paid after the intercalary month of
Addar II in his predecessor Ammiditana's final year. The explanation for its timing is
that most debts were due in the barley-harvesting month, Siman – the third month
of the Near Eastern calendar, corresponding to our own late May and early June.
The resources of cultivators normally were at their lowest ebb leading up to the harvest,
especially if a drought or other disruption occurred. In such cases creditors worried that
debts might be cancelled and anticipated matters by trying to extort whatever they could.

Ammisaduqa's edict aimed to prevent creditors from trying to collect debts prior
to the threshing time, and then refusing to refund the debtor's money when *mīšarum*
was proclaimed. § 5 prescribed that if a creditor "prematurely collected by means of
pressure, he must refund all that he received through such collection or be put to
death." If he had foreclosed on such debts, he had to "refund whatever he had received
through collection. He who does not make a refund in accordance with the royal
decree shall die."[415]

"The provisions of these acts anticipated a certain amount of skullduggery and
fraud aimed at circumventing the effect of the edict,"[416] notes Finkelstein.[417] One
way that creditors sought to evade *mīšarum* proclamations was to get debtors to waive
their rights under such royal edicts. A Mari text from the sixth year of Zimrilim
stipulates that "if an *uddurārum* is instituted, this silver will not be subject to that
measure."[418] This clause anticipates Hillel's prosbul waiver intended to get the debtor
to formally renounce any benefit of the debt remission.

---

[413] Finkelstein 1969; 1961 and esp. 1965 provides a thorough discussion. See also the bibliography
in Kraus 1984: 80. The special role of Sippar in this ritual act has not been explained.

[414] Finkelstein 1961: 93f.

[415] § 5, translated on pp. 526–528 of the paperback ANET (third ed.) lines 36–41.

[416] Finkelstein 1969: 58.

[417] In fact, it seems that Ammisaduqa's *mīšarum* proclamation in his first year led to lawsuits
brought to Sippar's Shamash temple for judgment concerning 60 GUR of barley taken from a
man. The case called for the rather infrequent addition of a judge from Babylon. The case is
cited in Eckart 1998: 127, citing BE 6/1 103 (Ams 1). See also his revised version (2008).

[418] ARM VIII 33, discussed by Durand 1982: 107 and Charpin 1987: 39.

Anticipating that creditors might try to use a similar deceptive ploy by drawing up their claims "as a sale or a bailment and then persist in taking interest," §6 of Ammisaduqa's edict voided such transfers. Creditors who attempted to "sue against the house of an Akkadian or an Amorite for whatever he had loaned him" were threatened with the death penalty. §7 laid down a similar punishment against creditors who claimed they had not given barley or silver as an interest-bearing loan, but as an advance for purchases or equity investment for mutual profit.

Ammisaduqa's edict devotes three paragraphs to ale wives. Their position apparently was a public one in which the palace provided beer on credit, while customers ran up tabs, to be paid on the threshing floor when the harvest was in. But §17 provides that after Ammisaduqa's *mîšarum* edict, "A tavernness who has given beer or barley as a loan may not collect any of what she had given as a loan." The obligations her customers had incurred *were* cancelled. Her net financial position did not suffer, because the edict also cancelled her own obligations to the royal beer suppliers.[419] The palace absorbed the loss, as it did with rent and tax collecting.

Some officials had prepaid wages or barley rations to infantrymen or sergeants harvesting crops on crown lands. Ammisaduqa's edict (§10) ruled that attempts to recover such advances could not be enforced, on pain of death. It was necessary to draw up new contracts. These rules confirm that the palace was the major relinquisher of claims, along with its officials, local headmen and private creditors.

Debt servitude and transfers of land as a result of poverty had not yet taken on the character of irreversibility they acquired in classical antiquity. §20 of Ammisaduqa's edict liberated Babylonian citizens. "If an obligation has resulted in foreclosure against a citizen … in consequence of which he placed his own person, his wife or his children in debt servitude for silver, or as a pledge – because the king has instituted mîšarum in the land, he is released; his freedom is in effect."

As was the case with bondservants, hereditary land that had been pawned for loans could be repurchased from the creditor by the debtor or his relatives. A key determinant as to whether a sale could be reversed was whether the "full price" had been paid. If there were full payment, properly witnessed as a voluntary transfer, the sale was considered genuine. But if the creditor had given only part of what the land was worth in a loan or tax lien, the transaction was subject to cancellation by the *mîšarum* decree.[420] Debtors who had pledged or sold their crop rights under such conditions had them restored.

The essence of royal restorations of the pre-existing order was recognition that the sale of land (or persons) usually was done only under conditions of economic distress. However, some transfers of property were socially desirable. Families whose numbers were dwindling sold land to families or clans increasing in size. *mîšarum*

---

[419] From Mesopotamia down through medieval Europe, women were the major tavern keepers. See Hartman and Oppenheim 1950.

[420] See Driver and Miles 1935: 287f. with regard to the Assyrian laws, and Lewy 1958: 26.

edicts did not annul these transactions. Nor did they affect the sale of townhouses or rooms in such buildings, which had passed into the investment market rather than being self-support land.

Such restorations of the *status quo ante* were made relatively easy by the fact that even when land was pledged, sold or relinquished to creditors, the debtors typically were not driven off their lands. Harvesting and other functions (including corvée labor duties) continued with the same personnel and in much the same way.[421] Unlike the case in Roman times, land passing into the hands of creditors was not stocked with slaves. What mainly changed was the distribution of crop yields between the former holder and the creditor. Smallholders still were able to survive without permanently losing their land and personal freedom, and hence without having to flee the country. That would become widespread practice throughout the Near East only by the Amarna Age c. 1400 BC.

There thus is little basis for the optimistic belief held by so many Victorian historians that the evolution of credit has been an ascent from primitive harshness to modern leniency. After Mesopotamia's initial financial takeoff in the third millennium the direction of evolution was from debt amnesties to the *reversal* of protecting debtors in classical antiquity. Even the militarized Neo-Assyrian rulers saw their self-interest to lie in liberating citizens from debt bondage, so that they could fight in the armies and provide corvée labor. The idea was anything but revolutionary. It was under the classical Greek and Roman oligarchies and their armies of mercenaries that bondage became irreversible and it took violent revolutions to annul debts, with most such revolutions failing.

---

[421] See Diakonoff 1969: 233.

19. Social Cosmology of Babylonia's Debt Cancellations

The year names, inscriptions and letters of Babylonian rulers describe how they cancelled back taxes and agrarian debts to save their economic order from being deranged. When simply used by itself, the phrase "to issue a *ṣimdatu*," an edict, usually referred specifically to a debt cancellation. Royal authority for such proclamations was built into the calendrical rhythms and cyclical renewal of nature. In an epoch when social rhythms were administered to coincide with celestial periodicities, these occasions were celebrated as a renewal of economic and social order along with the rhythms of nature.

Most studies of Bronze Age cosmology have focused on pantheons of the gods and goddesses, and how the creation myths and rituals of Mesopotamia provided prototypes anticipating their classical counterparts in Greece, Rome and the Jewish Bible. Less attention has been devoted to how this cosmology shaped the mundane details of everyday life, including the economic structuring of society, its debt and land tenure systems. Such attempts were discouraged during much of 20th century by the split of cuneiform studies into what Ignace Gelb has called "the struggle between Tammuz and onions" [422]: the aesthetic, cosmological and literary sphere as if it were distinct from the worldly economic sphere.

The New Year and coronation festivals were the paradigmatic celebrations, providing a cosmological context for Bronze Age debt cancellations. The essence of both festivals is renewal, restoring order cyclically. This principle applied above all when a new ruler took the throne to begin a new regnal cycle.

For nearly a thousand years, from Enmetena and Urukagina in the 25th century BC through Babylonian rulers in the 17th century BC, royal laws and debt cancellations appear to have been promulgated at the coronation festival. The New Year was celebrated at the spring equinox, the time for paying agrarian debts at the barley harvest. Payments of sharecropping debts and other obligations were weighed out on the threshing floor. It is not clear just when royal coronations took place, but inaugurating a new king was treated like a fresh start of time.

The New Year's festival fell outside the normal 360-day public administrative civic calendar, signifying the gap between the 354-day lunar year and the 365-day solar year. [423]

---

[422] Gelb 1967: 8. Our best records of prices from the Late-Babylonian period come from its astrological diaries, and its political history often is reflected better in astrological omen texts than in the formalized royal inscriptions.

[423] Bottéro 1961: 159 describes how, in the Neo-Babylonian period, the New Year festival was devoted to re-enacting the creation of order achieved by Marduk in his battle with the chaos-dragon Tiamat. "Like Marduk in the Creation Epic," observes Bottéro, the new ruler "finds himself confronted with a kind of chaos, and he must make a cosmos" re-establish "normal" order, free of the imbalances that have built up during the preceding period. The ruler acted the role of the sun-god in the staged battle against Tiamat, winning the cosmic struggle against disorder to create the social cosmos anew.

The incompatibility between the lunar and solar cycles leads to calendrical disorder between solar and lunar calendars. But calendrical order can be regularized by administrative fiat. So can economic and fiscal order. A propitious time was the New Year followed by a purging Saturnalia, a word that derives from Latin but whose basic practice goes back to Bronze Age Mesopotamia. It takes its name from the outermost planet visible in antiquity, Saturn, Babylonia's "Planet of Justice," reflecting that which is fixed (see the discussion of *kittum* in Ch. 16, p. 132).

Jupiter also was important. Driver and Miles cite an omen text warning that "if the planet Jupiter disappears, the gods will be angry and 'there must be justice,' meaning that there will be some disaster which will call for a special law to relieve the resultant distress."[424] The proper royal response to such an "act of god" is for the ruler to restore "straight order" by proclaiming *mīšarum*.

Charpin points out that Sumerian amar-gi signified the cyclical trajectory of the sun as well as the return of persons or property to their initial status.[425] The inference is that just as the sun returns each New Year to its equinoctial point of origin, so Mesopotamian "kings of justice" proclaimed a return to order out of chaos. The spirit combined rebirth of the physical cosmos with social justice, regenerating of society along with nature. Moral and physical blight were purged as men and beasts, houses, barns and temples were cleaned. During the course of the New Year's festival the rich and poor acted "ideally" towards each other in an auspiciously egalitarian atmosphere symbolizing a well-ordered state.

The years in which new rulers took the throne for the first annual coronation ceremony (commemorated in their second year-name) were the primary occasion for putting society back in order, to inaugurate their reign in an auspicious manner. Other important occasions for proclaiming *mīšarum* were years when new temples were dedicated or existing ones restored or renovated. As Frankfort has described the logic of these proclamations: "The inauguration of the temple took place on New Year's Day, so that the new beginning, which had been brought about by so great an effort of all, would be carried forward on the current of the new life which now set in."[426]

Assyriologists have not ventured to guess just where in the calendar Babylonian rulers raised the golden torch proclaiming *mīšarum* or its equivalent. If it was related to the twelve-day New Year's festival cycle, I suspect that it might have occurred on the eleventh day with the second Taking of Destinies by omen-reading.

Kraus warns that we do not know whether the golden torch was really burning, but a flaming torch certainly would have been the fastest way to signal a decree throughout the land. It may have been a preliminary sign that a detailed proclamation would follow.[427]

Reflecting the tradition of early Sumerian rulers as temple en officials, Babylonian kings depicted themselves as administrators first and foremost – builders of temples and later proclaimers of justice. Elizabeth van Buren found the characteristic

---

[424] Driver and Miles 1952: 22 f. See above for a similar text cited by Biggs.
[425] Charpin 1987: 39.
[426] Frankfort 1952: 11.
[427] Kraus 1984: 70ff.

iconography of kingship to be Ur-Namma or Hammurabi facing Shamash or an analogous sun god, holding the symbols of royal authority – the (measuring) rod and "ring" representing the coiled surveying rope used to lay out temple precincts – literally ruling.[428]

Among Bronze Age rulers, only the pharaohs are depicted in a military posture, receiving tribute or holding captured foreigners by the hair, about to smite them with a mace. In upstream Mari c. 1750, Zimrilim had a mural painted for his palace to reflect his military prowess, but found the only visual source to be Egyptian iconography – one of the rare instances of its being adopted outside of Egypt. "Even in the great imperial days of the second millennium, the Elamite kings, strongly influenced by adjacent Babylonia, seem to have stressed the nonmilitary aspect of kingship in their artistic representations." [429]

Military conflict and land pressure make *mīšarum* proclamations more frequent

Except for what may have been some military experiments in the fourth millennium, early Mesopotamian trade was conducted in a peaceful manner, if only because the means were lacking to sustain military imperialism. Yet city-states warred amongst themselves – and the larger the economic surplus grew, the greater a temptation it was for rival rulers and invaders to embark on military adventures.

Part of the explanation for this military dynamic lies in Mesopotamia's growth in population and the consequent pressure on its land and water resources. Towns and their surrounding rural areas and canals spread out until their boundaries collided, as in the long conflict between Lagash and Umma. From the Early Dynastic period onward, ambitious rulers sought imperial suzerainty for their cities – Kish, Uruk, Lagash, and then Akkad, Ur and finally Babylon. Nonetheless, Mesopotamia's "normal" condition was one of relative military and economic parity, as no city-state ever strongly dominated the others for long, much less put an end to local warfare. The "intermediate" Isin-Larsa period of small-statism represents the norm.[430]

However, the military overhead ended up absorbing the agricultural and commercial surplus. Local resources were taxed to sustain military campaigns. In addition to damaging the region's ecology, this dynamic forced much of the population into debt. In many parts of Babylonia the palace had difficulty collecting assessments, and found itself obliged to remit taxes and back debts in order to maintain the liberty and loyalty of the peasantry that formed the core of its army. Local collectors and headmen vied with the palace for the economic surplus being produced by the debtors who formed the bulk of the population.

Proclaiming *mīšarum* also no doubt enabled Hammurabi to consolidate popular support against an incipient oligarchy – not to speak of a legacy as a great and just ruler. But the ruler's limited ability to enforce his authority accelerated the buildup

[428] van Buren 1949: 434–450.
[429] Root 1979: 195.
[430] Hallo 1963: 12–15.

of wealth by individuals acting in their own self-interest, largely at the expense of the public institutions in which the surplus had long been concentrated. This privatization reduced Hammurabi's successors to "little more than figureheads, increasingly dependent on goods and services that were controlled by various traditionally ascribed and local groups. Finally, when the state was formally overthrown by a marauding Hittite army in 1595 BC, the locally recruited bureaucracy simply reverted to the position of a locally based aristocracy."[431] That is the underlying dynamic of Babylonian history. It recurred when the Mycenaean Greek economy collapsed after 1200 BC. Local headmen and the former palace bureaucracy accumulated wealth and patronage at the expense of the palace as its power waned.

Yet Assyriologists cannot trace for more than a few generations the family fortunes of men such as Balmunamhe of Larsa and his Babylonian counterparts, so conspicuous at the outset of the 18th century BC. There seems to have been a redistribution of such fortunes, partly by *mīšarum* acts and partly by royal re-assertion over commerce, by appointing *wakil tamkārī* overseers. Court records show that local officials tried to avoid returning property to their debtors and releasing debt servants after rulers proclaimed *mīšarum*, but were overruled when they overreached themselves. Yet despite rulings against them, headmen found leeway to take hitherto public or communally held property into their own hands, as long as they supplied the palace with its main objectives: crops, fighting men, corvée labor and money.

Charpin points out that when a local chieftain, Shunuhrahalu, wrote to Mari's ruler Zimrilim urging him to persuade a neighboring headman in Gashera to emulate Zimrilim's proclamation of *andurārum*, this was not "a reformist ideology."[432] The logic was conservative, socially expected and probably militarily necessary in view of the fact that, as Van De Mieroop observes: "The ideology of kingship of the time demanded that they [Babylonian kings] free people from such oppression."[433] Annulling debts at the start of a king's reign "made a new beginning, a clean slate onto which the king would make his mark." Such debt and tax amnesties were politically feasible because, as he explains, "the palace bore most of the losses. The benefit to the king was that the general population once again became directly responsible to him rather than to private financiers. In ideological terms, the edicts were further important as they showed the king as a guarantor of freedom, confirming his generosity and concern for the people."

Restoring the (idealized) order

Driver and Miles interpreted *andurārum* as "a release from a dependent position,"[434] because the major consequence was to liberate bondservants. Finet likewise translated *andurārum* as "liberation."[435] Such acts meant the freedom to return to one's original family after being freed by royal proclamation.

---

[431] Yoffee 1979: 13.
[432] Charpin 1987: 41.
[433] Van De Mieroop 2004: 11. ()

[434] Driver and Mile 1952, vol. I: 485 f. and 225.
[435] Finet 1983 [1973]: 134.

The essence of Mesopotamia's amar-gi, *andurārum* and *mīšarum* acts was to renew the status quo ante. Charpin objects to calling them "freedom" edicts, on the ground that house-born or purchased slaves who had been left with creditors as pledges were not manumitted, but were returned to their former masters (§ 21 of Ammisaduqa's edict).[436] Only formerly free debt pledges were liberated. Also not benefiting from *mīšarum* edicts were foreign slaves and aliens "resident within the ruler's territories for longer or shorter periods of time, usually as members of commercial or diplomatic missions."[437]

Perhaps we should call these edicts "renewal" acts, in the sense of restoring the economy to the way it was ideally "in the beginning" when the world presumably was created in good working order. A *mīšarum* decree

> was retroactive. Those measures aimed to restore legal, economic and social standards that had become downgraded. … within the mind of the people of ancient Mesopotamia there was no notion of what we would call social progress. Instead, the measures the king instituted under his *mîšarum* were measures to bring back the original order. The rules of the game had not been changed, but everyone had been dealt a new hand of cards. So it should not be a matter of surprise to us that these measures had to be regularly repeated, for recurring effects can be attributed to the same causes. There is no suggestion that any subsequent announcement of an edict of grace indicated that an earlier one had been ineffectively applied.[438]

Some modern commentators complain that debt cancellations were impractical because creditors would have avoided making loans if they anticipated the likelihood of a *mīšarum* act. But Charpin's review of the surviving documentation shows that just the opposite occurred: The volume of debt increased sharply prior to the royal edicts.[439] The vast majority did not reflect prior loans, but arrears on payments supposed to be made out of the harvest but which failed or was disrupted.[440] That is what prompted the royal edicts. They were responses to economic disorder, not the cause. They recognized the need to restore economic balance when the rural population's inability to meet its liabilities led to widespread insolvency.

Babylonia's *mīšarum* acts have suffered from much the same belittling as those of Urukagina levied by Samuel Kramer and, in a similar vein, Stephen Lieberman complains: "The need to repeat the enactment of identical provisions shows that the *mîšarum* provided relief, but did not eliminate the difficulties which made it

---

[436] Charpin 1987.

[437] Finkelstein 1969: 54. This is Finkelstein's ANET translation of Ammisaduqa's edict. He cites a similar provision "in Deut. 15:2 f. dealing with the remission (*šemittah*) of debts every seventh year: 'he (the creditor) shall not dun his neighbor or his kinsman, for the remission proclaimed is of Yahweh. You may dun the alien; but whatever is owing to you from your kinsman you must remit.'"

[438] Charpin 2013: 151.

[439] Charpin 1990: 186, elaborated in his article in Bongenaar (ed.) 2000: 186–203

[440] For a review of the various categories of debt see Wunsch 2002: 221–255.

necessary." True enough, but he follows up by leaping to the value judgment that: "What seems to have been needed was reform which would have eliminated all need for such adjustments, but the economic and political situation may not have allowed any such overall solution."[441]

No economy in history has found such a solution. The existence of debt and shortfalls in breaking even, or advances to smooth out gaps between planting and harvesting that could not be paid when normal production is interrupted – is inherent in the division of labor and the weather. The problem occurs when debt grows to exceed the ability to pay – all too frequent a phenomenon in our own modern world.

Today's economies still have credit cycles, personal debt crises and wartime emergencies – but no longer accept the idea of clean slates even when the alternative is debt-ridden austerity and economic polarization between creditors and debtors. The Jubilee 2000 movement and similar groups are calling for debt writedowns, and such calls have grown louder in the wake of the 2008 crash and subsequent debt deflation that is plaguing countries from Greece to Argentina. A clean slate would be progress to escape from instability.

Mesopotamia's "economic order acts" represent civilization's early legislation aimed at keeping the growth of interest-bearing debt within the economy's ability to pay. The basic principle was to leave "silver" loans to entrepreneurs to finance productive commercial investment intact. However, any society needs to annul financial claims that find no counterpart in productive capital and whose interest – and even payments of the principal – force debtors into insolvency. That often was the case with "barley" debts.

The distinction between productive commercial interest and parasitic usury is found in the 12th and 13th centuries AD. Church doctrine permitted interest to be charged when loans provided a gainful opportunity for the borrower as well as lender. Such loans usually were mercantile, and took the form of a foreign exchange transfer. An *agio* fee was permitted, on a logic akin to the Babylonian distinction between "silver" trade obligations and agrarian "barley" debts.

The end of the Old Babylonian Period

The 17th century BC was one of steady drains on the Babylonian economy. In addition to its military and debt problems, the ecological situation was worsening. Population growth led to over-cultivation and over-irrigation of the land, silting up of the canals, and abandonment of alternate fallow seasons.[442] An urban exodus ensued "toward the freedom of open and unpoliced regions," concludes Oppenheim: "The concentration of capital within the cities produced urban absentee landlords for whom tenant farmers worked; furthermore, it led to increased moneylending which, in turn, drove farmers and tenant farmers either to hire themselves out to

---

[441] Lieberman 1989.

[442] See for instance the comments of Adams and Jacobsen in Kraeling and Adams, eds., 1958; Gibson in Downing and Gibson, eds., 1974; Yoffee, 1977 :149, 13; Adams 1981; and Stone, 1987: 14 f.

work in the fields or to join outcast groups seeking refuge from the burdens of taxation and the payment of interest."[443] A class of what modern terminology calls "free laborers" came into being, lacking the traditional security and landholding rights of membership in the landed communities.

In addition to Mesopotamia's declining ability to generate a crop surplus, its export markets (and hence, supplies of raw materials) were shrinking. The north-westward expansion of Assur and Mari into Asia Minor compensated in part for the decline in the Indus trade, but the Hittites and local upheavals cut off this commerce, which had been an engine of the Mesopotamian takeoff.[444]

Land tenure was shedding its customary social responsibilities as usury spread throughout the Near East. Debt arrears led to "the dispossession of the [small] land-owners and, sometimes, even the flight of considerable numbers of them from their communities; by the widespread practice of bond slavery; and by the appearance of large individual and privileged estates," notes Diakonoff. Creditors foreclosed on land, and wealthy individuals bought it from poor holders. The new owners tended "to discontinue their communal services and, perhaps, even to stop paying taxes in kind, shifting this 'communal duty' to people dependent upon them. Thus ... what used to be a single group of people enjoying equal political rights (members of a territorial community), were now divided into a social estate of nobility free from community obligations, and an estate of working people who had to perform the community obligations for themselves and for their masters."[445]

The new appropriators – or at least some of them – were "immune from the redistribution of shares of land and from community control," and "could do essentially what they wanted with their holdings irrespective of whether at that time they performed any duties as community members or not."[446] Oppenheim makes a similar point: "The weakened central authority of the Middle Babylonian period was evidently ready to cede to persons of special status and to sanctuaries its right to collect taxes, to levy soldiers and workers, and to use the services of its subjects."[447]

The feeble reign of Ammisaduqa's successor, Samsuditana (1625–1595 BC), eleventh and last ruler of Hammurabi's dynasty, ended in a Hittite raid from Asia Minor in 1595. Although not a full-scale military campaign, it left Babylonia prone to occupation by the Kassites, apparently in conjunction with tribesmen from the Zagros region. These hitherto insignificant people from east of the Tigris ruled Babylonia until 1169, by delegating management to local headmen to a greater extent than Hammurabi and his successors had done.

The ensuing privatization terminated the economic renewal practices that had been customary throughout the Early and Middle Bronze Age. Babylonia entered its so-called Dark Age. "Babylonia never became a region of city-states again, but metamorphosed into a large territorial state with a single capital city whose rulers had

[443] Oppenheim 1967: 39 f.
[444] Muhly 1973: 453.
[445] Diakonoff 1982: 42 and 54 f.
[446] Diakonoff 1982: 54.
[447] Oppenheim 1972: 123.

varying degrees of control over the countryside. No competing city-states were ever to emerge again. That was the most lasting consequence of Hammurabi's rule in political terms."[448]

Yet at no time in the Old Babylonian period are there signs of popular protest or revolts, much less of revolutionary fervor. If palace coups occurred, they were not over social policy disagreements. Debtors fled the land and local rebellions threw off foreign control, but economic policy was not at issue. The Bronze Age political ideal, celebrated at New Year festivals and coronations, was that the tradition of royal proclamations of *mīšarum* and amar-gi could restore a primordial economic balance, less debt-ridden and with families able to support themselves on their cropland.

[448] Van De Mieroop 2005: 39.

20. Usury and Privatization in the Periphery, 1600–1200 BC

The Middle Bronze Age saw breakdowns of royal authority to protect small landholders and override privat creditors that occurred during 1600–1200 BC. Down through classical antiquity the power of the kings who remained was undercut by administrators and powerful families who broke free to pursue their self-interest. Officials and local headmen took over temple and palace land and workshops as their own personal estates. Labor hitherto dedicated to temple or state corvée projects was appropriated by the emerging oligarchies, which controlled the Councils of Elders (senates) that curtailed royal authority. The result was economic domination by wealth over land and labor.

Our modern era views the ending of royal power to proclaim clean slates as a progressive evolution toward private property and the security of creditor claims. But to populations living through these transition periods, the mid-second millennium was a period of disintegration and seizures of property and subjugation of conquered populations on an unprecedented scale. Land and urban economies were appropriated by the Kassite bands that occupied Babylonia, by the Hittites who conquered Asia Minor and Syria, by the Mycenaeans in Greece, and by the Vedic Aryan-speakers in the Indus Valley.

Appearing in Asia Minor slightly before 1900 BC, the Hittites are documented by 1770 blocking Assyrian caravan trade with central Anatolia. Under their New Kingdom dynasty (15th–12th centuries BC) they occupied the broad region from the Mediterranean to the Black Sea and rose to dominate Anatolia's former master, Assyria. Their trade is only scantily attested, and half the commercial Hittite vocabulary has been borrowed into their Indo-European language from other sources.

The Hittite laws are mainly political and social, not dealing with commerce or debt. The only known reference to debt in a royal amnesty occurs in an edict by the 12th-century BC ruler Tudhaliya that seems to allude to *wergild*-type compensation debts that had been paid by offenders to their victims:

> And if someone has given ransom for blood, and he has purchased himself from you; whether (the ransom be) a field or a person, no one shall release it.
>
> If he (the holder of the ransom) has taken those things along with his (the culprit's) wives and sons, he shall release them (?) to him.
>
> And if someone has given ransom for theft, if it is a field, they shall not release it. ... (II 3–10).[449]

The implication seems to be that exile and similar social punishments may have been forgiven by royal amnesties, but not property given as compensation to injured parties. If monetary lending existed for tax arrears and other agrarian obligations, the resulting debts likely would have been cited in this amnesty.

[449] Discussed in Westbrook and Woodard 1990: 641–659.

The Hittite concept of "release" is limited mainly to the release of subject populations from corvée duties so that they can serve in other capacities. "Hattušili I [1586–1556] states in the Hittite version of his annals that, upon capturing Hahhum, he freed (*arawe-*) its people from *šahhan* and *luzzi* [corvée] duties and released them to the sun goddess of Arinna; in the Akkadian version, he says he 'placed them in the house of the sun goddess of Arinna, and beneath the heavens I established their *andurārum*.'" Conversely, Queen Ashmunikkal "restored dedicated personal to secular jurisdiction, so that they could be levied for duties to the state."[450]

In Kassite Babylonia, political and economic power was decentralized, especially after 1380 BC. Its rulers erected *kidinnu* stones at the gates of major towns, and marked the boundaries of rural fields and the temples to attest to royal grants by the palace exempting communities or individuals from tribute, taxes or other obligations. These exemptions limited royal authority to the rural areas.

Such tax privileges and liberty from royal fiscal incursions were not sufficient to revive economic growth. Mesopotamia experienced rapid de-urbanization in the four centuries following the fall of Babylon. The period is dark in the sense that few records are known, which may be a sign that palace and temple accountability was curtailed.

Neighboring Elam's historical records disappear after 1500, not to resurface until the late 1300s.[451] By that time a different kind of society was emerging, a Late Bronze Age world peopled by Hittites and Hurrians (falling under the sway of a new Assyrian empire) as well as Kassites and a continuing influx of Amorites. Trade with the Indus Valley was not restored. Indo-European-speaking tribes swept into Persia, while Egypt was occupied by Hyksos tribesmen for over a century (1674–1567 BC), and subsequently was drawn into the Levant as a military power.

Seizures of palace and temple enterprise and land, often by warlords, became a dress rehearsal for antiquity's classical aristocracies to emerge after the region-wide devastation and demographic displacement at the dawn of the Iron Age 1200–800 BC.

Decentralization and grabitization gain momentum

The trends that gained momentum about 2000 BC reached their peak c. 1600. Nomadic pastoral Amorites from the west, Zagros mountain tribesmen and Kassites from the east, Hurrians from the northern Lake Van region east of Assur, and even a Hittite incursion from Asia Minor via Syria, as well as Sealand raids were led by tribal chieftains who parceled out the land and temple estates among their own followers.

As would become the case with the fall of Rome two millennia later, the two major causes of Babylonian collapse were economic polarization resulting from agrarian usury dispossessing the cultivators, and barbarian invasions. From Mesopotamia to the eastern Mediterranean, absentee appropriators stepped into the breach left by the weakening of central power. Large stretches of land were abandoned when crop yields declined and desertification spread throughout southern Mesopotamia. Canals silted up as royal authority and responsibility waned.

[450] Von Dassow 2013: 153.
[451] Hinz 1972: 221 f.

By 1400 BC most documented commerce was among royal households for their own use, mainly consisting of luxuries and presents among ruling elites. Documentation of commerce in this period primarily relates to gift exchange among rulers, not the bulk raw materials trade that had been dominant in the third millennium BC. This elitist trade was handled largely by ambassadors or messengers as a branch of diplomatic relations, not by mercantile traders. Documented Late Bronze Age trade throughout the Near East was largely "financed by the palace (and to a lesser degree by the temple – mainly in Egypt). The central administration employed its own merchants, who were institutionally set in the ranks of its subordinate personnel," observes Carlo Zaccagnini. "The role of private entrepreneurs seems to be rather limited."[452] In newly emerging areas such as Nuzi, *tamkāru* merchants belonged to the palace staff, receiving rations along with the royal scribes, shepherds and textile workers. In this reading, the role of independent traders diminished rather than expanded in areas where chieftains and warlords took over and sought to centralize economic control in their own hands and those of their supporters. As Zaccagnini summarizes the change:

> In the Old Babylonian period, the ideal of 'justice and equity' (*kittu u mēsharu*) which qualifies the king's figure and action, corresponds *inter alia* to an interest in limiting the consequences of excessive generalized indebtedness – hence the edicts of remission of debts. In the course of the Late Bronze Age, and specifically in the West, this situation undergoes a deep change: the traditional organization of the family groups, which are the basis of the social texture of the state, are disintegrating; the king emerges out of an elite of warrior nobles that hold completely different relations with the rural population: the exploitation of the peasant community is now common practice in the socio-economic activity of the palace. The edicts of remission are no longer issued.[453]

Or at least they were circumvented. Where they do survive in the textual record, they are cited "in documents written by private individuals: there we read that the transaction took place after the edict." Zaccagnini concludes that "the contracting parties expressly aimed at stating the invalidity of the clauses of the edict (in case an edict of remission were proclaimed)."

The process seems to have begun when Babylonian rulers turned over control of temples in Nippur and other buffer territories to chieftains in exchange for their providing contingents of fighting men, crops and/or money – or simply leaving southern Mesopotamia in peace. Financial, political and military power centered increasingly around these headmen, not institutions such as temples or independently wealthy professional families of traders and other entrepreneurs.

The main direction of social mobility was downward, mainly as a result of debt. Babylonian proverbs tell the story. "The strong man lives off what is paid for his

[452] Zaccagnini 1977: 171 ff.
[453] Zaccagnini 1977: 176 f.

strength, and the weak man off what is paid for his children," *i.e,.* through debt bondage or distress sale.[454] "The *awīlum* who makes loans as a creditor – his grain remains his grain, while his interest is enormous."[455] The Babylonian Theodicy deplores how "the opulent nouveau riche ... heaps up goods" and "has multiplied his wealth," while the gods "speak in favor of a rich man" and let riches go to him despite the fact that the rich "harm a poor man like a thief ... and extinguish him like a flame."[456]

The Kassite Age in Babylonia, 1600–1200 BC

In 1595 BC a Hittite army descended via Syria to raid Babylon and carried off its statue of Marduk. Meanwhile, Kassite tribesmen had been filtering into Babylonia from the Iranian highlands northwest of Elam since about 1750. Moving into the political vacuum, they held what power existed in Babylonia for nearly half a millennium, until 1157 – the longest rule in Babylonian history. Their personal names indicate that their language was neither Indo-European nor Semitic. They adopted the Babylonian language (Akkadian) for writing, while keeping Sumerian as the language of record-keeping and scholarly compilations of old epics and other literary works.

The Kassite conquerors held the support of older towns and chiefdoms by remitting their taxes and tribute, as it is made known on *kudurrus* (also called "boundery stones").[457] This left power in the hands of local headmen. There are no records of *mīšarum* acts or other signs of centralized control. In fact, economic records disappear, which is what makes the epoch "dark" to historians.

Babylonia was de-urbanized and its population shrank as the number of settlements was reduced by over 80 per cent in the half-millennium after the collapse of Hammurabi's dynasty, "leaving only small outposts scattered at wide intervals along watercourses which previously had been thickly settled."[458] Southern Mesopotamia was left in a condition scarcely more urban than the Indus Valley or Central Asia. Much of the land was not resettled until the Neo-Babylonian period, 539–331 BC. The Fertile Crescent's economic thread cannot be picked up again until the 1400s BC, and by that time a new world had emerged. The most important newcomers were the Hittites in Asia Minor and the Hurrian-speaking Mitanni east of the Middle Euphrates, in the Zab River and Lake Van region of what today is northeast Iraq.

---

[454] Lambert 1960: 248.
[455] Lambert 1960: 149, quoting the *Dialogue of Pessimism*.
[456] Lambert 1960: 52f.
[457] Brinkman 1974: 395–408. Slansky 2003 calls them "entitlement *narûs*" but this term failed to replace the customary "*kudurru*", see the new edition of *kudurrus* by Paulus 2014.
[458] Jacobsen and Adams 1958: 1254.

De-Urbanization of Babylonia[459]

Period	Percentage Nonurban (10 ha. or less)	Percentage Large Urban (more than 40 ha.)
Early Dynastic II/III	10.1%	78.4%
Akkadian	18.4	63.5
Ur III/Larsa	25.0	55.1
Old Babylonian	29.6	50.2
Kassite	56.8	30.4
Middle Babylonian	64.2	16.2

Figure 29: De-Urbanization of Babylonia in the Kassite period

Creditor stratagems in Nuzi, 1450–1400 BC

The town of Nuzi originally was Gasur, an Assyrian trade outpost about ten miles southwest of modern Kirkuk. Hurrian speakers dominated Assur from about 1700 BC onward, and spread south into Babylonia by 1600 BC as Hammurabi's dynasty lost control. Jankowska suggests that they "were first hired as warriors by the local kinglets and later seized power ... and merged or coexisted with the local population."

The Hurrian kings had Indo-Iranian names and their pantheon had Indo-European-type deities, yet their language was not Indo-European.[460] Like the Kassites, they adopted an Akkadian dialect for their written records, along with Babylonian economic practices including interest-bearing debt, and with it the stratagem of fictive adoptions enabling creditors to inherit the lands of their debtors.[461]

These practices are documented in tablets dating from 1450–1400 BC, including some of the largest cuneiform archives yet discovered. The most extensive text group concerns the family of Tehib-Tilla, a wealthy landowner and usurer whose business affairs were so extensive that he employed over forty scribes. Emulating the strategy that his father had used, he invested the money he obtained through usury (the typical annual rate of interest was 50 percent) to acquire land. Covering five generations, the archive documents the assembly of great estates in his family's hands.[462]

Land was not yet freely alienable at that time, but citizens had the right to adopt creditors as their legal heirs. "Soon after the discovery and first publication of the Nuzi texts," observes Zaccagnini,

---

[459] Adams 1965: 242.

[460] Landsberger 1939 and Jankowska 1991: 238 f.

[461] Fincke 2010: 35, cites various terms used for such transfers: "mock adoption," "sale-adoption," "real estate adoption."

[462] Jankowska 1969: 239, and 1991: 245f., describes the archive as including more than 150 contracts "by which the other parties conveyed to him, as to their adoptee, their hereditary plots," covering "a thousand hectares of land in seven different districts of the country. He preferred parcels situated along the roads; roads are the backbone of commerce, the control of which gives power."

it was noted that not a single contract of sale of land was represented among the hundreds of documents stemming from private archives. Apparently, the only way to transfer title of real estate to third parties was to let the purchaser enter into the family group of the seller(s), by conferring on him the position of 'son' (in a few cases 'brother') and thus enabling him to inherit a 'share' of the family patrimony; in most cases a plot of land. In turn, the 'adopted' son presented the adoptant with a 'gift,' consisting of commodities (in most cases barley, but also other staples).[463]

The prospective buyer/creditor circumvented traditional safeguards on land tenure by providing money or food to a landholder in exchange for being adopted as his heir, and waiting to inherit the land under disposition by the debtor's will. One scholar describes how women used this "sale-adoption" stratagem despite the fact that they could not inherit real estate under Hurrian law. They had themselves adopted as a son![464] "All Tehib-Tilla's deeds of acquisition of immovables took the form of adoption 'as son' into the family of the former owner of the parcel," summarizes Jankowska. "The parcels were alienated by the owners mainly for a miserable compensation because this happened during a period of drought."[465]

Adoptions in archaic communities "originally" aimed at helping ensure continuity of the clan or family lineage. But adopting creditors from outside the clan weakened its traditional cohesiveness. In addition to transferring land from poor families to wealthy ones, notes Diakonoff, "the obligation of communal labor-service continued, as a rule, to rest on the vendor's now very much curtailed allotment."[466] Nuzian usurers even took possession of canals.

The disruption was softened by leaving the debtor and his family in possession of the land for the duration of his life. However, "Tehib-tilla's tenants had to perform their *ilku*-services exactly as they did when they were still full owners of the land." The corvée-labor duty thus was shifted off finance onto debtors. "It would thus seem that, as long as the owner … stayed on the land which was liable for *ilku*-duties and worked it [even as tenants], they themselves were responsible for the performance of the *ilku*."[467]

Nuzi's first royal debt cancellations appear relatively late, "no doubt intended to lessen the social strain." The Hurrian word for such proclamations was *šudūtu*, the equivalent of a Babylonian *ṣimdatu* "proclamation." It connoted a general release for

---

[463] Zaccagnini 1984: 81. Fincke 2010 cites a creditor's warning to a family member not to sell his land to outsiders – a sign that this was being done.

[464] Lacheman 1973: 99f.

[465] Jankowska 1991: 245f.

[466] Diakonoff 1982: 55. To be sure, Jankowska 1969: 248 notes, "ownership based on adoption was always disputed by the kinsmen of the vendors ('adopters')." In the case of Tehib-Tilla's properties, lawsuits erupted after his death when sons of the numerous debtor/sellers protested the transfer of property to his son Ennamati and other heirs.

[467] Zaccagnini 1984: 91. He adds that inasmuch as the *ilku* consisted of personal labor services, "It would thus be physically impossible for a single person, such as Tehib-tilla or the like, to be personally liable for hundreds of *ilku* per year."

real estate as well as for bondservants, akin to Babylonian *andurārum*.[468] These *šudūtu* proclamations required "all who may have had claim upon the property involved to present them, doubtless within a certain period of time, to the authorities," notes the term's early explicator, Ernest Lacheman.[469]

Maidman finds that despite these proclamations, lands remained in the hands of wealthy appropriators.[470] But Tehib-Tilla's family lost their newly acquired property when Assyria attacked the region and Nuzi's garrison-fortress was occupied by a war leader from another clan, whose own family documents cite "the 'new liberation' of the citizens of Arrapkhe [the Nuzian region] from debts." Subsequent Nuzian contracts make much the same statements as are found in Babylonia, asserting that they were drawn up *after* the last royal proclamation and therefore were immune from debt cancellation until the ruler should announce a new such edict.

How indebtedness led to a dependent labor force

Until free-floating groups of able-bodied men for year-round hire came into being, the main dynamic forcing individuals to work for others was debt. Their employer was their creditor, and they worked off the interest with their labor service. They did not receive wages, because the emergency money or food already had been transferred as an interest-bearing loan.

The process had begun by pledging slaves, daughters and wives in third-millennium Sumer for what archaeologists politely call household services, and spread to harvest labor. By the second millennium this practice led to outright bondage. The characteristic Nuzian labor-service contract was called a *tidennu* agreement, a longterm antichretic loan in which creditors took their interest in the form of labor services or the land's crop.

One such contract clause stated explicitly: "The gold (exchanged commodity) does not bear interest." That meant that the servant provided by the debtor "does not receive his hire." As Eichler explains:

> The creditor's loan is covered in full by the person of the *tidennu* in 80% of the transactions. Furthermore, the phrase 'to stay in/enter the house of [the creditor]' signifies that the *tidennu* enters into a subservient relationship by becoming part of the creditor's household, and, in all likelihood, by receiving his support from him.[471]

Such contracts ran until such time as the debtor/servant could pay back the creditor/employer's advance, or until the ruler proclaimed *šudūtu*. Contracts often stipulated fines for non-compliance, typically twice the value of the original loan. The result

---

[468] Gordon 1935 cites a Nuzi text using the term *ina arki andurāri*.
[469] Lacheman 1962: vol. I., p. 233.
[470] Maidman 1996.
[471] Eichler 1973: 8, 27 and 40 f.

was "a type of indentured servitude. As long as the debt remains unpaid, the *tidennu* loses his freedom of movement." [472] The condition tended to be permanent.

The Hurrian-Hittite "Song of Release" extends the application of *andurārum*

Some time around 1600 BC the Hittites conquered the upstream town of Ebla. A lesser echo of the power that had dominated northern Syria a thousand years earlier, the city had passed from Amorite control to become part of the Hurrian kingdom. The "Song of Release" attributed Ebla's defeat to the refusal by its council of elders to follow the commandment of its god Teshub to liberate the population of Igingallish. The inhabitants of that town (west of the Euphrates) had been taken as war prisoners and turned over to serve, cook and wash clothes for Ebla's elite families.

Translated into Hittite c. 1400 BC in a bilingual edition, the poem describes the tension that had grown throughout the Bronze Age between wealthy families becoming an oligarchy and royal authority to proclaim liberation (Hurrian *kirenzi* = Hittite *para tarnumar* = Akkadian *andurārum*). At issue is is the morality of reducing citizens to bondage – not only indebted bondservants but entire populations taken as war prisoners.

The god Teshub commands the city's king Megi to "release the sons of Igingallish." Their captivity evidently had spanned the reigns of three local kings and six kings of Ebla prior to Megi's reign. Teshub tells Megi:

> If you (pl.) decree release [*nakk kirenzi*] for Ebla the fate is (this):
> you (pl.) decree release, to god-like (power) I shall exalt your weaponry,
> Your weaponry will beat the opponent,
> gloriously shall your field(s) thrive.
> If you (pl.) do not decree release, the fate for Ebla is (this):
> On the seventh day I shall come upon you. (I/II 1–23)

Megi goes before Ebla's council of elders and urges release of the captives. But the council's spokesman Zaralla rejects his demand, pointing out that the conquered population had become cooks, waiters and launderers. He tells Megi that if he wants a release, he should start by giving away his own son and return his wife to her father's household (Song of Release, IV 2–7.)

"Megi went weeping to Teshub and assured him that he tried to purify Ebla from sin, but was rejected (IV 15–19): 'I myself grant it, (but) my city does not grant release.'" [473] Teshub himself then goes before the assembly and insists that it free the sons of Igingallish from bondage. Zaralla replies that they will take care of his cult, feed it, give him silver and gold, and even pay his debts, but will not free the subject population because they need its services. Teshub threatens to destroy the city if it does not comply:

---

[472] Eichler 1973: 45.
[473] Von Dassow 2013: 127–165. My quotations from this poem are taken from this article.

And the city of Ebla I shall destroy,
Like a place of no habitation I shall make it,
The lower town I shall smash like a cup,
the upper town I shall trample in the dump,
the agora inside it, like a cup,
I shall crush underfoot.

The tablets break off here, and there is some question about their original sequence. A plausible re-ordering by Gernot Wilhelm depicts Teshub of abandoning Ebla and withdrawing to the underworld, leaving the city to be conquered by the Hittites. The Eblaites then mourn the departed god and hope to effect his return by restoring his directive to care for subjects who are needy, hungry and sick, not oppress them.[474]

The past few decades have seen a debate over just what kind of release was meant. The Hurrian word *kirenzi* corresponds to Akkadian *andurārum*, which typically referred to the remission of agrarian nonbusiness debts as described in the preceding chapters. But the *Song of Release* calls for manumitting populations enslaved by their conquerors. So debt bondage is not at issue in this poem, contrary to the assumption of its earliest translators.

As for just what "release" meant, Mary Bachvarova believes that Teshub punished Ebla because of the bad behavior of the city's elite in forcing "the people of Igingallish … to work for the Eblaite nobles" instead of dedicating them to fulfill the ritual obligations owed to Teshub and other gods or the royal ancestor cult of Ebla's dead kings. In her reading, Teshub wanted the prisoners to be liberated released from civic duties simply to be transferred to feed and serve his sanctuaries.

To support her reading she cites Hattushili I's *Annals*, reporting that he "took the hands of the female slaves from the millstone, and the hands of the male slaves from the sickles. I freed them from *shahhan* and *luzzi*. I ungirded their belts. I released them to my lady the sun goddess of Arinna in perpetuity."[475] What seems at first glance to be liberation thus would only shift the duties of slaves from serving its wealthy families to serve the temples.

This certainly is one meaning of *andurārum*, the word used in the Akkadian version of Hattushili's *Annals*. No doubt such diversion of dependent labor from temples and also state service occurred as oligarchies gained increasing power. But the central concern of the *Song of Release* is the ethic that "permanent subjection of free men is unjust" and violates the principle that "all are originally subjects of the

---

[474] Wilhelm 2013: 187–191.

[475] Bachvarova 2005: 52. *šahhan* were government-imposed services and payments in return for land use. *luzzi* referred to corvée labor tasks owed to the state or its officials, bailiffs, princes, or to the gods (temples), such as building fortifications and roads, or harvesting vineyards. See Hittite Laws § 56. She notes (p. 46) that a number of Hittite laws and treaties reflect "how labor obligations imposed on men prevent them from serving the gods, and how Hittite royalty displayed their piety through decrees which freed people from such obligations in order to better serve the gods or the royal dead."

gods alone."[476] Von Dassow's analysis shows that what is meant is indeed a return to the "original state" as in Sumerian amar-gi. That idea of liberation as restoring a norm is the key, not merely a transfer of civic servitude to temple service. Divine commandments to protect the economic and personal liberty of citizens is what gave the temples and their cults ideological authority in the first place.

Teshub's warning that he will destroy Ebla is akin to threats by the Biblical prophets, such as Amos (2: 6–7; 3: 10; 4: 1, etc.) that "Yahweh will wreck their mansions and strongholds" if they do not liberate their subjects, and Jeremiah 34 (discussed below in Chapter 23) warning that the Lord will withdraw his support and Judea will be conquered by Babylon as a result of Zedekiah's refusal to make good on his promise to free the bondservants.

Wilhelm's reading highlights a further Biblical parallel: The defeat of a city does not necessarily mean the defeat of its patron god. Just the opposite: It may mean that the city has behaved in a selfish way instead of obeying the god's commandments. "The divine power remains unaffected by the catastrophe; on the contrary, it becomes even more apparent."[477] Ebla was destroyed was not because its god was weak, but as punishment for holding its realm's subjects in bondage to its wealthy families.

Already in the mid–2nd millennium we thus find the literary trope or aetiology that became explicit in the preachings of the Biblical prophets. The consensus view of the poem's meaning is that "Accounts such as these reveal the limits of royal power in the face of elite privilege and appropriation."[478] Ebla's kings were constrained by rising power of their oligarchy, whose selfishness and oppression was responsible for Ebla being destroyed.

What was not destroyed was the ethic of *andurārum*, the traditional ethic that free citizens should not be reduced to bondage more than temporarily, and at some point should have their liberty restored.

Expropriation of cultivators from the land

Once debtor-cultivators or captured and enslaved populations faced the prospect of losing their land irreversibly, they were liable to flee. Some banded together to survive as outlaws in a world in which access to the land was closed off in one region after another. "One of the causes of flight certainly is personal indebtedness," finds Renger. "Entire villages had to flee to avoid bondage for debt."[479] Many fugitives became *hapiru*, landless have-nots working as migrant seasonal labor or mercenaries, or joined robber bands. Most seem to have been of Amorite stock, but the agrarian problem was so widespread that the term *hapiru* did not signify an ethnic identity. Diakonoff points to "the emergence all over the Near East of the characteristic social group of the *ʿapiru / hapiru*, who earlier were taken for the ancestors of the Hebrew tribes. …

---

[476] Von Dassow 2013: 159.
[477] Wilhelm 2013: 191.
[478] Scheidel 2017: 55.
[479] Renger 1994: 197.

They appear simultaneously with the mass enslavement for debt at the coming of the 2nd millennium BC, and disappear without leaving [a] trace when enslavement ceases to play an important role, shortly before the coming of the 1st millennium BC."[480]

Unable to conquer any major land, they were confined to less desirable areas such as the mountainous part of eastern Canaan, where records pick them up in the Amarna Age c. 1400 BC. A local Egyptian official administrator writes to the pharaoh complaining about incursions led by an opportunistic leader Abdi-Ashirta: "Behold now, Abdi-Ashirta has taken Shigata for himself and has said to the people of Ammiya: 'Kill your chiefs and become like us; then you shall have peace.' And they fell away in accordance with his message and became like GAZ/*hapiru*."[481]

Here for the first time we may speak of an uprising based on lines drawn between landowner and landless, and above all between creditors and debtors. Abdi-Ashirta is reported to have promised his army that "we shall drive the governors out of the midst of the lands, and all the lands will go over to the GAZ/*hapiru*." Cancelling debts and redistributing the land would become the insurgent cry throughout Greece from the 7th century BC onward.[482] The reported words of Abdi-Ashirta find their counterpart in the Jewish Bible: 1 Samuel 22:2 reports: "David left Gath and escaped to the cave of Adullam. When his brothers and his father's household heard about it, they went down to him there. All those who were in distress or in debt or discontented gathered around him and he became their leader. About four hundred men were with him."

The Middle Assyrian epilogue

The Hurrian kingdom of Arrapha (now Kirkuk in northeastern Iraq) made Assyria into a vassal-state during the Middle Assyrian period (1375–1047 BC). Its laws and surviving archives show cultivators driven into debt, losing their lands to a small group of wealthy creditors and facing bondage if they did not flee. Interest seems to have been charged only when payments were overdue, but Middle Assyrian loan contracts secured loans by obliging debtors to pledge the labor of their entire families to creditors, and also their land rights, leading "en masse to debtor-slavery."[483]

The records show three usurers, Rish-Nabiu, his son Iddin-Kube and grandson Kidin-Adad, plowing their gains back into land acquisition by purchase or foreclosure, obtaining much of their property at distress prices. As in Babylonia and other Middle Bronze Age societies, wealthy men managed "to liberate themselves totally from the actual performance of the community labor services and, possibly, also from the payment of taxes. These obligations were now transferred to the poorer part of the community peasantry, which performed it both for themselves and for their 'lords' and

---

[480] Diakonoff 1982: 55 f., 96.

[481] Greenberg 1955: 34, giving the extant references; see also Artzi 1964: 159–166, Mendenhall, 1973, and Liverani 1979 [1965].

[482] Finley 1973: 173; 1981: 161; and 1983: 108 f.

[483] Diakonoff 1969: 211 and 220–228. Most loans were for a year or less, denominated in tin or barley. Jankowska 1991: 253 points out that Assyria's labor force consisted partly of slaves (mainly captured war prisoners) but "seems to have been supplied mainly through debtor-slavery."

'patrons.' … [A]fter the period under discussion the 'nobility' actually left the communities and became a separate non-taxpaying estate."[484] The epoch of absentee land-ownership had arrived, and with it an avoidance of taxes and public duties by owners of wealth. This tendency of wealth to shift the tax burden onto labor is a thread that runs from ancient history down to today's world.[485]

The Middle Assyrian Laws give debtors "the right to redeem the pledge at any time on condition of paying the loan and the interest." But when their loan fell overdue they forfeited their children, servants or other pledges to the creditor.[486] § 39 of Tablet A deals with taking bond-servants into the creditor's household, ostensibly for the purpose of keeping them alive (called "reviving in distress"). Such pledges were to be treated well until the loan's due date had passed. After that time, if they had been pledged or purchased "for full price," they could be beaten or sold to third parties beyond the borders of Assyria (A 44 and C 3).

Diakonoff believes that the phrase "bought for the full price" meant any stipulated price or loan agreement, usually a distress price. But Lewy thinks that sales or foreclosures of servants and land at less than "the full price" were deemed to be loan transactions, and hence were liable to be annulled if the ruler proclaimed *andurārum*.[487] However, no such proclamations have been found from the Middle Assyrian period.

These Middle Assyrian Laws reflect how far usury had extended its corrosive impact. Children were accountable for their father's debts when he died. "Women pledged by their father to a creditor could be given in marriage (presumably for a brideprice) to another man, although the creditor had to ascertain that no one else had a financial claim on her. Numerous people seem to have been caught in this predicament, and no releases from the palace were forthcoming any longer, as had been the case in the early part of the millennium, for even the king himself obtained labor in this way."[488] Flight became the escape valve from the deteriorating physical environment, as well as from debt (as it still is today). Entire populations were put in motion, apparently from severe environmental and weather disruptions impoverishing the land as well as from the impact of debt.

Near Eastern records and inscriptions dwindle after about 1350 BC and stop altogether after 1200 BC, as they did in Mycenaean Greece.

---

[484] Diakonoff 1982: 96.

[485] I trace this trend in Hunt and Gilman, eds., 1998: 139–169.

[486] §§ 39, 44 and 48 of Tablet A and §§ 2–3 of Tablet C. See esp. **Pritchard YEAR**: 184 and Driver and Miles 1935: 287f. These laws draw the traditional distinction between inherited plots of land and those that already had entered the market process and hence were no longer subject to periodic re-allotment.

[487] Lewy 1958: 26.

[488] Van De Mieroop 2002: 79, citing Roth 1997: 163 and 169, citing §§ 28 and 39 of the Assyrian laws.

21. From the Dawn of the Iron Age to the Rosetta Stone

Most Near Eastern trade during the pivotal Amarna Age c. 1400 BC was conducted among royal households, whose rulers were nominally on a brotherly par with each other. Egypt's pharaoh was militarily the most powerful, but there was a polite (if stilted) egalitarianism among rulers as they exchanged gifts and women while maneuvering to influence the balance of power. Egypt kept pressure away from the Nile Valley by encouraging Assyria to fight the Hittites, whose leaders in turn tried to play Babylonia against Assyria.

The lack of interest-bearing debt attested in Hittite or in the linguistically kindred Mycenaean Greek society probably reflects the fact that control of resources derived mainly from military conquest, not commerce. Land was acquired not by purchase or debt foreclosure, but by being assigned to army commanders, officials and lesser royal servants and craftsmen in exchange for military and other services. There seems no evidence that commercial interest-bearing debt was passed on to the Aegean at this early time. The most likely point of transmission to Mycenaean Greece would have been the Phoenician port of Ugarit (Ras Shamra) in the northeastern (Syrian) corner of the Mediterranean. But where debts are attested in Ugarit, they are related mainly to trade with foreigners. Ugarit merchants differed from their Babylonian counterparts in that "money-lending operations, so characteristic for the Babylonian *tamkāru*, are very poorly represented in the hitherto published business documents from Ugarit."[489]

Heltzer rejects speculation that enslavement occurred in Ugarit as a result of high-interest credit, as is found in regions closer to the Mesopotamian core. In cases where land was foreclosed for debt, foreign creditors were obliged to relinquish it to the ruler of Ugarit, who compensated them for their loans. The effect of insolvency thus was to transfer family property into royal hands, not those of private appropriators.[490]

No interest-bearing debts appear in surviving Linear B records from Mycenean Greece, despite the Mesopotamian pedigree for many administrative and commercial practices diffusing to the Levant. Written on clay (a Mesopotamian medium), the tablets of Mycenaean Greece follow accounting formats that can be traced through earlier centuries moving up the Euphrates via Assur, Nuzi, Mari and on to Syria, to Ugarit and across the Aegean to Crete and Mycenae. Syllabic writing, seals and sealings as checks on the access to storerooms by palace servants were part of this transmission, but Mycenaean trade and Homeric exchange were more in the character of gift-exchange among aristocrats than production for profit.

Interest-bearing debt hardly seems likely to have flourished in the Dark Age centuries following the collapse of Mycenaean society. No debt bondage appears in the Homeric poems. The only male slave in the *Odyssey* whose origin is explained is the shepherd Eumaeus, captured and sold as a child. Male slaves are equally rare in Hesiod. Women who are bought are war prisoners, not debt pledges.[491]

[489] Astour 1972: 26.
[490] Heltzer 1984: 183 ff.

No interest-bearing debts appear in surviving Linear B records of Mycenaean Greece, despite the Mesopotamian pedigree for many administrative and commercial practices diffusing to the Levant. Written on clay (a Mesopotamian medium), the tablets of Mycenaean Greece follow accounting formats that can be traced through earlier centuries moving up the Euphrates via Assur, Nuzi, Mari and on to Syria, to Ugarit and across the Aegean to Crete and Mycenae. Syllabic writing, seals and sealings as checks on the access to storerooms by palace servants were part of this transmission, but Mycenaean trade and Homeric exchange were more in the character of gift exchange among aristocrats than production for profit.

Interest-bearing debt hardly seems likely to have flourished in the Dark Age centuries following the collapse of Mycenaean society. No debt bondage appears in the Homeric poems. The only male slave in the Odyssey whose origin is explained is the shepherd Eumaeus, captured and sold as a child.[491] Male slaves are equally rare in Hesiod. Women who are bought are war prisoners, not debt pledges.[492]

Diffusion to new contexts almost invariably involves mutation. The post-1200 BC Iron Age saw an adaptation of Mesopotamian commercial and agrarian debt practices by chieftains and headmen in Greece and Italy. In these new contexts usury became an intrusive wedge. Lacking a tradition of the checks and balances such as the royal debt cancellations and reversals of land forfeitures found in Sumer, Babylonia and Assyria, debt bondage became irreversible, at least prior to Solon's *seisachtheia* liberating Athenians.

The result was that agrarian usury, debt bondage and forfeiture of land rights became classical antiquity's most important economic dynamic. The classical aristocracies that emerged did not aim to preserve liberty, but to plunge as many of their clients as possible into bondage to themselves. As societies became oligarchic, they hired fighting men increasingly from the ranks of those they were dispossessing.

Debt amnesties in the Neo-Assyrian and Neo-Babylonian empires

Around 1160 BC the Elamites sacked Babylon (yet again), drove out the Kassite dynasty and carried off Hammurabi's stele with its inscribed laws. Nebuchadnezzar I (1125–1104 BC) liberated Babylonia, but a century later the Sealand dynasty from the south took over the region. Elam re-conquered it, followed by a series of mixed dynasties and, in 729, subjugation to Assyria.

The Neo-Assyrian empire (911–612 BC) bore little similarity to the Old Assyrian commercial empire. However, the new rulers still recognized the need to proclaim *andurārum* to maintain a free and loyal army. Although they did not adopt royal titles such as "preserver of law and lover of justice," they "might initiate an 'amnesty,' and ... this would lead to the cancellation of enslavement for debt."[493] The practice of royal debt remissions is documented in a number of Neo-Assyrian tablets from pri-

---

[491] Humphrey 1978: 161, citing the *Odyssey* 15.403–84.
[492] We can see this line of influence in Hesiod's *Theogony* describing Zeus, Kronos and the genealogy of the gods. The poem has been traced back to the Hittite myth of Kumarbi, which in turn reflects the Sumerian-Babylonian Creation Epic.
[493] Postgate 1973: 231 and texts nos. 10 and 248.

vate archives stipulating that silver was loaned "after the remission." Translators of these debt tablets explain that "the transaction is not annulled by the remission," implying that its meaning was like "the silver was borrowed/lent after the remission."[494]

Sargon II (722–705 BC) and his successors continued the practice of freeing debt-servants as a sacred royal duty as well as military necessity.[495] Assyrian bondservants in Babylon (under Assyrian domination from 729 to 626 BC) had to be "released absolutely from the debts which must have been the cause of their enslavement." Anticipation of such proclamations is attested in contracts for slave sales, obliging sellers to refund the price that buyers had paid, if and when bondservants were liberated.

In 626 BC, Nabopolassar established the Neo-Babylonian Dynasty, which held power until 539. In 597, Nebuchadnezzar II (604–562) conquered Judah and began deporting – but not enslaving – its inhabitants. From the 7th through 4th centuries BC "the practice of pledging one's [own] person for debt had completely vanished,"[496] in sharp contrast to what was happening in Greece and Rome.

This absence of debt bondage has prompted a controversy over whether Neo-Babylonian and early Achaemenid rulers found it necessary to annul debts. Hints of such acts come from private archives of debt tablets, and from Herodotus. Reconstructing their traces was one of the main issues at the 1998 colloquium at Columbia University on *Debt and Economic Renewal*. Michael Jursa noted that Herodotus (III. 67) "relates that an earlier 6th-century Smerdis (Bardiya) canceled taxes and conscription for three years."[497] Wunsch found an exceptional sample of convoluted debt and exchange transactions in the archive of the Egibi family from the year 522 that could have been "precisely what one might have done to protect himself against the possibility of a real estate redemption following the proclamation of a clean slate."[498]

In 1986, Stolper found "irregularities" in the Murashu family's archive of debt tablets for the year 424. Van Driel suggested that a usurper to the Persian throne after Darius sought to secure power by annulling debts. In reviewing the contemporary temple archives, Jursa proposes that the Persian king Darius II might have proclaimed not "a general debt remission comparable to the Old Babylonian *mīšarum* acts, but rather a cancellation of taxes and dues owed to the king, including debts resulting (indirectly) from these obligations."[499]

Such a proclamation would be in keeping with Neo-Assyrian evidence. Reflecting the timeless principle that *Debts that can't be paid, won't be paid*, proclaiming a tax or fiscal debt remission in the face of warfare or dynastic disruption was simply a practical matter when most debts were uncollectable in any event.

---

[494] Dalley and Postgate 1984 no. 59, p. 119, citing IM 75751 and IM 758.

[495] Postgate 1974: 417 and text no. 132.

[496] Dandamayev 1974: 438. His 1984 *Slavery in Babylonia*, esp. 157–180, shows how rare debt bondage had become in the Neo-Babylonian period.

[497] Jursa 2002: 212.

[498] Wunsch 2002: 245–247.

[499] Van Driel 1985–1986: 50–67, and Jursa 2002.

Egypt's pharaonic amnesties

We owe our modern understanding of hieroglyphics to the Rosetta Stone. Unearthed in 1799 by Napoleon's soldiers during France's invasion of Egypt, it is a trilingual ceremonial text honoring the 13-year old ruler Ptolemy V in 196 BC. The basalt stone has three parallel texts. Egyptian hieroglyphics (archaic official script) are on top, and Egyptian contemporary Demotic script is in the middle. On the bottom is a Greek text, reflecting the fact that the dynasty was founded by Alexander the Great's general Ptolemy, who seized Egypt in 305 BC after Alexander's death. By comparing its Greek, hieroglyphic and Demotic Egyptian scripts, the French decipherer Jean François Champollion was able to translate the old writing.

What is less well remembered is the Rosetta Stone's content – the Memphis decree. It commemorates an amnesty of tax debts and other royal fees. After more than a century of rule, the Ptolemies were getting into the flow of ancient tradition, acting more like the pharaohs of old than as military overlords. Encouraged by the priesthood to act as "the living image of Zeus/Amon, son of the Sun," the young ruler crowned at Memphis proclaimed an amnesty on the occasion of his coming of age and taking the throne, apparently in a spirit reminiscent of kindred proclamations that were traditional for pharaohs prior to the Greek conquest of Egypt.

The inscription reports that "he has remitted the debts to the crown which were owed by the people in Egypt and those in the rest of his kingdom, which were considerable, and he has freed those who were in the prisons and who were under accusation for a long time from the charges against them," as well as remitting various taxes and duties, including "the debts of the temples to the royal treasury up to the 8th year," 198/7 BC.[500]

Rostoftzeff describes this act as a *philanthropa* edict (royal good work) belonging to a time-honored tradition going back to the Bronze Age. They "were first and foremost proclamations of peace or grants of amnesty. They all began with the same formula: the kings give general pardon to all their subjects for 'errors, crimes, accusations, condemnations, and charges of all kinds' up to a certain date. ... There followed a general concession to all the population: a remission of taxes until a certain date."[501] The debt cancellation reflected a declining economy plagued by "pressure of taxes, rapid accumulation of arrears and ... confiscations, prisons full of criminals and public and private debtors ... fugitives scattered all over the country and living by robbery, [and] compulsion applied in every sphere of life," including military conscription. "The natural results were scarcity of labour, gradual depopulation of villages, abandonment of fields, deterioration of land, neglect of dikes and canals, and ... an atmosphere of war and unrest."[502]

Weinfeld likewise suggests a pedigree for such proclamations to be a general Near Eastern practice going back to the early pharaohs. He finds that the phrase signifying an Egyptian amnesty – literally "to let everyone return to his home" (or home town), *i.e.* a return to their origin – recalls Sumerian amar-gi. A paean composed for the accession or anniversary festival of Rameses IV (1153–1146 BC) proclaimed "that he

---

[500] The text is translated in Austin 1981: 374ff.
[501] Rostoftzeff 1941: vol. II, pp. 879 f.
[502] Rostoftzeff 1941: 713.

has caused those who had fled to return to their home(towns). … The naked are clothed … those who were in bonds are free again: those who were in chains rejoice."[503] In the same spirit, his father Rameses III (1184–1153) left an inscription on a temple block at Elephantine announcing that he freed temple personnel from corvée duties and performed other good works "after justice was established in this land."

The Egyptologist Ogden Goelet points out that "in the case of the Rosetta Decree, the synod of Egyptian priests who helped compose the text had been convened in the aftermath of the final suppression of a lengthy native revolt."[504] It seems that as debt became more important, debt amnesties were proclaimed as a logical extension of liberating rebels, criminals, exiles, and cities or their populations that owed taxes and fees to the palace, its collectors, and private creditors acting on their own.

Egypt's most important surviving edict is that of the Nineteenth Dynasty pharaoh Harmhab (13th century BC).[505] It is reminiscent of Urukagina's reform text in setting out to correct abuses and rectify social disorder in the land, freeing the people from unjust oppositions and protecting the poor from exploitation. However, Goelet emphasizes that Egypt's economy and royal practices under its early pharaohs differed from those of Mesopotamia. The royal amnesties of Egypt's Old Kingdom were "concerned with pardoning rebels or criminals, not with financial matters"[506] or redistributing land, for the simple reason that the pharaoh owned the land and creditors were in no position to appropriate it. "The theme of the pardoned being allowed to return home" occurs in literary sources, but for most of Egyptian history, personal debt and foreclosures by creditors "had not yet become a disturbing factor." But the Rosetta Stone explicitly forgave tax debts owed to the royal palace.

Like other Bronze Age laws, those of Egypt reflected principles of equity associated with the sun god of justice. Goelet finds that Egypt's coronations or the royal *Heb-sed* Festival were the most likely occasions for amnesties. In that sense the accession ceremonies were similar to Mesopotamia's coronation festival. Egypt's *sed* festival was long called a "jubilee" because of its kinship with the Hebrew *yobel* year of release.[507]

Egypt's "jubilee" or *sed* festival was celebrated in the pharaoh's 30th year of rule, when his reign was viewed as beginning a new cycle. This anniversary was celebrated by "the construction of an entirely new temple, at least the erection of a 'Festival Hall' within an existing sanctuary."[508] The basic idea of this 30-year periodicity for social re-orderings was "a month of years," at the end of which Egypt recreated its institutions and order afresh if no new ruler took the throne. But although the *sed* festival included a royal amnesty for prisoners, there is no indication of debts or their cancellation in

---

[503] Weinfeld 1982: 501 f. and 1985: 319. See also Smith 1968: 212.

[504] Ogden Goelet, Jr. 2002: 283, citing the review of the political situation that led up to the decree in Quirke and Andrews 1988: 7 f.

[505] Translated in Breasted 1906: vol. III, pp. 22 ff.

[506] Breasted 1906): 277.

[507] Helck 1975: 282 f.

[508] Fairman 1967

[509] Testart 2002: 197 spells out the logic: "A slave has but one master. He pays no taxes, and owes no military service. Every time a freeman was taken into slavery, the political powers-that-be lost a source of fiscal revenue and a soldier. Debt slavery, in itself, together with the sale of one's person or kin into slavery, weakens the central power."

the early period. No debt bondage in Early Dynastic times is documented. Where slaves are documented, they are captured war prisoners, not bondservants.

Nonetheless, Egyptian rulers are reported to have issued rules governing debt as it developed and spread throughout the economy. The New Kingdom lasted from 1552 to 664 BC. Near its end the pharaoh Bakenranef (720–715 BC), whose name is Grecianized as Bocchoris, is reported to have freed Egyptians from debt bondage and indeed, banned it much as Solon did in Athens over a century later. As one of the two rulers of the short Saite 24th dynasty, he was the last pharaoh to govern independent Egypt. Ethiopia invaded in the last year of his five-year reign and installed Kushite kings, inaugurating the Late Period of foreign rule over Egypt. It was in the midst of this military crisis that Bocchoris abolished debt bondage and, apparently in conjunction with this act, announced a reform requiring all contracts to be written rather than oral if they were to be deemed legally binding. Recognizing that creditors were prone to overstate the balances due, Bocchoris's policy ruled that if a debtor contested a claim that his creditor could not back up by producing a written agreement, the debt was nullified.

The Roman historian Diodorus of Sicily (I, 79) is our source of information on Bocchoris as told to him by contemporary Egyptians c. 40–30 BC. "If men who had borrowed money denied the indebtedness and had not signed a bond, they might take an oath to that effect and be cleared of the obligation." This insistence on written records remained in force into Ptolemaic times. It had long been standard Mesopotamian practice, attested in the laws of Hammurabi protecting debtors by requiring proper documentation. That is why archaeologists find debt records so dominant in their excavations.

Diodorus adds that Bocchoris also ruled "that the repayment of loans could be exacted only from a man's estate, and under no condition did he allow the debtor's person to be subject to seizure." Facing the military threat from Ethiopia, Egypt needed the services of men who had been expropriated for debt arrears. Diodorus explained that this was Bocchoris's rationale for abolishing debt bondage and cancelling undocumented debts: "The bodies of citizens should belong to the state, to the end that it might avail itself of the services which its citizens owed it, in times of both war and peace. For he felt that it would be absurd for a soldier, perhaps at the moment when he was setting forth to fight for his fatherland, to be haled to prison by his creditor for an unpaid loan, and that the greed of private citizens should in this way endanger the safety of all."[509]

That is the logic that must have guided Hammurabi to proclaim his laws blocking creditors from appropriating the crop surpluses produced by tenants on royal land, and on communal lands that owed manpower and military service to the palace. Creditor attempts to take the usufruct for themselves threatened to untrack Babylonia's ability to fill the military draft in an age when warfare was endemic.

Despite the inexorable trend of debt bondage that ultimately engulfed antiquity, most historians applaud the Iron Age Mediterranean West as bringing liberty and founding Western civilization. It was in this environment that the Jewish Bible gave the conflict between debtors and creditors a central role in shaping Judaic history and religion.

22. Judges, Kings and Usury: 8th and 7th Centuries BC

Much as Livy and Plutarch focused on the debt crises that wracked Greece and Rome throughout their recorded history, the Jewish Bible emphasizes the struggle between debtors and creditors as one of its central themes. A few good kings walking in righteousness are juxtaposed to many bad kings taxing the land and letting creditors prey on the weak and poor. Most kings failed to stop wealthy creditors from monopolizing the land and reducing populations to bondage. It was left to the prophets of the 8th and 7th centuries BC, and a few good rulers such as Josiah and the administrator Nehemiah, to counter the arrogance of the rich, elevating the idea of social justice to the moral core of their religion.

Few non-Biblical records exist for Israel and Judah prior to the 5th century BC. What has been presented as archaic tradition was edited many centuries after the epoch of the judges, David and Solomon. Only after the resettlement of Judah under Nehemiah in 458–432 BC was the Jewish Bible put into the form that has come down to us today, including the preachings of Amos and his younger contemporary Hosea in the 8th century BC. Its compilers interpolated melodramatic stories whose moral was that bad rulers or even entire peoples would meet unfortunate fates. Israel's destruction by Assyria in 722 was depicted as punishment for misrule, as was Judah's conquest by Babylonia in 597, and the deportation of much of its population.

The exiles returning from Babylonia codified what became the Torah ("Law"), the Bible's first five books, centered on the commandments received from the Lord by Moses on Mount Sinai. However, no dated contracts or court records for land sales survive to put matters in perspective. The denunciations of creditors by the prophets in the 8th and 7th centuries BC make no reference to the three Biblical law codes: the Covenant Code of Exodus 21–23, the Priestly Code of Deuteronomy 15 and 24 dealing with the septennial year of release, and the Holiness Code of Leviticus 25 dealing with the Jubilee Year.

These were the laws that made Yahweh a protector of the poor and needy, insisting on periodic debt cancellation, liberation of debt servants and a return of land to its former holders as a sacred covenant rather than royal policy of individual rulers. For many years Biblical scholars considered these laws to be more idealistic than practical. In contrast to Bronze Age debt cancellations whose enforcement is confirmed by legal records, the Biblical debt laws have been widely viewed as utopian statements not followed in practice. For starters, the Jewish lands were subject to foreign powers after 722. Even when kings were fully in control of Judah and Israel early in the first millennium, they are described as making taxes more onerous and backing wealthy creditors instead of proclaiming justice and equity.

It was in fact popular discontent when the Jewish kingdoms were subject to despotism that prompted the Torah's final authors to transform Near Eastern traditions of economic renewal into a Yahwistic religious covenant after the return from the Babylonian deportations (597–586). In an epoch when armies were raised increasingly by hiring mercenaries, kings taxed their subjects to hire professional soldiers instead of maintaining a free peasant army. Rulers permitted an oligarchy to take over the land, leading the prophets Jeremiah and Ezekiel, along with Isaiah, Amos and Micah, to denounce them for refusing to protect the poor from creditors or other takers of the land.

Led by Jeremiah (c. 626–586 BC, around the time of Solon's reforms in Athens) and his contemporary Ezekiel (622–570), the prophets were the major advocates of debt forgiveness. They were followed in the mid–5th century by the Persian-appointed governor Nehemiah, whose policies bore striking similarities to those of the popular tyrants who overthrew aristocracies in Sparta, Corinth and other prosperous Greek cities. What the Biblical laws did that was novel was to make clean slates automatic and periodic, not leaving them to the will of kings, who no longer could be trusted to give more than lip service to protecting the poor. The duty of cancelling debts, liberating bondservants and redistributing the land was woven into the foundation myth of Jewish religion, with the Lord making a moral pact with his followers when he freed them from bondage at the time of the Exodus.

The anti-royalist spirit of Biblical law

Israelite mistrust of kings had a long tradition. One of the most resonant passages of the Bible's historical books describes how the period of the judges gave way to that of kings. The elders came to Samuel the judge in his old age and complained that his two sons had turned to "dishonest gain, accepted bribes and perverted justice." The elders asked him to appoint a king to make Israel like other nations, above all to lead them into battle. Deploring their request, he listed the abuses to which kings were prone (1 Samuel 8):

> This is what the king who will reign over you will do: He will take your sons and make them serve with his chariots and horses, and they will run in front of his chariots. Some he will assign to be commanders of thousands and commanders of fifties [just as in Babylonian practice], and others to plow his ground and reap his harvest, and still others to make weapons of war and equipment for his chariots. He will take your daughters to be perfumers and cooks and bakers. He will take the best of your fields and vineyards and olive groves and give them to his attendants. He will take a tenth of your grain and of your vintage and give it to his officials and attendants. Your menservants and maidservants and the best of your cattle and donkeys he will take for his own use. He will take a tenth of your flocks, and you yourselves will become his slaves. When that day comes, you will cry out for relief from the king you have chosen.

No doubt these warnings were put into Samuel's mouth based on subsequent experience. Samuel designated Saul to become king c. 1010 BC, and his reign indeed was unhappy. After conquering Ammon in a surprise attack, Saul lost to the

Philistines in a pitched battle in which his sons were killed, and he killed himself to avoid capture. He was followed by the army commander David, son of Jesse of Bethlehem. Ruling c. 1006–966, David defeated the Philistines and later established a new capital at Jerusalem, not hitherto part of Israelite territory. Taken as his personal plunder, it was long known as the "city of David." He expanded its walled territory from 12 acres to about 32, and built up its religious importance to buttress his royal authority. Much as his Mesopotamian predecessors had done, David appointed palace officials as priests of its temple, and centralized the royal and temple treasuries.[510]

In the absence of non-biblical sources citing David or his son Solomon, Israelite history must be inferred from the sketchy comments in the Bible's historical books. It seems that in the long tradition extending from Amorite warlords down through the Viking and Norman invaders of medieval Europe, David parceled out the land among his companions. His army leader Joab is reported to have been a large landlord.[511]

Moise Weinfeld contends that when 2 Samuel 8 reports that "David reigned over all Israel, doing what was just and right," a *deror* edict proclaiming justice and right-eousness is to be understood.[512] But the Bible depicts David as levying taxes, not as alleviating the fiscal burden. His impositions became so onerous that Israel attempted to withdraw from Judah. Sheba, son of Bikri, "sounded the trumpet and shouted, 'We have no share in David, no part in Jesse's son! Every man to his tent, O Israel!'" (2 Samuel 20).

After David's army defeated Sheba he ordered a census to enroll the land's fighting men, placing Adoniram in charge of forced labor (2 Samuel 24). Even his army commander Joab protested. The census imposed on Israelites was precisely the kind of corvée labor-tax from which Moses was said to have delivered them in Egypt!

David's personality also is depicted as autocratic in lusting after Bathsheba, wife of his military commander Uriah the Hittite. He arranged for the husband to be killed fighting the Philistines, and then married Bathsheba, who bore him Solomon (c. 966–926 BC), who gained the throne through palace intrigue despite the fact that he was not the first-born. He lived in splendor, taking foreign wives belonging to numerous religions (following the example of Late Bronze Age rulers throughout the Near East), and maintained a class of royal charioteers. Organizing trade as a royal monopoly, he undertook commercial ventures to trade with Arabia in partnership with Hiram of Tyre.

To finance these activities, Solomon imposed onerous taxes and labor services, dividing Israel into twelve fiscal provinces, each of which was obliged to support the royal budget for one month a year. An overseer was appointed for each district, headed by the royal scribal administrator, a position that had not existed under David. The kingdom was burdened with an annual tax of 666 talents of gold (about 25 tons).[513]

---

[510] See de Vaux 1961: 139f. 1 Kings 14:26 reports that the treasuries later were looted by the Egyptians.

[511] 2 Samuel 14:30. See McKenzie 1983: 31. Noth 1960: 179–202 gives a military summary of David's reign.

[512] Weinfeld 1972: 153.

[513] Noth 1961: 212; see 1 Kings 4 and 14.

There is no indication that Solomon cancelled the land's debts when he built Jerusalem's temple (1 Kings 8: 12ff.), *e.g.*, as did Gudea in similar circumstances a millennium earlier in Lagash. The corvée labor Solomon and his son Rehoboam imposed were so harsh that Solomon's labor overseer Jeroboam rebelled and fled to Egypt to avoid being killed (1 Kings 11).

The Lord warned Solomon to be upright and observe his laws, or else He would cut off the Israelites from their land in punishment for having "forsaken the Lord their God, who brought their fathers out of Egypt." De Vaux notes that the Bible's historical books "never allude to any legislative power of the king."[514] Rulers are depicted as having authority to appoint officials, but do not enact laws. Good rulers are simply those who uphold priestly influence, such as Josiah (640–609) who "recovered" the laws of Deuteronomy.

Proverbs 29:14 instructs the Israelites: "If a king judges the poor with fairness, his throne will always be secure." But not many kings proved fair after the turn of the first millennium. When Solomon died c. 930 BC, his son Rehoboam initiated a crisis that split the kingdom. Instead of inaugurating his reign with a fiscal amnesty, he increased the tax burden. The Israelites sent a delegation asking him to lighten their yoke, and his advisers urged him to comply. But in a hubristic show of force Rehoboam promised to make their taxes "even heavier. My father scourged you with whips; I will scourge you with scorpions" (1 Kings 12). The ten tribes of Israel withdrew from the southern kingdom of Judah, echoing the cry of Sheba son of Bikri a generation earlier: "Look after your own house, O David!" They chose as their king Solomon's rebellious administrator Jeroboam (930–910 BC). Israel's subsequent history depicts the land as suffering punishment for having left only the smaller kingdom of Judah to worship Yahweh.

After Rehoboam, only eight good kings are cited in Judah, headed by Hezekiah and Josiah. In Israel, within half a century an army leader, Omri (880–873), usurped the throne. His son Ahab (873–853) sought to tax the Israelites as heavily as the Judean kings had done. The prophet Elijah led a revolt, campaigning against the Ba'al cult and its astral deities that Ahab had permitted to flourish after he married the Phoenician princess Jezebel from the wealthy port of Sidon. Soon thereafter, supporters of the prophet Elisha obtained the throne for Jehu (841–814), who eliminated the house of Omri and suppressed the Ba'al worship, presumably along with the most offensive fiscal and financial practices.

Land tenure threatened by debt foreclosure

Abraham is described as a merchant from Ur in Sumer, but the Israelites did not view themselves as a mercantile nation. During the period of their kings they used the word "Canaanite" to indicate a trader.[515] In the face of intensifying commercial forces, they sought to preserve family ties to hereditary land to support themselves. This

---

[514] de Vaux 1961: 150.
[515] David 1950: 157, citing Isaiah 23.

meant not pledging or selling an inheritance irrevocably but preserving the family's right to reclaim it.[516] The essence of their hereditary tenure was to preserve access to the land as the paramount means of self-support, in contrast to absentee ownership.

The traditional ethic is illustrated in the story of Omri's son Ahab's machinations to acquire Naboth's vineyard (1 Kings 21). Naboth protests: "The Lord forbid that I should give you the inheritance of my fathers." Ahab returns home without pressing the point, but his Ba'al-worshipping Phoenician wife Jezebel prods him to arrange for Naboth's judicial murder to confiscate his land. The moral of this story is that her mercenary character corrupted Ahab and let him repudiate the family ties that traditionally had consolidated communal self-support against the appropriation of the land by outsiders.

To punish his chosen people for falling away from his commandments, the Lord condemned Israel to be conquered by Sargon II of Assyria in 721, and later let Judah be subjugated by Babylonia's king Nebuchadnezzar. The Assyrian army captured Israel's capital city of Samaria in 722, and invaded Judah in 705, reducing it to little more than Jerusalem and its environs. Judah held out in shrunken form until 587, when Babylonia destroyed it. The prophets blamed these disasters on the failure to free the poor from debt bondage and return the lands that indebted families had forfeited. In a fitting retaliation for having dispossessed their own brethren, the rich who had enslaved the poor ended up being deported from their land.

The prophets lead a revolt

Archaeological excavations in Israel show small 10ᵗʰ-century BC towns with houses of similar size and arrangement. Each house, summarizes de Vaux,

> represents the dwelling of a family which lived in the same way as its neighbors. The contrast is striking when we pass to the eighth century houses on the same site: the rich houses are bigger and better built and in a different quarter from that where the poor houses are huddled together. Between these two centuries, a social revolution had taken place. The monarchical institutions produced … a class of officials who drew a profit from their posts and the favors granted them by the king. Others, by hard work or good luck, made vast profits from their lands. … Isaiah 2: 7 says: 'The land is full of silver and gold, and treasures past counting.' The prophets condemn their contemporaries for their luxury in building, in entertainment and in dress. … The wealth of the day was in fact badly distributed and often ill-gotten: 'If they covet fields, they seize them; if houses, they take them' (Micah 2: 2). The rich landlords would speculate and defraud others, the judges took bribes, and the creditors knew no pity.[5176]

[516] See North 1954:. 167ff.
[517] De Vaux 1961: 72f.

The 8th and 7th centuries were a time of rising prosperity for Judah, Israel and the rest of the Mediterranean. Iron-using technology made tools that increased crop yields, as well as more affordable arms for fighting. Commerce expanded, and with it came interest-bearing debt, much as had occurred throughout the Mesopotamian periphery a millennium earlier. A wealthy class emerged and found markets for pottery and luxury export crops such as olive oil and wine. The ensuing money economy caused debt strains as usury turned debtors into clients, dependents and bondservants, prying away their land.

The Bible's passages that deal with lending refer to agrarian usury and loans to the poor in dire need, not to commercial advances. "Every time lending on interest is mentioned in the Bible, it is spoken of with disapproval."[518] The loan market was depicted as predatory, driving people into debt and taking their land and thus threatening to destroy what today are called family values.

Having lost faith in kings, the populist prophets prepared the ground for the Biblical debt laws by assigning protection of the poor to Yahweh. More concerned with protecting cultivators from their creditors than with astral cosmology, Yahweh demanded a moral economic order in stronger terms than did other gods who, like Ba'al (and their priesthoods), became tools of the emerging aristocracies.

Yet the prophets of Israel and Judah were well-connected men of influence, as were the Greek and Roman reformers and the Stoics who later influenced the Gracchi and other disaffected aristocrats in Rome. Although these reformers spoke on behalf of the poor against wealthy predators, they did not arise out of the poor classes. "Motivated by idealism or personal ambition they sought, with the support of the affluents, to commit the rulers to programs of social amelioration and regeneration."[519]

Rabbinic tradition describes Amos, influential in Israel in the time of Jeroboam II (786–746), as "a moderately wealthy stockraiser and landowner."[520] He "speaks to the people of the northern kingdom generally and to the privileged classes particularly." In Judah, Isaiah was an aristocrat (as was Zephaniah) who became an advisor of Uzziah (767–740), Ahaz (732–716) and Hezekiah (716–687) and chronicled their reigns.[521]

What these prominent reformers shared was the perception that instead of leading to greater overall prosperity, leaving moneylending and land tenure to what today are called "market relations" and the "sanctity of debt" meant dispossessing debtors from the land – and in due course to the kingdom's military defeat. Opposing the aggressiveness of their fellow prosperous classes, these reformer-prophets presented their program as conservative. They accused rulers of deviating from the higher authority of religion, succumbing to Ba'al worship and an addictive compulsion to amass property without limit – what the Greeks called hubris, the arrogance of wealth. What the prophets claimed to restore was an idealized "original" economy in which families were self-sufficient on the land, free from bondage and able to support themselves without running into debt more than temporarily.

[518] Hillel Gamoran 1971: 131, 127.
[519] Silver 1983: 248f.
[520] Huffmon 1983: 109.
[521] See Isaiah 37–382 and Chronicles 26: 22 and 32: 32.

Robert North summarizes the sermons and oracles of Amos and his fellow reformers as implying that "there can be wrong even when the poor man parts with his
land freely and for a fair price. Justice demands that the land remain more or less in-
alienably distributed among numerous small holders. When property is concentrated
in the hands of a few, monopolistic oppression is the inevitable result."[520] Inasmuch
as lending and land sale occurred mainly among unequals, this was held to be akin
to coercive robbery and was implicitly opposed by the Eighth Commandment: Thou
shalt not steal.

Land consolidation to assemble great estates – *latifundia* – was blamed for the
downfall of Israel and Judah, as it was in Rome a half-millennium later. "Woe to you
who add house to house and join field to field till no space is left and you live alone
in the land," spoke Isaiah (5: 8), the most influential prophet during 740–700, around
the time of the radical Lycurgan economic reforms in Sparta. Isaiah continues (5:9ff.):
"Surely the great houses will become desolate, the fine mansions left without occupants. ... Woe to those who call evil good and good evil, who put darkness for light
and light for darkness, who put bitter for sweet and sweet for bitter."

Likewise the prophet Micah (740–670), an aristocrat who advised Hezekiah,
declaimed: "Woe to those that devise iniquity ... they covet fields and houses, and take
them by force. They defraud a man of his home and his inheritance" (Micah 2: 1–2).
He adds (7: 3): "Both hands are skilled in doing evil; the ruler demands gifts, the judge
accepts bribes, the powerful dictate what they desire – they all conspire together."

Isaiah 13: 11 promises to "put an end to the arrogance of the haughty and ... humble the pride of the ruthless." He warns (3: 14f.): "The Lord enters into judgment
against the elders and leaders of his people: 'It is you who have ruined my vineyard; the
plunder from the poor is in your houses. What do you mean by crushing my people
and grinding the faces of the poor?'" Indeed, Isaiah starts off (1: 10–23) by declaiming:

> See how the faithful city has become a harlot! She once was full of justice;
> righteousness used to dwell in her – but now murderers! ... Your rulers are
> rebels, companions of thieves; they all love bribes and chase after gifts. They
> do not defend the cause of the fatherless; the widow's case does not come
> before them.

Amos 2: 6ff. bears a similar message about the Lord's wrath at Judah's elite:

> They sell the righteous for silver, and the needy for a pair of sandals. They
> trample on the heads of the poor as upon the dust of the ground and deny
> justice to the oppressed.
>
> They lie down beside every altar on garments taken in pledge. In the
> house of their god they drink wine taken as fines.

Continuing this theme later, Amos 5: 12–16 accuses:

> You oppress the righteous and take bribes, and you deprive the poor of justice
> in the courts. Therefore the prudent man keeps quiet in such times, for the
> times are evil.

[520] North 1954: 39.

Hate evil, love good; maintain justice in the courts. Perhaps the Lord
God Almighty will have mercy on the remnant of Joseph.

The end of Israel was coming because the kingdom and its leaders had permitted
wealth-seekers to exploit the poor and deny them justice.

Hosea's speeches in the 8th century BC allude to similar wrongs. He warns (in a
passage written retroactively) that Israel's riches will be taken by the Assyrians, because
instead of sowing righteousness the Israelites "have planted wickedness, reaped evil,
and eaten the fruit of deception" (Hosea 10). Its merchants stir the Lord's wrath by
using false weights and measures. "They make many promises, take false oaths and
make agreements; therefore lawsuits spring up like poisonous weeds in a plowed field."

This metaphor alludes to Greek *hubris*, literary an overgrowth of vegetation. Such
imagery, according to Gottwald, suggests "that the oaths and agreements condemned
had to do with land transactions or loans to debtor farmers. Especially striking is the
use of the Genesis traditions about Jacob cheating his brother to epitomize the
northern kingdom as a land of greed and plunder (12:8–9). Finally, the climactic
'true confession' of Israel in 14:1–3 states that 'in you (Yahweh) the orphan finds
mercy,' a code phrase for the socioeconomic program of tribal Israel for protecting
the weak."[523]

The prophets wanted to restore an idealized *status quo ante*, but their preachings
show no trace of Mesopotamia's clean slate tradition, or even of the Biblical law codes
such as the Jubilee year. "Nowhere in the Bible do the prophets explicitly base themselves on the Mosaic legislation as a norm of their decrees," points out North.[524]
Lemche adds that the main ingredient of the Exodus story, "the covenant, does not
seem to have played any significant role in the religious life of Israel before the sixth
century. … it was only in relatively late times that Moses was understood as a lawgiver."[525] The first 39 chapters of Isaiah (the later ones are attributed to Deutero- and
Third-Isaiah) do not mention Exodus traditions.

What we find prior to Jeremiah and Ezekiel are straightforward denunciations of
usury, leavened occasionally by miracles. For instance, in 2 Kings 4 (c. 850 BC) a
follower of the prophet Elisha dies. His widow calls out to Elisha in distress that "now
his creditor is coming to take my two boys as his slaves." All she owns is some oil to
light her lamps. Elisha saves her by performing a miracle: He tells her to borrow as
many jars from her neighbors as she can, and fill them all with oil. She is able to
miraculously fill them all from her own small jar, and sells the oil to repay her debts.

This obviously was not a solution available to everybody. That is why the message
of the prophets was so pessimistic. Their solution was simply to exhort rulers and the
wealthy to behave more charitably.

---

[523] Gottwald 1985: 361.
[524] North 1954: 205.
[525] Lemche 1985: 435, citing Nielsen.

II REGUM IV

Sic oleum Viduæ precibus pius auxit Elias,
Ut redimat natus, ac alat inde ſuos
Diſce; Deo charus pro te ſi tollit ad aſtra
Quam fortes habeat, que is juvet, ille manus

Elisa mehrt das Oel. Der Wittwen Noth verschwindet.
Sie löst die Kinder aus und nehrt sie durch die Gab.
Wer Gott lieb, und für dich die Hand gen Himmel windet,
der zieht mit starker Faust, für dich, die Hilf
herab.

Figure 30: A widow redeems her child after Elisha's intervention by C. Luyken, 1697..

How the Ten Commandments pertain to the usury problem

The Ten Commandments (Exod. 20, repeated in Deut. 5), immediately preceding the Covenant Code, bear on the debt issue in ways not immediately apparent to modern eyes. For instance, as Gottwald points out: "The crimes listed in Hosea 4:1 by a series of nouns, that is, false swearing [the Third Commandment], stealing [the Eighth Commandment], and murder [the Sixth Commandment], were all involved in the debt foreclosures, land-grabbing, and court corruption pinpointed by Amos."[526]

Dictating his laws to Moses, Yahweh warns his followers to adhere to the law (Torah) and shun other gods (the First Commandment), *e.g.* as Jezebel worshipped Baʿal. In the spirit of Hosea 10: 1–2 a century earlier, Deut. 12: 2–6 calls for tearing down altars and destroying the temples of other gods. Yahweh exhorts his followers to remember that "I am a jealous god" (Second Commandment), and directs them not to worship idols by making images or physical representations of any gods. The Third Commandment forbids them to misuse Yahweh's name – a prohibition blocking creditors from forcing debtors to waive their sacred rights by making them swear not to avail themselves of the Biblical laws protecting their welfare. Related to this is the Ninth Commandment, prohibiting Israelites from accusing or testifying falsely against one another in lawsuits.

The Fourth Commandment enjoins Israelites from working on the Sabbath day. Deuteronomy extends this principle to the Sabbatical Year of Release (a week of years). The Exodus story frames this law, as the Lord repeatedly reminds the Israelites of their own origin in slavery, by the refrain, "Remember, thou wast a bondsman in the land of Egypt" (Deut. 15: 15, 24: 18, *et al.*), not to mention under Solomon and his successors.

The Tenth Commandment prohibits Israelites from coveting members of other households – including their servants, property or family members pledged for debt. As such, it was related to the Eighth Commandment ("Thou shalt not steal"), which was long perceived to ban creditors from taking what the poor needed for their self-support. To foreclose on land and not ultimately return it to the defaulting debtor was held to constitute theft. The most relevant Biblical chapter defining interest charges in this way is Ezekiel 18, where the prophet of the Exile describes the Lord's threat that a "father will die for his own sin, because he practiced extortion, robbed his brother and did what was wrong among his people."

Martin Luther's 1516 AD sermon on the Eighth Commandment condemns usury as a form of theft, warning that it destroys cities much as a worm destroys an apple from within its core. A generation later John Calvin, in a commentary on Ezekiel written in the final year of his life (published in 1565 AD), likewise defined usury and mercantile fraud as theft, accusing wealthy lenders of being as guilty of breaking the Eighth Commandment as highwaymen and robbers.[527] Jews were forbidden to take interest from one another – which is why Jesus overturned the tables of moneylenders in the temple.

---

[526] Gottwald 1985: 361.
[527] On these points of medieval doctrine see Hyma 1951: 283 ff. and 443 ff.

Figure 31: Jesus expels the moneylenders from the Temple by El Greco (1600).

The Revised Standard Version of the Bible translates "usury" as referring to "excessive" interest, that is, to usury over and above the legal rate approved by civil authorities. This anachronism distorts the text's meaning. Neither Hebrew, Greek nor Latin had separate words to distinguish between interest and usury. That distinction is the product of medieval Canon Law, which carved out a form of commercial gain (*inter-esse*) that Christians could take legitimately in the face of the biblical strictures. Lending among merchants and their backers (what the Babylonians categorized as "silver loans") is not discussed in the Bible.

Throughout antiquity there was a perception that interest on loans to pay taxes or simply to survive (as distinct from commercial investment) normally was charged only to unequals, to persons whose status was below that of the creditor. Prosperous Greeks, for instance, gave their slaves money to lend out to clients at usury, but lent each other money interest-free in *eranos* societies organized to raise friendly loans for their peers.[528] In contrast, the poor had to pay for their loans. They were treated as outsiders, as economic prey rather than brethren whose self-sufficiency was to be protected.

---

[528] Viz. Plato, Laws Bk V, 742f.; Aristotle, Politics I.10; Aristophanes, Clouds 1283ff., and Cato cited in Cicero, De Officiis, II.25.

Earlier Near Eastern societies had laws to prevent the mercantile classes from converting their wealth into landholding at the expense of general communal self-dependency, but there were no religious sanctions against charging usury to fellow community members such as are found in Biblical law, to say nothing of the Biblical injunctions to aid the poor even to the point of leaving the land fallow so that the stranger or freedman may glean food in the year of release.

These radical laws were the culmination of Jewish experience codified after the return of exiles from Babylonia. The economic strains they addressed were occurring throughout the entire classical world. In Greece, for instance, contemporary 7th-century BC records describe clans that had taken over the land in Corinth and other prosperous cities being overthrown by popular leaders called "tyrants" who exiled them and redistributed the land among their followers. In Sparta the semi-mythical Lycurgus is said by Plutarch to have gone so far as to have replaced silver with iron fiat money and replaced the oligarchy with a re-distributive equality. In early 6th-century BC Athens, Solon ended debt bondage for citizens. All this was kindred in spirit to what was happening in Judah.

23. Biblical Laws Call for Periodic Debt Cancellation

The Bible interprets Israel's defeat by Sargon II in 722 BC as divine punishment for falling away from the covenant with the Lord. Israel's punishment fit the crime: Just as its creditor elite had dispossessed their brethren from the land, so the ten tribes of Israel were deported to Mesopotamia and Media, and Judah's size was reduced to only the region surrounding Jerusalem.

Apart from fundamentalist literal readers of the Bible, one of the few modern writers who believe that the Biblical debt laws actually were applied in the 8th century BC is Morris Silver. He believes that in trying to help the poor by implementing pro-debtor laws, Israel and Judah not only weakened their economic progress but also antagonized their aristocracy, whose ranks included the cavalry and in time defected to Assyria and Babylonia.[529]

This reading recalls the Athenian aristocrats who sought Sparta's aid to protect their wealth from the democracy. History certainly has shown financial wealth and creditor strategy for power to be cosmopolitan, not patriotic. The Israelite prophets did indeed condemn the cavalry, synonymous with the aristocracy, in an epoch when "class" reflected a citizen's military rank, based on the amount of land one possessed to support the expense of his arms and training.

Throughout the ancient world military tactics were shifting to rely more on the *demos*-infantry. After the Assyrian king Sennacherib (705–681) captured all of Judah except Jerusalem in 701, chariot troops never again were raised.[530] A citizen-infantry and mounted cavalry were complemented by navies manned by the poorest citizens.

By the closing decades of the 7th century BC the aristocracy's power throughout the Mediterranean region was based largely on commercializing land use. Converting Athenian land to grow olive and wine for export, the aristocracy obtained labor initially from debtors dispossessed from their land. In Solon's day these *hektemoroi* or "sixth-parters" were left on their land and obliged to turn over much of their surplus (there is debate over whether it was ⅙ or ⅚) as interest or rent usufruct to their creditors.

Around the time creditor aristocracies were being overthrown by tyrants in Corinth and other leading Greek city-states, the eight-year old Josiah (born in 648 BC) ascended Judah's throne, reigning from 640 to 609. His upbringing was shaped by populist advisors influenced by the prophet Jeremiah (655–586). Their teachings inspired Josiah to oppose the oligarchs who had killed his predecessor Amon.

Josiah's biography resembles that of the earlier Israelite ruler Joash (798–782 BC, described in 2 Kings 11:17). Coming to the throne as a seven-year old after a danger-

---

[529] Silver 1983: 221 ff. and 227. He defended this view in Silver 1993.
[530] De Vaux 1997 [1961]: 224 .

ous conspiracy, Joash had sought to stop social abuses and restore the Yahweh-worship by supporting the priest Jahoiada. Josiah supported Jeremiah in a kindred program to uplift the people from economic oppression by Judah's oligarchy. (Both biographies are based only on the Bible, as no contemporary records mentioning Josiah or Joash have survived.)

In both cases the economic war between creditors and debtors took on a religious dimension. The reformer prophets promoting Yahweh worship accused Judah and its inhabitants of being "full of superstitions from the East" (Isaiah 2:7–11), and recalled Isaiah's warning that the Lord will not forgive the rich and greedy, and that "the eyes of the arrogant man will be humbled, and their pride brought low."

Josiah's accession occurred at a time when the Assyrian Empire was weakening and Chaldean Babylonia had not yet reached full imperial strength. This military vacuum left Judah able to embark on far-reaching reforms. The great watershed occurred in 610, when Josiah used his tax money to rebuild Jerusalem's temple. Priests are said to have found an ancient law scroll, the P document, which formed the basis for Deuteronomy (the "Second Law").

It was in the spirit of the times for religious texts to be found in temples, or for oracles from the distant past to be discovered at opportune moments and be interpreted in keeping with the times. Reforms could be based on references to a lost golden age, a sacred past presented not as an innovation but as a return to former traditions. That is why in Athens oligarchic and democratic politicians each had their own version of Solon's laws.

The P document has been compared to that of Numa's alleged laws in Rome, which the senate rejected and destroyed, claiming that they were not genuine. The P document appears to have originated in Israel rather than Judah.[531] The original presented to Josiah has not survived, only the post-exilic elaboration in Deuteronomy after being edited by Ezekiel and nearly two centuries of the Jewish community in exile in Babylonia. Accusing the self-centeredness of wealth of deranging the sacred past, the P document made economic behavior the moral test to judge good and evil. This dovetails with the preachings of Jeremiah and Ezekiel. The fact that no traces of Deuteronomy's ideas appear in the preachings of Amos, Hosea and Isaiah suggests that the P document was re-composed after its discovery in 610 BC.

As reported in 2 Kings 22–23, Josiah, twenty-six years old in that year, became angry that the Deuteronomic laws were not being followed. Either they had been forgotten or never were applied. Counseled by the reformers, he made them official policy. Calling together the elders and summoning the people to the temple, he read the law and got them to re-affirm its stipulations by acclamation. Josiah then set about removing priests who worshipped Ba'al and other gods. Deuteronomy became the required Judean religious text, as Leviticus would be after the return from captivity late in the 5th century BC.

---

[531] De Vaux 1997 [1961]: 144 suggests that the P-document may have been brought to Judah after the fall of Samaria in 722 BC. For a recent review of the controversy over whether it was written by the priesthood under Josiah or re-composed after the exile, see Schmid 2007. Finkelstein and Silberman 2001 suggest that it was an idealistic invention, pointing out that no archaeological confirmation has been found for the reforms cited in Deuteronomy.

Lending and interest in the Covenant Code of Exodus

The Covenant Code (Exodus 21–23) depicts Yahweh as ruler and protector of Israel, making a covenant with its people (or their proxy, the priesthood) to protect the economically weak even without the intermediary of kings. This idea of an independent priesthood – and a populist one at that – does not reflect how David, Solomon and subsequent kings are said to have behaved.

Instead of cancelling agrarian debts by royal or temple fiat to resolve the strains stemming from agrarian usury, the Covenant Code condemns the charging of interest outright, at least against fellow Israelites. It is as if all are equals, to whom charging interest would be asocial. The Lord says (Exod. 22:22f.):

> Do not take advantage of a widow or an orphan. If you do and they cry out to me, I will certainly hear their cry. My anger will be aroused, and I will kill you with the sword; your wives will become widows and your children fatherless.
>
> If you lend money to one of my people among you that is needy, do not be like a moneylender; charge him no interest.

This is considered to be the oldest Elohistic law. Its silence as to commercial lending has led many readers unfamiliar with Near Eastern precedents to jump to the conclusion that it prohibits charging interest on commercial loans as well as those to the needy poor. Neufeld is typical in believing that the fact that neither this passage nor Deuteronomy 23: 20f. mention the borrower's economic status means that all interest-bearing loans must have been banned.[532] But it is clear that the Exodus lawgiver had in mind lending to the poor, not commercial lending among the well to do.[533]

Ezekiel 18. 22, Proverbs 28. 8 and Psalm 15. 5 likewise condemn charging interest as oppressive. Yet there is "no trace of an attempt to prohibit the charging of interest in Accadian law as there is in Hebrew and Moslem law," note Driver and Miles. The distinction between commercial loans and rural usury existed from the outset in Sumer and Babylonia, but "In Hebrew law, however, it is lending upon interest to a poor man which is forbidden, while it is expressly permitted if the borrower is a foreigner."[534] By implication the foreigner is a merchant.

---

[532] Neufeld 1955: 305.

[533] Silver 1983: 70 is comically modernist in arguing that the rising number of debt servants stems not from "economic depression but in an expanding economy in which an increased number of people are borrowing in order to invest. Naturally, some of these investors ultimately fail due to inabilitly to run a business or bad luck." But it hardly is "bad luck" not to be able to repay loans bearing 33⅓% or 50% interest. At such rates it is inevitable that many debtors will fail in subsistence-oriented economies such as those of antiquity. In any case, as Finley has shown, there is no evidence for productive borrowing to finance capital investment in antiquity. The Bible's concern is with personal consumer debt.

[534] Driver and Miles 1952, vol. I, pp. 174f. They add: "The religious feeling against usury [found in Exod. 22.25, Lev. 25.35f., and Deut. 23.19f. with regard to foreigners] was entirely absent from the Sumero-Babylonian world where payment of interest upon a loan is regarded as a normal and respectable phenomenon."

Having banned the charging of interest, Exodus 20: 26–27 deals with the taking of security for loans: "If you take your neighbor's cloak as a pledge, return it to him by sunset, because his cloak is the only covering he has for his body.[535] What else will he sleep in? When he cries out to me, I will hear; for I am compassionate."

Debt bondage was permitted, but was limited to six years duration. This law often has been compared to that of Hammurabi (§117) freeing debt pledges after three years of service. Exodus 21 describes the Lord as instructing Moses:

> If you buy a Hebrew servant, he is to serve you for six years. But in the seventh year he shall go free without paying anything.
>
> If he came in alone, he shall go free alone; but if he has a wife when he comes, she is to go with him. If his master has given him a wife and she has borne him sons or daughters, the wife and her children shall belong to her master, and only the man shall go free.
>
> But if the servant declares, 'I love my master, my wife, and my children and do not want to go free,' then his master must take him before the judges. He shall take him to the door or the doorpost and pierce his ear with an awl. Then he will be his servant for life.

One factor prompting this latter choice no doubt was the habit, common almost down to modern times, to treat house slaves as family members.[536] The bondsman may have chosen to remain in the creditor's family when he realized what his master was giving him along with his freedom was not enough to make a better life.

Gender also is important. Most female slaves and bondservants were taken as concubines for the creditor or his sons, for whom they bore children.[537] Exodus does not call for their liberation, but prescribes that they should be treated humanely:

> If a man sells his daughter as a servant, she is not to go free as menservants do. If she does not please her master who has selected her for himself, he must let her be redeemed. He has no right to sell her to foreigners, because he has broken faith with her. If he selects her for his son, he must grant her the rights of a daughter. If he marries another woman, he must not deprive the first one of her food, clothing and marital rights. If he does not provide her with these three things, she is to go free, without any payment of money.

---

[535] Amos 2: 8, cited above, denounces creditors who "lie down beside every altar on garments taken in pledge."

[536] The most poorly treated slaves were those who belonged to the public sector or large economic enterprises as "means of production" rather than providers of family services. They typically were war prisoners, not debt bondsmen. Such distinctions between various types of servitude and conditions of service must always be borne in mind when discussing archaic slavery, debt bondage and liberty.

[537] De Vaux 1997 [1961]: 86.

Exod. 23: 9–13 makes the more radical demand to leave the land open for all people in need to glean its yield:

> Do not oppress an alien; you yourselves know how it feels to be aliens, because you were aliens in Egypt.
>
> For six years you are to sow your fields and harvest the crops, but during the seventh year you let the land rest unplowed and unused. Then the poor among your people may get food from it, and the wild animals may eat what they leave. Do the same with your vineyard and your olive grove.
>
> Six days you shalt work, but on the seventh day do not work, so that your ox and your donkey may rest and the slave born in your household, and the alien as well, may be refreshed.

This call for a fallow Sabbath year recurs in Deuteronomy and Leviticus. The parallelism with the Sabbath day of the week suggests the idea of rest from working for masters. Some interpreters find the logic to reflect a program for a crop rotation to renew the soil, but Ginzberg and North believe that the Exodus laws simply let freedmen and other needy individuals take the crops so that they would not have to relapse into debt bondage.[538] North points out: "The cultic 'fallow' suggests workstoppage, but is more explicitly related to poor relief; an unprejudiced literal retranslation of the text greatly diminishes the number of passages which seem to forbid farm-work."[539] Cultivators would still plow and use the land, but would leave access to the harvest freely available to the needy.

The Priestly Code of Deuteronomy

The Priestly Code (P document) expands the meaning of the "seventh year" from that of Exodus 23 (referring to a six-year term for each bondservant) into a society-wide release for land. This made the Sabbatical year (šemittah) universal instead of being counted individually for each bondsman as in Exodus and the Laws of Hammurabi. And instead of sending out the freed bondservant as he came in, empty-handed as in Exodus 21, his former master was to give him sufficient resources to ensure his self-support. He was still allowed to glean what he needed from the fields so that he would not starve, and the debts that had caused his bondage were annulled. "At the end of every seven years you must cancel debts," Deuteronomy 15: 2–18 explains:

> This is how it is to be done: Every creditor shall cancel the loan he has made to his fellow Israelite[540] He shall not require payment from his fellow Israelite or brother, because the Lord's time for cancelling debts has been proclaimed.

---

[538] Ginzberg 1932: 363, asserts bluntly: "It must be obvious to anyone that Exodus is not at all interested in permitting the land to lie fallow. And such immature analogies as comparing the lying fallow of the land with the rotation of crops are worthless."

[539] North 1954: 131.

[540] North 1954: 187 translates this line: "Every holder of a pawn at his disposition shall release what he *contracted over by pawnbrokerage* with his neighbor" (his italics).

You may require payment from a foreigner, but you must cancel any debt your brother owes you. However, there should be no poor among you, for in the land the Lord your God is giving you to possess as your inheritance, he will richly bless you, if only you fully obey the Lord your God and are careful to follow all these commands I am giving you today. For the Lord your God will bless you as he has promised, and you will lend to many nations but will borrow from none. You will rule over many nations but none will rule over you.

Deuteronomy 24:6 protects the debtor – and the functioning of society at large – by prohibiting the basic means of self-support from being pledged to creditors: "Do not take a pair of millstones – not even the upper one – as security for a debt, because that would be taking a man's livelihood as security." This injunction finds its counterpart in the laws of many societies from the Middle Ages to modern bankruptcy proceedings. Also repeated is the sanction against taking garments as pledges: "If the man is poor, do not go to sleep with his pledge in your possession. Return his cloak to him by sunset so that he may sleep in it." And in a ruling that recalls the laws of Hammurabi, Deuteronomy 24:10–13 stipulates: "When you make a loan of any kind to your neighbor, do not go into his house to get what he is offering as a pledge. Stay outside and let the man to whom you are making the loan bring the pledge out to you."

Deuteronomy 24:14–15 does uphold one kind of debt: the wages that landowners owe their help. It insists that the wages of migratory workers are to be paid at the close of each working day: "Do not take advantage of a hired man who is poor and needy, whether he is a brother Israelite or an alien living in one of your towns. Pay him his wages each day before sunset, because he is poor and is counting on it. Otherwise … you will be guilty of sin."[541]

Finally, Deutonomy 24:17–18 places its laws in the context of the Mosaic experience: "Do not deprive the alien or the fatherless of justice, or take the cloak of the widow as a pledge. Remember that you were slaves in Egypt and the lord your God redeemed you from there. That is why I command you to do this." This passage alludes to Jeremiah 34 describing the Lord's compact with the Israelites fleeing Egypt in their collective liberation from servitude.[542]

[541] The concern here is a timeless one. When the Allies proclaimed the world's most recent national debt cancellation on record, wiping Germany's internal debts off the books in 1948 (paving the way for its Economic Miracle), wage obligations owed by employers since the last paycheck were kept inviolate.

[542] Ginzberg 1932: 349: "Exodus has no such theocratic explanation, and it is perhaps reasonable to believe that Exod. 21 is therefore a very old Semitic law."

Jeremiah depicts the Babylonian captivity as divine retaliation for violating the Covenant

Josiah's attempt to implement reforms plunged Judah into a class war waged on the field of religious doctrine, best attested in the preachings of Deuteronomy's leading proponent Jeremiah (born 655 BC). Coming from a wealthy priestly family, he was the last major pre-exilic prophet. Active from the time of Josiah's accession through the second wave of Babylonian deportations from Judah in 587, he focused on social justice, accusing the mainstream priesthood of being dominated by self-centered idolatrous Ba'al worshippers among the aristocracy and their followers.

In the face of Babylonia's growing military threat, Jeremiah 7: 6–7, 11 warned his compatriots: "If you do not oppress the alien, the fatherless or the widow and do not shed innocent blood in this place … then I will let you live in this place, in the land I gave your forefathers for ever and ever … Has this house, which bears my Name, become a den of robbers to you? I have been watching! declares the Lord." This is the passage Jesus cited when he entered Jerusalem's temple to overturn the benches of the moneychangers, calling it a "den of thieves."

The extent to which Deuteronomy's laws were elevated from moral status enjoying religious sanction to legally binding rules enforceable within the royal justice system is unclear. The experiment in administering these laws was followed too quickly by Judah's military collapse to see whether they would have worked.[531] Josiah died on the battlefield in 604, fighting at Megiddo against Egypt's pharaoh Neco, who was making an incursion against Babylonia to support Assyria. A few months later Neco captured Josiah's son Jehoahaz, held him for ransom, and chose another son (Eliakim) to become king of Judah under the name of Jehoiakim.

When the Babylonians conquered Judah again they kept Jehoiakim as a vassal king. He subsequently rebelled and was defeated when Nebuchadnezzar captured Jerusalem in 597. Babylonians looted its temples and palace of whatever movable property they could carry, along with craftsmen, officers and soldiers – reportedly ten thousand men.

The next king, Zedekiah (596–587), likewise rebelled and was counter-attacked. Jeremiah 34: 8–10 describes him making a covenant in response to Nebuchadnezzar's new siege of Jerusalem. The story is filled out in 2 Chronicles 32 and 2 Kings 25. It is similar to Rome's legend of Coriolanus in the face of the secession of the plebs later in the 6th century:

> The word came to Jeremiah from the Lord after King Zedekiah had made a covenant with all the people in Jerusalem to proclaim freedom (*deror*) for the slaves. Everyone was to free his Hebrew slaves, both male and female; no one was to hold a fellow Jew in bondage. So all the officials and people who entered into this covenant agreed that they would free their male and female slaves and no longer hold them in bondage. They agreed, and set them free.

[543] Kaufman 1960: 290.

This is the first documented instance of a society-wide debt cancellation in Judah, for there is no evidence that Josiah had ever attempted to enforce the Sabbatical Year. This passage also contains the earliest biblical usage of the Levitical term *deror*, suggesting that the word may be a retrojection by the compilers of the Holiness Code. Deuteronomy only uses the word *shemittah*. Zedekiah's freeing Jewish bondservants and thereby canceling the debts that bound them in servitude was not related to any existing law. It was a military act, much as Greek and Roman tacticians resorted to in similar military crises.[544]

As often is the case with the promises of rulers and politicians, Zedekiah rescinded his *deror* act after the crisis had passed. The creditors who backed his regime

> changed their minds and took back the slaves they had freed. …
>
> Then the word of the Lord came to Jeremiah: This is what the Lord, the God of Israel, says: I made a covenant with your forefathers when I brought them out of Egypt, out of the land of slavery. I said, "Every seventh year each of you must free any fellow Hebrew who has sold himself to you. After he has served you six years, you must let him go free." Your fathers, however, did not listen to me or pay attention to me. Recently you repented and did what is right in my sight: Each of you proclaimed liberty (*deror*) to his countrymen. You even made a covenant before me in the house that bears my Name. But now you have turned around and profaned my name; each of you has taken back the male and female slaves you had set free to go where they wished. You have forced them to become your slaves again.
>
> Therefore, this is what the Lord says: "You have not obeyed me; you have not proclaimed freedom for your fellow countrymen. So I now proclaim 'freedom' for you," declares the Lord – "freedom to fall by the sword, plague and famine. I will make you abhorrent to all the kingdoms of the earth …I will hand Zedekiah king of Judah and his officials over to their enemies who seek their lives, to the army of the king of Babylon, which has withdrawn from you. I am going to give the order," declares the Lord, "and I will bring them back to this city. And I will fight against it, take it and burn it down. And I will lay waste the towns of Judah so that no one can live there. (Jeremiah 34: 8–22)

Judah's defeat in this war was inevitable. Babylonia controlled the territory west of Mesopotamia down to the Egyptian border. Jeremiah 39 describes Jerusalem's fall. The Babylonians burned its palace, temple and houses, broke down its walls, captured Zedekiah and killed his sons before his eyes, "and also killed all the nobles of Judah." They then "carried into exile to Babylon the people who remained in the city," leaving behind only "some of the poor people, who owned nothing." Jeremiah reports that Nebuchadnezzar deported some 4,600 persons in 597, 587 and 582 BC.[545]

---

[544] The Greek military writer Aeneus Tacticus (4th century BC) urged debt cancellations to win over populations in times of siege.

[545] Toynbee 1976: 161 and 164 finds this compatible with Assyria's official figure of 27,290 persons deported in 721 BC from the larger and most populous kingdom of Israel. In his view, "The years 597–582 saw the end of the Kingdom of Judah and the beginning of the history of the Jews and of Judaism."

As in Greece and Rome, Judah's creditor-debtor war overshadowed the conflict with foreigners. Jeremiah appealed to the Babylonians to implement the social program that he and his supporters were unable to achieve until the Judean aristocracy was overthrown.

It seems that a redistribution of land was done by the Babylonians to win the peace after their victory. They freed Jeremiah from captivity, and the Babylonian commander echoed his prophecy: "The Lord your God decreed this disaster for this place. … he has done just as he said he would. All this happened because you people sinned against the Lord and did not obey him." The aristocracy's debt claims were cancelled and their lands redistributed by the Babylonians, not by populist domestic reforms. The victors carried off the wealthiest families – the class that had been the major force opposing Josiah's reforms. As 2 Chronicles 36: 21 reports sardonically, the land finally got its Sabbath rest.

Jeremiah's biography (Jeremiah 40, apparently written by his secretary, Baruch), describes how the Babylonians set the prophet free and gave him provisions. He is said to have stayed in Judah along with the poorest former inhabitants, many of whom presumably became part of his following. The Babylonia-appointed governor Gedaliah advised them to "Settle down in the land and serve the king of Babylon, and it will go well with you."[546] The prophet Zephaniah (3: 12) wove these events into the Yahweh tradition by predicting that the poor and humble who trusted in Yahweh would be the sole survivors when the Lord would drive out Baʿalism from Judah. Such prophecies, along with Psalm 73's warning that the land would be destroyed if it did not adhere to the covenant protecting the poor, have a long pedigree.

The biblical narrative leaves a gap until Nehemiah and Ezra with their followers returned to Judah a century and a half later.

---

[546] The degree to which Jewish families were assimilated in Babylonia is documented by Pearce and Wunsch 2014, and Wunsch (in preparation).

24. The Babylonian Impact on Judaic Debt Laws

Jewish law protecting the poor from debt bondage was codified in an epoch when debt crises already had led the 7th-century tyrants of Corinth, Megara, Olbia and Cumae to break the power of their local oligarchies, redistribute the land and cancel the debts. Like the *hapiru* leader Abdi-Ashirta c. 1400 BC, the appeal of these early populists did not (as far as is known) go much beyond the patronage principle of rewarding their supporters. Likewise, Zedekiah's debt cancellation when Babylon attacked Jerusalem was simply a tactic to hold the population's loyalty in a military emergency – one which showed that the promises of rulers could not be trusted.

When Solon of Athens and Sparta's semi-mythical Lycurgus liberated their populations from debt bondage, they did so as authors of a new civic order, not as drawing on an ancient covenant. Solon's successors, the Peisistratids, sponsored social reforms as secular leaders, building up the Dionysus festival and Homeric recitations as counterweights to the Eleusan religion controlled by the old aristocratic families. The compilers of the Jewish Bible likewise rejected religion that had become oligarchic, characterizing it as Baʿal worship. But instead of juxtaposing a civic order as in Sparta and Athens, the Judaic authors sanctified their economic reforms as part of Mosaic Law, which they made the core of post-Exile Judaism.

This new religious synthesis was created by the elites exiled to Babylonia in 597–582 and their descendants, who absorbed much Babylonian culture. Returning to Judah in 539, with more to come a century later in 444, they recast their religion in a way that wove the Near Eastern tradition of royal clean slates, such as were proclaimed by Neo-Assyrian and Neo-Babylonian rulers, into the recorded Biblical tradition.

Judah lacked the autonomy to make such proclamations, and also had no tradition of rulers protecting debtors. So it hardly is surprising that its advocates found religious reform to be the path of least resistance to liberate the population from debt. The *Precepts and Admonitions to a Prince* exemplifies the doctrine that Babylonian rulers were expected to follow to regulate credit and the dynamics of rural debt:

> If a king does not heed justice, his people will be thrown into chaos, and his land will be devastated.
>
> If he does not heed the justice of his land, Ea, king of destinies, will alter his destiny and will not cease from hostilely pursuing him.
>
> If he does not heed his nobles, his life will be cut short.
>
> If he does not heed his adviser, his land will rebel against him.
>
> If citizens of Nippur are brought to him for judgment, but he accepts a present and improperly convicts them, Enlil, lord of the lands, will bring a foreign army against him to slaughter his army, whose prince and chief officers will roam his streets like fighting-cocks.[547]

---

[547] Lambert 1967: 113

Such warnings, traditional in Babylonian wisdom literature, form the prototype for those of the prophets, as when Ezekiel 34.2–4 declaimed:

> Woe to the shepherds of Israel who only take care of themselves! Should not shepherds take care of the flock? You eat the curds, clothe yourselves with the wool and slaughter the choice animals, but you do not take care of the flock. You have not strengthened the weak or healed the sick or bound up the injured. You have not brought back the strays or searched for the lost. You have ruled them harshly and brutally.

Ezekiel's apocalyptic message in the face of Judah's defeat by Babylonia

Much as the preachings of Jeremiah are associated with Deuteronomy, those of Ezekiel, "the great prophet of the Exile, the architect of the Restoration,"[548] provide the key to Leviticus and its Holiness Code. Taken to Babylonia in 597 BC as a military hostage, Ezekiel dominated the priestly school that edited the Torah's earliest sources into a version that was finalized by Ezra's school after the Jews returned from Baby-

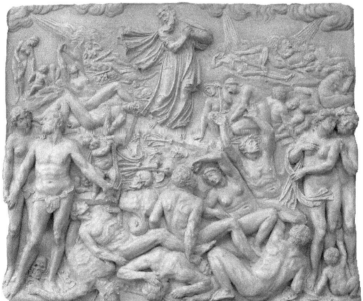

Figure 31: The Vision of Ezekiel by L. Kern.

lonia. Many phrases occur frequently in Ezekiel and the Holiness Laws but seldom elsewhere. "The theory that the Lord is the true owner of all the land and the Hebrews are but his tenants is surprisingly absent in Exodus," notes Ginzberg.[549] Evidently the theory of eminent domain of the Lord was intended to strengthen the laws, which were further sanctified by linking them to the Sabbath principle that took on a more emphatic symbolism during the exile.

[548] Gordon 1965: 268.
[549] Ginzberg 1932: 353.

In an apocalyptic tone Ezekiel 7 announces: "The word of the Lord came to me: …"The end is now upon you and I will unleash my anger against you. I will judge you according to your conduct and repay you for all your detestable practices." Against the corruption of riches associated with mercantile contacts with foreigners he declaims:

> "Like mother, like daughter." … Your mother was a Hittite and your father was an Amorite. Your older sister was Samaria, who lived to the north of you with her daughters; and your younger sister, who lived to the south of you with her daughters, was Sodom. You not only walked in their ways and copied their detestable practices, but in all your ways you soon became more depraved than they. …
>
> Now this was the sin of your sister Sodom: She and her daughters were arrogant, overfed and unconcerned; they did not help the poor and needy. They were haughty and did detestable things before me. Therefore I did away with them as you have seen.   (Ezek. 16:1–3, 15, 44–51)

From Ezekiel to Third-Isaiah

The most archaic land tenure was intended to enable families to feed themselves and produce their basic needs while providing corvée labor (and in time a crop tax), not to concentrate property in a few hands. Deutero-Isaiah decries Judah's falling away from social equity in its prevalent greed for money (Isaiah 46:6–7):

> Some pour out gold from their bags and weigh out silver on the scales; they hire a goldsmith to make it into a god, and they bow down and worship it.

The prophets had made no reference to the Covenant or to the injunction of Leviticus 25 that land should not be sold forever because it belongs to God. Third-Isaiah calls for a plan of action based on the Levitical *deror* principle. Isaiah 61:1–2 interpolates the passage that Jesus selected to define his own program when he returned to Nazareth and gave the sermon reported in Luke 4 (cited above in Chapter 2; see below, Chapter 26).

So familiar have its phrases become – they permeate the New Testament and subsequent evangelism – that it is easy to overlook this passage as their source. To "proclaim good news (gospel) to the poor" has become so common that its original association with *deror* has been lost. God's reign ("the Year of the Lord's favor") is proclaimed by one anointed to be a messenger of the Holy Spirit as an amnesty (*deror*) for captives and the poor. Although not every subsequent "reference to 'proclaiming good news' is a citation of Isaiah 61:1," points out Sharon Ringe, "three principal images come together to characterize the Jubilee: the announcement of God's reign by one anointed by the Holy Spirit to be a messenger, the proclamation of good news to the poor, and the declaration of 'release' from captivity to various forms of imprisonment and enslavement."[550]

---

[550] Ringe 1985: 34, xiv and 85.

Decrying the fact that the Judeans failed to enact the Levitical Year of Redemption, Third-Isaiah (61.5, 8) has Yahweh threaten: "Aliens will shepherd your flocks, foreigners will work your fields and vineyards … 'For I, Lord, love justice; I hate robbery and iniquity.'" These interpolations were based on the Holiness Code, the H document whose raw material was combined with long-established Babylonian traditions and the P document that underlay Deuteronomy, reworked into their final form during the resettlement of Judah.

The reforms of Nehemiah and Ezra

When Cyrus (559–530 BC) conquered Babylonia in 539, he absorbed its dependency Judah into the Persian Empire. Tolerant of local elites and their religious practices as long as they supplied the stipulated tribute, Cyrus is said to have issued an edict in 538 permitting 40,000 families to return to Jerusalem to rebuild its temple. (The restoration was completed a quarter-century later, in 515.)

However, Cyrus "did not guarantee that Judeans would recover their former lands or take possession of other lands within their new areas of settlement," points out Baruch Levine. "It was undoubtedly necessary in many cases to repurchase land from non-Judeans, and there was probably conflict over rights of ownership." [551] This problem occurred nearly again a century later.

In 458 BC, around the time of the rising tide of democracy in Athens under the Peisistratid "reform tyranny," Persia's king Artaxerxes (465–425) authorized the Babylonian scribe Ezra to lead 1,760 fellow Jews to Jerusalem (Ezra 8.15 ff.). Then, in 445, another Babylonian Jew, Nehemiah, rose to the position of cupbearer to Artaxerxes. Nehemiah's Biblical memoir describes the king giving him permission to rebuild Jerusalem after local attacks. It was a personal favor, unconnected with any particular policy beyond re-establishing the normal flow of tribute.

The next year, in 444, Artaxerxes permitted Nehemiah to resettle more Babylonian Jews in their former homeland. A conflict ensued over land ownership, alongside the problem of bondage to Persian debt collectors of the less affluent Jews who had been left in Judah. Announcing a series of reforms twelve years later, in 432, Nehemiah told how he found cultivators facing the harvest-time obligation to pay interest to creditors or the loss of their land. This was the situation that inspired his populist program denouncing usury, debt bondage and land monopolization.

Morton Smith compares Nehemiah's actions as leader of the Jewish return to those of the earlier Greek tyrants and reformers. Like Solon, Nehemiah

> dwelt on the efforts of his party to ransom Judeans sold into slavery; he contrasted this with the local gentry's practice of selling Judeans for debt; he paused dramatically to hear what his opponents had to say; without pausing too long, he pointed out that they were silent; he denounced their practices, emphasizing their impiety and the disgrace to which they had exposed the

---

[551] Levine, ed., 1989: 74. This chapter's reconstruction relies strongly on Levine's reconstruction of events and the two volumes we have co-edited.

Judeans in the eyes of the neighboring peoples; he slipped in the admission that he and his family and staff had also been lending money and grain at interest; and he demanded the abolition of interest and the return of the properties seized. Of course – in front of the crowd – the offenders consented. He made them swear to it on the spot. The consequent increase of his popularity can be imagined.[552]

Nehemiah and Ezra sponsored debt forgiveness beyond anything comparable in Greece. The Jewish Bible's core reference point became Moses's walkout from Egypt, capped by the Lord making a covenant to protect the country they formed from ever again falling into bondage. This frame for Jewish history depicted Judah's kings – allied with venal creditors monopolizing the land – as violating the laws of Exodus, Leviticus and Deuteronomy.

In a description reminiscent of Genesis 47: 18 describing the Egyptian pharaoh (noted earlier), Nehemiah 5 reports that cultivators complained:

> "We are mortgaging our fields, our vineyards and our homes to get grain during the famine." Still others were saying, "We have had to borrow money to pay the king's tax on our fields and vineyards. Although we are of the same flesh and blood as our countrymen and though our sons are as good as theirs, yet we have to subject our sons and daughters to slavery. Some of our daughters have already been enslaved, but we are powerless, because our fields and our vineyards belong to others."

To win favor at the expense of the landlord-dominated assimilationist party that had gained control of Jerusalem and its temple, Nehemiah remitted all personal debts, released the land from mortgage and freed bondservants who had lost their liberty:

> When I heard their outcry and these charges, I was very angry. I pondered them in my mind and then accused the nobles and officials. I told them, "You are exacting usury from your own countrymen!" So I called together a large meeting to deal with them and said: "As far as possible, we have bought back our Jewish brothers who were sold to the Gentiles. Now you are selling your brothers, only for them to be sold back to us!" They kept quiet, because they could find nothing to say.
>
> So I continued, "What you are doing is not right. Shouldn't you walk in the fear of our God to avoid the reproach of our Gentile enemies? I and my brothers and my men are also lending the people money and grain. But let the exacting of usury stop! Give back to them immediately their fields, vineyards, olive groves and houses, and also the usury you are charging them – the percentage of their money, grain, new wine and oil."
>
> "We will give it back," they said. "And we will not demand anything more from them. We will do as you say."
>
> Then I summoned the priests and made the nobles and officials take an oath to do what they had promised.

[552] Smith 1971: 131 and Yamauchi 1980: 269–292.

Nehemiah found no Persian opposition to the anti-creditor reforms he introduced. Persian elites traditionally were free of debt (Herodotus I. 138), and had no desire to see the land pass into the hands of creditors taking crops as interest before the palace received its share. As governor of Judah, Nehemiah operated in the political sphere while the redactors around Ezra concerned themselves mainly with religious practice. Under their sponsorship the book of Deuteronomy was revised and the Torah's other four books were edited in the context of an absolute Yahweh monotheism, weaving clean slates into the core of Jewish religion.

Debt cancellation, freeing bondservants and returning land that had been forfeited was made the defining act of Jewish post-exilic identity, and was grounded in long-established Near Eastern practice. Nehemiah's contemporary, Herodotus (VI. 59), describes the common tradition he found throughout the Near East: "When a new [Spartan] king comes to the throne on the death of his predecessor, he follows a custom which obtains in Persia on similar occasions: he remits, that is, all debts owed by Spartan citizens either to the king or to the treasury. This corresponds with the Persian custom whereby a king, on his accession, remits arrears of tribute from all his subject states." Having been universal Mesopotamian practice for thousands of years, this practice was henceforth to be applied in Judah.

Nehemiah is "acting in his authority as governor and representative of Artaxerxes I, so it is in fact a royal decree of amnesty."[553] But he did not use the word *deror* or cite Deuteronomy or Leviticus – a clue that the Jubilee Year is a later neo-archaism.[554] Subsequent historians have confirmed Morton Smith's observation that "none of this [Levitical] social legislation is known to have been enforced before Nehemiah's time."[555] The word *deror* appears only in Leviticus 25:10, Third-Isaiah 61:1, Jeremiah 34:8, 15 and 17, and Ezekiel 46:17.

Finding the temple hierarchy controlled by the landed aristocracy, Nehemiah – despite being only a layman – expelled a leading ally of the assimilationist party, Tobias the Ammonite, from the room the High Priest had given him in Jerusalem's temple. For good measure Nehemiah ordered that the rooms be purified of the pollution Tobias's residence had created![556] Installing a reformist Levite priesthood to wrest control from Judah's former religious hierarchies, Nehemiah financed its administration with a tithe of the land's produce (recalling Zadok the priest and hence the Melchizedek tradition).

---

[553] Ringe 1985: 23 and 25.

[554] De Vaux 1961: 82 and Levine 1989: 273.

[555] Smith 1971: 141. Lemche 1985: 314 ff., 384 and 435 adds that although Isaiah mentions Egypt a few times, neither he nor Micah refer to the Exodus tradition or Moses. The main ingredient of the Sinai revelation, where the Lord hands Moses the laws and establishes the covenant, "does not seem to have played any significant role in the religious life of Israel before the sixth century." He therefore attributes the social legislation and idea of a united Israel to the post-exile period.

[556] Smith 1971: 132 f. The Tobiads will reappear in the Hasmonian period.

No doubt some well-to-do families in Judah had retained their land, especially if they agreed to act on behalf of the new regime. But much land must have been contested between the exiles who returned and those who had remained on the land and worked it. However, Nehemiah's description of how he found Jews oppressed by their creditors shows that debtor-creditor tensions continued in Judea after the exile, along the lines that the Prophets had been describing for centuries. But not even when Nehemiah denounced the behavior of the wealthy did he mention a Jubilee Year. That appears to have been introduced in the subsequent codification of the Jewish Bible.

The return of Babylonian Jews must have thrown matters into some disarray. The first wave fought for control of Jerusalem's Temple, bringing back the sacred implements and cult objects from Babylon as insignia of their authority. The Bible gives traces of this conflict, but says nothing about the implicit conflict over landownership that must have arisen between the returnees and local owners. No doubt during the exile there would have been resentful tales about what one's ancestors had lost, much as one hears from the former Russian nobility about their castles and estates taken in the 1917 revolution – dreaming about recovering their ancestral property.

We can only imagine how the returnees may have maneuvered. During the exile Judah's land was farmed by the families who had appropriated it when the former elites were deported, and by the relatively few who managed to keep their land under Babylonian suzerainty. Some returnees likely demanded "Give us back our ancestral land" – and no doubt the existing holders resisted such claims. The question became one of how to legitimize title to land in dispute. No records survive to tell who recovered land, or how.

In Mesopotamian tradition the aim of these proclamations was to free the land from debt and promote widespread citizen-tenure. But in Judah any such "return" of the land would have involved "returning" it to the descendants of the large landowners and magnates who had been deported. If descendants of the original deportees indeed demanded a return of "their" ancestral lands, this would have been an ironic twist to the deror act. The returnees would have used the Levitical laws to take this property from those whom Babylonia had left in possession, or at least from creditors who had dispossessed them.

Egypt substituted for Babylonian oppression

Julius Wellhausen demonstrated over a century ago that the Biblical narrative was edited after the return from exile, telescoping the formulation of its laws into a dramatic episode in which Moses receives them as a unit after leading the exodus from Egypt.

For instance, the famine story about Joseph advising the pharaoh (Genesis 47) to buy up all the grain and then sell it to the population in exchange for their land does not reflect Egyptian land tenure as much as how poor Israelites became dependent by pledging their land and indenturing themselves to creditors.[557] Israelites and

---

[557] Levine 1989: 272.

Judeans from the Late Bronze Age onward sought to escape not from Egyptian oppression but that of Assyrians, Babylonians and their own wealthy families and rulers, capped by the Persian takeover. Nehemiah 5: 3–5 describes Judah's inhabitants mortgaging their fields, vineyards and houses to buy bread, and consigning their children to bondage, unable to buy back their liberty.

Transplanting Mosaic laws to a mythical Egyptian setting provided Judaism with a non-Babylonian heritage. This avoided isolating the returnees from the Judeans whom Nebuchadnezzar had left in the land. The story of Moses leading the Exodus from economic oppression became a foundation myth sanctifying the laws of Leviticus and the other law codes, and for Yahweh to repeatedly remind the Israelites that He had given them the land for their heirs to enjoy on the condition that they preserve liberty (*deror*) and economic self-sufficiency for their fellow citizens. To save themselves from being enslaved ever again, they were to adhere to the covenant of periodic debt remission of bondservants and land restitution.

This tradition was supposed to save Judaism from degenerating into a vehicle for the leading aristocratic families to justify their harsh creditor laws. Judaic law made the Lord "not merely a guarantor of the Covenant, he was a party to it. ... Because it was designed to safeguard the Covenant, it enjoins severe penalties for all crimes against God, idolatry and blasphemy."[558] The Jewish people as a whole became liable, not only individual wrongdoers.

Assyria and Babylonia were depicted as having carried out the Lord's retribution for Israel and Judah violating this covenant – that is, the laws redacted by the returnees from Babylon. Levine explains the framework of Leviticus in terms of "the loss of land by Israelites and their families. ... Leviticus 25.45f. recalls the complaints of the citizenry in Nehemiah 5" describing Judeans being "indentured to non-Israelites, suggesting a mixed population. The prohibition against the permanent alienation of family land may also have been motivated by the fear of the loss of land to gentiles and foreigners to whom Israelites were indebted."[559]

Athens coped with this problem by forbidding foreigners to own land in Attica. This rule blocked them from foreclosing on land as a pledge for unpaid debts, or even buying it from needy citizens. But that was civil law, not part of Greek religion.

Recasting Babylonian *andurārum* proclamations in a Yahwist context

Untangling the threads woven together in the Holiness Code of Leviticus is one of the thorniest problems of Biblical scholarship. The idea of periodic economic renewal transmitted via Leviticus, the writings of Ezekiel and the wisdom literature dealing with debt (Psalms, Proverbs and much of Job) reflect Babylonian prototypes that also are found in the religion of Ba'al and other rivals to that of Yahweh.

---

[558] De Vaux 1961: 149.
[559] Levine 1989: 274.

Having adopted many aspects of Babylonian culture during the preceding century, the group around Ezra seems to have found an economic model in Babylonia's *andurārum* acts. What made Nehemiah, Ezra and their contemporary compilers of the Jewish Bible unique was their reworking of these Near Eastern Clean Slates to the plane of sacred covenant. Economic renewal in the form of periodic debt cancellation, land restitution and liberation of bondservants was to be enforced by the priesthood rather than civic rulers.

What also is unprecedented – and indicates that Leviticus is relatively late – is that its Holiness Laws are not merely listed, but their purpose and intent are explained. That is "something rare in P,"[560] and also is absent from its Bronze Age Sumerian and Babylonian antecedents.

In his introduction to the Jewish Publication Society's translation of *Leviticus*, Bernard Bamberger summarizes the findings of modern scholarship with regard to its underlying P document. Despite the fact that the P document contains the most archaic elements incorporated into the Torah,[561] "The nineteenth-century Bible critics considered P the latest part of the Torah, composed during or after the Babylonian exile. It was intended as a sort of constitution for the Second Commonwealth, when the Jews had no king and the High Priest was leader and spokesman of the nation."[562] The Holiness Code was appended to the P document, which itself was "a composite of various sources. The substance of P was not created in the fifth century B.C.E., but it seems probable that the priestly materials were given their present form at that time."

So Leviticus as we know it is a composite, reflecting the 5th-century BC difficulties of enforcing the laws of Deuteronomy (and Exodus) with regard to releasing indentured bondservants. Deuteronomy's limitation of debt bondage to six years of service is extended to the 50-year Jubilee period.

The books of Deuteronomy and Leviticus democratized ritual and liturgical texts hitherto the provenance of temple priesthoods throughout the Near East. Only trained scribes could read Hammurabi's stele with its laws and contemporary royal *mīšarum* edicts in public places. But by the first millennium literacy had become widespread. The Torah was made accessible to the population through the institution of the synagogue, and the entire book of Leviticus was to be read aloud publicly every seven years.

It seems that the returning exiles framed Jewish history and the warnings of the prophets for two main purposes. One was to frame the Jubilee Year and explain the (undocumented) land redistribution that seems to have taken place while winning the hearts and minds of the majority of indebted Judeans by annulling the debts that had built up, as described by Nehemiah. A second aim was to emphasize social justice, above all with regard to personal debt and land tenure, thereby rescuing the reputation of the Jewish God Yahweh despite the defeat of his people by the Babylonians (and

---

[560] Bamberger 1979: xviii.

[561] *E.g.*, the rite of the scapegoat (Lev. 16), household gods, and especially the *deror* proclamation. See Kaufmann 1966.

[562] Bamberger 1979: xix.

earlier by the Assyrians). In the Biblical frame of reference, Judah's defeat did not occur because its god was weaker than that of the Babylonians. It was attributed to Yahweh's anger and disapproval over how his people, led by their kings and the wealthy, ignored his commandments and veered away from the path of righteousness.

This latter view of the role of Yahweh as a justice god has long been held.[563] It places the Jewish god in the tradition of Shamash and other Mesopotamian gods of justice, combining his role with that of Nanshe, Nemesis and other justice goddesses charged with punishing hubris. But more than any prior Near Eastern narrative, Jewish religion and its Biblical narrative reflected an economic conflict that culminated in taking the role of protecting debtors out of the hands of kings and placing it at the center of Mosaic Law. Much as Solon had freed Athenians from debt bondage, the Jewish Bible liberated the Jews from bondage to their creditor class.

25. From Religious Covenant to Hillel

As the preceding chapter has described, the Holiness Code that comprises Chapters 17 through 26 of Leviticus is considered to be a post-exile addition to the P document that formed the basis for Deuteronomy. Elaborating the Priestly Code, it schedules the Jubilee Year on the basis of sevens, reflecting the Sabbath day of rest each week and Deuteronomy's septennial year of fallow. Leviticus 25 directs the Israelites to celebrate the Jubilee Year by "counting off seven sabbaths of years – seven times seven years … a period of forty-nine years. Then have the trumpet sounded everywhere on the tenth day of the seventh month; on the Day of Atonement sound the trumpet throughout your land." [564]

The ram's horn (Heb. *šofar*) replaces the sacred torch raised by Babylonian rulers. "The sounding of the trumpet may be explained as a public proclamation required in ancient oriental law-codes as a sort of registration-formality prerequisite to the exchange of property administration." [565]

Superseding Deuteronomy's septennial release of bondservants, the 50-year Jubilee periodicity only freed bondservants pledged during the preceding half century who were still alive. [566] Property restitution is the overarching principle. "Where communism decrees 'None shall have property,' Leviticus decrees 'None shall *lose* property'; but both are against unhealthy latifundism." [567] What is upheld are communal safeguards against expropriation of the poor, not private appropriation.

Only in Jubilee years may clan members return to their own land to provide themselves with the means of subsistence. As the Lord explains (Lev. 25:23f.): "The land must not be sold permanently, because the land is mine and you are but aliens

---

[563] Most recently elaborated by Thomas Römer in *The Invention of God* (2016): "if YHWH can make use of the Babylonians, that means he can control them; therefore, he is more powerful than the gods of Babylon."

[564] North 1954: 193f. The seventh month of the year (a "second" New Year; see Numbers 36.4) opened by sounding the ram's horn to signify the special festivals of that month. North, Ginzberg and de Vaux review the convoluted debate about whether the 49th or 50th year is meant, and the hardship that observation of double fallow years would have caused, in their publications cited in this chapter.

[565] North 1954: 174 and 2. For the horn's significance see Gaster 1953: 113.

[566] Exod. 23:10f. frees each bondservant upon completion of six years of service. This former seventh year for each servant in Exodus and Deuteronomy 15:12 became fixed (as in Jer. 34) and linked to the seventh-year fallow, a kind of "rest" associated with the weekly Sabbath. Levine 1989: 271 notes that the only reference to redeeming bondsmen every seventh year in Leviticus is 25:47f., "which exhorts Israelites of the same clan to redeem relatives who have become indentured to gentiles." Otherwise the indentured Israelite, "bereft of means or of concerned relatives, must await the Jubilee year." As was the case throughout the Near East, houseborn slaves or household slaves bought from dealers (usually captured prisoners) were not freed. Only Jewish bondservants taken as collateral for debt were redeemed.

[567] North 1954: 158 and 175, drawing on Salomon 1931: 45.

and my tenants. Throughout the country that you hold as a possession you must provide for the redemption (*ge'ullah*, "ransom") of the land."[568] The Lord appears here as the ultimate redeemer, rescuing his followers from bondage and giving them their liberty and means of subsistence once again. This became the model for Jesus to redeem his followers from sin, just as from debt.

In keeping with traditional land allotment, redeemers from the same clan as the seller are permitted to regain title for themselves. The aim is to keep the land in the hands of the original clan, evidently to deter an acquisitive oligarchy from developing. For the expropriated, however, waiting until the Jubilee year was a last recourse:

> If one of your countrymen becomes poor and sells some of his property, his nearest relative is to come and redeem what his countryman has sold. If, however, a man has no one to redeem it for him but he himself prospers and acquires sufficient means to redeem it, he is to determine the value for the years since he sold it and refund the balance to the man to whom he sold it; he can then go back to his own property. But if he does not acquire the means to repay him, what he sold will remain in the possession of the buyer until the Year of Jubilee. It will be returned in the Jubilee, and he can then go back to his property.

Land alienated under economic duress (the usual motive for sale or forfeiture) was thus to be redeemed as rapidly as possible. "The effect of this law," explains Levine, "is to obligate the purchaser to accept the redemption payment of the original owner. He may not refuse to do so."[569]

Leviticus repeats the strictures found in Exodus and Deuteronomy against charging interest or otherwise extorting money and property from the poor:

> If one of your countrymen becomes poor and is unable to support himself among you, help him as you would an alien or a temporary resident, so he may continue to live among you. You must not lend him money at interest or sell him food at a profit. I am the Lord your God, who brought you out of Egypt to give you the land of Canaan and to be your God.   (Lev. 25:35–38)[570]

---

[568] The term *ge'ullah* derives from *go'el*, meaning a kinsman in his role as redeemer. The principle of landownership at work "is the conviction that every parcel of the promised land must remain forever in the same clan to which it was originally apportioned in Numbers 36:7." North 1954: 35.

[569] Levin1989: 175. As in Bronze Age Babylonian law, urban real estate constituted a separate category of transactions. Belonging to the commercial sphere, it was exempt from the laws designed to protect society's basic self-sufficiency on the land for smallholders. The details for redeeming houses in walled cities are spelled out in Lev. 25:29–31.

[570] The Holiness Code adds the terms *tarbīt* or *marbīt* to indicate accrued interest, rather than neshek or "bite," which seems to refer to the deduction ("bite") of interest in advance, as often was the practice in personal lending. Commercial loans and investments stood outside the purview of Biblical law.

Creditors who monopolize land and take their fellow citizens as bondservants usurp what belongs to society in trust from the Lord. The Biblical laws characterize keeping fellow citizens in servitude or depriving them of the means of self-support as sacrilege. Repeating the Holiness Code's two most characteristic expressions, "fear thy God" and "for I, the Lord, am your God," the concluding lines of Lev. 25 use the Exodus tradition as divine sanction. These two phrases, not found elsewhere in the Torah, recur nearly fifty times.[571] In keeping with the preaching of the prophets, Judah's conquest by foreign powers is construed as divine warning not to forego the laws of Leviticus. The Jubilee Year was an attempt to sanctify economic renewal in an archaizing way. The Lord will punish widespread disobedience by returning the Israelites to foreign oppression.

The twilight of economic renewal and the Jubilee

The Book of the Covenant in Exodus, the Priestly Laws of Deuteronomy and the Holiness Code of Leviticus retain the central element of Bronze Age royal proclamations: periodic renewal of liberty from debt and the reversal of resulting land forfeitures. However, North finds "an absolute silence in the later books of the Bible regarding the theory and practice of the jubilee."[572]

This silence has led to a debate that touches a modern nerve. Today's economies rely on "market equilibrium" in which a rising volume of creditor claims overwhelm the shrinking ability of debtors to pay. Society's response to economic imbalance is to leave matters to the marketplace to resolve – and "market" dynamics typically increase inequality. Interest-bearing debt leads to a polarization of wealth. In antiquity it led to a shift in land ownership away from cultivators growing their own food crops to absentee owners assembling vast estates by "joining field to field till no space is left and you live alone in the land" (Isaiah 5. 8). Cultivation on these *latifundia* shifted to export crops, headed by wine and olive oil, produced increasingly by servile labor.

Creditor misbehavior in the story of Job

The story of Job illustrates mercantile and creditor misbehavior in ways often glossed over by modern readers. Job is a wealthy landowner, indeed "the greatest man among all the people of the east." The devil decides to test his faith, to see if he will stand firm as a paragon of good behavior. At issue is whether lending and wealth can be made moral.

Job's friend Zophar reflects the traditional resentment against large accumulations of personal wealth, on the assumption that it is achieved by exploitation. "How fleeting is the mirth of the wicked in their pride," he muses (Job 20). To set things right, equity must be restored. The rich man's

> children must make amends to the poor;
> his own hands must give back his wealth ...

---

[571] Bamberger 1979: xviii-xix.
[572] North 1954: 36.

He will spit out the riches he swallowed. …
He will not enjoy the streams,
    the rivers flowing with honey and cream.
What he toiled for, he must give back uneaten;
    he will not enjoy the profit from his trading.
For he has oppressed the poor and left them destitute;
    he has seized houses he did not build.
Surely he will have no respite from his craving;
    he cannot save himself by his treasure.
Nothing is left for him to devour;
    his prosperity will not endure.
In the midst of plenty, distress will overtake him. …
A flood will carry off his house,
    rushing waters on the day of God's wrath.
Such is the fate God allots the wicked,
    the heritage appointed for them by God.

Job asks Zophar why this moral balance has not in fact materialized. Why are the wicked rich not punished:

Why do the wicked live on, growing old and increasing in power? …
They spend their years in prosperity and go down to the grave in peace.
Yet they say to God, "Leave us alone! We have no desire to know your ways.
Who is the Almighty, that we should serve him?
What would we gain by praying to him?"

Another friend, Eliphaz, picks up the theme of how badly creditors behave:

Is not your wickedness great? Are not your sins endless?
You demanded security from your brothers for no reason;
    you stripped men of their clothing, leaving them naked.
You gave no water to the weary and you withheld food from the hungry, though
    you were a powerful man owning land – an honored man, living on it.
And you sent widows away empty-handed, and broke the strength of the
    fatherless. …

Job replies that he himself has behaved righteously and used his wealth honorably:

I rescued the poor who cried for help,
    and the fatherless who had none to assist him.
The man who was dying blessed me; I made the widow's heart sing.
I put on righteousness as my clothing; justice was my robe and my turban. …
I was a father to the needy; I took up the case of the stranger.
I broke the fangs of the wicked and snatched the victims from their teeth.

The "fangs" in this passage may allude to the Hebrew word for interest, *neshek*, the "bite" taken off the loan principal in advance for loans made to the poor. Job continues:

Have I not wept for those in trouble? Has not my soul grieved for the poor?
Yet when I hoped for good, evil came; when I looked for light,
    then came darkness.

Elihu steps in and poses the moral puzzle that wealth is rewarded by conquering the earth despite its evil methods, while the meek and moral men suffer. Where is the Lord in all this? "Job says, 'I am innocent, but God denies me justice.'" Yet

it is unthinkable that God would do wrong,
    that the Almighty would pervert justice.
Who appointed him over the earth? Who put him in charge
    of the whole world? … Can he who hates justice govern?
Will you condemn the just and mighty One?
Is he not the One who says to kings, "You are worthless," and to nobles, "You
    are wicked," who shows no partiality to princes and does not favor the
    rich over the poor, for they are all the work of his hands. …
His eyes are on the ways of men; he sees their very step.
There is no dark place, no deep shadow, where evildoers can hide. …
He punishes them for their wickedness. …

The Lord intervenes at this point and addresses Job out of the whirlwind: "Would you discredit my justice? Would you condemn me to justify yourself?"

To encourage faith the Lord doubles Job's wealth to reward him for suffering in the face of his good behavior.

The moral is left hanging. Is it that wealthy people can earn their money and the Lord's reward by being good? Or do they grow wealthy regardless of whether they are moral? Proverb 11:4 answers this on the purely individual plane: "Wealth is worthless in the day of wrath, but righteousness delivers from death."

In practice, neither the Lord nor society punished wealthy Judeans for their gains. The prophets explained what the Lord did not tell Job: It was not individuals but entire nations that would be punished for breaking the Lord's covenant and permitting the rich to victimize the poor. That is why society and its religion had to prevent the arrogant hubris of wealth.

The post-exilic prophets, psalms and proverbs

Psalm 73 is a prayer for divine retaliation against the greedy:

Surely God is good to Israel, to those who are pure in heart.
But as for me, my feet had almost slipped; I had nearly lost my foothold.
For I envied the arrogant when I saw the prosperity of the wicked.
They have no struggles; their bodies are healthy and strong.
They are free from the burdens common to man;
    they are not plagued by human ills.
Therefore pride is their necklace; they clothe themselves with violence.
From their callous hearts comes iniquity. (Hebrew: Their eyes bulge with fat).

The evil conceits of their minds know no limits.
They scoff and speak with malice; in their arrogance they threaten oppression.
Their mouths lay claim to heaven, and their tongues take possession of the earth.
…
That is what the wicked are like – always carefree, they increase in wealth.
Surely you place them on slippery ground; you cast them down to ruin.
How suddenly are they destroyed, completely swept away by terrors!

Proverbs abound in this morality: "The wicked man flees though no one pursues, but the righteous are as bold as a lion" (28. 1). "When a country is rebellious, it has many rulers, but a man of understanding and knowledge maintains order" (28. 2). "A ruler who oppresses the poor is like a driving rain that leaves no crops" (28. 3). "Those who forsake the law praise the wicked, but those who keep the law resist them" (28. 4). "Better a poor man whose walk is blameless than a rich man whose ways are perverse" (28. 6).

But the prophets offered only a jeremiad, not a program to reverse the monopolization of the land. Malachi 4: 1–3 caps this tradition, promising that:

> "Surely the day is coming; it will burn like a furnace. All the arrogant and every evildoer will be stubble, and the day that is coming will set them on fire," says the Lord Almighty. "Not a root or a branch will be left to them. But for you who revere my name, the sun of righteousness will rise with healing in its wings. And you will go out and leap like calves released from the stall. Then you will trample down the wicked; they will be ashes under the soles of your feet on the day when I do these things," says the Lord Almighty.
>
> "Remember the law of my servant Moses, the decrees and laws I gave him at Horeb for all Israel … or else I will come and strike the land with a curse."

The Jewish Bible thus ends with a call to return to the laws of Exodus, Deuteronomy and Leviticus. Looking backward, the *yobel* trumpets provide a linkage to Bronze Age festivals where debts were cancelled. Looking forward, they call for a messenger to redeem Israel, followed by the Christian Testament whose own closing book of Revelation (8: 11) returns to the sabbatical theme with seven *yobel* trumpets played by seven angels.

From royal to Levitical rhythms of economic renewal

Most Near Eastern religions shared an astral cosmology centered on the coronation festival's re-creation of order. If debt cancellations were to be proclaimed, these were the ceremonial occasions to do it. Such New Year-type festivals typically were highlighted by a ritual battle between the forces of order and chaos, in which the king vanquished his enemies.

The authors of Judaism found that by the first millennium the royal rhetoric of justice and righteousness had become a hollow bombast. Babylonia's Chaldean kings and most of their contemporary monarchs brought a new imperial domination of subject populations under a despotic god-king cult. The Judaic prophets and their intellectual circles diabolized rival deities so as to distinguish their religion's moral program from that of Baʿal and related astral gods.[573] "Baʿal worshipper," "Sodomite" and "Gomorran" were typical epithets for creditors.

The redactors of Leviticus took debt cancellations out of the hands of kings by making them calendrically regular. The timing of Bronze Age clean slates had depended on the ascent of new rulers to the throne, or when military or agricultural conditions called for such action. The closest approximation to a uniform periodicity was that for rulers who lived long enough to celebrate their 30th year on the throne, as did the pharaohs who presided over many of Egypt's *sed* festivals, and also Hammurabi. The number 30 was linked to the solarized 360-day public administrative (non-lunar) calendar, referring to "a month of years."

Judaism emphasized its break with this tradition by reverting to a lunar-based periodicity. Taking the 28-day month of lunar visibility as its starting point, the Fourth Commandment sanctified the seven-day week with its compulsory day of rest on the Sabbath. During the exile this rest day grew in importance. Upon the resettlement of Judah, Nehemiah (10:31) had the people pledge: "When the neighboring peoples bring merchandise or grain to sell on the Sabbath, we will not buy from them on the Sabbath or on any holy day. Every seventh year we will forego working the land and will cancel all debts." Based on "seven weeks of years," being the year *following* the seven septennial cycles (49 years), the Jubilee year of Leviticus extended the cyclical principle of economic renewal to 50 years.[574]

Making this periodicity fixed rather than variable made the cycle independent of the transition from one ruler to the next. That transformed the concept of time from cyclical to linear, catalyzing the Judeo-Christian idea of linear time.

The implicit conflict underlying Judah's first Jubilee

No loan contracts or land sales survive to tell us whether a land restitution and Jubilee Year occurred in Judah fifty years after Nehemiah and Ezra's generation of returnees. Writing was on parchment, not clay, leaving no wills or dowry agreements, land-sale or debt records to document debt and land tenure in Judah from the time of Babylonian domination and the two return waves of the exiled Jews down to the time of Jesus. After Nehemiah, the next political narrative occurs under the Hasmonian monarchy, whose revolt in 168 BC gave way to a new landowning creditor oligarchy. During the intervening centuries Judah experienced renewed tensions between debtors and creditors, landowners and the disenfranchised, as shown in the Dead Sea scrolls, culminating in the preachings of Jesus as reported by his apostles.

[573] Gordon 1990 describes how Habi, a zodiac god in Ebla c. 2400 and a similar astro-deity at Ugarit a millennium later, appears as the devil in the Hebrew text of Isaiah 26:20.

[574] Ginzberg 1932: 381ff. speculates that the 49th/50th year timing may have been an attempt to reconcile solar and lunar rhythms. Ranging far afield, he finds an analogy in an Aztec three-day festival celebrated every 52 years, but this idea seems forced. North 1954: 127 cites an obscure set of computations in a 1778 book by Johann G. Franke showing "that the period of 49 sun-years is exactly equal to 50 moon-years plus 6 synodic months, but he then concludes that the entire debate would rest on a mistake if, as he believes, the 50th and 49th year were really the same."

Judah revolts and a new oligarchy emerges

After Alexander the Great conquered Judah and the rest of the Levant in 332 BC, his general Ptolemy succeeded him as ruler of Egypt and the Levant, founding a dynasty that raised taxes on Judah higher than the Persians had imposed. The Greek warlords bled as much as they could as quickly as possible.

Judean resistance found an ally in the successors of another of Alexander's generals, Seleucus, who had seized Syria, Mesopotamia and much of Asia Minor. When war erupted in 246–241 between the Seleucids and Egypt, Jerusalem's high priest Onias II refrained from paying the regular imperial tribute to the Ptolemies. But he was forced to pay the tribute by the Tobiads, a Transjordanian Jewish family of landed aristocrats that had taken the lead in fighting against Nehemiah's reconstruction program in Judah two hundred years earlier. One of its members, Joseph, became a military commander under the Ptolemies, acting as a tax farmer for Judah and Syria while governing an outpost guarding the Arab desert frontier.[575]

Wealthy Judeans profiteered from the Ptolemaic trade monopolies in wine, oil and other exports produced mainly on large estates, as well as from tax-collecting contracts. Most of their income was plowed into usury and more land acquisition to turn crop land to luxury export production. This was the opposite of the owner-occupancy land tenure that Leviticus had sought to maintain. Many displaced Judeans were obliged to hire themselves out as mercenaries, especially to Egypt in the Jewish settlement at Elephantine. Another Jewish community was planted in Alexandria.

In 168 BC, under the leadership of its Hasmonean rulers, Judah revolted. 1 Maccabees 6: 49–53 reports that during the siege of Jerusalem by Antiochus VII (Sidetes) in 163 "there were no provisions in the city, because it was the sabbath year," implying that this law of Deuteronomy was being adhered to, although the details remain obscure.

The economic strains suffered under the Ptolemies and Hasmoneans led to religious sectarianism. A Hellenistic version of Judaism emerged in Alexandria, where the Jewish Bible was translated into Greek (as the Septuagint) around 200 BC.

At home, Judaism fragmented among the well-to-do Sadducees, the populist Pharisees and austere groups such as the Essenes. Zoroastrian proselytizers from Parthian Mesopotamia spread a Persian influence, especially among the Essenes, drawing a "simple dualism between the two creative spirits, the spirit of good and evil, light and darkness, truth and falsehood."[576]

How Hillel's *prosbul* yielded power to creditors and land appropriators

Backed by Roman force, creditor oligarchies consolidated their power throughout the Mediterranean and Levant. Judaism's priestly hierarchy joined other priesthoods in being drawn under the oligarchic sway. Credit was privatized, headed by usurers involved in imperial tax collection. A thriving commercial oligarchy had come into being under the Hasmonean expansion, supported by Jewish Hellenizers and Romans. Advocates

[575] Gottwald 1985: 442f.
[576] Albright 1960: 214.

of the poor and weak – the activist Pharisees and the Essenes – were excluded from temple offices and left to form their own sects. By Herod's time (1ˢᵗ century BC) the various pro-oligarchy groups joined to counter a populist reaction led by the Pharisee legalist school, while the Essenes withdrew into self-sufficient subsistence-based communities.

Adherence to the laws of Leviticus and Deuteronomy could not be enforced under such conditions. Buyers of Judean property denied sellers their customary one-year right to redeem urban properties, and also refused to comply with the redemption of rural land by the seller or his relatives, to say nothing of returning it in a Jubilee Year. Recent buyers who had bought lands since the last Jubilee Year, "attempted to avoid the old sellers during the 1ˢᵗ day of the year in order to retain possession," writes Ginzberg.[577] This evasive tactic became so prevalent by the first century of the modern era that Rabbi Hillel, in the *Mishna Arakin* 9.4, "established a special board with which the seller was permitted to place the money equal to the price for which he had sold a year previously and regain possession of his old property." This would not have helped the poor or insolvent sellers, of course.

Hillel's *prosbul* superseded the Biblical commandments cancelling agrarian debts and restoring forfeited lands. It was a legal clause by which borrowers waived their rights to avail themselves of the Sabbatical and Jubilee years.[578] This waiver mirrored earlier subterfuges by Babylonian creditors to circumvent royal clean slates .

Hillel framed the problem as one where "people refused to loan to one another" – as if debt or forced sale resulted from an actual loan, not merely from tax arrears or other charges. "To ease the conscience of a few law-believing if not law-abiding individuals, Hillel finally officially permitted the law to be disregarded by a technicality."[579] No mention is made of debts that accrued as tax arrears or other unpaid bills in contrast to actual money loans. Matthew 23:1 reports Jesus's response, saying to the crowds and his disciples: "The teachers of the law and the Pharisees sit in Moses' seat. … They tie up heavy loads and put them on men's shoulders, but they themselves are not willing to lift a finger to move them."

The fact that Hillel could establish the *prosbul* waiver as part of rabbinical orthodoxy showed how far Judaism was swept up in the tide of privatization and debt. Roman law made debt obligations sacrosanct, not their cancellation. The practice of releasing bondservants and land from the hands of creditors gave way to debt foreclosure being made irreversible and the loss of status permanent.

---

[577] Ginzberg 1932: 390.

[578] Schaeffer 1915: 159 f., quoting *Shebi'it* 10:4 *Gittin* 37a, reproduces the formula to be used: "I so and so deliver unto you the judges of such and such a place (the declaration) that I may at any time I choose demand the payment of all my outstanding debts." He adds lugubriously: "The enactment was a salutary one in that it served the debtor to make a loan whenever he needed it," although it subsequently inured him by enabling creditors to take advantage of his need by appropriating his land and personal service. North 1954: 91 recognizes: "This is commonly referred to even by sympathetic commentators as a subterfuge, to evade the (presumed) obvious terms of the law for the benefit of the individual and of the general economic structure."

[579] Ginzberg 1932: 363. Most Biblical historians state that the *prosbul* predates Jesus. For a discussion see Drake 2014, citing Jacob Neusner 1971: 117–120; Zeitlin 1947: 341–362.

The *prosbul* pragmatically acknowledged the status quo that had come into being between creditors and debtors – and Rome's tax collectors. Its senators bid lavishly for the right to exploit colonies as governors. Having polarized and dried up the agrarian economy at home, Rome became a confederacy of wealthy families feeding on the Levantine economies. Unlike the rulers of old kingdoms, Roman imperial administrators saw no reason to maintain a free land-tenured body of citizen-soldiers subject to the draft. The new armies were mercenary-based. Displacing indebted cultivators from their lands actually helped fill the ranks of the imperial legions.

Legal and philosophical glosses to the Jewish Mishna and Talmud composed around the turn of the modern era do not elaborate on the Jubilee Year. The Book of Jubilees deals only with the calendar, not Clean Slates, indicating that Jubilee years were counted but not observed. Of all the major Biblical laws, this most radical one – that the Lord owns the land, not private appropriators – was the first to be cast aside.

To be sure, creditors who failed to avail themselves of Hillel's *prosbul* stratagem lost their opportunity to avoid relinquishing their properties in the Jubilee year. "In the time of the Mishna," notes Ginzberg, "the Jewish courts would not permit any recognition of the right to collect a debt when the lender had not safeguarded himself by drawing up the contract according to the Prosbul prior to the beginning of the Sabbatical Year." [580]

This obedience paid to the Jubilee year debt forgiveness remained strong enough as late as 12th-century AD Spain to inspire Maimonides and Ibn Adret to insist that without the *prosbul* waiver, debts among Jews were to be forgiven. [581] But North points out that the papal Jubilee instituted around that time had no connection with the original Biblical institution; "indeed, the first Holy Year proclamation issued in Rome in 1300 does not even mention the name of jubilee," [582] which appears for the first time in a papal bull of December 25 of that year. Such papal Jubilee celebrations forced many medieval European economies *into* debt to the Italian bankers to meet the papacy's levies (as detailed by the English annalist Mathew Paris). Church doctrine meanwhile narrowed the scope of the Jewish teachings from a society-wide policy to one of charity on the personal plane, leaving intact the market-oriented practices that the Old Testament prophets had sought to constrain.

From Judah through the Christian West, a religious otherworldliness gained momentum as hopes for worldly improvement faded. This turning within culminated in Essene and Christian withdrawal. "The pre-exilic prophets had not been concerned with salvation for the individual," writes Cyrus Gordon, "but rather for the nation." [583] Henceforth, religions dealt more with personal salvation. Their morality shifted away from denouncing social injustice to apocalyptic preaching about the judgment of souls. The ideas of social equity and literal debt redemption that had inspired the prophets and the authors of the Torah became etherealized into spiritual metaphors.

---

[580] Ginzberg 1932: 363.
[581] Neuman 1942: 219 f. and 295.

[582] North 1954: 213.
[583] Gordon 1965: 265 ff.

26. Christianity Spiritualizes the Jubilee Year as the Day of Judgment

Neither Greek nor Roman religion had a counterpart to the Jewish reformer-prophets preaching on behalf of the poor against creditor aggressiveness. The major Greek and Roman critiques of usury came from secular philosophers, above all the Stoics. Plato and Aristotle condemned usury in the 4th century BC,[584] and by the 1st century AD creditor behavior, corruption and violence was a constant theme running through the historical narratives of Livy and Plutarch to explain Rome's economic polarization. But their philosophizing had no effect on policy or religion. The Greek and Roman religious bureaucracy was drawn from oligarchic ranks and sanctified civic laws favoring creditor power over the debtors. Greek religion did denounce hubris, the arrogance of wealth and power victimizing society's weaker members. But the idea of debt remissions was becoming utopian, a nostalgic memory of a lost Golden Age. The Greeks were so far from having a Clean Slate tradition that civic officials in some cities were obliged to swear oaths not to cancel debts or redistribute the land.

Also different in the first millennium BC was the role of kings and civic oligarchies that emerged in Greece and Rome. The Biblical kings from the time of Solomon, like the Roman Senators, are reported to have been rapacious as they burdened their populations with taxes and debts, becoming the largest landowners and also the major creditors. In contrast to Babylonian *mišarum* acts restoring royal tax claims and control over labor from debt claims by creditors, the Biblical Jubilee Year and Deuteronomy's Sabbath year would have been at the expense of Iron Age kings and their allied aristocracies. That is why Roman aristocrats killed populist leaders advocating protection for debtors and land redistribution during the century spanning the murder of Tiberius Gracchus in 133 BC down through the civil war that culminated in the crowning of Augustus in 29 BC.

---

[584] Aristotle pointed out in his *Politics*, I.9, 1258 (c. 350 BC) that unlike goats, sheep and cattle monetary metal was barren, not capable of reproducing itself. This is why "The most hated sort (of wealth getting) and with the greatest reason, is usury, which makes a gain out of money itself and not from the natural object of it. For money was intended to be used in exchange, not to increase at interest. ... Wherefore of all modes of getting wealth, this is the most unnatural."

In the *Republic*, Book VIII, 555d–556b (c. 380 BC), Socrates talks with Glaucon, pointing to the "negligence and encouragement of licentiousness in oligarchies." Their greed, Socrates explains, inserts the parasitic "sting of their money into any of the remainder who do not resist." The effect is to burden many Athenians with debt, to suffer foreclosure on their land and disenfranchisement, fostering "the drone and pauper element in the state." This leaves the people (the *demos*) to "conspire against the acquirers of their estates and the rest of the citizens, and be eager for revolution." Earlier, in Book I, Socrates likens paying back an interest-bearing loan to a greedy usurer to be analogous to returning borrowed weapons to a lunatic.

In a spirit similar to Livy's and Plutarch's descriptions of the harsh creditor behavior and land grabbing of Roman elites, the Jewish Bible depicts most kings as rapacious, with their power resting largely on their financial wealth. In response to this situation, Deuteronomy "assigns no significant role to the king (such as appointing judges or commanding the army), but severely restricts the king's freedom to accumulate capital and describes him as a figurehead whose main role is studying God's Teaching so that he will not become arrogant."[585] The epoch of Near Eastern "divine kingship" proclaiming "justice and equity" was over. The Biblical Jubilee Year would have been at the expense of kings, civic aristocratic regimes, and the imperial Roman Empire.

Coronation and New Year festivals were stripped of their Bronze Age association with economic renewal and debt amnesty. The New Year degenerated into a Roman Saturnalia, keeping the ritual drunkenness and disorder but dropping any ensuing restoration of economic balance and equity by freeing society from agrarian and personal debt. The Stoics focused on inward personal values rather than on reversing monopolization of the land and privatization of credit. Although most Stoics condemned usury, many (such as Seneca) enriched themselves through it. Mutual aid was restricted mainly within the aristocracy with its interest-free eranos loans.

Underlying Bronze Age periodic renewal and debt amnesty was a circular idea of time. Society's landholding patterns, financial balance and liberation of indebted citizens from bondage were to be restored to a state of equity, conceived as a timeless status quo ante. The classical idea of linear progress means not restoring any such past, and hence not reversing economic inequity and the accumulation of indebtedness. The epoch of secular progress made social polarization and the monopolization of land irreversible.

The early history of Christianity saw Jesus expand the Jubilee tradition into a radical agenda to redeem the poor from debt bondage. Yet as his movement became more universal, reaching beyond Judaism to encompass all humanity, it was constrained to become otherworldly in the face of the Roman oligarchy's victory. The "Year of the Lord" came to symbolize an equity to be achieved more in heaven than on earth. Jesus was transformed from the Lord's messenger bringing good news of a Clean Slate, to become the Christ preaching forgiveness on a more abstract spiritualized plane.

Christianity did not sponsor the debt cancellations and land redemption that Yahweh had stipulated as part of his covenant with the Israelites. By stripping away his character as a Lord of economic redemption sponsoring reordering of debt and land tenure on earth, these transformations dropped the focus on debt that Jesus had emphasized.

Jesus' teachings on debt forgiveness

Luke 4:16–30 describes Jesus' first public act upon returning to his native town of Nazareth. Visiting its synagogue, he is handed the scroll of Isaiah, and unrolls it to the passage in (Third-) Isaiah 61, where the prophet (as noted above in Chapter 24) announces that the Lord has sent him "to preach good news (gospel) to the poor" and "to proclaim freedom (deror) for the prisoners and ... to release the oppressed, to proclaim the year of the Lord's favor," that is, the Jubilee Year. Jesus informed the

---

[585] Tigay 1996: 461.

congregation that he had come to fulfill that destiny. Treating debt bondage literally, not as merely a metaphor for spiritual bondage, Jesus the Redeemer set about preaching literal redemption from debt. With the sounding of the yobel trumpet the old order is to yield to one of equity and righteousness restoring the poor to dignity.

Among the four gospel writers, only Luke describes this inaugural sermon. Matthew and Mark merely say that after delivering it, Jesus was violently rejected by his fellow Nazarines. Luke explains why, by grounding Jesus's message in the Jubilee tradition. For many years Biblical scholarship interpreted his version as being an idiosyncratic elaboration of Mark 6: 1–6, perhaps drawing on non-Mark traditions. But discovery of the Dead Sea scrolls suggests that it was Mark and the other gospel writers who skipped over the significance of Jesus' *deror* citation from Isaiah, and subsequent Christianity, not Jesus, that treated "release" as a metaphor for a more spiritualized advent of God's reign and "forgiveness of humankind … a metaphor for God's work of redemption and reconciliation."[586] For subsequent Christianity, the coming sovereignty of God was to end the old worldly order, rescuing "the poor" but not by taking the specific worldly policy of cancelling the debts that held them in poverty and stripped them of their land and means of self-support.

Jesus' Parable of the Unmerciful Servant (Matthew 18) leaves little doubt that the poor literally should be forgiven their debts. Admonishing Peter to excuse his brother's sins, Jesus explains that admission to heaven depends on how one conducts his life in accordance with the principle of Leviticus 19: 18: "Love thy neighbor as thyself." This precept forms the basis for the Golden Rule that we should not do unto others what we would not wish them to do unto us.

Jesus' parable applies this ethic to debt forgiveness. A king calls his officials and administrators together to settle accounts with them. The first man brought in is a satrap who owes him ten thousand talents. Unable to pay this enormous amount, he asks for more time to collect more taxes from his subjects. But the king orders that the insolvent satrap, his wife, children "and all that he had be sold to repay the debt. The satrap fell on his knees before him and begged, 'Be patient with me and I will pay back everything.' His master took pity on him, canceled the debt and let him go. But when that satrap went out, he found one of his subordinate officials who owed him a hundred *denarii*. He grabbed the official and began to choke him. 'Pay back what you owe me!' he demanded. His fellow royal servant fell to his knees and begged him, 'Be patient with me, and I will pay you back.'" But the satrap refused, and had his subordinate thrown into prison until he could pay the debt.

When the royal servants told the king what had happened, he called his satrap back. "'You wicked servant,' he said, 'I canceled all that debt of yours because you begged me to. Shouldn't you have had mercy on your fellow servant just as I had on you?' In anger the king turned him over to the jailers until he should pay back all he owed." Jesus warns: "This is how my heavenly Father will treat each of you unless you forgive your brother from your heart."

[586] Ringe 1985: 38 ff., 42 and 66. The Greek term for "release," *aphesis,* found in the Septuagint translation of Isaiah 61: 1 and 58: 6, places as much emphasis as Hebrew *deror* on release from economic obligations, and does not have religious connotations of a covenant.

The relation of this parable to the Lord's Prayer seems obvious enough, but the gospels have different versions. Matthew 6: 12 reads "Forgive us our debts, as we forgive our debtors (*tois opheiletais*)." But as Chapter 4 has traced, in many languages the words "debt," "trespass," and "sin" have interchangeable meanings (as in German Schuld). Luke 11: 4 breaks the parallelism, saying "forgive us our 'sins' (*tas hamartias*) as we forgive our debtors (*tois opheiletais*)." On this ground Ringe interprets the Lord's Prayer as a "Jubilee Prayer." [587]

London Drake cites two reasons why monetary debts rather than non-financial moral sins must be meant. First, the Lord's Prayer "petition is unusual because it incorporates human action into a prayer, and uses the language of debt." Creditors can forgive debts and the wealthy can give to charity, but only God can forgive sins. Also, there are philological reasons for its use of a word meaning specifically monetary debts. [588]

Luke 6: 35 cites Jesus' admonition to "lend, without expecting to be repaid." That is the opposite of the intent of Hillel's *prosbul* clause. Charity toward the poor called for forgiving their debts, and many early Christians used their own money to redeem their brethren from debt bondage. Christ's title of the Redeemer includes the idea of saving debtors from bondage. The ultimate test of a well-to-do person's spiritual goodness was to relinquish his financial power over his debtors, as in the story of Job. In Luke's passage, as in Job and in Matthew 18's parable above, lending is represented as the characteristic test for admission to heaven. It is the most prevalent mode of exerting either generosity or coercive power toward one's fellow beings.

All four gospels (Luke 19, Matthew 21, Mark 11 and John 2) tell the story of how Jesus drove home the conflict between his religious values and those of creditors. Upon entering Jerusalem he went directly to its temple, where business contracts and oaths, including debt agreements, were sworn to the Lord (as they had been at Babylonia's temple gates). This oath taking sanctified the repayment of debts. Jesus overturned the benches of the moneychangers and emptied out their moneybags on the floor, threw over the tables of merchants, made a scourge of cords and "drove them all out of the temple, and the sheep, and the oxen" (John 2: 15). Echoing the words of Jeremiah 7: 11 some four centuries earlier, Jesus announced: "My house will be a house of prayer, but you have made it 'a den of thieves.'"

This is the only report in the Scriptures of his using violence. It is the act that inspired the city leaders to plot his death. Matthew 23: 16 reports Jesus's explanation for his criticism: "You say, 'If anyone swears by the temple, it means nothing; but if

---

[587] Ringe 1985: 77–81. Indeed, Ringe (p. 105) finds "the Beatitudes found in the Sermons on the Mount and on the Plain (Matt. 5: 3–6/Luke 6: 20–22) … to be a meditation on the content of Isaiah 61: 1–2."

[588] Drake 2014: 239 "The Qumran documents do use חוב for sin rather than debt, but only in a few places (just over twenty occurrences for חוב and חובה). From the evidence we have, in the first century חוב was a comprehensible but still unusual word for sin, and would not become the conventional term until later." Also, most "occurrences [of ὀφείλημα or its cognates] in the New Testament all refer to debts or obligations (especially debts in the Gospels), not sins, and other words referring to sin are used much more frequently (286 occurrences of αράπτωμα, ἁμαρτάνω, and their cognates)."

anyone swears by the gold of the temple, he is bound by his oath.' You blind fools! Which is greater: the gold, or the temple that makes the gold sacred?"[589]

Quoting Jeremiah was doubly significant in that the prophet describes the Lord as warning the Israelites not to turn their land and temples into a den of thieves by oppressing the most seriously afflicted debtors – aliens, orphans and widows – upon pain of breaking the covenant and losing their own liberty. Poverty goes hand in hand with its cause: covetous greed. To prey on the weak, to monopolize the land and wealth, is to seize what belongs to the Lord and his followers. The law applicable to creditors accordingly is the Eighth Commandment: Thou shalt not steal. Usurers were stealing the land and liberty of the Israelites. The people would suffer national perdition if they failed to heed the Lord's spirit and rectify matters.

From the Jubilee Year to the Day of Judgment

Only Luke turns the Jubilee into an eschatological frame of reference. The "reign of God" is a clean slate, a Jubilee Year marking the end of the old order. A new equality was to be proclaimed, benefiting mainly the poor. The final chapter of Luke (24:47) describes Jesus explaining what is written in the Scriptures: "The Messiah will suffer and rise from the dead on the third day, and repentance and forgiveness of sins [*hamartia*] will be preached in his name to all nations, beginning at Jerusalem."

One can well imagine the impact such preaching had from Jerusalem to Rome, whose poor had lost their struggle for social equity by the time Augustus was crowned emperor in 29 BC. For debtors, the arrow of time threatened to bring only a deepening poverty. As hopes for worldly reform became gloomier, more eyes turned to the hereafter to await the Millennium. Christianity promised a renewal, but ultimately in an eschatological Day of Judgment to occur at the end of history.

From redemption to charity

Cancelling debts and returning land and debt servants to their former family holders had become politically impossible by imperial Roman times. Christianity turned the spirit of righteousness into one of charity – by those who had accumulated wealth that, from the archaic perspective, was gained inequitably in the first place.

Acts 4:32–35 reflects the new ideal: "No one claimed that any of his possessions was his own, but they shared everything they had. … There were no needy persons among them. For from time to time those who owned lands or houses sold them, brought the money from the sales and put it at the apostles' feet, and it was distributed to anyone as he had need." This was a distributive response, not a clean slate wiping out the debt overgrowth.

The Christian Lord shifted the moral focus away from economy-wide personal debt amnesties to saving the souls of individuals, especially those of the wealthy. Private charity was substituted for the Mosaic covenant to periodically cancel debts

---

[589] Jesus adds (Matthew 23:25): "You clean the outside of the cup and dish, but inside they are full of greed and self-indulgence."

and restore the land.[590] This left the worldly patterns of debt and landholding intact as economies sunk into clientage to the wealthy, whose charitable activities typically amounted to a tithe of their takings. The rich monopolized the land as the imperial Roman world polarized into feudalism.

By the time Christianity came to dominate the Roman Empire in the 3rd and 4th centuries of the modern era, the money economy was drying up except at the top of the social pyramid. Usury was banned among the Christian clergy, while slavery yielded to feudalism. But usury and slavery were ended more as a result of economic collapse and depopulation than by Christian opposition.

From Stoic Philosophy to the Church Fathers

In line with Jesus's contrast between worldly riches and the treasures in heaven, Matthew 7:19–24 exhorts Christians not to "store up for yourselves treasures on earth, where moth and rust destroy, and where thieves break in and steal. But store up for yourselves treasures in heaven ... For where your treasure is, there your heart will be also. ... No one can serve two masters. Either he will hate the one and love the other, or he will be devoted to the one and despise the other. You cannot serve both God and Money [Mammon]."

Worldly ideology became increasingly embittered as Roman society sank into deepening poverty in the glare of gaudy displays of wealth. 1 John 2:15–17 urges Christians: "Do not love the world or anything in the world. If anyone loves the world, the love of the Father is not in him. ... The world and its desires pass away, but the man who does the will of God lives forever." In much the same vein, Timothy exhorts:

> We brought nothing into the world, and we can take nothing out of it. But if we have food and clothing, we will be content with that. People who want to get rich fall into the temptation and a trap and into many foolish and harmful desires that plunge men into ruin and destruction. For the love of money is a root of all kinds of evil. Some people, eager for money, have wandered from the faith and pierced themselves with many griefs. ...
>
> Command those who are rich in this present world not to be arrogant nor to put their hope in wealth, which is so uncertain, but to put their hope in God, who richly provides us with everything for our enjoyment. Command them to do good, to be rich in good deeds, and to be generous and willing to share. In this way they will lay up treasure for themselves as a firm foundation for the coming age, so that they may take hold of the life that is truly life.   (1 Timothy 6:6–12, 17–19)

Economic and moral contrasts were drawn in melodramatic terms, along with dreams of a utopian Golden Age at the start of history – the "mother condition," as it were. The philosopher Seneca, tutor to the emperor Nero, endorsed the view of the Stoic

---

[590] Islam picked up Christianity's emphasis on charity. The Koran's prohibition of interest (2.276) "stands between verses dealing with almsgiving." Not charging interest was like a charitable gift to the borrower.

encyclopediast Poseidonius of Apamea that a utopian Golden Age of Saturn had been a communalistic state in which arts and crafts were as yet unknown but whose government "was under the jurisdiction of the wise" who "protected the weaker from the stronger. ... No ruler tried his power against those to whom he owed the beginnings of his power ... But when once vice stole in and kingdoms were transformed into tyrannies, a need arose for laws," such as those framed by the wise Lycurgus of Sparta and Solon of Athens. In this fortune-favored Second Age,

Figure 33: Allegory of avarice by Albrecht Dürer

the bounties of nature lay open to all, for men's indiscriminate use, before avarice and luxury had broken the bonds which held mortals together, and they, abandoning their communal existence, had separated and turned together.

No ploughman tilled the soil, nor was it right
To portion off or bound one's property.
Men shared their gains, and earth more freely gave
Her riches to her sons who sought them not. (Virgil, *Georgics*, i, 125 ff.)

What race of men was ever more blest than that race? They enjoyed all nature in partnership ... But avarice broke in upon a condition so happily ordained, and, by its eagerness to lay something away and to turn it to its own private use, made all things the property of others, and reduced itself from boundless wealth to straitened need. It was avarice that introduced poverty and, by craving much, lost all. And so, although she now tries to make good her loss, although she adds one estate to another, evicting a neighbor either by buying him out or by wronging him, although she extends her country estates to the size of provinces and defines ownership as meaning extensive travel through one's own property – in spite of all these efforts of hers, no enlargement of our boundaries will bring us back to the condition from which we have departed. ... What there was, was divided among un-quarrelling friends. Not yet had the stronger begun to lay hands upon the weaker. Not yet had the miser, by hiding away what lay before him, shut off his neighbor from even the necessaries of life; each cared as much for his neighbor as for himself. Armor lay unused, and the hand, unstained by human blood, had turned all its hatred against wild beasts.   (Seneca, *Epistle* xc)

By the 4th century AD the Christian father Lactantius (tutor to Constantine's son Crispus) presented history in similar terms:

> The source of all these evils was cupidity, bursting forth from the contempt of true virtue. The wealthy did not share with others, but seized the property of others as their own, drawing in all things for their own private gain. Goods which individuals were producing for the use of all were taken into the homes of the few. In order to enslave the many, the greedy began to appropriate and accumulate the necessities of life and kept them tightly shut up, so that they might keep these bounties for themselves. They did this not for humanity's sake (which was not in them at all), but to rake up all things as products of their greed and avarice. In the name of justice they made unfair and unjust laws to sanction their thefts and avarice against the power of the multitude. In this way they availed as much by authority as by strength of arms or overt evil.
>
> (Lactantius, *Divine Institutes*, V,vi.)

The Virgin Mary replaces Nanshe and Nemesis

From Sumerian Nanshe to Greek Nemesis, the role of punishing arrogance, fraud and injustice by the rich and powerful often was assigned to goddesses. Nemesis carried the scales of justice and punished merchants, other wealthy individuals and above all creditors for their hubristic arrogance of wealth.

Each archaic town had its own patron deity, although each tended to follow a similar regional pantheon headed by a sun god of justice. Protection of the poorest individuals—those consigned to temple and palace workshops—typically was assigned to a goddess, sometimes depicted as spouse of the sun god. No such female deity is found in Judaism. The Lord Yahweh protected the poor, "absorbing" the feminine function so to speak. As Pauline Christianity reached out to new constituencies, local pantheons were telescoped into what became the Christian trinity. Cyril of Alexandria elevated the Mary cult largely as a means of excluding the Jews, who were unwilling to accept a female consort deity. Cyril's iconography of the Virgin Mary stripped away the earlier aspect of the avenging goddess punishing hubris as Nanshe and Nemesis had done. She became simply the patroness of the suffering poor.

Figure 34:
Nemesis with writing board and wheel

The End Time and the Day of Judgment

The Jewish Mishnah calls the first day of Nisan (the springtime Babylonian New Year) the New Year of kings. "According to the Mishna," observes one Biblical historian, "at New Year all the inhabitants of the earth pass before God, as the scripture says: 'He fashioneth their hearts alike; and considereth all their works' (Psalm 33.15). ... The spring thus has its 'day of judgment' for determining the harvest of grain, the autumn for determining the water, and at the official New Year mankind is judged."[591] This Day of Judgment involves a trial as well as "establishment of cosmic order which takes place at each new season. ... in which the cosmos begins anew, after the chaos that has gone before."

A similar imagery is found in Isaiah 24. After warning that Egypt, Babylon and other kingdoms are about to be subjugated, Isaiah describes the Lord's devastation of the earth in words that sound like part of the Saturnalia-type narrative for the Babylonian New Year ceremony:

The earth dries up and withers, the world languishes and withers,
    the exalted of the earth languish.
The earth is defiled by its people; they have disobeyed the laws,
    violated the statutes and broken the everlasting covenant.
Therefore a curse consumes the earth; its people must bear the guilt. ...
    The city is left in ruins, its gate is battered to pieces.
So will it be on the earth and among the nations ...
The floodgates of the heavens are opened, the foundations of the earth shake.
The earth is broken up, the earth is split asunder, the earth is thoroughly shaken.
The earth reels like a drunkard, it sways like a hut in the wind;
    so heavy upon it is the guilt of its rebellion that it falls – never to rise again.
In that day the Lord will punish the powers in the heavens above
    and the kings on the earth below.
They will be herded together like prisoners bound in a dungeon.

There follows a hymn praising the Lord, who has expelled the foreigners and exploiters (Isaiah 25–26): "You have been a refuge for the poor, a refuge for the needy in his distress, a shelter from the storm and a shade from the heat." The Lord restores justice, trampling evil.

On the Day of Judgment all the souls ever born stand shoulder to shoulder. 2 Timothy 3: 1–5 warns: "There will be terrible times in the last days. People will be lovers of themselves, lovers of money, boastful, proud, abusive, disobedient to their parents, ungrateful, unholy, without love, unforgiving, slanderous, without self-control, brutal, not lovers of the good, treacherous, rash, conceited, lovers of pleasure rather than lovers of God – having a form of godliness but denying its power. Have nothing to do with them."

[591] Wensinck 1923: 182.

James 5:1–5 continues in the same vein (recalling Matthew 7:19ff. quoted above):

> Now listen, you rich people, weep and wail because of the misery that is
> coming upon you. Your wealth has rotted, and moths have eaten your clothes.
> Your gold and silver are corroded. Their corrosion will testify against you
> and eat your flesh like fire. You have hoarded wealth in the last days. Look!
> The wages you failed to pay the workmen who mowed your fields are crying
> out against you. The cries of the harvesters have reached the ears of the Lord
> Almighty. You have lived on earth in luxury and self-indulgence.

This denunciation recalls the cries of Sodom, as well as Ezekiel 16:49. The Book of
Revelation reports John's vision of the Lord with a voice like a trumpet to announce
the Day of Judgment – the occasion for re-ordering the world, much as Mesopotamian rulers restored order out of chaos. Like the Babylonian New Year festival, at
which the newly ordered world begins only when Tiamat has been defeated, the
apocalyptic Christian vision welcomes "the last days" as an end time of chaos
heralding the Lord's proclamation of order and equity. Good will vanquish evil, and
order will replace disorder.[592]

The Book of Revelation depicts the Lord destroying the world – "Babylon," a
metaphor for "merchants of the earth [growing] rich from her excessive luxuries. ...
no one buys their cargoes any more – cargoes of gold, silver and precious stones and
pearls ... cattle and sheep; horses and carriages; and bodies and souls of men. ... The
merchants who sold these things and gained their wealth from her will stand far off,
terrified at her torment ... and cry out ... 'In one hour such great wealth has been
brought to ruin!'" The multitude in heaven will shout "Amen, Hallelujah!" The New
Jerusalem will appear on earth, the millennium restoring equity and righteousness,
the Year of the Lord that Jesus prophesied.

Redemption, the arrow of time and the Christian Millennium

The essence of the idea of progress is its irreversible arrow of time. Replacing the
tradition of periodic social renewal and clean slates, Christianity promises to restore
equity only at the end of time, at the Last Judgment. Until then, one must suffer on
earth, where deepening poverty and debt for most of the population has been made
immune from periodic restorations of equity.

Eschatology is the doctrine of ends and final things. When theologians speak of
Christian eschatology, they mean the end towards which history is moving – Christ's
second coming at the Day of Judgment. Cyril of Alexandria, the 5th-century AD
ideologue of the doctrine of a holy trinity, wrote: "There will be a time of release
(*aphesis*) for us all, over all the world, at the end I mean, when each one will run to his
own possession, that is to the destiny suited to him and apportioned by God."[593]

---

[592] Wensinck 1923: 183. See also Isaiah 53.
[593] *De Adoratione* Mg 68, 1125, quoted in North 1954: 229.

Commenting on this passage, North observes that in contrast to the Jewish Bible and its prophets seeking to end poverty, the New Testament "elevates the spirit of poverty to a value in its own right. The old law controlled the acquisition of material wealth, the new praises those who use this world as if they used it not, 1 Corinth. 7:31 ['For the world in its present form is passing away.']; whose business is in heaven, Philippians 3:20 ['Our citizenship is in heaven']." The ultimate Jubilee year is no longer on earth; it exists only in Heaven.

*   *   *

The debt write-offs that once stood at the core of social renewal and religious ethics have long been all but unthinkable. Only quite recently in history have people stopped questioning and criticizing the social, moral and economic consequences of debt.

Today's theology lacks the Biblical idea of liberty in the sense of Hebrew *deror* and its Near Eastern antecedents – liberty from unpayably high debts and monopolization of land. "Although theologians of liberation clearly recognize the importance of gospel imagery pointing to 'good news to the poor,'" concludes Ringe, "they seem not to be drawn to the theological motif of forgiveness."[584] In its modern sense this word appears to connote forgiving one's oppressors, accepting the unfair world as it is. "Before 'forgiveness' can find its way back into the lexicon of liberation, it must be linked to justice," specifically to the concept of economic equity found in the Jubilee tradition. Yet to date, hopes for major religious statements on debt and land reform have not been rewarded.

A modern Isaiah or Jeremiah might interpret today's economic and environmental devastation as a sign from the Lord that societies have veered from the righteous path and the End Time is drawing near – by earth (poisoned and quaking), air (polluted and with "extreme weather"), fire (global warming and Fukushima) and water (rising sea levels and flooding). The recent scourges of disease and other disasters might appear as portents confirming that the Day of Judgment is at hand.

Jesus would find the domestic and international debt burden to pose a moral test of self-centeredness *versus* openheartedness, Mammon *versus* God. Medieval Canon Law would find that most of today's debts have no counterpart in creating mutual gain between borrower and lender, but constitute parasitic usury, a form of theft.

If their values are right in deeming today's debt burden to be wrong, then political philosophy and religious fervor should aim at a higher concept of equity to restore economic and social order.

27. A Byzantine Echo

Like Babylonia in Hammurabi's epoch, the Eastern Roman Empire's army and tax base consisted mainly of peasant freeholders. To defend against Slavic and Muslim invasions in the 6th and 7th centuries, Emperor Heraclius (610–641) assigned soldiers self-support land in military districts called themes. The countryside accounted for 90 to 95 percent of the population, with scattered villages more like the towns of ancient Babylonia than the cities of classical antiquity. "Their populations consisted mostly of peasants, who farmed the adjoining land," with the usual array of small cottage industries and defensive fortifications.[594]

Down through the 10th and the early 11th century these fiscal theme districts provided Constantinople with a standing army as a hereditary land-tenured class under commanders (*strategoi*). "The vast bulk of the military forces now consisted of free peasant smallholders who held land ... in exchange for which they (or one person per household) had to give military service. The peasant-soldiers, as they are commonly called, also drew a salary every four years. They owned their horse and military equipment."[595]

As in Babylonia, a rising aristocracy of military leaders sought to pry away the land of smallholders and villages. Their aim was to gain control of the crop surplus and labor at the expense of the palace and its tax collectors. In the 9th and 10th centuries, emperors of Basil I's "Macedonian" dynasty (867–1056) issued laws (called Novels) to counter this takeover by reversing transfers of village land to the wealthy and banning future such takeovers. Romanos I spelled out their fiscal and military logic in his Novel of 934 barring the wealthy and "powerful" from taking village land: The population's "contribution of taxes and the fulfillment of military obligations ... will be completely lost should the common people disappear."[596]

Roman fiscal reform from Diocletian to Justinian

Upon becoming Roman Emperor, Diocletian (284–305) sought to stem the decline in tax revenue by creating a bureaucracy of decurion tax administrators. They were held responsible for fiscal shortfalls, but corruption was rife. Many simply kept what they collected, while powerful families resisted paying taxes, forcing poorer ones to make up the deficit. By the 4th century "the peasants were ruined economically, crushed by heavy burdens, defenceless before the arrogance and abuse of the government officials. This was the reason why they placed themselves under the patronage

---

[594] Dagron 2002: 394.

[595] Laiou 2002: 15. See also Haldon 1997: 208–253, and Danstrup 1946: 234.

[596] Romanos, Edict of 934, I.2, in McGeer 2000: 56. This is the only English-language translation of these Novels, drawing heavily on Lemerle 1979.

Figure 35: Summa on the Codex of Justinian.

of the great landowners, becoming their bondsmen and surrendering to their protectors a freedom which had become almost intolerable."[597]

Attempts to tighten imperial tax collection were bound to alienate these officials, and especially the large landholders, who backed military warlords against emperors strong enough to restrain their grabbing. They overthrew Emperor Majorian (457–461), a former general, when in 458 he assigned tax collection to governors instead of local administrators as one of his first acts, his Novel No. 2, "On the Remission of Past-Due Accounts," despite proclaiming an amnesty for land-tax arrears.

The fiscal problem worsened over the next two centuries. Officials were notorious for taking the land of smallholders and keeping the crop surplus for themselves at the expense of central authority. Justinian (527–565) banned self-dealing and related conflict of interest by officials when he codified Roman law in his *Corpus Juris Civilis* (I.53):

> 1. Those who administer public affairs … cannot purchase any movable or immovable property, or build any houses without obtaining from Us [the Emperor] a special rescript authorizing them to do so.
> (1) Moreover, they must refuse donations of every description … no matter what they may consist of, and what their value is, unless the donor specially ratifies the donation in writing, after the term of office of the person who received the gift has expired, or the term of five years has elapsed …[598]

The historian Procopius criticized Justinian for not following earlier emperors and cancelling agrarian debts, but tightening the fiscal screws on landowners. Officials unable to collect the stipulated tax revenue were obliged "to abandon their property to the informers or to the confiscation of the state."

> It had formerly been the long-established custom that each Roman ruler should, not only once during his reign but often remit to his subjects whatever public debts [that is, taxes] were in arrears, so that those who were in financial difficulty and had no means of paying their delinquencies would not be too far pressed. … But Justinian, during thirty-two years' time, made no such concession to his subjects, and consequently those who were unable to pay had to flee their country and never return.[599]

It was indeed normal for Byzantine emperors to protect widespread land tenure by cancelling tax arrears to maintain the solvency (and hence, loyalty) of landowners, especially to help regions recover from warfare. In 401, Honorius had remitted arrears

---

[597] Ostrogorsky 1969: 53.

[598] Scott 1932. *Enactments of Justinian. The Code.* Book I, para 53. A translation is available at https://droitromain.univ-grenoble-alpes.fr/Anglica/CJ1_Scott.htm#53. Brown 1971: 157 discusses this problem. Self-dealing is still subject to modern prohibitions of emoluments while in public office.

[599] Procopius, *Secret History* ch. 23 (tr. Atwater 1992: 111). Born in Roman Palestine, Procopius became legal advisor to the Roman general Belisarius, and apparently had a seat in the Constantinople Senate as an *illustres*. He died in 554, some 17 year into Justinian's reign, for whose details he is the major contemporary source.

up to 386. A. H. M. Jones summarizes how in 414 the Eastern Roman Emperor Theodosius II wrote off all arrears from 368 to 407, indicating "that there had been no general indulgence in the East since the latter part of Valens' reign [364–378]. In 433 the arrears of 408 to 427 were remitted, and there must have been another indulgence (not recorded in the Novels) early in the 440s covering the years 428–437. Marcian on his accession (450) remitted the arrears of 438 to 447, which was over-indulgent. In the West, Valentinian III was lax also, cancelling arrears up to 436 in 438, and up to 447 in 450; many powerful taxpayers who had held up payment for two or three years must have profited. Majorian went even further, remitting on his accession all fiscal debts up to the previous financial year."[600]

Justinian tightened up tax collection, but "probably on his accession (527), remitted arrears up to 522. His next indulgence, which covered the years 523 to 544, did not come until 553. Justin II soon after his accession (November 565) remitted arrears up to 560." Jones explains the economic dynamic as being pragmatic, as "general remissions were intended not so much to relieve the taxpayers as to clear up the public accounts by writing off bad debts. They chiefly benefited the public by preventing ingenious officials from raking up ancient claims against taxpayers who had failed to keep their receipts. To guard against this form of extortion Marcian ruled that if a taxpayer could produce receipts for three continuous years no earlier claim was admissible."

Figure 36: Emperor Justinian

These imperial debt amnesties thus applied mainly to tax arrears. Other debt secured by land did not play nearly the role that it had done in antiquity. Tax forgiveness was traditional Byzantine practice for lands that suffered military or natural disasters. Tiberius II Constantine (578–582) remitted a year's taxation to restore morale, as did Irene (797–802), mainly to gain support against opponents who ultimately overthrew her.

[600] Jones 1964, vol. I: 467.

In the 11[601] century, Basil II "waived two years' worth of land and hearth taxes."[601] That century's Zavorda tax treatise explains how to stop the abandonment of land by proclaiming a sympatheia tax remission:

> When a village has been found wiped out, either wholly or in part, its tax is investigated. … The inspector who comes out grants them a *sympatheia*. And thereafter they [the lands] are handed out in leaseholding by the inspector. Or else the tax collectors lease them to the villagers; for before the passage of thirty years it is not allowed that devastated properties be made *klasma* or otherwise alienated, specifically on account of the owners' absence. For if they return within the thirty-year period, they have back their own property. … But often, before having been made *klasma*, it is offered in pasturage [to other villagers], until the owners' return.[602]

While the West fragmented into feudal lordships,[603] the post-Roman aristocracy in the Eastern Empire fades from the historical record in the 7th and 8th centuries, "increasingly to be replaced by new men, typically of military background, and commonly of Armenian or Caucasian descent. In the countryside and the provinces … landowners and notables were either slaughtered or took flight."[604] Based in the free peasant communities, the new magnates used their administrative position to increase their holdings "by absorbing, often through dubious means, the properties of the small peasants."[605]

Strong emperors restored the role of peasant freeholders as the basis for the steady flow of Byzantine tax revenue, which peaked in the early 10th century. But large landowners sought to gain control of rural land and labor. By the 12th century they succeeded in enthroning their own proxies as emperors.

---

[601] Treadgold 1997: 577. He describes Basil's act simply as reflecting the fact that Constantinople didn't need the money.

[602] Brand 1969: 58. Citing the early 10th-century Marcian Treatise, and the mid-11th-century Zavorda Treatise, he notes (p. 45): "The principal affliction threatening peasants, to judge by the space accorded it in the two treatises, was devastation by an enemy incursion; the chronicles show raids to have been frequent. Many villagers, the Marcian Treatise implies, would be killed or carried off, or would take flight. The problem which faced the tax inspector was how to keep the remaining farmers at work, for according to the principal of mutualness (*allelengyon*) they were obligated to pay the taxes of the devastated land. To prevent the remaining farmers from fleeing, the central government sent an inspector, who was empowered to grant total remission of taxes (*sympatheia*) for any land which seemed worthy of it: the whole village, part of the village land, certain individual parcels, or parts of individual parcels. In this last case, the parcel would owe a certain tax and have a *sympatheia* for the rest. A number of entries in the surviving Boeotian tax register show such partial *sympatheiai*."

[603] Ostrogorsky 1969: 96–100 and 133f.

[604] Sarris 2012: 434, endorsing Whittow 2009: 134–153, characterizing "the Middle Byzantine Empire of the eighth to tenth centuries as a 'world of peasants,' in which the concerns and complaints of peasant farmers, freeholders, and their families emerged to the fore of imperial legislation and the workings of justice as never before."

[605] Charanis 1953: 415–423, repr. in Eisenstadt, ed., 1986.

The Novels of Basil and Romanus protecting smallholders from the *dynatoi*

In Byzantine practice each emperor selected his successor as co-ruler so as to take office with a running start when his predecessor died. Michael III (842–867) was named emperor at the age of two. The way in which he chose Basil I as his successor illustrates the role played by chance in shaping political turning points – and what the adjective "byzantine" means.

When Michael turned fifteen (the age of male adulthood at the time), his mother Theodora forced him into an arranged marriage. But he was in love with Eudocia Ingerina, the daughter of a Verangian (Viking Russian) guard in the imperial retinue. When she got pregnant a decade later, in 866, Michael did not want the child (the future Leo VI) to be born out of wedlock, so he asked one of his favorite companions, Basil to marry her. To comply, Basil had to divorce his own wife. Eudocia continued to be Michael's mistress, and Michael assigned his older sister Thecla to serve as Basil's mistress.[606] As a reward, he named Basil his co-emperor, citing his bravery in combat.

Within a year Basil and his supporters killed the 27-year-old Michael in his bedchamber, sleeping off a drinking bout. Basil was 56. The son of a peasant soldier, he had spent most of his life in modest circumstances.[607] Arnold Toynbee called him a "self-made man," yet also "the most statesmanlike East Roman Emperor since his self-made predecessor Leo III."[608]

Taking the throne as first emperor of the "Macedonian" dynasty (although probably of Armenian descent), Basil (867–886) set to work restoring Byzantine fiscal solvency. Toward this end he immersed himself in the actual court process where smallholders protested their tax burden or the appropriation of their land by the wealthy. According to the chronicler Theophanes Continuatus: "Whenever he was free from the other cares of state, he would go down to the Genikon, the main fiscal bureau, to sit and hear the complaints lodged by aggrieved taxpayers … 'he defended the injured and through lawful punishment stopped the perpetrators of injustice from daring to do anything similar again.'"[609]

Michael III had exhausted the treasury by giving vast sums to his favorites. Basil made them repay half of what Michael had given away, raising 4.3 million *nomismata*, equal to more than a year's imperial revenue.[610] To put fiscal policy and a free peasantry on a more self-sustaining basis, Basil started composing the great Byzantine law compilation, the Epanagoge (completed by Leo). From the Code of Justinian it forbid public officers from buying land during their term of office or receiving "gifts" (as noted above). From the edict of Theodosius in 391 (*Codex Theodosianus* III.1.6) it prevented land from being sold freely to anyone except near kinsman and co-owners

---

[606] Treadgold 1997: 453.

[607] The only modern biography of Basil is Tobias 2007, but it says little about his economic administration.

[608] Toynbee 1973: 583. His discussion of the biography written by Basil's grandson Constantine VII is highly informative, pp. 581–598.

[699] Theophanes Continuatus, *Vita Basilii* 260–261, summarized in Magdalino 1994: 99.

[610] Treadgold 1997: 456.

of village land. Likewise incorporated into the Epanagoge were the edicts "by Leo and Anthemius in 468 (*Corpus juris civilis*, XI.55) [which] served 'to prevent the owner of land from transferring the same to a stranger, under any circumstances.'"[611] Basil fought with his sons, especially with his nominal second son Leo after his first son Constantine died. As was the case with Michael III, a forced marriage played a role. Basil's wife Eudocia chose a relative whom Leo did not want. He had his own girlfriend, a tavern keeper's daughter. Basil backed Eudocia, beat up Leo, and married off the girl to someone else. There were rumors that Leo, who viewed Michael as his real father, planned to mount a palace coup. Basil imprisoned him for a while, but died soon after in what was reported to be a strange hunting accident. That enabled Leo VI (886–912) to take the throne at the age of twenty.

In contrast to Basil, Leo favored the aristocracy and its land acquisition. He reversed Basil's protections against absentee appropriators, and also Basil's forbidding "the receipt of interest by any persons except orphans and minors."[612] Leo permitted interest of 4% to be charged, claiming that the ban on rural mortgages burdened the economy.[613]

Most important, Leo issued a Novel repealing Basil's limitation of the right of first refusal to members of the local tax district. "The holder of a property is permitted to sell to any person he wishes without interference and without giving notification."[614] Leo's rationale for tis policy was that giving neighbors the right of first refusal instead of letting outsiders bid would enable them to block outside bidders so as to buy the land of the most impoverished peasants for themselves at a distressed price. Leo's ruling gave neighbors only a six-month window to acquire land from fellow villagers, after which time it could be sold to outsiders.[615]

That policy opened the way for wealthy creditors or other buyers to acquire the land of village smallholders by extending loans against it. In his 907 *Procheiros Nomos*, Leo reversed his earlier ruling and "described the charging of interest as 'unworthy of a Christian state' and banned it completely, without exceptions, laying down furthermore that any interest paid was to be applied to the principal of the debt."[616]

After Leo caught an intestinal disease and died in 912, his younger brother Alexander ruled for a year (912–913). Designated as co-emperor by Basil 33 years earlier, in 879, he was reported to be dissolute, and died of exhaustion after a sporting game. He was followed as co-emperor by Leo's 8-year old son, the future Constantine VII.

---

[611] McGeer 2000: 50, citing Scott 1932, 15: 214.

[612] Gofas 2002: 1100, citing the Epanagoge 28.2 as issued at the end of Basil I's reign in 885 or 886.

[613] Ostrogorsky 1969: 189 f.: "Justinian law (*Cod. Just.* IV, 32, 26) limited the rates of interest as follows: persons of high rank were allowed to charge 4 per cent (*trientes usurae*), merchants 8 per cent (*besses usurae*), all others 6 per cent (*semisses usurae*)," including the state (*Cod. Just.* X,8.3).

[614] Translated in McGeer 2000: 35 f.: "Leo VI permits the unrestricted alienation of property."

[615] To be sure, Leo was not a free marketer in the modern sense. Byzantine practice was to strictly control trade, regulating its prices and charging tariffs to the point of driving commerce into the hands of Venetians (part of the Byzantine empire at this time) and other Italians.

[616] Gofas 2002: 1101.

But until Constantine could formally take his position as an adult six years later, court turmoil led the crown to pass to the remarkable Romanos Lecapenus (920–944).

A soldier's son growing up outside of Constantinople's palace bureaucracy, Romanos I was nearly fifty years old. Renowned for his strength and bravery, he had been given rapid promotions within the army, rising to command a naval fleet. That position enabled him to seize power when a political vacuum developed after the deaths of Leo and Alexander. Romanos consolidated his rule by marrying his daughter Helena to Constantine instead of simply killing the child as so often was Byzantine practice. For this forbearance he was called "the gentle usurper." Later, he favored Constantine as his successor over his own children.

Figure 37: Leo Phokas' supporters surrender to Romanos Lekapenos.

Upon taking the throne, Romanos reversed Leo VI's rule "freeing" land markets, on the ground that this enabled the wealthy – whom he called the *dynatoi* – to displace peasant cultivators. Romanos defined the *dynatoi* as those "capable of intimidating sellers or satisfying them with a promise of some benefaction." They were "the powerful," from *dyne* (force), hence *dynastes* (lord) for power made hereditary.[617] In a subsequent Novel issued in 934 he listed their status in the civil, military or ecclesiastical hierarchies: "the illustrious *magistroi* or *patrikioi* ... persons honored with offices, governorships, or civil or military dignities ...|those enumerated in the Senate... thematic officials or ex-officials ... metropolitans, archbishops, bishops, *higoumenoi*, ecclesiastical officials or supervisors or heads of pious or imperial houses."[618] They all were prohibited from acquiring village land from smallholders.

Romanos' father, like Basil's, had held a military fief, so Romanos was familiar with incursions by outsiders buying up the land of soldiers and peasant freeholders. To save the peasantry from being reduced to the status of landless dependents and

---

[617] Plutarch used the word *dynatoi* in his life of Tiberius Gracchus (8.5) to describe the wealthy Roman opponents of the land reform proposed by the consul Gaius Laelius c. 140 BC, anticipating the subsequent reform proposals of the Gracchi.

[618] Romanos, 934 edict, I.2 (McGeer 2000: 55). See also his 922 edict, II.2 (McGeer 2000: 46).

clients, he revived the Law of Pre-Emption giving kinsmen and village neighbors the right of first refusal. His intention was to ban the sale of such land:

> We forbid the *dynatoi* henceforth to acquire any land, whether by way of adoption or gift, ordinary or *mortis causa*, by testamentary disposition, by use alone, or by some form of protection or support, from the less well to do unless they are their relatives. Nor are they to arrange new purchases, rents, or exchanges with the owners in any villages and hamlets where they do not have their own properties.[619]

Dynatoi who attempted this sort of intrigue were to be deprived of the land they had acquired, and were to pay the treasury a fine equal to its full price. Specifying who was permitted to buy village land, Romanos ranked groups in terms of their right of first refusal, starting with one's immediate family to neighbors and other members of the tax district, followed by outsiders who already had some share in such land. Only those who already held property in the village were allowed to buy more, lease it from smallholders or receive it as a "gift." Any "military lands alienated in any manner whatsoever" for the last thirty years were to be restored to their original holders or heirs, without compensation. For abandoned klasmatic land that the public treasury might sell off, neighbors were to be given preference. Only if they all declined could dynatoi or other outsiders buy it.

The problem of wealthy individuals buying up land designated for soldiers or local villagers was age-old. Already c. 1750 BC, Hammurabi's laws had blocked the purchase or foreclosure of land assigned to soldiers:

> §35 If a man should purchase from a soldier either the cattle or the sheep and goats which the king gave to the soldier, he shall forfeit his silver.
> §36 (Furthermore), the field, orchard, or house of a soldier, fisherman, or a state tenant will not be sold.
> §37 If a man should purchase a field, orchard, or house of a soldier, fisherman, or a state tenant, his deed shall be invalidated and he shall forfeit his silver; the field, orchard, or house shall revert to its owner.[620]

What made Romanos' reform urgent was the historically cold winter of 927/928. The ground was reported to have frozen for four months, causing the crops to fail. Famine ensued and many families died, or survived by selling their land to buy food and provisions. Land takeovers increased, despite the sanctions that Romanos' earlier Novel had imposed. The three-year right to repurchase land, granted by earlier Novels, did not help much because smallholders were too broke to earn enough to buy it back. "As a rule, the 'powerful' was both a landed proprietor and an official," notes Ostrogorsky. "Those who were responsible for executing the orders of the Emperor were largely interested in frustrating them."[621]

---

[619] Romanos, novel reviving the Law of Pre-emption, Clause II.1 translated by McGeer 2000: 46. Ostrogorsky 1969: 275 f. and most other historians date it to April 922, but some scholars believe it was just before the cold winter of 927/8. See McGeer's discussion, pp. 37 ff. and that of Toynbee 1973: 149 f.
[620] Roth 1997: 87.
[621] Ostrogorsky 1969: 275.

Romanos' Novel of 934 barring *dynatoi* from acquiring village land

Romanus issued a new Novel in 934, characterizing land purchases in the wake of the crop failure as "pillaging...–for how could I say 'purchase' and not 'greedily gulp down'?– the possessions of the poor at a very cheap price."[622] Accusing the greedy of using "the indigence of the poor...as the opportunity for business instead of charity, compassion, or kindness when they saw the poor oppressed by famine, they bought up the possessions of the unfortunate poor at a very low price," some merely "with grain or other forms of payment.... [T]hey were like a pestilential attack of disease to the miserable inhabitants of the villages, having entered like gangrene into the body of the villages and causing total destruction."[623]

Aiming to reverse these takeovers, Romanos' preamble uses the Biblical terms *penates* and *ptochoi* for the poor. Decrying "the great confusion of affairs, hence the great tide of injustices, hence the great and widespread oppression of the poor, and the great sighing of the needy, for whose sake the Lord rose from the dead," the emperor depicts himself as protector of the poor and downtrodden His concluding paragraph denounces the greedy as "enemies of the natural order, of the Creation, and of justice."[624]

Celebrating Byzantium's military victory securing its eastern frontier, Romanos asks: "How will we, after accomplishing so much against the onslaught of external enemies, not rid ourselves of our own enemies within?"[625] His ruling promised to save the realm from "people who, in their passionate greed and mean-spiritedness, are engrossed in so great a pursuit of gain, who consider none of the ways to achieve wealth disgraceful, and who impose the burden of their interference on the freedom [of others]." By imposing limits on such people, Romanos promises that the *dynatoi* no longer shall

> dare either on their own or through an intermediary to intrude into a village or hamlet for the sake of a sale, gift, or inheritance – either whole or partial – or on any other pretext whatsoever. As this sort of acquisition has been ruled invalid, the acquired properties, along with the improvements since added, are to return without refund to the owners or, if they or their relatives are no longer alive, to the inhabitants of the villages or hamlets. For the domination of these persons has increased the great hardship of the poor, and ... will cause no little harm to the commonwealth unless the present legislation puts an end to it first. (I.2.)

Spelling out the logic behind his Novel, Romanos' prologue describes his rulings as "beneficial to the common good, acceptable to God, profitable to the treasury, and useful to the state.... Those concerned with the stability of the state must eliminate the cause of disturbance, expel what is harmful, and support the common good" (I.2). Otherwise, the greedy would undercut Byzantium's tax revenue and the supply of soldiers.

---

[622] III.3, McGeer 2000: 55.

[623] II.1. McGeer (2000: 57) notes: "The comparison of speculators with pestilence and gangrene is drawn from novels 32, 33 and 34 of the emperor Justinian," citing Scott 1932: 16: 183–187.

[624] VII.I, McGeer 2000: 27.

[625] McGeer 2000: 60. Toynbee 1973: 153 provides a more eloquent translation: "Now that we have achieved these magnificent successes in putting an end to the aggression of the foreign enemy, what about the domestic enemy in our own household? How can we refrain from dealing severely with him?"

To block stratagems that might enable the *dynatoi* to acquire village land by distress sales, Romanos ruled that "if the true value of the lands sold is found to be over twice the price paid, the purchasers are to be expelled without refund," and to restore ownership to its original holders (III.3). Such buyers "are to be evicted therefrom without refund and deprived of [the results of] their own labors and improvements" (VII.1.)

However, large landholders had devised "a law-abiding pretext … for the transfer of property from the debtors to the creditors; and the pretext used was that of antichresis," taking interest in the form of the crop yield. By using this stratagem, creditors could obtain the yield of land by making a loan secured by the crop as interest, year after year. This did not require formally transferring land held by smallholders into their possession. Relinquishing the crop yield "would not appear to be alienations but temporary arrangements, which [nominally] would result in the return of the land to its original owner, as soon as he had repaid the debt to his creditor. In reality the property was never returned, as Manuel Comnenus [Emperor from 1143 to 1180] expressly admits. … It was this devious method through which land [later fell] into the hands of the already powerful" by the time of Manuel Comnenus, who ruled it illegal on the ground that the result was indeed an alienation, of the sort which Romanos' Novel banned by blocking assignment of land as a "gift."[626]

What occurred was the same opportunistic innovation that is first found on a grand scale in first-millennium BC Babylonia: making loans to cover taxes and fees or extending much needed consumption loans in times of crop failure, secured by either alienable or otherwise unalienable land. Once the debtor is unable to pay current interest rates, the pledge is converted to terms of antichresis, *i.e.*, the creditor receives the full income of the field in lieu of interest payments.[627] This leads, in practice, to the debtor becoming the tenant of the creditor, ending up with only a fraction of the yield, which makes it even more difficult to repay interest and principal.[628]

Such "inverted" relationships can last for decades and do not require the transfer of property title. The creditor usually has no intention of ending such relationship as he can rely on the most dependable kind of tenant in a quasi serf-like state. This tactic can be found in 6th-century BC Babylonian archives of private entrepreneurs but it is especially well attested in the records of the Murashu family of Nippur in the Achaemenid period.

McGeer points out how similar Romanos' policy of restoring Byzantine land tenure to the *status quo ante* was to that of the Biblical Jubilee Year. He suggests "that the emperor's reasoning and provisions were guided by a passage in Leviticus 25:23–38, in which God ordains that every fifty years all dispossessed homes and lands must revert to their original owners; this measure defends the interests of the lowly, in that it

---

[626] Papadatou 2008: 209–220.

[627] Babylonian records express this concept literally by *ebūr eqli iānu ḫubul kaspi iānu* "there is no yield of the field and no interest of the silver."

[628] The legal details of such conversions of hypothecarial loans into antichretic loans and their consequences are best described by Cardascia 1951: 27–41 and Stolper 1985: 104–107; Stolper (p. 105) refers to it as a "tendency to transform politically insecure tangible titles to real property into more resilient, intangible debt title." See also chapters 7 and 17 above.

restores their ancestral properties, relieves them of debt obligations, and counters the injustice of the few gaining more and more while the many have less and less." [629]

Common denominators linking Byzantine policy to that of Babylonia were, first, recognition that wealth tended to polarize; and second, that reversing this dynamic required royal action. Inequality was seen to be inherent in the way economic life was organized, subject to the rhythms of nature that included periodic crop failure leading to dependency on the wealthy, as occurred after the great winter of 929. The policy to restore stability was to return land to smallholders who had sold it to the powerful.

For Babylonia this economic renewal started by liberating bondservants and wiping out debts when they grew too heavy. In Byzantine times, bondage and rural usury were less important, but the key to restoring an idealized status quo ante was still a strong royal power to counter the maneuverings of powerful families to concentrate land, financial wealth and political office in their own hands.

The oligarchic response was to gain control of the fiscal bureaucracy and weaken central oversight authority. The dynamic is age-old. Greece and Rome had replaced kings with aristocratic senates to enact laws that served the oligarchy, administered by themselves as heads of the judiciary system. And as religious officials, they sanctified pro-creditor laws and made property transfers irreversible, along with personal dependency and bondage. The counter-movement from the Biblical prophets to Jesus– and later, by Byzantine emperors of the 9th and 10th centuries – was to denounce personal greed.

The Byzantine *dynatoi* responded by political and military intrigue to undermine public regulatory and tax authority by shifting control of resources and political office into their own hands. Toward this end they allied themselves with opponents of Romanos, including his own sons. Romanos' health was failing in 944 and, as he became more religious, his sons were persuaded by powerful courtiers to order him exiled to a monastery on the island of Prote, where he became a monk.

Romanos' son Stephen hoped to become senior emperor, but a popular demonstration supported his co-emperor Constantine, now nearly forty years old. When his wife – their sister Helena – backed her husband, the two brothers plotted to kill him, in league with the general Bardas Phokas, who was hoping to become a warlord. But Constantine moved first, having Stephen and Constantine Lekapenos arrested and exiled to join their father (who died in 948).

In 945 the crown thus passed to Constantine VII (913–959), son of Leo VI. Citing Basil as his official grandfather, Constantine faced the same tension between the imperial government's authority and the powerful local military and landowning magnates that Toynbee describes as having confronted Basil I and Romanos I. "On the Imperial throne to which they had climbed, as in the humble surroundings in which each of them had been born, they were still … under the thumb of a corrupt and oppressive civil service. In the East Roman Empire, neither the people nor the Emperor had the last word. The true masters of the Empire were the officials acting in collusion with the *dynatoi*." [630]

That tension became the focus of Constantine's Novels and those of Basil II.

28. Zenith and Decline of Byzantium: 945–1204

In 947, two years after taking the throne, Constantine VII issued a Novel strengthening that of Romanos thirteen years earlier. "The majority of the powerful have not abstained from transactions most ruinous to the poor," he complained (1.1). "Neither law nor fear of the emperor has restrained their greed" (Prologue, 2nd version). Singling out the central Anatolian plateau south of the Black Sea as the heartland of the military aristocracy, the Novel's Prologue accuses the *dynatoi* of "infiltrating into village communities by means of sales, gifts, and inheritances … oppressing the miserable poor and making them fugitives from their own properties."[631]

To counter this grabbing, Constantine ruled that "Every gift and inheritance, and the settlements and ratifications between those persons already under exclusion, contrived with a view to circumventing this law, are inoperative and will be considered null and void" (II.1). All properties that had been sold should to be restored "to the sellers, or to their heirs and members of the same tax community" (II.3).

To ensure enforcement, Constantine's Epilogue directs his officials to "read out this pronouncement and legislation to all in the theme, from the powerful persons down to the lowest and last man." This wording recalls Hammurabi's epilogue to his laws:

> Let any wronged man who has a lawsuit come before the statue of me, the king of justice (*šar mīšarim*), and let him have my inscribed stela read aloud to him … and let my stela reveal the lawsuit [*dīnum*, judgment] for him.[632]

A follow-up Novel sought to make official the "unwritten custom" of forbidding owners of military estates from selling land that was supposed to maintain soldiers. Many had relinquished their property to the *dynatoi* and entered their private service, creating "private armies loyal to powerful military magnates."[633] To stop this, Constantine ruled that buyers and other takers of such properties "shall pay six gold *nomismata* as punishment, half of which the *stratiotes* [seller] will receive towards the resumption of his former position" (III.1). The other half was for the treasury.

To restore imperial control over military land and recover the tax yield and services of its soldiers, ostensibly by preventing sales "below the fair price," Constantine "set a minimum inalienable value upon the military lands" at four pounds of gold, and two pounds for sailors' land. These high minimum prices established "a criterion by which to compel the return of alienated military properties to their original owners." Two decades later Nikephoros II Phokas tripled this official transfer price to

---

[629] McGeer 2000: 50, fn 3.

[630] Toynbee 1973: 184.

[631] McGeer 2000: 30. He describes the more densely populated areas of Syria and western Asia Minor as being "more resistant to the intrusions of the powerful." (He translates Constantine's 947 Novel on pp. 63–67, the source of my quotations.)

twelve pounds of gold as a minimum sale value! That set "a limit so high as to … effectively rule transactions in military property illegal and non-binding."[634]

Constantine defended these price constraints by stating the moral premise guiding his Novel. The affliction of greed was spreading from the dynatoi to their underlings, "for the habits of the high and mighty as often as not prove contagious to the populace as a whole."

> There was a time which saw a general upheaval of affairs and an irresistible onslaught of misery, when every last one of the high and mighty in his haste to carve out unlimited lands for himself enrolled the wretched owners in a list of slaves, with nary a thought that his actions were reprehensible, but instead believing himself ill-treated if someone else seemed to surpass him in greed. (III.1.)

Constantine's successor, Romanos II (959–963), ruled that any lands sold since Constantine took the throne in 945 were to be "restored without obligation to reimburse the buyers, who thereby suffer the consequences of ignoring the laws barring acquisitions of lands from poor persons to *stratiotai*."[635] The last paragraph of Romanos' novel (III.1) states: "From the time of the rule of our deceased emperor [Constantine] you will restore without exception all stratiotai as well as civilians to their own land without repayment."

Tax exemption for Church property

Military land was not the only category being absorbed into great estates. Monastery lands and personal shrines also were controlled by the aristocracy, which obtained tax exemption by creating endowments on their own land.

Late Roman exemptions were granted to the clergy and other public bodies that "could easily be considered as hereditary, especially when granted to members of large and powerful families." Exemption of nominally devotional land from the land tax (klerikotopion) "profited mainly the bishop, who received at least part of the exemption," keeping the tax abatement for himself or simply "offering prospective lessees more advantageous conditions than those of non-exempt landowners."[636]

At least the Byzantine Church never achieved the power over secular rulers that the Roman papacy wielded in the West. In line with age-old practice from Sargon through Babylonian rulers appointing their family members to administer the major temples, younger sons of emperors were castrated so that they could not become emperors, who could not be eunuchs, but could head the Eastern Church. Michael I Rangabe (811–813) appointed his son Ignatios as Patriarch of Constantinople (847–858 and again 867–877). Leo VI followed suit with his son Stephen I (886–893), and Romanos I appointed his son Theophylact Lekapenos (933–956).

---

[632] Laws of Hammurapi, xlviii: 3–15; translation from Martha Roth 1997: 88.
[633] McGeer 2000: 70.
[634] McGeer 2000: 105 and 18 f.
[635] McGeer 2000: 81. *Stratiotai* were the designated managers of military lands. Many sought to become landlords themselves instead of protecting their smallholders.

Romanos II's successor, Nikephoros II Phokas (963–969), issued a Novel in 964 banning the endowment of new monasteries. His prologue castigates their lust for land and other wealth, "the evident disease of the monasteries and even the pious foundations (for a disease is what I call this insatiety)." To counter their avarice, he ruled that "no one is allowed to transfer fields and properties in any way to monasteries, homes for the aged, or hostels ... for this does them no good," as they already had too much land (I.4).[637] He "advised people wishing to support monasteries, convents, hostelries, hospices, archbishoprics [and] bishoprics" to limit their contributions to "workers (slaves, *oiketas*), as well as large and small livestock; for it is pointless to give land, which the law of the church forbids it to sell again, to establishments which lack the means to work it."[638]

Thirty-two years later (in 996, discussed below), Basil II issued a Novel decrying the fact that in addition to the incursions of secular dynatoi, the spread of the monasteries had driven many village communes to "the verge of extinction" (III.1). A buyer obtaining village or theme land, probably in a distress sale or in payment for a loan, might put up a chapel and call it a monastery, enabling the local bishop later to claim possession. Such ploys were nullified and these lands were "all to be restored to the poor." Monasteries that "stood on peasant land and which had only a small number of monks were to be regarded not as monasteries but as chapels of ease," that is, for attendance by those who could not reach the local parish church. They were made "subordinate to the village community and exempt from paying tribute to the bishop."[639]

The 10th century's emperors heaped favors on what Lemerle's *Agrarian History of Byzantium* calls "the latifundiary Church," whose metropolitans, bishoprics and convents forced smallholders "to hand over their land, and [outmaneuvered] those who resisted ... striving with success to obtain exemption from fiscal liabilities, and even from the basic tax." That was not good for the economy, because monastic "methods of cultivation were less efficient," yielding less rental value and tax revenue than land farmed by village or *theme* smallholders. "Peasants or *stratiotes*, having granted their land, were themselves reduced, usually on their own land, to a condition of dependence on the new owner."[640]

The fight by Basil II (976–1025) against the *dynatoi*

The nearly 50-year reign of Basil II, nominal grandson of Constantine VII, was the longest of any Byzantine emperor. He resembled Hammurabi not only in his long rule but also by establishing the security of land held by soldiers and freeholders, reversing its transfer to absentee buyers. He was the last emperor strong enough to curtail the power of the military and landed aristocracy to pry land and revenue away from palace control.

[636] Oikonomides 1988: 321–325.
[637] McGeer 2000: 91–95.
[638] Lemerle 1979: 109.
[639] Ostrogorsky 1969: 306.
[640] Lemerle 1979: 190 f. and 216. See also Charanis 1948: 53–64.

Basil's predecessor John I Tzimisces (969–976) had died without issue, leaving the 19-year old Basil and his 16-year old brother (the future Constantine VIII) under the guardianship of Lord Chamberlain Basil Lecepanus, the son of Romanos I by his mistress, castrated at birth to prevent him from ever claiming the throne for himself. He became the power behind the throne while the young princes played a merely ceremonial role in court formalities.

Civil war broke out almost immediately. Bardas Scleros, a general from one of the richest families, had married the sister of Tzimisces, who he claimed had promised him the emperorship. Backed by the military aristocracy, he had his troops acclaim him as Emperor that year.

Basil's court hired another major military leader with his own army, Bardas Phocas from a Cappadocian military family, to defend Constantinople against Scleros. But Bardas teamed up with Scleros a decade later, in 987. Their agreement called for Phocas to take Constantinople and the Western European provinces (apparently backed by the Church with the support of the Lord Chamberlain Basil), while Scleros would take Asia Minor. However, Phocas had Scleros arrested, and marched on Constantinople with his own troops in 988. His offensive collapsed when he died in battle the next year, after having fought for 13 years, until 989.

Figure 38:
Michael Psellos and his student Michael VII.

In due course Scleros submitted to Basil, and was assigned a rank second only to the emperor in exchange for promising not to revolt. The chronicler Michael Psellus (1017–1078) reports that the two leaders concluded their reconciliation meal with a long conversation, at which Basil asked how his Empire "could be preserved free from dissension" in the future.

Scleros had an answer to this, although it was not the sort of advice one would expect from a general ... 'Cut down the governors who become overproud,' he said. 'Let no generals on campaign have too many resources. Exhaust them with unjust exactions, to keep them busied with their own affairs. ... Be accessible to no one. Share with few your most intimate plans.'[641]

This advice was similar to that which Thrasybulus, tyrant of Miletus is said by Herodotus (5.92) to have given a herald sent by Periander, tyrant of Corinth in the late 7th century BC. In Herodotus' telling, Thrasybulus led the man to a field of grain and cut off the highest ears. Upon hearing this, Periander killed or exiled his city's wealthiest and most powerful citizens.

---

[641] Psellus, *Chronographia* I.29, translated by Sawter 1966: 43. The word "unjust" seems Psellus's own view.

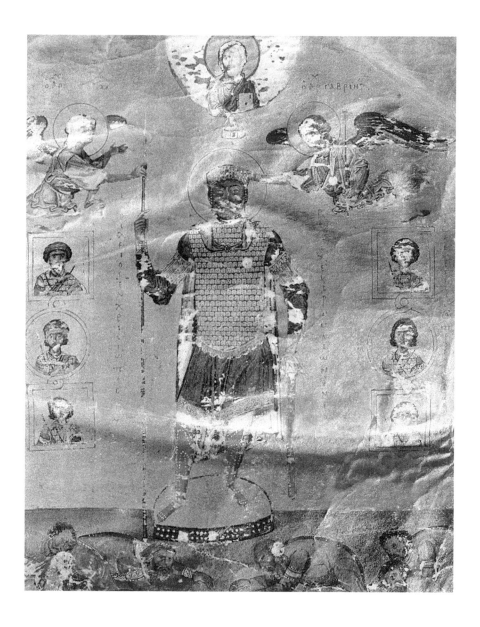

Figure 39:
Miniature of Emperor Basil II in triumphal garb, exemplifying the Imperial Crown
handed down by Angels. Psalter of Basil II (Psalter of Venice), BNM, Ms. gr. 17, fol.
3r, detail References: Paul Stephenson: A note on the portrait illumination of Basil
II in his psalter

Basil did not go anywhere near so far, but moved fiscally, taxing the landed elites to save smallholders from falling into dependency and thus keeping them available to pay taxes and serve in the army. He saw the main threat to his rule and the stability of the Byzantine state to be the military aristocracy of Cappadocia and Anatolia, along with the wealthy families dominating the Byzantine court and church leaders who had backed the civil war against him. "Whatever happened to contribute to his own (the emperor's) welfare, or to the good of the state, was allowed to remain on the statutes. All those decrees, on the other hand, which referred to the granting of favors or positions of dignity, were now rescinded."[642]

As had occurred seven decades earlier under Romanos I, a cold winter in 989 caused widespread distress. The sea froze and an earthquake toppled the towers or *cupolas* of forty churches, including the Hagia Sophia. The crisis enabled the large landowners to obtain the property of military themes and villages, prompting Basil to issue a Novel on January 1, 996, reinforcing that of his great-grandfather Romanos I in 934.

Basil's key ruling was to abolish the 40-year limit on the right of smallholders to repossess land that had been sold in the aftermath of the cold winter 68 years earlier. "No matter how much time goes by," the Prologue promises, "the poor man shall not be restricted in seeking and recovering what is his," *i.e.*, what belonged to his forebears as village members prior to the winter of 928. Only *dynatoi* who could produce documents showing that their ownership rights predated the famine could keep their land (I.1).

To counteract falsified local records, Basil "declared null and void the recent local *periorismoi*, the registers of estates, drawn up by the great landowners in their capacity of local authorities, and gave preference to the former records lodged with the central administration."[643] He added: "There is no time limit against the fisc," which "may invoke its legal claim" for eminent domain as a right "extending back to the time of Caesar Augustus" (IV.1).

Confiscating the property mainly of leading families who might threaten his claim to the throne, Basil singled out the Phocas and the Maleini *dynatoi* in central Anatolia.[644] As an anecdotal example of the injustice that had occurred, Basil cited Philokales, "originally one of the poor and the villagers, but afterwards one of the illustrious and wealthy." When he became a bureaucrat, "he took possession of the entire village commune and made it into his own estate." When Basil "learned of the matter in a complaint brought forward by the poor," he felt that it would be wrong to let Philokales keep what he "wrongfully took." So he demolished the man's lavish dwellings down to the foundations, gave back to the poor what was theirs, left him with the fiscal property which he had at the beginning, and made him one of the villagers once more."[645]

---

[642] Psellus, *Chronographia* I.19-20, Sawter 1966: 37 f. The emperor also exiled the Lord Chamberlain Basil for having conspired with the *dynatoi*.

[643] Danstrup 1948: 197.

[644] Ostrogorsky 1969: 305, endorsed by McGeer 2000: 112.

[645] McGeer 2000: 112, 116 and 118. In a second version of Basil's Novel (I.2A) the emperor prides himself that by removing the forty-year limit, "the children of the *dynatoi*, upon being deprived of this ill-gotten inheritance … will descend into poverty and utmost hardship" just as other village members must endure.

Basil's next step was to shift the allelengyon land tax onto the large landowners, including the monasteries. This stabilized revenue for the Byzantine treasury by falling on the wealthy classes best able to pay the land tax, while saving smallholders from having to abandon their land, flee or become clients of the larger landowners. This strong rulership prompted aristocrats to assemble their own armies of clients to resist the emperor. In 1022, Basil had to suppress "a revolt of Nikephoros Xiphias, strategos of Anatolia, and Nikephorus Phocas, the son of Bardas."[646] The military and landed aristocracy backed weak emperors over the next two centuries, hollowing out the Byzantine state in their struggle to privatize village and military land, avoid taxes and reduce the status of free smallholders to that of serfs.

Land monopoly leads to fiscal and military dismantling

Basil II died in 1025, leaving a reported 200,000 talents of gold as well as enormous stores of jewels from his military conquests at the disposal of his brother Constantine VIII (1025–1028).[647] Constantine was 65 years old and had shown little interest in co-governing. "He was by no means the man to expend his own energies on cares of State," writes Psellus. Although "already an old man … he plunged into a life of pleasure, determined to squander and spend everything," on entertainment and banquets, court extravaganzas and gifts, "gluttony and sexual passions. … To members of his court he threw wide open the gates of his favor, heaping gold on them as though it were sand."[648] He also spent enormous sums on renovating churches as memorials to his piety.[649]

Constantine was followed by a series of self-indulgent emperors and empresses who further dissipated the treasury's money. He chose the aristocrat Romanos III Argyrus (1028–1034) to marry his daughter Zoe. Ruling for six years, Romanos viewed the *dynatoi* as his power base, not as a class to be subordinated to the empire's overall welfare. Buying support from the military class and civil population by distributing "largess on a generous scale, thus adding to a body which was already gross,"[650] Romanos "revoked Basil II's law making magnates liable for unpaid taxes in their tax districts, forgave debts to the treasury, and tolerated embezzlement by his tax collectors."[651] This set imperial tax collection on a long two-century decline, while ending the effort to stop the growth of large estates.

For many centuries Byzantine land tenure had been based on the archaic principle of small parcels of land, stable taxation and community-based production. This structure discouraged the emergence of large estates and motivated farmers to expand cultivation and raise output. Even dependent peasants (*paroikoi* , *i.e.* by the house) were not

---

[646] Louis Brehier 1977: 150.
[647] Psellus, *Chronographia*, I.31 and VII.53: 308. The Roman talent was about 33 kilograms (75 pounds). During Basil's rule the vaults of his treasure chambers "were not big enough, [so] he had spiral galleries dug underground."
[648] Psellus, *Chronographia*, II.3 and II.6–9, pp. 45, 56f. and 54.
[649] Psellus, *Chronographia*, III.15, p. 72.
[650] Psellus, *Chronographia*, VII.53, p. 308.
[651] Treadgold 1997: 584. See also Psellus, *Chronographia.*, III.13–15, pp. 70ff.

slaves in the traditional sense, but rather "half-free". They had no right to leave the land, but their master had no right to dislocate them either. In contrast, the economy in the West took a dive after the fall of the Western Roman Empire. Adam Smith notes that "it seldom happens that a great proprietor is a great improver."[652]

That is what happened from Romanos III onward. What made his rule "more terrible was the fact that while the great majority were being plundered and stripped, the imperial treasury enjoyed not a penny of the profits built up from these embezzlements, for the rivers of money were being diverted elsewhere."[653]

Zoe became empress upon her husband's death, and appointed her lover Michael IV "the Paphlagonian" (1034–1041) as her successor. Their wasteful rule was followed by the intrigues of Michael V (1041–1042) and then by Zoe's joint rule with her younger sister Theodora (1042). Psellus writes that neither of these two empresses "was fitted by temperament to govern. … For the most part they confused the trifles of the harem with important matters of state." Zoe's passion was for "gold – not for the sake of mere possession or hoarding of it, but so that she could satisfy her instinct for generosity," emptying the treasury on gifts to those who praised her.[654]

Three decades of such rule "exhausted the imperial treasures on personal whims. The public revenues were expended not on the organization of the army, but on favors to civilians and on magnificent shows." Funerals were made impressive, and monuments were erected to the emperors, surrounded by churches to sanctify them. Then, as they had to enrich their places of meditation (the name they invented for these buildings) with money and possessions, they not only emptied the palace treasury, but even cut into the money contributed by the people to the public revenues.

> … The imperial wealth was divided into three parts: one to pay for their pleasures, another to glorify their new-fangled buildings, and a third to enable those who were naturally lazy … while the military were being stinted and treated harshly.[655]

Zoe and Theodora were followed by Constantine IX (1042–1055), who "failed to realize that [the emperorship] entailed responsibility for the well-being of his subjects." Delegating to others "the administration of public affairs," justice and the armed forces, "he had entered the harbor of the palace, so to speak, to enjoy the advantages of a calm retreat and to avoid the duties of helmsman."[656] His rule was followed by the return of Zoe's younger sister Theodora (1055–1056) and then briefly by her favorite, Michael VI (1056–1057).

These post-Macedonian emperors were self-indulgent figureheads who did not challenge the aristocracy. The *allelengyon* and *epibole* land taxes disappeared as fiscal

---

[652] Christodoulakis 2015: 49, quoting Smith 1776, Book 3, ch. 2.

[653] Psellus, *Chronographia*, III.13, p. 71.

[654] Psellus, *Chronographia*, VI.5, p. 157. He concludes (VI.62–64 and VI.157, pp. 185f. and 238) that even when she grew old, Empress Zoe's "judgment was completely warped by the vulgar extravagance that prevailed in the palace."

[655] Psellus, *Chronographia*, VII.59, p. 311.

[656] Psellus, *Chronographia*, VI.48, p. 179.

policy and command of the army was relinquished to the large landholders. "The peasants were no longer in a position to pay the tax, and the 'powerful' were not willing to do so," Ostrogorsky summarizes the empire's decline into insolvency. "The privilege most sought after by large landowners was that of exemption from taxes, immunity, or as it was termed in Byzantium, *exkousseia*. … The great secular and ecclesiastical estates were exempted from certain taxes, and the most powerful and influential among them from all taxes, enjoying full immunity. Thereafter the taxes and the other dues of the serfs on those estates no longer went into the imperial treasury, but came to the land owners" as rent.[657]

Instead of the crop surpluses of village communities being paid as taxes, the Byzantine fiscal system was monetized and levied on individuals.[658] Treadgold summarizes the result: "After centuries of capable emperors had brought Byzantium to an apex of power under Basil II, a mere fifty-six years of misgovernment had squandered half the empire's territory, nearly all of its huge army and ample treasury, and a long tradition of growing security and stability. The preponderance of incompetent emperors after Basil was striking, but no accident. Powerful bureaucrats and generals had guarded their influence by repeatedly promoting nonentities to the throne, undermining the few leaders who showed some initiative." Byzantium lost "its heartland to some disorganized nomads, and was reduced to fighting for its life again. After 120 years more, the empire came to pieces and fell to a small foreign army [of Crusaders] assembled almost by chance."[659]

The ground for this collapse was prepared by two centuries of Byzantine court intrigue "between the rival forces of the civil nobility of the capital and the military aristocracy of the provinces. The latter was the stronger party."[660] To be sure, some 11th-century emperors sought "to reduce the power of the military magnates in the administration of the empire," fearing that "the powers which they exercised as military commanders made them extremely dangerous to the central government."[661] But on balance the large landowners became the state.

The Byzantine Empire stopped restoring land rights to the cultivators who manned the army and paid taxes. McGeer finds that "No further legislation on the military lands appears after the reign of Nikephoros Phokas," not even in Basil II's novel of 996. The Comneni Dynasty (1081–1184) disbanded military land tenure, shifting the army to fully equipped professionals and foreign mercenaries, who were paid out of tax revenues.[662] Military and village smallholders were driven to sell or

---

[657] Ostrogorsky1969: 329. He adds: "The great estates, which enjoyed full fiscal and legal immunity, slipped out of the net of the central administration and imperial officials were even forbidden to enter the territory of these estates."

[658] See Laiou, ed., 2002: 1131: "Whereas the new fiscality may have facilitated the circulation of money, it overtaxed the peasant and undertaxed the privileged estate owner … and eventually had negative political and social repercussions as far as the state was concerned."

[659] Treadgold 1997: 611 and 667. See also Ostrogorsk 1969: 323.

[660] Ostrogorsky 1969: 322 and 330f.

[661] Charanis 1953: 415–423, repr. in Eisenstadt, ed, 1986.

[662] McGeer 2000: 20f.

abandon their land, becoming clients of the wealthy landholders (including the Church) or simply ran away,[663] as inhabitants were squeezed dry, "though not to the government's profit."[664]

What formerly had been paid as taxes was privatized as land rent. "The army of the themes ceased to exist, and even the word 'theme,' for troops of the provincial army of stratiotai, fell out of use in the eleventh century." This weakened Byzantium fiscally, impairing its ability to defend itself, and leading to debasement of the coinage. Constantinople started to farm out tax collection, even to foreigners.

Isaac Comnenus (1057–1059) recalled Romanus I and Basil I by usurping the throne as a strong military leader from outside the aristocratic elite. He tried to reverse the decline and refill the treasury in the wake of the corruption and waste that had become ingrained during the preceding 32 years. But the rot had become so ingrained that Isaac "seems to have considered most of the thematic troop past saving, since he made no effort to enforce the laws that had protected their military lands."[665]

Isaac did cancel some land grants made by Michael VI and Constantine IX and reclaimed imperial estates that the aristocracy had taken over, headed by "all imperial estates that had been granted to churches and monasteries, which under Nicephorus II's law of 964 were forbidden to receive land from anyone."[666] Summarizing Isaac's moves, Psellus reports that he "had little sympathy for the court party. All kinds of economy were practised. The monasteries suffered first and many noble families were forced to give up property and wealth; certain allowances given to men in office were cancelled; taxation became heavier and was merciless; donations made by other rulers were withheld."

There seemed no middle ground between leaving things the way they were and radically redistributing the land to restore the theme and village tax system. It is a reflection on how far the aristocracy's takeover had spread that even Isaac's admirers such as Psellus thought that so drastic a change was not politically feasible:

> In matters other than the civil [military] administration he advanced the welfare of his Empire by gradual progress, and had he followed the same policy in the non-military sphere also, by purging the State of its rotten elements, first reducing the gross evil and then applying his remedy, two things would have happened: he himself would have earned undying honor; and the body politic would not have been brought to utter ruin. But Isaac wanted to revolutionize everything. He was eager to lose no time in cutting out the dead wood which had long been accumulating in the Roman Empire. … He attempted to get rid of the bulges and restore the body to a normal shape, to take away this and build up that, to heal the intestines and breathe into this monster some live-giving breath; but the task was beyond him.[667]

[663] See Treadgold 1997: 577
[664] Ostrogorsk1969: 331f. and 393.
[665] Treadgold 1997: 599.
[666] Treadgold 1997: 598f.
[667] Psellus, *Chronographia*, VII.52, p. 307.

Psellus described Byzantine society as having already passed the tipping point. And as matters indeed turned out under the century-long Comneni dynasty "the army swallowed up the resources of the Empire. The people were crushed by intolerable burdens" while the great estates expanded, particularly those of the laity."[668]

As noted above, Isaac Comnenus did take away from certain monasteries a sum of money "hardly less than the imperial fortune."[669] And in 1158 a Novel of Manuel Comnenus "took back all imperial estates that had been granted to churches and monasteries" since Nikephorus II's law of 964, which apparently had fallen into abeyance.[670] Despite these largely rhetorical Novels, Church property experienced a rapid growth in the 11th and 12th centuries.

The beginning of the end occurred when Crusaders began to arrive in 1096. First came the ragged bands that had looted their way along the road from Belgrade toward Constantinople. Most of these informal troops were massacred when they tried to rob the Turks. The escapees made their way to Constantinople, where the lords and knights arrived later in the year, pledged to support Byzantium against the infidels.[671] They were awed by how much richer the city was than their own Western lands.

Figure 40: Conquest of Constantinople by the crusaders in 1204.

[668] Ostrogorsky 1969: 392f.
[669] Lemerle 1979: 216f.
[670] Treadgold 1997: 599.
[671] Treadgold 1997: 621. The classic account is Steven Runciman's *History of The Crusades* (Cambridge: 1951, 3 vols.), along with his *Byzantine Civilization* (New York, 1956 [1933]).

A century later, in 1202, the Fourth Crusade marched to Venice, having agreed to pay its leaders 85,000 silver marks for transport to Egypt. But fewer Crusaders showed up than were expected, and they were only able to pay 51,000 marks. The Venetian doge, Enrico Dandolo, let them pay the balance by conquering the Christian port of Zara (Zadar) in Hungary.

The Comneni Prince Alexius sent a welcoming embassy promising to accept papal authority over the Eastern Church and to provide the Crusaders with ten thousand soldiers and 100,000 marks if they would make him Byzantine emperor. His father, Isaac II Angelus (1185–1204) agreed to this deal to deter the Crusaders from attacking Constantinople. So Alexius IV (1203–1204) was crowned at age 21. He announced a reunion of the Byzantine and Roman churches, and confiscated the Church treasury to pay half the money he had promised.

The Venetians took half, and the Crusaders used their share to pay their own debts – and then decided to plunder Constantinople. The local population rioted, fires broke out, and Alexius IV was removed. Alexius V Ducas Murtzuphlus replaced Alexius IV and his father when most administrators fled, but ruled less than a year.[672] The Crusade's leaders reckoned their loot to be 900,000 marks, out of which they paid off the Venetians.

The sacking of Byzantium was a climax to the economy's erosion during the 11th and 12th centuries. Isaac Comnenus and his successors had not found a way to field an army and promote prosperity without strengthening the landholding nobility to overpower imperial control. Ever since the ancient Near East, powerful families have rivaled the palace for control of land, labor and their economic surplus. Their drive to avoid fiscal labor, crop and monetary taxes on their own land and that of their clients traditionally has been at the expense of public obligations for military service and corvée labor.

From Babylonia though Rome, most landed estates were assembled by foreclosing on collateral pledged by debtors. In Byzantium they were appropriated mainly by purchase and clientage arrangements under distress conditions. The common denominator from Babylonia to Byzantium was the transfer of subsistence land to large property owners. Making such transfers irreversible impaired government fiscal revenue and the supply of military manpower, leading ultimately to economic collapse.

Acts by Byzantine emperors (like those of Babylonian rulers) to reverse this takeover by the powerful thus were not part of a utopian idealism to protect the weak and poor. Toynbee endorsed Ostrogorsky's explanation of the Byzantine struggle between emperors and the dynatoi over land tenure and its associated fiscal policy:

> In protecting the small freeholders, civilian and military, against the designs of the large-scale landowners, the East Roman Government was not contending for the rights or for the independence of the small fry. The truth is that it was defending its own rights – its rights to the peasants' payments and services, which the feudal lords were trying to capture from the Government.

---

[672] The details are summarized in Treadgold, *History of the Byzantine State and Society*, pp. 662–666.

The tenth-century domestic context (in the Empire) was not a contest between big and small landowners; it was a contest between the Imperial Government and the feudal potentates. The small landowners were merely the object of that context; their payments and services were the prize that was at stake.[673]

Elaborating on the contest for power between the Government and the *dynatoi*, Toynbee comments that it "gave the penates the opportunity of choosing between their two potential masters. When an increasing number of them came to the conclusion that it was a worse fate to be the Government's serf than to be a private magnate's serf, the magnates' victory over the Government was assured." As Ostrogorsky summarized in his History of the Byzantine State: "The whole trend of the times, with the growth of the great estates, and the overburdening and impoverishment of the lower classes, made it inevitable that ever wider strata of the population were bartering their freedom to become, if not slaves, then at least serfs. In the end, the triumphant advance of feudal processes weakened the authority of the state and undermined the Byzantine polity's power of resistance."[674]

Ultimately at issue was who would manage the economy, and in whose interests. In Hammurabi's day, annulling grain debts helped block the rising power of independent officials, creditors and merchants as rivals to the palace. His andurarum acts restored land to smallholders while maintaining royal control of their labor as soldiers in the army and as taxpayers. Byzantine emperors likewise reversed land transfers to the dynatoi. But in their epoch, foreclosing on mortgage loans was not nearly as important as direct buyouts after the devastating winters of 927/28 and 989.

The common denominator spanning Western Europe and Byzantium was the growing control over the army, church and ultimately the state by large landowners. Leaving the land's rent to Byzantine military commanders (especially in Asia Minor and Anatolia) and their allied clerical and political bureaucracy in Constantinople led to the fiscal crisis that undercut the empire's ability to field an army composed of smallholders. Byzantium ended up being conquered and looted.

* * *

Most fortunes throughout history have been obtained by appropriating the public domain and other land by military seizure, insider dealing, foreclosure by creditors, or purchase at distress prices – followed by a shedding of tax obligations. At some point this appropriation of land and natural resources reaches a high enough degree to enable the expropriators to become the de facto government.

Acceptance of a polarizing status quo and weakening fiscal position is abetted by civic religion or secular ideology defending any given distribution of land and financial wealth as being a result of nature (or "the market"). No matter how unequal this distribution of wealth becomes, the alternative is said to be anarchy and collapse – as if the main cause of systemic collapse throughout most recorded history has not actually been over-indebtedness and the transfer of land to large appropriators.

---

[673] Toynbee 1973: 175f., citing Ostrogorsky 1956: 16.
[674] Ostrogorsky 1969: 394.

Mainstream ideology now denies a positive role for government policy to constrain the large-scale concentration of wealth. Purporting to explain the history of inequality since the Stone Age, for instance, Stanford historian Walter Scheidel's 2017 book *The Great Leveler* downplays the ability to substantially reduce it without natural disasters wiping out wealth at the top. He recognizes that the inherent tendency of history is for the wealthy to win out and make society increasingly unequal. But the only "solution" to inequality that he finds at work are the four "great levelers": mass warfare, violent revolution, lethal pandemics or state collapse. He does not acknowledge progressive tax policy, debt writeoffs or return of land to smallholders as means to prevent or reverse the concentration of wealth in the absence of external crisis.

The Book of Revelation forecast these plagues as punishment for the greed and inequity into which the Roman Empire was falling. By Late Roman times there seemed no alternative to the Dark Age that was descending. Recovery of a more equitable past seemed politically hopeless, and so was idealized as occurring only by divine intervention at the end of history. Yet for thousands of years, economic polarization was reversed by cancelling debts and restoring land tenure to smallholders who cultivated the land, fought in the army, paid taxes and/or performed corvée labor duties. That was the essence of Babylonia's royal proclamation of clean slates, and Byzantine policy to avoid polarization from the 7ᵗʰ through 10ᵗʰ centuries.

Opposition to government policies to limit the concentration of wealth promotes an unhistorical and hence unwarranted political surrender to the status quo. Widening inequality is claimed to be natural, as if no countervailing power of government could promote more widespread prosperity. This rationalization of an inequitable status quo has no room to acknowledge the historical success of policies that have deterred inequality from developing to the point of impoverishing the poor, or that have reversed such polarization when it does develop.

Neither the Bronze Age, classical antiquity nor the Byzantine emperors of the 9ᵗʰ and 10ᵗʰ centuries shared Scheidel's apocalyptic idea of external crisis being the only way to reverse economic inequality. These epochs had a much more active political view of how to promote economic stability and equality. Plato observed that "an oligarchy becomes 'two cities,' Rich and Poor, as great wealth is opposed to extreme poverty for the masses, and almost everyone outside the ruling class is a pauper."[675] Aristotle wrote that cities could be democratic or oligarchic, so that when the politeia changes, a city becomes a different kind of city. The task of Athenian democracy, and later of Byzantine imperial Novels, was to prevent oligarchic polarization.

I attended a lecture by Prof. Scheidel at Columbia University in 2017 where he insisted that debt was not a significant factor in Rome's decline. The audience let out a gasp, recognizing how radically his claim was at odds with the writings of Plutarch, Livy, Diodorus and other historians who indeed attributed the fall of the Roman Republic to the aggressive behavior and political violence of its creditor oligarchy.

In the tradition of the "Oriental despotism" view, a 2017 book by Yale professor

---

[675] This point is discussed by Ste. Croix 1981: 286f., citing Aristotle, *Politics* III.3 at 1276ᵇ 3–4, and Plato, *Republic*, VIII.551d, 552b–d.

James C. Scott, *Against the Grain: A Deep History of the Earliest States* sees state authority and power as emerging from the Neolithic agricultural revolution only in a despotic way as taxer and oppressor. This one-sided view of the state fails to recognize how Hammurabi's Babylonian dynasty and his contemporaries enabled their citizen armies to remain self-supporting on the land, free from bondage – and much later, how the 9th- and 10th-century Byzantine emperors likewise preserved village self-support land in the hands of a tax-paying peasant army.

The key was not so much to prevent inequality as such. Even in Sumer, palace elites and temple heads received as high a multiple of revenue relative to manual labor as do today's corporate CEOs. But throughout the Bronze Age, as long as citizens could obtain their basic needs and self-support, they do not seem to have protested immense wealth at the top. Stability was promoted by continually restoring the "normal" condition where everyone could be self-sustaining on their land, free from bondage.

Historians who start out by assuming that the sanctity of debt is a universal prerequisite for economic stability and growth – and therefore not a policy issue – remove the concepts of freedom and liberty from the question of how society manages its debt relationships. Moses Finley, for instance, juxtaposed classical antiquity's idea of freedom to that of the ancient Near East, finding it "impossible to translate the word 'freedom,' *eleutheria* in Greek, *libertas* in Latin, or 'free man,' into any ancient Near Eastern language, including Hebrew, or into any Far Eastern language either, for that matter."[676] Yet as this book has noted, America's Liberty Bell's inscription, "Proclaim freedom throughout the land," is a translation of Hebrew *deror*, recalling Akkadian *andurārum*.

A blind spot when it comes to recognizing the linkage between debt writedowns and freedom is widely shared today. The reality is that Greek and Roman political liberty was economically precarious. For Greeks and Romans, falling into debt subjected them to the risk of bondage without much hope of recovering their liberty. They lacked the prospect of royal amar-gi and *andurārum* amnesties annulling personal debts in Sumer, Babylonia and their neighboring realms, liberating citizens who had fallen into debt bondage or lost their land tenure rights. *Eleutheria* and *libertas* signified freedom from bondage, but not liberation from liability to creditors. A rising proportion of the Greek and Roman populations lost this liberty without hope of any authority liberating them. That is why, as Finley noted, the great political cry throughout antiquity was for debt cancellations and land redistribution. But these were achieved only rarely, as when Greece's 7th-century BC "tyrants" overthrew their cities' archaic aristocracies. The word "tyrants" quickly became a term of invective, as if liberating Greek populations from bondage to a narrow hereditary ethnic aristocracy was not a key precondition for establishing subsequent democratic freedom.

Greek and Roman oligarchies suppressed advocacy of Clean Slates, often violently. Memory of Greece's 7th-century BC populist "tyrants" inspired the tradition of civic officials in some cities being obliged to swear that they would not cancel the debts. Sparta's kings Agis and Cleomenes were killed for advocating debt cancellation late in the 3rd century BC, and Rome suffered violence and assassination of populist

---

[676] Finley 1975: 28, cited in Larsen 2015: 101.

leaders who urged debt cancellation. I intend to trace this history in this volume's sequel, *The Collapse of Antiquity.*

Arnold Toynbee described Rome's patrician idea of "freedom" or "liberty" as limited to oligarchic freedom from kings or civic bodies powerful enough to check creditor power to indebt and impoverish the citizenry at large. "The patrician aristocracy's
monopoly of office after the eclipse of the monarchy had been used by the patricians
as a weapon for maintaining their hold on the lion's share of the country's economic
assets; and the plebeian majority of the Roman citizen-body had striven to gain access
to public office as a means to securing a more equitable distribution of property and
a restraint on the oppression of debtors by creditors."[677] The latter attempt failed,
and European and Western civilization is still living with the aftermath.

Historians who believe that inequality is natural depict freedom and the way to
save economies from poverty as being to downsize government. In this school's reading, the success of Byzantine *dynatoi* in installing emperors too weak and self-indulgent to check the overgrowth of debt and concentration of land ownership should
have promoted freedom and prosperity. The reality is that the powerful reduced
village smallholders to a state of quasi-feudal dependency.

"The state" is an arena in which creditors, landholders and rulers vie for control.
History's eternal tension is between strong rulers and ambitious landlords or creditors
over whether to deter or permit (indeed, encourage) inequality, economic polarization
and poverty. The central focus of historiography therefore should be policy choices
regarding debt, taxation and land tenure.

The characteristic view of history from Ibn Khaldun's *Muqaddimah: An Introduction to History* in 1377 through the 18th-century Scottish Enlightenment was one
of rise and fall. So we are brought back to the idea of circular time to renew basic
social balance. Ibn Khaldun described successful societies as those of mutual aid, declining as a result of their failure to constrain greed and selfishness. Machinations by
the wealthy to concentrate land, money and credit in their own hands undercut the
initial social ethic that promoted economic growth. The destiny of such societies was
to replace their leaders by reformers from within, or to be conquered by outsiders.

That is the story of the ancient Near East, Greek and Roman antiquity, the Biblical lands and Byzantine society. From the Biblical prophets through Roman Stoic
historians to Byzantine chroniclers, the causes of decline were seen to be the weakness
and failure of rulers to block the economically corrosive self-seeking drives of creditors,
military warlords or wealthy land appropriators. Strong governments checked the
power of creditors and absentee landlords in order to save the citizenry from being
reduced to indebted bondservants, renters, clients or serfs. When such societies fell
to conquerors from outside their society, it was blamed on their being weakened from
within. The classic example was Rome's creditor class corrupting the law and using
political assassination to destroy democratic checks and balances, and later the power
grabbing of Byzantine *dynatoi.*

[677] Toynbee 1965, vol. I: 316.

29. Epilogue: Western Civilization is Rooted in the Bronze Age Near East

A market economy usually is seen to be grounded in making credit and land ownership secure, that is, not reversible by royal fiat. Turning financial wealth and credit into land ownership and control of labor is seen as progress toward efficiency. In this view, Bronze Age laws to prevent the emergence of a creditor class from disenfranchising the citizenry appear to have been a false start, not as regulating economic relations and markets to preserve economic growth and military stability.

Despite the fact that our civilization calls itself Judeo-Christian, it abhors the admonition to cancel debts placed at the core of Mosaic Law and the sermons of Jesus. The idea of restoring economic balance by cancelling debts is radically at odds with how modern ideology thinks society should be organized. Most economists and historians imagine that periodic debt amnesties must always have been inherently unworkable in practice. If not outright utopian, the practice is assumed to have been economically destructive and tyrannical.

How creditor appropriation turned land into "private property"

From the origins of civilization down through feudal Europe, fiscal policy was based on the land and its crop surplus. When William the Conqueror led the Norman invasion of England in 1066, his military chieftains replaced the traditional clan heads as collectors. Twenty years later he ordered compilation of the Domesday Book to assess the realm's ability to pay crop tribute and supply contingents of fighting men. In due course the lords rebelled and sought to keep the land's rent for themselves instead of turning it over to the Crown. Much the same resistance to royal taxing power had occurred in Byzantium as the dynatoi appropriated the land and reduced its military themes and village labor to dependency on themselves. And three millennia earlier, Hammurabi faced the same centrifugal economic pressure as commercial wealth became increasingly concentrated outside of palace control.

Traditional land tenure in England was untracked when nobles donated or pledged their land to the Knights Templar and Hospitallers for loans to embark on the Crusades. The religious prestige of these banking orders helped loosen customary restrictions against alienating land outside of local communities. Henceforth, lending money against land rights was a major way to obtain land, leading to its outright free salability. In fact, financial wealth always has sought to absorb land and its rent.

A byproduct of writing this history of debt has been to highlight the role of creditors in creating property as our modern epoch knows it – land freely alienable, increasingly stripped of the fiscal obligations that underlay archaic land tenure.

Families in Bronze Age economies needed land to support themselves. And their communities needed their members to serve in the military and provide corvée labor on civic construction projects.[678] Land tenure emerged out of this fiscal need. It was allocated on the basis of how much a family needed to support its basic needs and fulfill its obligations to help build town walls and defenses, temples and other infrastructure and, in time, pay crop taxes or their money equivalent.[679]

These fiscal obligations defined the community's rules of land tenure. But starting in the Old Babylonian period, the interest of creditors and other absentee owners has been opposed to that of rulers and their fiscal needs, not to mention the freedom and self-reliance of smallholders. The new buyers sought to shift liability for palatial tax claims onto the sellers-become-renters. Making tax-paying land marketable thus involved a radical political transformation

Land rights were privatized by being financialized. Creditors sought "freedom" to foreclose or otherwise obtain crop or land rights, overriding the right of citizens to self-support land along with the palace's fiscal claims for labor services and crop payments. Byzantine emperors likewise were deprived of taxes by permitting the land of smallholders to be alienable, that is, subject to forfeiture for debt or saleable under duress.

A precondition for making land alienable was to define just what was being transferred – the land alone, or its public obligations? Creditors sought to separate the land from its customary labor and crop obligations. As for the sellers' fate, their land became socially decontextualized from economic consideration.

Today's free-enterprise ideology deems property rights a precondition for economic stability and progress, and treats taxes as state "interference" with individual rights, not as having defined property rights in the first place. Friedrich Engels went so far as to describe the state as being created as a vehicle to protect the property of archaic elites, not to deter their appropriation. Protecting absentee landlordship certainly has been a role of the state since the Roman Empire. However, paying creditors the crop surplus and owing work-time as debt service was antithetical to the Bronze Age palace's needs for corvée and military labor.

Transferability of land outside of the kinship-based community is the first hallmark of what our epoch defines as property rights. The second hallmark is the irreversibility of such transfers – making them immune from Clean Slates. Bronze Age rulers proclaimed these restorations of economic order to restore customary land tenure and fiscal viability. Much of the population would have run away or defected if widespread irreversible forfeiture of land to absentee owners was permitted. As creditors won this political battle, flight from the land did indeed occur. That is the essence of modern land tenure during the industrial capitalist epoch: to drive rural labor off the land.

This dynamic became a basic economic feature of the modern world. The 16th to 18th centuries saw a series of Enclosure Movements privatize England's Commons by legal stealth and political insider dealing. Today the World Bank is facilitating a modern Enclosure Movement by promoting land registries in Third World and post-

---

[678] See for instance the articles in Steinkeller and Hudson 2015.

[679] I describe how money initially evolved largely as a means of denominating such contributions. in Hudson 2018.

Soviet countries. Official registration of title is a precondition for privatizing land ownership. The security of credit finds its counterpart in the insecurity of land tenure for the indebted population at large.

The Peruvian mining official Hernando de Soto euphemizes this process: "In the midst of their own poorest neighborhoods and shantytowns, there are … trillions of dollars, all ready to be put to use," if only land rights can be borrowed against, by enabling them to be pledged "as collateral for mortgages."[680] Giving squatters in villages or urban slums legal title is a precondition for stripping them of their customary rights.

It turns out that the absence of formal property rights has been a major virtue for such families. Nobody can dispossess them, because they are protected by custom. Registering their homes as their personal property would indeed enable them to borrow emergency money to make ends meet – but also to be evicted when they could not earn enough to pay their mortgage (with interest).

Forfeiture is the aim, of course! Registering customary land tenure in the holder's name is the first step toward making it transferable to creditors. While De Soto euphemizes borrowing against the land as "equity extraction," *The Economist* magazine aptly notes that there are "two sides to collateral: enforcing the bank's right to repossess an asset is as important as recognising the owner's right to possess it." Borrowers end up losing their security, leaving the newly legalized property rights with foreclosing creditors.[681] That is what a free land market means today. Describing some of the "problems associated with land titles," another writer tells how, "in Thai villages where the duck pond was common property there is now one person owning it and the rest of the village is excluded; in Cambodia unscrupulous property developers have forced land holders off the land."[682]

It is an age-old story. Privatizing credit in classical Greece and Rome, Judah and Israel, led to privatization of the land by wealthy absentee owners. To retain control over the land's tax yield and labor services, strong rulers sought to reverse such transfers. Creditors responded by overthrowing royal power capable of enforcing debt amnesties and reversing land sales or foreclosures. The right of citizens to self-support on the land was replaced by its opposite principle – the right of creditors to foreclose, or buyers with money to buy land irreversibly. This dynamic transformed the classical world. It led to economic polarization, fiscal crisis and ultimately to being conquered – first in the Western Roman Empire and then in Byzantium. At issue is what economic

[680] De Soto 2000: 37, 86. As president of the Geneva-based International Council of Copper Exporting Countries, de Soto lobbied to counter national sovereignty over subsoil mineral rights. Ames and Levine 2013 call him the "Friedrich Hayek of Latin America." Claiming "that foreign mining firms should have exclusive rights to gold from traditionally communal Peruvian lands, De Soto came up with a clever end-around idea: giving property title to the masses of Peru's poor living in the vast shanties and shacks in the slums of Lima and cities beyond. … The point was to align the masses' assumptions about property ownership with those of the banana republic's handful of rich landowning families."

[681] "The mystery of capital deepens: Giving land titles to the poor is no silver bullet," *The Economist*, August 24, 2006.

[682] Makewell, 2013: 133.

progress means. Linear progress is irreversible. It means that transfers of property and the loss of personal liberty cannot be reversed by restoring a status quo ante in good order.

This book has traced debt's role in this long transformation, and reviewed the repertory of policies to reverse its socially destructive effects. Archaic restorations of order ended when the loss of self-support land rights no longer could be reversed. The economic status for much of the population deteriorated into debt dependency and serfdom, while creditors and landlords shifted the tax burden off themselves.

The meaning of economic liberty

A constant dynamic of history has been the drive by financial elites to centralize control in their own hands and manage the economy in predatory, extractive ways. Their ostensible freedom is at the expense of the governing authority and the economy at large. As such, it is the opposite of liberty as conceived in Sumerian times. Yet instead of appreciating the success of early policies to keep the volume of agrarian and personal debt within the ability to be paid, creditors and privatizers have written history from their own vantage point. Demonizing royal authority, today's orthodoxy depicts clean slates as an exercise in Oriental Despotism, an autocratic version of the Temple State approach popular a few generations ago. Bronze Age curbs on creditors are characterized as a despotic repression of individualism, without recognizing just how despotic creditor control of economies becomes in disabling protection of debtors.

On the ostensibly anti-authoritarian left, Moses Finley excluded the Near East from the epoch that he demarcated as "ancient history." This seems to have been a result of accepting Karl Polanyi's dichotomy between redistributive markets and market pricing as being distinct historical stages rather than co-existing in most economies, ancient and modern alike. Failing to recognize the extent to which the West's entrepreneurial and financial techniques, money and prices, interest and land tenure were innovated in "mixed" Near Eastern economies, Finley wrote:

> The Near Eastern economies were dominated by large palace- or temple-complexes, who owned the greater part of the arable, virtually monopolized anything that can be called "industrial production" as well as foreign trade (which includes inter-city trade, not merely trade with foreign parts), and organized the economic, military, political and religious life of the society through a single complicated, bureaucratic, record-keeping operation for which the word "rationing", taken very broadly, is as good a one-word description as I can think of. ...The exclusion of the Near East is therefore not arbitrary ...

In this view, Bronze Age palaces were antithetical to enterprise rather than sponsoring it. Rejecting Finley's assertion, Steven Garfinkle notes:

> The use of the term "primitive" ... becomes particularly objectionable when applied to the Mesopotamian economy because it feeds into the traditional removal of the ancient Near East from the mainstream of history. ... To

Finley, the ancient Near East was not just primitive, it was strange and, therefore, not part of "our" history. By placing the ancient Near East outside of the western experience, Finley was able to justify its exclusion from ancient history; but only if we understand the term "ancient history" to apply exclusively to the carefully screened origins of the "West."[683]

Overlooking the Bronze Age genesis of Western civilization, "private enterprise" models treat the Near Eastern takeoff as a blind alley, not as providing classical Greece and Rome with their basic commercial and financial techniques, interest-bearing debt, and monetary weights and measures. It is as if Western civilization evolved directly from tribal savagery to classical Greece and Rome, without Bronze Age catalysts or antecedents. Silver's monetary role is not recognized as being the designated means of paying debts to the large institutions, or as a byproduct of their account keeping, or even as needing official oversight of purity and publically standardized weights and measures. The individualistic "barter" approach imagines that money emerged simply as a commodity being traded by individuals acting on their own.

Anthropologists have described how "primitive" reciprocity debts helped integrate archaic communities, not polarize them. Wergild-type reparations for inflicting injury (and also marriage obligations or bride price) retained the symmetry of gift exchange. Such debts were kept within the ability of families or clans to pay without disrupting their ability to support themselves on the land and perform normal community duties. The Bronze Age still treated this underlying balance as an "original" and normal condition – a status quo ante of economic liberty based on self-support. Royal amnesties and clean slates kept restoring this state of affairs on a timely basis.

Bronze Age money as a means of palatial production and trade accounting

The time gap between planting and harvesting, or embarking and returning from trade ventures, required agricultural and mercantile debt. Defining the monetary function to settle these balances typically spread from the palace and temples to the economy at large. Citizens owed corvée labor duties and fees for palace and temple services, while merchants owed debts for Mesopotamian palace consignments of export goods or money to import copper and tin to make bronze tools and weapons, and for luxury goods such as silver and precious stone.

Most commercial debts were denominated in silver, the key prestige metal for the palace and temples. The palace obtained it by providing consignments of handicrafts for entrepreneurial merchants to export, and was the major customer for the silver and other imports they brought back. Temples sanctified the purity of this silver for payments within the economy at large.

The weights and measures created for palatial accounting to distribute rations on a standardized monthly basis divided the "bushel" of barley into 60 "quarts." For commercial payments owed to the palace, the value of a silver shekel was set as equal to that of a quart of grain. A silver mina was divided into 60 shekels. This parallel fractional division created a bimonetary system of credit and money that interlinked

[683] Garfinkle 2012: 6f., citing Finley 1985: 28.

commercial loans and advances to traders on the one hand with debts owed by cultivators to pay fees and tax-like charges to the palace.

Each of these spheres – mercantile silver debts, and crop debts owed by cultivators – had its own interest rate and terms of payment. Commercial "silver" debts bore interest at 1 shekel per mina per month, 12 shekels a year, to be paid on the return of the boats or caravans from sea and overland trade. Agrarian debts were paid in barley on the threshing floor at harvest time, and typically charged the sharecropping ratio of one-third for late payment or for agrarian loans and advances.

The origins of money thus lay in fiscal arrangements with the palace, not in barter or trade among isolated individuals. Commerce was entrepreneurial, as was the supervision of herds, the leasing of sharecropping land and other agricultural enterprise, boating and kindred managerial functions. These typically involved profit-sharing agreements with the palace or the increasingly active mercantile class.

By the Middle Babylonian period, agrarian usury became a sideline for such wealth to gain control of labor and, in due course, cropland. Creditors spent their usurious gains on gaining control of dependent labor as clients, at the expense of palace levies of taxes and corvée labor. This conflict of interest created a fiscal problem that was still found three thousand years later in 10th-century Byzantium.

The inherent inability of personal and agrarian debts to be paid over the long run

Until about 1600 BC agrarian debts customarily were subject to royal amnesties when new rulers took the throne, or existing rulers consolidated support after military victories, or when crops failed. These clean slates survived into the Neo-Assyrian and Neo-Babylonian empires – long enough to inspire the debt Jubilee of Leviticus 25. But by the end of antiquity the buildup of debt was made immune from such proclamations. Debtors lost their liberty and land to foreclosing creditors irreversibl. When Sparta's kings Agis and Cleomenes tried to cancel debts in the 3rd century BC, local oligarchs called on the Achaean League and Rome to defeat Sparta.

Roman law favored a creditor oligarchy that disenfranchised indebted citizens and concentrated land ownership. This led to debt servitude, depopulation, and to serfdom at the end of the Roman Empire. Stoic philosophers blamed debt for the collapse of the Republic, and grew sentimental for the Bronze Age as having been a Golden Age of mutual aid and equity.

The modern world retains the Roman legal principle protecting the claims of creditors against the economic solvency of debtors. No modern tradition does what Urukagina, Gudea, Ur-Namma, Lipit-Ishtar, Hammurabi and their contemporaries did in proclaiming "justice and equity" to forgive tax debts when they grew top-heavy. As Dominique Charpin has quipped, the French term "redressment" corresponding to Babylonian *mīšarum*, "to restore balance," has taken on the connotation of governments balancing budgets by raising taxes.[681] After the 2008 financial crash, banks

---

[684] Charpin 1990: 13.

and bondholders were bailed out instead of having to take losses on their bad and often fraudulent loans. This left the economy to limp along with its debt burden kept in place.

The commitment by Urukagina and subsequent rulers to protect widows and orphans ("the naked") has become a stock phrase expressing society's obligation to protect the poor. But today's feigned concern for protecting widowed heiresses and orphaned heirs living on trust-fund portfolios of fixed-income securities has become a shorthand phrase for opposing wage increases (and presumably price inflation) that would lighten the economy's debt burden. These affluent heirs are trotted out as proxies for banks, bondholders and other creditors, in contrast to antiquity's widows and orphans who were poor debtors.

A study of the long sweep of history shows a universal principle to be at work: The burden of debt tends to exceed the ability of debtors to pay. This has been the major cause of economic polarization from antiquity to modern times. Yet today's popular ideology blames debtors, as if when their arrears are a personal choice rather than stemming from economic strains that compel them to run up debts simply to survive.

To cap matters, modern prejudice assumes that writing down debts would cause a crisis (losses by creditors) instead of being necessary to save economies from crisis and insolvency. A finance professor, William Goetzmann, found a Babylonian-era *mīšarum* act at Larsa. Imagining this to be an isolated clean slate, he called it "the crash of 1788," as if it caused financial disaster. Misreading Rim-Sin's edict as "eliminating all debt by royal decree," he did not realize that only barley debts were annulled, not commercial "silver" debts.[685]

Depicting debt only in a positive light, Goetzmann makes a wild guess that "Perhaps he [Rim-Sin] himself or those close to him had gotten into debt." He has managed to avoid reading even the most basic Assyriological research, which would have taught him that Bronze Age palaces and their bureaucracies were their epoch's major creditors, not debtors! The agrarian debts that Rim-Sin cancelled were those that the population owed to his palace and other creditors, not those that he owed. He proclaimed a clean slate in a war situation, as was normal to liberate cultivators to serve in the army. In a similar move to gain support, Larsa's conqueror Hammurabi proclaimed a clean slate specifically for Larsa after he defeated Rim-Sin, following numerous debt cancellations to benefit his own citizen army.

To insist that all debts must be paid ignores the contrast between the thousands of years of successful Near Eastern clean slates and the debt bondage into which Greco-Roman antiquity sank. The tendency of debt is to expand to the point where it becomes too large to be paid. But today's pro-creditor orthodoxy rejects any logic that would justify resolving this problem by debt writedowns.

The policy lesson of Bronze Age economics is rejected as being too radical by those who believe that creditor interests should take priority over those of the indebted economy at large. The insights by Assyriologists over the last decades are mostly ignored in the academic curriculum and popular discussion. Western civilization is still

---

[685] Goetzmann 2016: 57f.

depicted as going back to Greece but not any further in time or eastwards in place. And just as today's mainstream economists recoil from the idea that Babylonian Clean Slates helped sustain growth and stability, most theological training belittles the Biblical laws of debt forgiveness as merely a utopian dream. When I recently gave a lecture at a theological seminary, some professors informed me that they had gone through divinity school without learning about how central the role of debt was in the Jewish Bible and Jesus's teachings from his first sermon to his parables.

Economic ideology plays the role today that religious morality did in times past. Mainstream economists depict money and debt as only a veil, not affecting the distribution of income and wealth except to finance growth. Even in the wake of the 2008 debt crisis and subsequent Greek national bankruptcy, this ideology is silent as to the socially corrosive effects of debt prying away control of the land, natural resources and the organs of government.

The thousands of years of political and religious conflict over the debt issue traced in the preceding chapters provide a repertory of how the early millennia of our civilization dealt with this problem. If their policy in many cases was more successful than today's, it is because they recognized that insisting that all debts must be paid meant foreclosures, economic polarization and impoverishment of the economy at large.

Indexes

General Index

1st month (Nisan)
30-day administrative month 17
30-day month 59
30-year periodicity 179
360-day administrative
　calendar 59
50th year 5
60-year reign 127
see also interest rate

A

a month of years 179, 223
a week of years 194
able-bodied 97, 169
Abrams, Robert (Attorney
　General) 148
absentee
　acquirer 143
　appropriator 164, 241
　landowner 64, 67, 92, 174
　owner 68, 108, 124, 189,
　　219, 264, 265
accounting 21, 22, 23
　practice 56
　of cost 17, 21
acquisition 248
act of god 147
administrative calendar of 360
　days 59
administrative month of 30 days
　17
adoption 65, 66, 168
　fictive 167
　transfer of title 168
aetiology 172
Afghanistan 109
agio 25, 160
agoranomoi 22
Akkad 29, 70, 72, 73, 89, 90,
　91, 92, 93, 97, 108, 109,
　128, 149, 157
Akkadian dynasty 29, 71, 89, 119
Akkadian Empire 87
Akkadians 90, 92, 98, 112,
　113, 114, 116, 117
alcoholic beverages 136
ale wives
　see tavern keeper
alienation

restrictions 66, 123
　of property by debtors to
　　creditors 64
allelengyon 253
alliances 37, 70, 119, 129
allocation of resources 21
amar-gi (return to the "mother
　condition") 5, 19, 29,
　69, 76, 85-86, 89, 94, 96,
　107, 114, 116, 149, 156,
　159, 162, 178, 261
Amarna Age 154, 173, 175
ambassador 165
amnesty
　see also cancellation of debt
　for debt-servants 114
　for lawbreakers 84
Amorite(s) 23, 29, 30, 70, 91,
　102, 105, 106, 117, 119,
　122, 125, 128, 129, 130,
　131,149, 152, 153, 164,
　170, 172, 187, 209
Amorite dynasty of Babylon 30
Amorite invasion 70
Anatolia 29, 54, 90, 109, 113,
　117, 118, 163, 252, 253,
　259
ancestors 56, 172, 213
　honoring of 35
Anglo-Saxon law 38
Antasura 74, 76
Anthropological approach 35,
　42, 47, 53, 56, 58
antichresis 169-170
aphesis 225, 232
apprentice 83, 146
arbitrage, agrarian 48
arbitrary power 136
arbitrators 38
archive 19, 98, 99, 100, 103,
　116, 119, 125, 126, 167,
　168, 173, 176, 177, 245
aristocracy 6, 25, 30, 31, 34,
　53, 89, 133, 151, 158,
　164, 176, 186, 190, 197,
　203, 205, 212, 227, 224,
　235, 239, 241, 247, 248,
　249, 250, 252, 253, 254,
　255, 256, 261, 262

army 104, 254
　contingents or phalanges of
　　fighting men 88, 165, 263
　of citizens 17, 107, 131, 197
　of free land-tenured peasants
　　32
　service in 46, 106, 108, 252,
　　269
Arrapkhe 169
arrears 4, 6, 25, 49, 75, 76, 83,
　96, 131, 149, 150, 159,
　161, 163, 178, 180, 212,
　225, 237, 238, 269
arrogance of wealth *see* hubris
arrow of time 232
artisan 83
Ashmunikkal 164
Asia Minor 3, 24, 25, 32, 33,
　43, 59, 61, 70, 90, 92,
　109, 115, 116, 121, 123,
　125, 161, 163, 164, 166,
　224, 247, 250, 259
asset stripping 53, 94
asset 33, 38, 45
　not necessarily reflecting
　　value of debt 45
　of the offending party being
　　distrained, 44
Assur 3, 19, 29-30, 97, 107-
　108, 109-118, 125, 128,
　132, 150-151, 161, 164,
　167, 175-176
Assyria 30, 44, 115-116, 125,
　163, 169, 173-176, 181,
　189, 197, 203-204, 214
astral cosmology 190, 222
Athenian citizen 133
Athens 31, 57, 65-66, 105,
　141, 180, 186, 196, 198,
　207, 210, 214, 229
austerity 7, 27, 53, 88, 160
authority of palace 30, 64, 97
autocracy 100

B

Babylon passim
Babylonian captivity 203
Babylonian economic practices,
　adoption of 167

Historical Persons

Modern Authors

Bibliographical Abbreviations

ABAW	Abhandlungen der Bayerischen Akademie der Wissenschaften
AfO	*Archiv für Orientforschung*
ANET	see Pritchard 1955 [1958].
ArOr	*Archív Orientálni*
BiOr	*Bibliotheca Orientalis*
CA	*Current Anthropology*
HUCA	*Hebrew Union College Annual*
JAA	*Journal of Anthropological Archaeology*
JANESCU	*Journal of the Ancient Near Eastern Society of Columbia University*
JAOS	*Journal of the American Oriental Society*
JBL	*Journal of Biblical Literature*
JCS	*Journal of Cuneiform Studies*
JEH	*Journal of Economic History*
JESHO	*Journal of the Economic and Social History of the Orient*
JJS	*Journal of Jewish Studies*
JNES	*Journal of Near Eastern Studies*
NABU	*Nouvelles assyriologiques brèves et utilitaires*
Or	*Orientalia*
PIHANS	*Uitgaven van het Nederlands Historisch-Archaeologisch Instituut te Istanbul*
RA	*Revue d'Assyriologie et d'Archaéologie Orientale*
RAI	*Rencontre Assyriologique Internationale*
REA	*Research in Economic Anthropology: An Annual Compilation of Research*
RHist	*Revue Historique*
RIDA	*Revue Internationale des Droits de l'Antiquite*
RlA	*Reallexikon der Assyriologie*
RSO	*Rivista degli Studi Orientali*
SciAm	*Scientific American*
ZA	*Zeitschrift für Assyriologie und vorderasiatische Archäologie*

Bibliography

Adams, Robert McC.
   1960 "Factors Influencing the Rise of Civilization in the Alluvium Illustrated by Meso-
      potamia," in Kraeling and Adams, eds., *City Invincible* (Chicago University of Chicago
      Press) 24–45.
   1981 *Heartland of Cities. Surveys of Ancient Settlement and Land Use on the Central Flood-
      plain of the Euphrates* (Chicago—London: University of Chicago Press).
Adelson, H. L.
   1995 "The Origins of a Concept of Social Justice" in Irani and Silver, eds., *Social Justice in the
      Ancient World* (Westport, Conn.: Greenwood Press) 25–38.
Alexander, John B.
   1938 "A Babylonian Year of Jubilee?" JBL 57: 75–79.
Algaze, Guillermo
   1993 *The Uruk World System: The Dynamics of Expansion in Early Mesopotamian Civilization*
      (Chicago: University of Chicago Press).
Alster, Bendt
   1974 *The Instructions of Shuruppak: A Sumerian Proverb Collection* (Mesopotamia: Copen-
      hagen Studies in Assyriology 2, Copenhagen: Akademisk Forlag).

Andreau, Jean, P. Briant and R. Descat, eds.
  1994 *Économie antique: les échanges dans l'antiquité: le rôle de l'état* (Entretiens d'archéologie et d'histoire Saint-Bertrand-de-Comminges 1, Saint-Bertrand-de-Comminges: Musée archéologique départemental).
Archi, Alfonso
  2002 "'Debt' in an Archaic Palatial Economy: The Evidence from Ebla," in Hudson and Van De Mieroop, eds., *Debt and Economic Renewal* (CDL press: Bethesda, Maryland) 95–108.
Archi, Alfonso, ed.
  1984 *Circulation of Goods in Non-Palatial Context in the Ancient Near East* (Incunabula Graeca 82) Rome: Edizioni dell'Ateneo.
Artzi, Pinhas
  1964 "'Vox Populi' in the El-Amarna Tablets," *RA* 58: 159–166.
Astour, Michael C.
  1965 *Hellenosemitica. An Ethnic and Cultural Study in West Semitic Impact on Mycenaean Greece* (Leiden: Brill).
  1972 "The Merchant Class of Ugarit," in Edzard, ed., *Gesellschaftsklassen* 11–26.
Atwater, Richard
  1992   Procopius, *Secret History.* New York: Dorset Press.
Austin, M. M.
  1981 *The Hellenistic World from Alexander to the Roman Conquest: A Selection of Ancient Sources in Translation* (Cambridge: Cambridge University Press).
Bachvarova, Mary
  2005 "Relations between God and Man in the Hurro-Hittite Song of Release," JAOS 125: 45–58.
Balkan, Kemal
  1974 "Cancellation of Debts in Cappadocian Tablets from Kültepe," in Bittel, Houwink Ten Kate and Reiner, eds., *Anatolian Studies presented to Hans C. Güterbock* (PIHANS 35. Istanbul: Nederlands Instituut voor het Nabije Oosten) 29–36.
Bamberger, Bernard J.
  1979 *Leviticus: A Modern Commentary* (New York: Union of American Hebrew Congregations).
Baron, Salo Wittmayer
  1952 *A Social and Religious History of the Jews*, vol. I: *To the beginning of the Christian Era* (2nd ed., New York [1937]).
Barton, George A.
  1929 *The Royal Inscriptions of Sumer and Akkad* (New Haven: American Oriental Society).
Benveniste, Emile
  1973 *Indo–European Language and Society* (Miami Linguistic Series 12. Coral Gables, Florida: University of Miami Press).
Bernal, Martin
  1987 *Black Athena. The Fabrication of Ancient Greece 1785–1985.* New Brunswick, New Jersey: Rutgers University Press.
Biggs, R. D.
  1967 "More Babylonian Prophecies," *Iraq* 27: 117–132.
Binchy, D. A.
  1970 "Celtic Suretyship, A Fossilized Indo-European Institution," in Cardona, Hoenigswald and Senn, eds., *Indo-European and Indo-Europeans Papers Presented at the Third Indo-European Conference at the University of Pennsylvania* (Philadelphia: University of Pennsylvania Press) 355–367. Reprinted in *The Irish Jurist* 7 (1972): 360–372.

Black-Michaud, Jacob
  1975   *Cohesive Force: Feud in the Mediterranean and the Middle East.* New York: Blackwell.
Blackstone, Sir William
  1765–1769 *Commentaries on the Laws of England.* Book IV chapter 23: *Of the Several Modes of Prosecution.* Oxford: Clarendon Press.
Bleeker, C. J.
  1967   *Egyptian Festivals. Enactments of Religious Renewal* (Leiden: Brill).
Boas, Franz
  1913–1914 "Ethnology of the Kwakiutl, Based on Data Collected by George Hunt," *Bureau of American Ethnology, Annual Report* 35: 41 –794, i–xii.
Bogaert, Raymond
  1966   *Les origines antiques de la banque de dépôt: une mise au point accompagnée d'une esquisse des opérations de banque en Mésopotamie* (Leiden: Sijthoff).
von Böhm-Bawerk, Eugen
  1890   *Capital and Interest: A Critical History of Economic Theory* (London).
Bongenaar, A. C. V. M., ed.
  2000   *Interdependency of Institutions and Private Entrepreneurs. Proceedings of the 2nd MOS Symposium, Leiden, December 11–12, 1998* (PIHANS 87. Istanbul: Nederlands Instituut voor het Nabije Oosten).
Bottéro, Jean
  1961   "Désordre économique et annulation des dettes en Mesopotamie à l'epoque paléo-babylonienne," *JESHO* 4: 113–164.
  1992   *Mesopotamia: Writing, Reasoning, and the Gods* (Chicago: University of Chicago Press [Paris 1987]).
Bourboilis, Photiene P.
  1964   *Ancient Festivals of the "Saturnalia" Type* (= *Hellennica* 16, Thessaloniki) Hetaireia. Peloponnēsiakōn Spoudōn.
Brand, Charles M.
  1969 "Two Byzantine Treatises on Taxation," *Traditio* 25: 58.
Breasted, James Henry
  1906   *Ancient Records of Egypt* (Chicago).
Brehier, Louis
  1977   *Life and Death of Byzantium.* Amsterdam.
Brinkman, John A.
  1974 "The Monarchy in the Time of the Kassite Dynasty," in Garelli, ed., *Le Palais et la Royauté,* 395–408.
Bromberg, Benjamin
  1942 "The Origin of Banking: Religious Finance in Babylonia," *JEH* 2: 77–88.
Brown Peter
  1971   *The World of Late Antiquity.* London.
Bryant, Sophie
  1923   *Liberty, Order and Law under Native Irish Rule: A Study in the Book of the Ancient Laws of Ireland* (New York).
Cardascia, George
  1959 "La concept babylonien de la propriete," *RIDA* 6: 19–32.
Charanis, Peter
  1948   "The Monastic Properties and the State in the Byzantine Empire," Dumbarton Oaks Papers IV: 53–64.
  1953 "Economic Factors in the Decline of the Byzantine Empire," *JEH* 13: 415–423.

Charpin, Dominique

1980   *Archives familiales et propriété privée en Babylonie ancienne: Étude des documents de Tell Sifr* (Geneva-Paris).

1986   *Le Clerge d'Ur au siecle d'Hammurapi* (Geneva-Paris).

1987   "Les decréts royaux à l'époque paleo-babylonienne, à propos d'un ouvrage récent," *AfO* 34:36–44.

1990a   "L'andurârum à Mari," *M.A.R.I.* 6: 253–270.

1990b   "Les édits de 'restauration' des rois babyloniens et leur application," in Claude Nicolet, ed., *Du pouvoir dans l'antiquité: Mots et réalités* (Geneva): 13–24.

1992   "L'application des édits de *mîšarum*: Traces documentaires," *NABU* 1992/3, 57f.

1995   "The History of Ancient Mesopotamia: An Overview," in Jack Sasson, ed., *Civilizations of the Ancient Near East* (New York): 807–829.

2000   "Les prêteurs et la palais: Les édits de *mîšarum* des rois de Babylone et leurs traces dans les archives privées," in A C.V.M. Bongenaar, ed., *Interdependency of Institutions and Private Entrepreneurs. Proceedings of the Second MOS Symposium, Leiden 1998.* Leiden: Nederlands Historisch-Archaeologisch Institut te Istanbul: 185–211.

2003   *Hammurabi of Babylon* (London and New York).

2013   "I am the Sun of Babylon: Solar Aspects of Royal Power," in Jane A. Hill, Philip Jones and Antonio J. Morales, eds., *Expressing Power, Generating Authority: Cosmos, Politics and the Ideology of Kingship in Ancient Egypt and Mesopotamia.* Philadelphia: University of Pennsylvania Press: 65–96.

Chirichigno, Gregory C.

1993   *Debt-Slavery in Israel and the Ancient Near East.* Sheffield.

Christodoulakis, N.

2015   *How Crises Shaped Economic Ideas and Policies.* Springer.

Cooper, Jerrold S.

1983   *Reconstructing History From Ancient Inscriptions: The Lagash-Umma Border Conflict* Malibu, Cal.

1986   *Sumerian and Akkadian Royal Inscriptions*, vol. I: *Presargonic Inscriptions.* New Haven.

Crawford, Harriet E. W.

1973   "Mesopotamia's Invisible Exports in the Third Millennium BC," *World Archaeology* 5: 232–241.

Crawford, Sidnie White and Cecilia Wassen, eds.

2016   *The Dead Sea Scrolls at Qumran and the Concept of a Library.* Leiden: Brill.

Dagron, Gilbert

2002   "The Urban Economy, Seventh-Twelfth Centuries," in Angeliki E. Laiou, ed., *The Economic History of Byzantium: From the Seventh through the Fifteenth Century.* Washington D.C.: Dumbarton Oaks Research Library and Collection: 393–461.

Dandamayev, Mohammed A.

1974   "Social Stratification in Babylonia," *Acta Antiqua Hungarica* 22:438–443.

1984   *Slavery in Babylonia, from Napopolassar to Alexander the Great (626–331 BC).* De Kalb, Ill.

1988   "The Neo-Babylonian Popular Assembly," in Petr Vavroušek and Vladimir Souček, eds., *ŠULMU: Papers on the Ancient Near East Presented at International Conference of Socialist Countries (Prague, Sept. 30– Oct. 3, 1986).* Prague: 63–71.

1994   "Babylonian Popular Assemblies," Lecture given at the Metropolitan Museum of Art, March 31, 1993, ms.

1996   "An Age of Privatization in Mesopotamia, 7th to 4th Centuries BC," in Hudson and Levine, *Privatization* 197–210.

Dandamayev, M. A., I. Gershevitch, H. Klengel, G. Komoróczy, M. T. Larsen, J. N. Postgate, eds.
   1982   *Societies and Languages of the Ancient Near East: Studies in Honour of I. M. Diakonoff* (Warminster: Aris & Phillips).

Danstrup, John
   1946   "The State and Landed Property in Byzantium to 1250," *Classica et mediaevalia* 8: 22–267.
   1948   "Manuel I's Coup against Genoa and Venice in the Light of Byzantine Commercial Policy," *Classica et mediaevalia* 10: 195–219.

David, Martin
   1948   "The Manumission of Slaves under Zedekiah," *Oud-testamentische Studien* V: 63–79.
   1950   "Hammurapi and the Law in Exodus," *Oud-testamentische Studien* VII: 149–178.

Deimel, Anton
   1931   *Sumerische Tempelwirtschaft der Zeit Urukaginas und seiner Vorgänger.* Rome.

Dercksen, J. G., ed.
   1999   *Trade and Finance in Ancient Mesopotamia (MOS Studies 1) [Leiden 1997].* Istanbul 1999.

De Soto, Hernando
   2000   *The Mystery of Capital.* New York: Basic Books.

de Vaux, Roland
   1961   *Ancient Israel, I: Social Institutions.* New York.

Diakonoff, Igor M.
   1958   "Some Remarks on the 'Reforms' of Urukagina," *RA* 52: 1–15.
   1959   "Ancient Near East in Soviet Research," *ArOr* 27.
   1971   "On the Structure of Old Babylonian Society," in Horst Klengel, ed., *Beiträge zur sozialen Struktur des alten Vorderasien.* Berlin: 15–31.
   1972   "Socio-Economic Classes in Babylonia and the Babylonian Concept of Social Stratification," in D. O. Edzard, ed., *Gesellschaftsklassen*: 41–52.
   1974   *Structure of Society and State in Early Dynastic Sumer* (MANE 1/ 3). Malibu.
   1975   "The Rural Economy of the Ancient Near East," *JESHO* 18: 121–133.
   1976   "Slaves, Helots and Serfs in Early Antiquity," in J. Hermatta and G. Komoroczy, eds., *Wirtschaft und Gesellschaft im alten Vorderasien.* Budapest.
   1982   "The Structure of Near Eastern Society before the Middle of the 2nd Millennium BC," *Oikumene* 3: 7–100 (originally published in Russian, *VDI* 1967/68).
   1985   "Extended Families in Old Babylonian Ur," *ZA* 75: 41–65.
   1991   "The City-States of Sumer" and "Early Despotisms in Mesopotamia," in *Early Antiquity.* Chicago: 67–97.

Diakonoff, Igor M., ed.
   1969   *Ancient Mesopotamia: Socio-Economic History: A Collection of Studies by Soviet Scholars* Moscow.
   1991   *Early Antiquity.* Chicago and London.

Dossin, George
         "Sur le prophétisme à Mari," in *La divination en Mésopotamie et dans les régions voisines* (XIV RAI). Paris: Presses universitaires: 77–86.

Douglas, Mary
   1965   *Purity and Danger: An Analysis of Concepts of Purity and Taboo.* New York.

Drake, Lyndon
   2015   "Did Jesus Oppose the *prosbul* in the Forgiveness Petition of the Lord's Prayer?" *Novum Testamentum* 56: 233–244.

Driver, G. R., and John C. Miles
  1935   *The Assyrian Laws.* Oxford.
  1939   "Code of Hammurapi, §§ 117–119," in Paul Koschaker Festschrift (Leiden): 65–75.
  1952   *The Babylonian Laws* (Oxford, 2 vols.)
Eckart, Otto,
  2008   "Soziale Restitution und Vertragsrecht: mīšaru(m), (an)-duraru(m), kirenzi, para tarnu-mar, šemitta und deror in Mesopotamien, Syrien, in der Hebräischen Bibel und die Frage des Rechtstransfers im Alten Orient," *RA* 92 (1998) revised as "Institutionen sozialer Restitution im Alten Orient und im Alten Testament," in his *Altorientalische und biblische Rechtsgeschichte:* 135–160.
Edzard, Dietz Otto
  1957   *Die zweite Zwischenzeit Babyloniens.* Wiesbaden.
  1967   "The Old Babylonian Period," in Jean Bottéro, *et al.,* eds., *The Near East: The Early Civilizations.* New York.
  1968   *Sumerische Rechtsurkunden des III. Jahrtausends aus der Zeit vor der III. Dynastie von Ur* (ABAW, N.S. 67) Munich.
  1974   "'Sociale Reformen' im Zweistromland bis Ca. 1600 v. Chr.: Realität oder Literarischer Topos?" *Acta Antiqua Hungarica* 22: 145–56.
  1991   "Irikagina (Urukagina)," in P. Michaelowski, P. Steinkeller, E. E. Stone, and R. L. Zettler, eds., *Velles Paraules: Ancient Near Eastern Studies in Honor of Miguel Civil on the Occasion of his Sixty-Fifth Birthday* (Aula Orientalis 9) Barcelona: 78–80.
  1996   "Private Ownership of Land and Slaves, and its Relation to the 'God' and the 'State' in Sumer and Akkad," in M. Hudson and B. Levine, eds., *Privatization,* 109–128.
  1997   *Gudea and his Dynasty* (The Royal Inscriptions of Mesopotamia. Early Periods , Vol. 3/1) Toronto.
Edzard, Dietz Otto, ed.
  1972   *Gesellschaftsklassen im Alten Zweistromland und in den angrenzenden Gebieten. XVIII. Rencontre assyriologique internationale, München, 29. Juni bis 3. Juli 1970* (ABAW 75) Munich: Bayerische Akademie der Wissenschaften.
Eisenstadt, ed.,
  1986   *The Origins and Diversity of Axial Age Civilizations.* Albany, NY.
Barry L. Eichler
  1973   *Indenture at Nuzi.* New Haven.
Bidez, J.
  1943   *La Cité du monde et la cité du soceil chez le Stoïciens.* Paris: Les Belles Lettres.
Eilers, W.
  1973   "Reflexions sur les origines du droit en Mesopotamie," *Revue historique de droit français et étranger,* 4e serie, 51: 195–215.
Eliade, Mircea
  1959   *Cosmos and History.* New York (= *The Myth of the Eternal Return,* Chicago 1954).
Ellis, Maria de Jong
  1972   "ṣimdatu in the Old Babylonian Sources," *JCS* 24: 74–82.
  1976   *Agriculture and the State in Ancient Mesopotamia: An Introduction to Problems of Land Tenure.* Philadelphia.
Evans, Geoffrey
  1958   "Ancient Mesopotamian Assemblies," *JAOS* 78: 1–11.
Fairman, H. W.
  1958   "The Kingship Rituals of Egypt," in Hooke, ed., *Myth, Ritual, and Kingship.* Oxford: Clarendon: 74–104.

292

Falkenstein, Adam
    1954 "The Sumerian Temple City," *Journal of World History* I: 784–814 (trans. Undena 1974) and in Donald Kagan, *Problems in Ancient History* 2: *The Ancient Near East and Greece.* New York 197).
    1956 *Die neusumerischen Gerichtsurkunden.* Teil I: *Einleitung und systematische Darstellung.* ABAW, phil.-hist. Kl., N. F. 39.
    1966 *Die Inschriften Gudeas von Lagash* (AnOr 30) Munich.

Fincke, Jeanette C.
    2010 "Zum Verkauf von Grundbesitz in Nuzi," in *Festschrift für Gernot Wilhelm.* ISLET: Dresden: 135–141.

Finet, André
    1973 *Le Code de Hammurapi.* Paris, 2ⁿᵈ ed. 1983).

Finkelstein, Jacob J.
    1961 "Ammisaduqa's Edict and the Babylonian 'Law Codes,'" *JCS* 15: 91–104.
    1965 "Some New *misharum* Material and its Implications," in Hans G. Güterbock and Thorkild Jacobsen, eds., *Studies in Honor of Benno Landsberger on his Seventy-Fifth Birthday.* (Assyriological Studies 16) Chicago: 233–246.
    1969 "The Edict of Ammisaduqa: A New Text," *RA* 63: 45–64.
    1975 "The Laws of Ur-Nammu," in ANET II: 31–34.
    1981 "The Ox that Gored," *Transactions of the American Philosophical Society*, 71/2: 1–89.

Finley, Moses I.
    1973 *The Ancient Economy.* Berkeley and London.
    1981 *Economy and Society in Ancient Greece.* London.
    1983 *Politics in the Ancient World.* Cambridge.

Foster, Benjamin R.
    1982 *Umma in the Sargonic Period.* Hamden, Conn.
    1995 "Social Reform in Ancient Mesopotamia," in K. D. Irani and Morris Silver, eds., *Social Justice in the Ancient World.* Westport, Conn.: 165–178.
    2005 *Before the Muses: An Anthology of Akkadian Literature.* 3ʳᵈ ed. Bethesda, Md.: CDL Press.

Frankfort, Henri
    1951 *Kingship and the Gods.* Chicago.
    1952 "State Festivals in Egypt and Mesopotamia," *Journal of the Warburg and Courtauld Institute* 15: 1–12.

Frayne, Douglas R.
    1987 *Assyrian Rulers of the Third and Second Millennia BC* (RIM I) Toronto.
    1990 *The Royal Inscriptions of Mesopotamia: Old Babylonian Period (2003–1595 BC)* (RIM 4) Toronto.
    1997 *The Royal Inscriptions of Mesopotamia: The Ur III Period (2112–2004 BC)* (RIME 3/2) Toronto.
    2008 *The Royal Inscriptions of Mesopotamia:Presargonic Period (2700–2350 BC)* (RIME 1) Toronto.

Fuks, Alexander
    1984 *Social Conflict in Ancient Greece.* Leiden.

Gadd, C. J.
    1930 "Entemena: A New Incident," *RA* 27: 125–126.
    1939 "Text of the 'Babylonian Seisachtheia,'" in J. Friedrich *et al.*, eds., *Symbolae ... Paul Koschaker* Leiden: 102–105.
    1948 *Ideas of Divine Rule in the Ancient East.* London.

Gamoran, Hillel
    1971 "The Biblical Law Against Loans on Interest," *JNES* 30:127–133.

Garelli, Paul (ed.)
    1974 *Le Palais et la Royaute* (= XIXe RAI). Paris.

Garfinkle, Steven J.
    2004 "Shepherds, Merchants, and Credit: Some Observations On Lending Practices in Ur III Mesopotamia," *JESHO* 47: 1–30.
    2004 "Public versus Private in the Ancient Near East," in Daniel C. Snell, ed., *A Companion to the Ancient Near East.* Blackwell: 384–396.
    2012 *Entrepreneurs and Enterprise in Early Mesopotamia: A Study of Three Archives from the Third Dynasty of Ur (2112–2004 BC).* Bethesda, Maryland.

Gaster, Theodor
    1950 *Thespis: Ritual, Myth and Drama in the Ancient Near East.* New York.
    1953 *Festivals of the Jewish Year.* New York.

Gelb, Ignace J.
    1965 "The Ancient Mesopotamian Ration System," *JNES* 24: 230–243.
    1967 "Approaches to the Study of Ancient Society," *JAOS* 87: 1–8.
    1967 "Growth of a Herd of Cattle in Ten Years," *JCS* 21: 64–69.
    1971 "On the Alleged Temple and State Economies in Ancient Mesopotamia," in Pietro De Francisci, ed., *Studi in Onore di Edoardo Volterra.* Milan: vol. VI: 137–154.
    1972a "The Arua Institution," *RA* 66:1–21.
    1972b "From Freedom to Slavery," in D. O. Edzard, ed., *Gesellschaftsklassen*: 87–92.

Gelb, Ignace; Piotr Steinkeller and Robert M. Whiting Jr.
    1989 *Earliest Land Tenure Systems in the Near East: Ancient Kudurrus* (OIP 104) Chicago.

Gernet, Louis
    1981 *The Anthropology of Ancient Greece.* Baltimore and London.

Gibson, McGuire
    1974 "Violation of Fallow and Engineered Disaster in Mesopotamian Civilization," in Theodore Downing and McGuire Gibson, eds., *Irrigation's Impact on Society* (Anthropological Papers of the University of Arizona 25) Tucson:, Arizona 7–19.

Ginnell, Laurence
    1894 *The Brehon Laws: A Legal Handbook.* London.

Ginzberg, Eli
    1932 "Studies in the Economics of the Bible," *Jewish Quarterly Review* 22: 342–408.

Gledhill, John and Mogens Larsen
    1982 "The Polanyi Paradigm and a Dynamic Analysis of Archaic States," in Colin Renfrew, Michael J. Rowlands, and Barbara Abbott Segraves, eds., *Theory and Explanation in Archaeology.* New York: Academic Press.

Goelet, Jr., Ogden
    2002 "Fiscal Renewal in Ancient Egypt: Its Language, Symbols and Metaphors," in Hudson and Van De Mieroop, eds, *Debt and Economic Renewal*: 277–326.

Gofas, Demetrios
    2002 "The Byzantine Law of Interest," in Angeliki E. Laiou, ed., *The Economic History of Byzantium: From the Seventh through the Fifteenth Century.* Washington D.C.: Dumbarton Oaks Research Library and Collection: 1095–1104.

Goetzmann, William
    2016 *Money Changes Everything. How Finance Made Civilization Possible.* Princeton.

Golb, Norman
    1995 *Who Wrote the Dead Sea Scrolls?* New York: Scribner.

Gordon, Cyrus
 1935 "Paralleles nouziens aux lois et coutumes de l'Ancien Testament," *Revue Biblique* 44: 1–8.
 1965 *The Ancient Near East* (3rd ed., New York).
Gordon, Edmund
 1968 *Sumerian Proverbs: Glimpses of Everyday Life in Ancient Mesopotamia.* New York.
Gottwald, Norman K.
 1985 *The Hebrew Bible: A Socio-Literary Introduction.* Philadelphia.
Graeber, David
 2011 *Debt: The First 4000 Years.* New York: Melvillle House.
Grayson, A. K.
 1972 *Assyrian Royal Inscriptions.* Wiesbaden.
 1987 *Assyrian Rulers of the Third and Second Millennia BC* (RIM I) Toronto.
Greenberg, Moshe
 1955 *The Hab/piru* (AOS Ser. 39) New Haven.
Gress, David
 1989 "The Case Against Martin Bernal," *The New Criterion* 1.
 1998 *From Plato to NATO: The Idea of the West and its Opponents.* Free Press.
Grierson, Philip
 1978 "The Origins of Money," *REA* I: 1–35.
Halbherr, Federico
 1897 "Cretan Expedition III. Epigraphical Researches in Gortyna," *American Journal of Archaeology* 1/3: 159–238.
Haldon, John
 1997 *Byzantium in the Seventh Century. The Transformation of a Culture,* 2nd ed. Cambridge.
Hallo, William W.
 1957 *Early Mesopotamian Royal Titles: A Philologic and Historical Analysis.* New Haven.
 1958 Review of Schmoekel 1957 in *JAOS* 78: 305–308.
 1960 "A Sumerian Amphictyony," *JCS* 14: 88–116.
 1963 "Royal Hymns and Mesopotamian Unity," *JCS* 17: 112–115.
 1972 "The House of Ur-Meme," *JNES* 31: 87–95.
 1990 "Proverbs Quoted in Epic," in Tzvi Abusch, John Huehnergard and Piotr Steinkeller, eds., *Lingering over Words: Studies in Ancient Near Eastern Literature in Honor of William L. Moran* (Harvard Semitic Studies 37) Atlanta: Scholars Press: 203–217.
 1992 *The Book of the People.* Atlanta.
 1995 "Slave Release in the Biblical World in Light of a New Text," in Z. Zevit *et al.*, eds., *Solving Riddles and Untying Knots* (FS J.C. Greenfield). Winona Lake 79–93.
 2005 "New Light on the Gutians," in R. Kalvelagen, D. Katz, W. H. van Soldt, eds., *Ethnicity in Ancient Mesopotamia. Papers Read at the 48th Rencontre Assyriologique Internationale, Leiden 1–4 July 2002* (PIHANS 102) Leiden 147–159.
Harmatta, J. and G. Komoroczy, eds.
 1974 *Wirtschaft und Gesellschaft im alten Vorderasien.* Budapest.
Harris, Rivkah
 1960 "Old Babylonian Temple Loans," *JCS* 14: 127–137.
 1964 "The *nadītu* Women," in *Studies Presented to Leo Oppenheim.* Chicago 106–135.
 1975 *Ancient Sippar. A Demographic Study of an Old-Babylonian City (1894-1595 B.C.)* (PIHANS 36) Leiden.
Hartman, L. F., and Leo Oppenheim
 1950 "On Beer and Brewing Techniques in Ancient Mesopotamia According to the XXIIIrd tablet of the series ḪAR.r a = *ḫubullu*," (Supplement to the *Journal of the American Oriental Society* 10) Baltimore: American Oriental Society.

Hawkins, J. D.

1988 "Royal Statements of ideal prices: Assyrian, Babylonian, and Hittite," in J. V. Canby *et al*., eds., *Ancient Anatolia: Aspects of Change and Cultural Development* (*Essays in Honor of Machteld J. Mellink*). Madison: 93–102.

Heichelheim, Fritz M.

1958 *An Ancient Economic History, from the Palaeolithic Age to the Migrations of the Germanic, Slavic and Arabic Nations, I.* (rev. ed.) Leiden.

Helck, Wolfgang

1975 *Wirtschaftsgeschichte des alten Ägypten im 3. und 2. Jahrtausend* (Handbuch der Orientalistik I. 5) Leiden.

Heltzer, Michael

1978 *Goods, Prices and the Organization of Trade in Ugarit: Marketing and Transportation in the Eastern Mediterranean in the Second Half of the II Millennium, B.C.E.* Wiesbaden.

1982 *The Internal Organization of the Kingdom of Ugarit.* Wiesbaden.

1984 "Private Property in Ugarit," in Archi, ed., *Circulation of Goods* 161–193.

Hildebrand, Bruno

1864 "Natural-, Geld- und Creditwirtschaft" in Hildebrand, *Jahrbücher für Nationalökonomie und Statistik.*

Hinz, Walther

1972 *The Lost World of Elam.* London.

Hocart, A. M.

1927 *Kingship.* London.

Hoebel, Edward Adamson

1968 [1964] *The Law of Primitive Man: A Study in Comparative Legal Dynamics.* New York.

Homer, Sidney

1963 *A History of Interest Rates.* New Brunswick, N. J.

Hooke, S. H.

1928 *New Year's Day: The Story of the Calendar.* New York.

1958 *Myth, Ritual, and Kingship.* Oxford.

Hudson, Michael

1968 "The Sieve of Gold," *Ramparts*, May–June 1968.

1969 "Epitaph for Bretton Woods," *Journal of International Affairs* 23 (Winter 1969).

1972 *Super Imperialism: The Economic Strategy of American Empire.* Holt, Rinehart.

1981 "The Logic of Regionalism in History and Today," "The Objectives of Regionalism in the 1980s," and "A Regional Strategy to Finance the New International Economic Order," in Davidson Nicol, Luis Excheverria and Aurelio Peccei, eds., *Regionalism and the New International Economic Order.* Pergamon Press for UNITAR.

1992 "Did the Phoenicians Introduce the Idea of Interest to Greece and Italy — And If So, When?" in Günter Kopcke and Isabelle Tokumaru, *Greece Between East and West: 10th– 8th Centuries BC.* Mainz 128–143.

1994 "Land Monopolization, Fiscal Crises and Clean Slate 'Jubilee' Proclamations in Antiquity," in Hudson, Miller and Feder, eds., *A Philosophy for a Fair Society.* London 33–79 (also in Robert Hunt *et al*., ed., *Property: The Economic Context.* Society for Economic Anthropology, 1995).

1996 "Privatization in History and Today: A Survey of the Unresolved Controversies," and "The Dynamics of Privatization, from the Bronze Age to the Present," in M. Hudson and B. Levine, eds., *Privatization.*

1999 "The Economic Roots of the Jubilee," *Bible Review* 15 (Feb. 1999): 26–33, 44.

2000 "How Interest Rates Were Set, 2500 BC–1000 AD: *Máš, tokos* and *fænus* as metaphors for interest accruals," *Journal of the Economic and Social History of the Orient* 43: 132–161.

2002 "Reconstructing the Origins of Interest-Bearing Debt and the Logic of Clean Slates," in M. Hudson and M. Van De Mieroop, eds., *Debt and Economic Renewal:* 7–58.

2002 "Debt Forgiveness and Redemption: Where do the Churches now stand," *Geophilos* 2: 8–33.

2003 "The Cartalist/Monetarist Debate in Historical Perspective," in Edward Nell and Stephanie Bell, eds., *The State, The Market and The Euro.* Edward Elgar.

2004 "The Development of Money-of-Account in Sumer's Temples," in M. Hudson and C. Wunsch, eds., *Creating Economic Order:* 303–329.

2004a "The Archaeology of Money in Light of Mesopotamian Records," in L. Randall Wray, ed., *Credit and State Theories of Money: The Contributions of A. Mitchell Innes.* Edward Elgar.

2005/2006
Review of Ph. Chancier, F. Joannès, P. Rouillard and A. Tenu, eds., *Autour de Polanyi: vocabularies, théories et modalities des échanges* (Paris 2005) and J. G. Manning and Ian Morris, eds., *The Ancient Economy: Evidence and Models* (Stanford: 2005) in *Archiv für Orientforschung* 51: 405–11.

2010 "Entrepreneurs: From the Near Eastern Takeoff to the Roman Collapse," in David S. Landes, Joel Mokyr, and William J. Baumol, eds., *The Invention of Enterprise: Entrepreneurship from Ancient Mesopotamia to Modern Times.* Princeton: Princeton University Press: 8–39.

2019 "Origins of Money and Interest: Palatial Credit, not Barter," in S. Bartelossi, Y. Cassis, K. Yago, eds., *Handbook of the History of Money and Currency.* Springer.

Hudson, Michael and Baruch Levine, eds.
1996 *Privatization in the Ancient Near East and Classical Antiquity.* Cambridge, Mass.: Peabody Museum.

1999 *Urbanization and Land Ownership in the Ancient Near East.* Cambridge, Mass. Peabody Museum, Harvard.

Hudson, Michael and Marc Van De Mieroop, eds.
2002 *Debt and Economic Renewal in the Ancient Near East.* Bethesda, Maryland: CDL Press

Hudson, Michael and Cornelia Wunsch, eds.
2004 *Creating Economic Order: Record-Keeping, Standardization and the Development of Accounting in the Ancient Near East.* Bethesda, Maryland: CDL Press.

Hudson, Michael and Fred Harrison
1984 "The Archaeology of Economic Collapse: A 4000 Year Perspective," in Hudson, Miller and Feder, eds., *A Philosophy for a Fair Society.* London: 7–31.

Huffmon, H. B., F. A. Spina and A. R. W. Green, eds.
1983 *The Quest for the Kingdom of God: Studies in Honor of George E. Mendenhall.* Winona Lake, Ind.

Huffmon, Herbert B.
1983 "The Social Role of Amos' Message," in Huffmon, *et al., The Quest for the Kingdom of God:* 109–116.

Humphreys, Sally C.
1978 *Anthropology and the Greeks.* London.

Hussey, Mary Inda
1912 *Sumerian Tablets in the Harvard Semitic Museum. Part I: Chiefly from the Reigns of Lugalanda and Urukagina of Lagash.* Cambridge.

Hyma, Albert
1951 *Renaissance to Reformation.* Grand Rapids.
Irani, K. D., and Morris Silver, eds.
1995 *Social Justice in the Ancient World. A Conference at City College of New York, March 10–12, 1993.* Westport, Conn.
Jacobsen, Thorkild
1943 "Primitive Democracy in Ancient Mesopotamia," *JNES* 2: 159–173.
1953 "The Reign of Ibbi-Suen," *JCS* 7: 40–43.
1967 "Some Sumerian City-Names," *JCS* 21: 100–110.
1987 *The Harps that Once…. Sumerian Poetry in Translation.* New Haven.
Jacobsen, Thorkild and Adams, Robert M.
1958 "Salt and Silt in Ancient Mesopotamian Agriculture," *Science* 128: 1252–1258.
Jankowska, Ninel B.
1969 "Extended Family Commune and Civil Self-Government in Arrapha in the Fifteenth–Fourteenth Century BC," in Diakonoff, ed., *Ancient Mesopotamia*: 235–252.
1978 "Provisioning of the Cult in Arrapha," in B. Hruska and G. Komoroczy, eds., *Festschrift Lubor Matouš.* Budapest: vol. I, 171–178.
1991 "Assur, Mitanni, and Arrapkhe," in Diakonoff, ed., *Early Antiquity*: 228–260.
Jastrow, Morris
1909 "Sun and Saturn," *RA* 7: 163–78.
Jones, A. H. M.
1964 *The Later Roman Empire 284–602.* Baltimore.
Jursa, Michael
2002 "Debts and Indebtedness in the Neo-Babylonian Period: Evidence from Institutional Archives," in Hudson and Van De Mieroop, eds., *Debt and Economic Renewal*): 197–220.
Kaufmann, Yehezkel
1966 *The Religion of Israel.* Chicago.
Khalidi, Tarif, ed.
1984 *Land Tenure and Social Transformation in the Middle East.* Beirut.
King, L. W.
1900 *The Letters and Inscriptions of Hammurapi* (3 vols.) London.
Klein, Ernest
1971 *A Comprehensive Etymological Dictionary of the English Language.* Amsterdam: Elsevier.
Klengel, Horst
1973 "Die Geschäfte des Babyloniers Balmunamche," *Das Altertum* 19: 199–207.
1989 *Handel und Händler im alten Orient.* Vienna.
1991 *König Hammurapi und der Alltag Babylons* (2nd ed.) Zurich.
Klima, Josef
1947 "La base religieuse et éthique de l'ordre social dans l'orient ancien," *ArOr* 16: 334–55.
Knapp, Georg Friedrich
1924 "*The Cartalist/Monetarist Debate in Historical Perspective*," in Edward Nell and Stephanie Bell, eds., *The State, The Market and The Euro.* Edward Elgar.
Kobelski, Paul J.
1981 *Melchizedek and Melchireša* (Catholic Biblical Quarterly, Monograph Series 10) Washington: Catholic Biblical Association of America.
Kohl, Philip L.
1978 "The Balance of Trade in Southwestern Asia in the Mid-Third Millennium BC," *CA* 19: 463–492.

1977 "The 'World Economy' of West Asia in the Third Millennium BC," in M. Taddei, ed., *South Asian Archaeology*. Naples 55–85.

1989 "The use and abuse of world systems theory: the case of the 'pristine' West Asian state," in Lamberg-Karlovsky, ed., *Archaeological Thought in America*: 218–240.

Komoroczy, G.

1982 "Zur Frage der Periodizität der altbabylonischen *misharum*-Erlasse," in M. A. Dandamaev *et al.*, eds., *Society and Languages*. Warminster 196–205.

Korošec, Viktor

1971 "The Growth of Legislation in Ancient Mesopotamia and Asia Minor," in *Studi in Onore di Giuseppe Grosso*. Turin, vol. IV: 267–284.

Koschaker, Paul

1917 *Rechtsvergleichende Studien zur Gesetzgebung Hammurapis, Königs von Babylon*. Leipzig.

1942 "Zur staatlichen Wirtschaftsverwaltung in altbabylonischer Zeit, inbesondere nach Urkunden in Larsa," *ZA* 47: 179–80.

Kraeling, Carl H. and Robert M. Adams, eds.

1960 *City Invincible: A Symposium on Urbanization and Cultural Development in the Ancient Near East, Held at the Oriental Institute Dec. 4–7, 1958*. Chicago: Chicago University Press.

Kramer, Samuel Noah

1954 "The Ur-Nammu Law Code," *Or* 23: 40–51.

1959 [1956] *History Begins at Sumer*. New York.

1963 *The Sumerians: Their History, Culture, and Character*. Chicago.

1971 "Aspects of Mesopotamian Society, Evidence from the Sumerian Literary Sources," in H. Klengel, ed., *Schriften zur Geschichte und Kultur des Alten Orients*. Berlin, vol. I: 1–13.

1981 "Gov. Urukagina's Message for Mr. Reagan," *The New York Times*, January 30, 1981. http://www.nytimes.com/1981/01/30/opinion/l-gov-urukagina-s-message-for-mr-reagan–245065.html

1983 "The Ur-Nammu Law Code: Who Was its Author?" *Or* 52: 453–456.

Kraus, Fritz R.

1958 *Ein Edikt des Königs Ammi-saduqa von Babylon* (Studia et documenta 5) Leiden.

1958 "Ein zentrales Problem des altmesopotamischen Rechtes: Was ist der Codex Hammurabi?" *Genava*, n.s. 8: 283–296.

1954 "Le role des temples depuis la troisième dynastie d'Ur jusqu' à la première dynastie de Babylone," *Journal of World History* 1: 578–545.

1965 "Ein Edikt des Königs Samsu-iluma von Babylon," in H. G. Güterbock and T. Jacobsen, ed., *Studies in Honor of Benno Landsberger on His Seventy-fifth Birthday, April 21, 1963* (Assyriological Studies 16): 225–231.

1966 *Staatliche Viehhaltung im altbabylonischen Lande Larsa*. Amsterdam.

1969 "Another Look at Hammurabi's Ancestors," *JCS* 22: 1–2.

1970 *Sumerer und Akkader* (Amsterdam).

1984 *Königliche Verfügungen in altbabylonischer Zeit* (Studia et documenta 11) Leiden.

Kugel, James

1997 *The Bible As It Was*. Cambridge, Mass.

Kwasman, Theodore and Simo Parpola

1991 *Legal Transactions of the Royal Court of Nineveh, Part I*. Helsinki.

Labat, René

1939 *Le caractère religieux de la royauté assyro-babylonienne*. Paris.

Lacheman, Ernest. R.

1962 "The Word *sŭdūtu* in the Nuzi Tablets," in *25th International Congress of Orientalists 1960.* Moscow, vol. I: 233–238.

1973 "Real Estate Adoption by Women in the Tablets from Uru NUZI," in Harry A. Hoffner, Jr., ed., *Essays presented to Cyrus H. Gordon on the Occasion of his Sixty-fifth Birthday.* Neukirchen.

Lamberg-Karlovsky, Carl C.

1986 "The *longue durée* of the Ancient Near East," in L. Huot, ed., *De l'Indus aux Balkans, Receuil á la mémoire de Jean Deshayes.* Paris.

1989 "Mesopotamia, Central Asia and the Indus Valley: So the Kings Were Killed," in C. C. Lamberg Karlovsky, ed., *Archaeological Thought in America.* Cambridge 241–267.

1996 "The Archaeological Evidence for International Commerce, Public and/or Private," in Michael Hudson and Baruch Levine, eds. *Privatization in the Ancient Near East and Classical Antiquity* (Cambridge, Mass.: Peabody Museum).

1999 "Households, Land Tenure, and Communications Systems in the 6th–4th Millennia of Greater Mesopotamia," in Hudson and Levine 1999: 167—202.

Lamberg-Karlovsky, Carl C., ed.

1989 *Archaeological Thought in America.* Cambridge.

Lambert, Maurice

1952 "La période présargonique," *Sumer* 8: 52–77 and 198–216.

1953 "Textes commerciaux de Lagash," *RA* 47: 37–69 and 105–20.

1955 "Le code d'Ur-Nammu," *RA* 49: 169–177.

1956 "Les 'reforms' d'Urukagina," *RA* 50: 169–184.

1960 "La naissance de la bureaucratie," *RHist* 224: 1–26.

1961a "Le premier triomphe de la bureaucratie," *RHist* 225: 21–46.

1961b "Recherches sur la vie ouvriers," *ArOr* 29: 427–438

1963 "L'usage de l'argent-metal à Lagash au temps de la IIIᵉ Dynastie d'Ur," *RA* 57: 79–92 and 193–200.

1966 "La guerre entre Urukagina et Lugalzaggesi," *RSO* 41: 29–66

1971 "Une Inscription nouvelle d'Entemena prince de Lagash," *Revue du Louvre*, 21: 231–236.

1972 "L'expansion de Lagash au temps d'Entemena," *RSO* 47: 1–22.

Lambert, Wilfred G.

1960 *Babylonian Wisdom Literature.* 2nd ed. Oxford 1967.

1965 "Nebuchadnezzar King of Justice," *Iraq* 27: 1–11.

1970 "The Reading of the Name uru.KA.gi.na," *Or* 39: 419.

1979 "Interchange of Ideas between Southern Mesopotamia and Syria-Palestine as Seen in Literature," in H. J. Nissen and J. Renger, *Mesopotamien und seine Nachbarn* (RAI 25) Berlin 311–316.

1990 "Old Testament Mythology in its Ancient Near Eastern Context," in J. A. Emerton, ed., *Congress Volume Jerusalem 1986* (Vetus Testamentum Suppl.): 124–143.

Landsberger, Benno

1939 "Die babylonischen Termini für Gesetz und Recht," in *Symbolae Koschaker* (Studia et documenta 2) Leiden 219–234.

1974 "Three Essays on the Sumerians," http://www.undena.com/EL-UP/Landsberger_1974_Three_Essays_on_the_Sumerians_-_MANE_1.2.pdf

Larsen, Mogens Trolle

1976 *The Old Assyrian City-State and Its Colonies.* Copenhagen.

2015 *Ancient Kanesh. A Merchant Colony in Bronze Age Anatolia.* Cambridge University Press.

Laum, Bernard
   1924   *Heiliges Geld.* Tübingen.
Leemans, W. F.
   1950   *The Old Babylonian Merchant: His Business and Social Position.* Leiden.
   1960   *Foreign Trade in the Old Babylonian Period.* Leiden.
   1975   "The Role of Landlease in Mesopotamia in the Early Second Millennium BC," *JESHO* 18: 134–145.
   1968   "King Hammurapi as Judge," in J. A. Ankum, *Symbolae Martino David dedicatae,* Leiden: Brill, vol. 2: 107–129.
Lemche, Niels Peter
   1979   "*andurārum* and *mīsharum*: Comments on the Problems of Social Edicts and their Application in the Ancient Near East," *JNES* 38: 11–18.
   1985   *Ancient Israel.* Leiden.
Lemerle, Paul
   1997   *The Agrarian History of Byzantium.* Galway, Ireland.
Levine, Baruch A.
   1989   *Leviticus: The Traditional Hebrew Text, with the New Jewish Publication Society Translation.* Philadelphia.
   1993   "The Social Parameter of Biblical Law: Kingship and Justice," in K. D. Irani and M. Silver, eds., *Social Justice.*
   1996   "The Hebrew Bible as a Repository of References to Economic Developments in the Ancient Near East," in M. Hudson and B. Levine, eds., *Privatization in the Ancient Near East.*
Lewy, Hildegard
   1947   "Marginal Notes on a Recent Volume of Babylonian Mathematical Texts," *JAOS* 67: 305–320.
   1952   "Nitokris-NAQIA," *JNES* 11: 264–286.
Lewy, Julius
   1956   "On Some Institutions of the Old Assyrian Empire," *HUCA* 27: 1–80.
   1958   "The Biblical Institution of *deror* in the Light of Akkadian Documents," *Eretz-Israel* 5: 21*–31*.
   1958b "Some Aspects of Commercial Life in Assyria and Asia Minor in the Nineteenth Pre-Christian Century," *JAOS* 78: 89–101.
   1961   "Amurritica," *HUCA* 32: 31–74.
Lieberman, Stephen J.
   1989   "Royal 'Reforms' of the Amurrite Dynasty, *BiOr* 46: 241–59.
Lipinski, Eduard, ed.
   1979   *State and Temple Economy in the Ancient Near East.* 2 vols. Leuven.
Liverani, Mario
   1969   "Sydyq e Misor," in *Studi E. Volterra.* Milano, vol. VI, 59–62.
   1979   *Three Amarna Essays* (Monographs on the Ancient Near East 1/5) Malibu.
   1987   "The Collapse of the Near Eastern Regional System at the End of the Bronze Age," in T. C. Champion, ed., *Center and Periphery* 66–73.
   1993   *Akkad: The First World Empire.* Padova.
   2005   "The Near East: The Bronze Age," in J. G. Manning and Ian Morris, *The Ancient Economy: Evidence and Models.* Stanford University Press: 47–57.
Loewenstamm, Samuel
   1969   "M/Tarbit and Neshek," *Journal of Biblical Literature,* 88: 78–80.

Lundquist, John M.

   1983 "What is a Temple? A Preliminary Typology," in H. B. Huffmon, F. A. Spina and A. R.
        W. Green, eds., *The Quest for the Kingdom of God: Studies in Honor of George E. Menden-
        hall.* Winona Lake, Ind. 205–219.

MacCormack, Carol P.

   1981 "Exchange and Hierarchy," in Alison Sheridan and Geoff Bailey, eds., *Economic Anthro-
        pology: Towards an Integration of Ecological and Social Approaches* (BAR International
        Series 96) Oxford 159–166.

Maekawa, Kazuya

   1973–74 "The Development of the É-MI in Lagash during the Early Dynastic III."
           Mesopotamia 8–9: 77–144.

Magdalino, Paul

   1994 "Justice and Finance in the Byzantine State, Ninth to Twelfth Centuries," in Angeliki
        E. Laiou and Dieter Simon, eds., *Law and Society in Byzantium Ninth-Twelfth Centuries*
        Washington D.C.: Dumbarton Oaks 93–116.

Magen, Yitzhak and Yuval Peleg

   2006 *The Site of the Dead Sea Scrolls: Archaeological Interpretations and Debates.* Leiden: Brill.

Maidman, Maynard

   1996 "'Privatization' and Private Property at Nuzi: The Limits of Evidence," in M. Hudson
        and B. Levine, *Privatization.*

Maine, Henry

   1888 *Lectures on the Early History of Institutions* (*A Sequel to 'Ancient Law'*, 3rd ed.) New York.

Makkay, J.

   1983 "The origins of the 'temple-economy' as seen in the light of prehistoric evidence," *Iraq*
        45: 1–6.

Malinowski, Bronislaw

   1922 *Argonauts of the Western Pacific.* New York.

Manning, J. G. and Ian Morris

   2005 *The Ancient Economy: Evidence and Models.* Stanford University Press.

Marx, Karl

   1889 *Capital: A Critical Analysis of Capitalist Production.* London.

Matouš, Libor

   1956 "Purchase of Landed Property in Ur by Balmunamhe," *Charisteria Orientalia J. Rypka.*
        Prague 179–186.

Mauss, Marcel

   1952 [1925] *The Gift.* New York.

McKenzie, John L.

   1983 "The Sack of Israel," in Huffmon *et al.*, eds., *The Quest for the Kingdom of God* 25–34.

McGeer, Eric

   2000 *The Land Legislation of the Macedonian Emperors.* Toronto.

Meek, Theophile J.

   1958 "The Code of Hammurapi," in ANET. Princeton: 138–167.

Mellaart, James

   1987 "Common Sense vs. Old-Fashioned Theory in the Interpretation of the Cultural Devel-
        opment of the Ancient Near East," in Linda Manzanilla, ed., *Studies in the Neolithic
        and Urban Revolutions. The V. Gordon Childe Colloquium, Mexico, 1986* (BAR Interna-
        tional Series 349) Oxford.

Mendelsohn, Isaac

   1949 *Slavery in the Ancient Near East.* New York.

Mendenhall, George E.
1973   *The Tenth Generation: The Origins of the Biblical Tradition.* Baltimore.

Michel, Cécile
2013   "Economic and Social Aspects of the Old Assyrian Loan Contract," in F. d'Agostino, éd. *L'economia dell'antica Mesopotamia (III-I millennio a.C.).* Rome 41–55.

Milik, J. T.
1972   "Milki-sedeq dans les anciens écrits juifs et chrétiens," *JJS* 23: 95–144.

Miller, Daniel
1985   "Ideology and the Harappan Civilization," *JAA* 4: 34–71.

Mitchell, Robert
1993   "Demands for Land Redistribution and Debt Reduction in the Roman Republic," in K. D. Irani and M. Silver, eds., *Social Justice in the Ancient World:* 199–214.

Moscati, Sabatino
1960   *The Face of the Ancient Orient.* Chicago.

Muhly, James David
1973   *Copper and Tin: The Distribution of Mineral Resources and the Nature of the Metals Trade in the Bronze Age.* Hamden, Conn.

Müller, M.
1982   "Gold, Silber und Blei als Wertmesser in Mesopotamien während der zweiten Hälfte des 2. Jahrtausends v.u.Z," in J. N. Postgate *et al.*, eds., *Societies and Languages*: 270–278.

Murakawa, Kentaro
1957   "Demiurgos," *Historia* 6: 385–415.

Murra, John V.
1962   "Cloth and its Functions in the Inca State," *American Anthropologist* 64: 710–728.
1980   *The Economic Organization of the Inka State.* Westport [1956].

Murphy, Arthur, ed.
1822   *The Works of Cornelius Tacitus: With an Essay on his Life and Genius, Notes, Supplements, &c.* (New York, Printed for P. A. Mesier [etc.]).

Nagy, Gregory
1993   "Metaphorical Definitions of Justice in Early Greek Poetry: A Comparative Perspective," in K. D. Irani and M. Silver, eds., *Social Justice in the Ancient World.*

Nelson, Benjamin
1949   *The Idea of Usury: From Tribal Brotherhood to Universal Otherhood* (2nd ed. 1960) Princeton.

Nemet-Nejat, Karen Rhea
1993   *Cuneiform Mathematical texts as a Reflection of Everyday Life in Mesopotamia* (AOS Series 75) New Haven.

Neufeld, Edward
1955   "The Prohibition Against Loans at Interest in Ancient Hebrew Laws," *HUCA* 26: 355–412.
1953   "The Rate of Interest and the Text of Nehemiah 5: 11," *Jewish Quarterly Review* 44: 194–197.
1958   "Socio-Economic Background of *Yobel* and *Semitta*," *RSO* 33: 53–124.

Neuman, Abraham A.
1942   *The Jews in Spain: Their Social, Political, and Cultural Life during the Middle Ages.* Philadelphia, 2 vols.

Neusner, Jacob
1971   *The Rabbinic Traditions about the Pharisees before 70.* Leiden: Brill.

Neusner, Jacob, ed.
1975 *Christianity, Judaism and Other Greco-Roman Cults: Studies for Morton Smith at Sixty.* Leiden, 4 vols.

Nissen, Hans J.
1988 *The Early History of the Ancient Near East, 9000–2000 BC.* Chicago.

Nissen, Hans, Peter Damorow and Robert Englund
1993 *Archaic Bookkeeping: Writing and Techniques of Economic Administration in the Ancient Near East.* Chicago.

North, Robert
1950 "Biblical Echoes in the Holy Year," *American Ecclesiastical Review* 123: 416–436.
1954 *Sociology of the Biblical Jubilee.* Rome.

Noth, Martin
1960 *History of Israel: Biblical History.* New York.

Oates, Joan
1972 "Prehistoric Settlement Patterns in Mesopotamia," in Ucko *et al.*, eds., *Man, Settlement and Urbanism. Proceedings of a Meeting of the Research Seminar in Archaeology and Related Subjects Held at the Institute of Archaeology, London University* London 300–309.
1978 "Mesopotamian Social Organization: Archaeological and Philological Evidence," in J. Friedman and M. J. Rowlands, *The Evolution of Social Systems.* London and Pittsburgh 457–485.
1979 *Babylon.*

Oikonomides, N.
1988 "Tax Exemptions for the Secular Clergy under Basil II," in J. Chrysostomides, ed., *Kathegetria Essays Presented to Joan Hussey for her 80th Birthday.* Camberley: Porphyrogenitus 321–325.

Olivier, Hannes
1988 "The Periodicity of the *misharum* Again," in W. Claasen, ed., *Text and Context: Old Testament and Semitic Studies for F. C. Fenshan* (JSOT Suppl. 48) Sheffield 227–235.

Oppenheim, A. Leo
1949 "The Golden Garments of the Gods," *JNES* 8: 172–193.
1954 "The Seafaring Merchants of Ur," *JAOS* 74: 6–17.
1957 "A Bird's-Eye View of Mesopotamian Economic History," in K. Polanyi, C. M. Arensberg and H. W. Pearson, eds., *Trade and Market in the Early Empires.* Glencoe 27–37.
1967a *Letters from Mesopotamia.* Chicago.
1967b "A New Look at the Structure of Mesopotamian Society," *JESHO* 10: 1–16.
1972 *Ancient Mesopotamia.* Chicago (1st ed. 1964).

Orlin, Louis L.
1970 *Assyrian Colonies in Cappadocia.* The Hague.

Ostrogorsky, George
1969 *History of the Byzantine State* (rev. ed.) New Brunswick, NJ.

Otto, Eckart
1998 "Soziale Restitution und Vertragsrecht: *mišaru(m) (an)-durāru(m) kirenzi, parā tarnumar, šemitta* und *deror* in Mesopotamien, Syrien, in der hebräischen Bibel und die Frage des Rechtstransfers im Alten Orient. *RA* 92: 125–160.

Papadatou, Dafni
2008 "Antichresis in Byzantine Law," *Revue des Études Byzantines* 66: 209–220

Parrot, André
1948 *Tello.* Paris.

Pettinato, Giovanni
1981 *The Archives of Ebla: An Empire Inscribed in Clay.* Garden City, N.Y.

Polanyi, Karl, Conrad M. Arensberg and Harry W. Pearson, eds.
  1957   *Trade and Market in the Early Empires: Economies in History and Theory.* New York.
Postgate, J. N.
  1969   *Neo-Assyrian Royal Grants and Decrees.* (Studia Pohl s. maior 1) Rome.
  1972 "The role of the temple in the Mesopotamian secular community," in Peter J. Ucko,
         Ruth Tringham and G. W. Dimbleby, eds., *Man, Settlement and Urbanism.* London
         811–825.
  1973   *The Governor's Palace Archive* (Cuneiform Texts from Nimrud II) British School of Ar-
         chaeology in Iraq.
  1974 "Royal Exercise of Justice under the Assyrian Empire," in Paul Garelli, ed., *Le Palais et
         la Royauté.* Paris: 417–426.
  1976   *Fifty Neo-Assyrian Legal Documents.* Warminster.
  1992   *Early Mesopotamian Society and Economy at the Dawn of History.* London and New York.
  1995 "Royal Ideology and State Administration in Sumer and Akkad," in Jack Sasson, ed.,
         Civilizations of the Ancient Near East. New York 395–412.
Powell, Marvin A.
  1977 "Sumerian Merchants and the Problem of Profit," *Iraq* 39: 23–29.
  1985 "Salt, Seed, and Yields in Sumerian Agriculture. A Critique of the Theory of Progressive
         Salinization," *ZA* 75: 7–38.
  1986 "The Economy of the Extended Family According to Sumerian Sources" (Oikumene 5)
         Leuven 9–14.
  1990 "Identification and Interpretation of Long-Term Price Fluctuations in Babylonia: More
         on the History of Money in Mesopotamia," *AoF* 17: 95–118.
  1999 "Wir müssen alle unsere Nische nuzten: Monies, Motives, and Methods in Babylonian
         Economics," in J. G. Dercksen, ed., *Trade and Finance in Ancient Mesopotamia.*
         (PIHANS 84) Istanbul 5–23.
Procopius (tr. Richard Atwater)
  Secret History, New York (1992).
Psellus, Michael (tr. E. R. A. Sawter)
  1966 *Chronographia*, as *Fourteen Byzantine Rulers: The Chronographia of Michael Psellus.*
         London.
Pritchard, James B.
  1969   Ancient Near Eastern Texts Relating to the Old Textament (3rd ed. with suppl.)
         Princeton, New Jersey: Princeton University Press.
Purves, Pierre M.
  1945 "Commentary on Nuzi Real Property in Light of Recent Studies," *JNES* 4: 68–76.
Quiggen, Alison (Hingston)
  1949   *A Survey of Primitive Money.* London.
Quirke, Stephen and Carol Andrews
  1988   *The Rosetta Stone: Facsimile Drawing with an Introduction and Translation.* New York
         and London.
Raglan, Lord
  1936   *The Hero: A Study in Tradition, Myth, and Drama.* London.
Renger, Johannes
  1972 "Flucht als soziales Problem in der altbabylonischen Gesellschaft," in D. O. Edzard, ed.,
         Gesellschaftsklassen im Alten Zweistromland und in den angrenzenden Gebieten (ABAW
         75) Munich: Bayerische Akademie der Wissenschaften 167–182.
  1979 "Interaction of Temple, Palace, and 'Private Enterprise' in the Old Babylonian Econ-
         omy," in Lipiński, ed., *State and Temple Economy* vol. I, 249–256.

1984 "Patterns of Non-Institutional Trade and Non-Commercial Exchange in Ancient Mesopotamia at the Beginning of the Second Millennium BC," in Archi, ed., *Circulation of Goods* 31–115.

1994 "On Economic Structures in Ancient Mesopotamia," *Orientalia* 18: 157–208.

2002 "Royal Edicts of the Old Babylonian Period – Structural Background," in M. Hudson and M. Van De Mieroop, eds., *Debt and Economic Renewal* 139–162.

Revillout, E.

1907 "Boccoris et son code," *Revue egyptologique* 12: 124–141.

Ringe, Sharon H.

1985 *Jesus, Liberation and the Biblical Jubilee*. Philadelphia.

Roberts, J.J.M.

2002 "Melchizedek (11Q13 = 11QMelch)," in J. H. Charlesworth, ed., *Pesharim, Other Commentaries, and Related Documents*. Tübingen: Mohr Siebeck 264–273.

Root, Margaret Cool

1979 *The King and Kingship in Achaemenid Art: Essays on the Creation of an Iconography of Empire* (Acta Iranica, 3rd series, vol. 9) Leiden.

Roscher, Wilhelm

1878 *Principles of Political Economy*. New York.

Rosengarten, Yvonne

1959 "La notion sumérienne de souveraineté divine: Urukagina et son dieu Ningirsu," *Revue de l'Histoire des Religions* 156: 129–160.

1960a *Le Concept sumérien de consommation dans la vie économique et religieuse*. Paris.

1960b *Le Régime des offrandes dans la société sumérienne, d'après les textes présargoniques de Lagash*. Paris.

Ostrogorsky, Georgije

1956 *Quelques problèmes d'histoire de la paysannerie byzantine*. Brussels.

Roth, Martha

1997 *Law Collections from Mesopotamia and Asia Minor* (2nd ed.) Atlanta: Scholars Press.

Rowlands, Michael, Mogens T. Larsen and Kristian Kristiansen, eds.

1987 *Center and Periphery in the Ancient World*. Cambridge.

Runciman, Steven

1951 *History of the Crusades*. 3 vols. Cambridge.

1956 [1933] *Byzantine Civilization*. New York

Sahlins, Marshall

1972 *Stone Age Economics*. Chicago.

Sallaberger, Walther

2007 "From Urban Culture to Nomadism: A History of Upper Mesopotamia in the Late Third Millennium," in Catherine Kuzucuoğlu and Catherine Marro, eds., *Sociétés humaines et changement climatique à la fin du troisième millénaire: Une crise a-t-elle eu lieu en Haute Mésopotamie? Actes du colloque de Lyon, 5-8 décembre 2005*. Paris: de Boccard 417–456.

2007 "The Palace and the Temple in Babylonia," in Gwendolyn Leick, ed., *The Babylonian World*. New York and London: Routledge 265–275.

2013 "The Management of Royal Treasure: Palace Archives and Palatial Economy in the Ancient Near East," in Jane A. Hill, Philip Jones, and Antonio J. Morales, *Experiencing Power, Generating Authority: Cosmos, Politics and the Ideology of Kingship in Ancient Egypt and Mesopotamia*. University of Pennsylvania Museum of Archaeology and Anthropology, Philadelphia 213–255.

306

Sallaberger, Walther *et al.*, eds.

2013 *Tempel im Alten Orient. 7. Internationales Colloquium der Deutschen Orient-Gesellschaft, 11.-13. Oktober 2009, München.* Wiesbaden.

Salomon, Kurt

1931 *Lösung des sozialen Problems: Die Bibel.* Breslau.

Sanders, James A.

1973 "The Old Testament in 11Q Melchizedeq," *JANESCU* 5: 373–382.

1975 "From Isaiah 61 to Luke 4," in Neusner 1975: I 75–106.

Ste. Croix, G. E. M

1981 *The Class Struggle in the Ancient World.* Ithaca.

Sarris, Peter

2012 "Large Estates and the Peasantry in Byzantium c. 600–1100," *Revue Belge de Philologie et d'Histoire* 90: 434.

Sasson, Jack, ed.

1995 *Civilizations of the Ancient Near East.* New York: Scribner.

Sauren, H.

1975 "Die Einweihung des Eninnu," in *Le temple et le culte* (CRRAI 20) Leiden 95–103.

Sawter, E. R. A.

1966 *Fourteen Byzantine Rulers: The Chronographia of Michael Psellus.* London.

Schaeffer, Henry

1915 *The Social Legislation of the Primitive Semites.* New Haven.

Schauss, Hayyim

1938 *The Jewish Festivals: From Their Beginnings to Our Own Day.* New York.

Schmökel, Hartmut

1957 *Geschichte des alten Vorderasien.* Leiden.

Schneider, Anna

1921 *Die Anfänge der Kulturwirtschaft: Die Sumerische Tempelstadt.* Essen.

Schorr, Moses

1915 *Eine babylonische Seisachthie aus dem Anfang der Kassitenzeit* (Sitzungsberichte der Heidelberger Akademie der Wissenschaften, Phil.-hist. Kl.) Heidelberg.

Scheidel, Walter

2017 *The Great Leveler: Violence and the History of Inequality from the Stone Age to the Twenty-First Century.* Princeton.

Schrakamp, Ingo

2013 "Die 'Sumerische Tempelstadt' heute. Die sozialökonomische Rolle eines Tempels in frühdynastischer Zeit," in W. Sallaberger *et al.*, eds., *Tempel im Alten Orient* 445–465.

2015 "Urukagina und die Geschichte von Lagash am Ende der Präsargonischen Zeit," in Reinhard Dittmann and Gebhard J. Selz, eds., *It's a Long Way to a Historiography of the Early Dynastic Period(s)*. Münster, Ugarit-Verlag 303–386.

Scott, James

2017 *Against the Grain. A Deep History of the Earliest States.* Yale.

Scott, Samuel P.

1932 *The Civil Law, XII.* Cincinnati.

Scott, William Robert

1912 *The Constitution and Finance of English, Scottish and Irish Joint-Stock Companies to 1720,* 3 vols. Cambridge.

Senchus Mor (Thom *et al.*, eds.)

Ancient Laws of Ireland. 2 vols. Published under direction of the commissioners for publishing the Ancient Laws and Institutes of Ireland. Dublin 1869.

Silver, Morris
  1983   *Prophets and Markets: The Political Economy of Ancient Israel.* Boston–The Hague.
  1993   "Prophets and Markets Revisited," in K. D. Irani and M. Silver, eds., *Social Justice in the Ancient World.*
Skaist, Aaron
  1994   *The Old Babylonian Loan Contract: Its History and Geography.* Ramat Gan: Bar Ilan University Press).
Smith, Adam
  1776   *Wealth of Nations.*
Smith, Carol A.
  1976   *Regional Analysis.* 2 vols. New York.
Smith, H. S.
  1968   "A Note on Amnesty," *Journal of Egyptian Archaeology* 54: 209–212.
Smith, Morton
  1971   *Palestinian Parties and Politics that Shaped the Old Testament.* New York.
Snell, Daniel
  1982   *Ledgers and Prices: Early Mesopotamian Merchant Accounts.* New Haven.
Sollberger, Edmond and J. R. Kupper.
  1971   *Inscriptions royales sumériennes et akkadiennes.* Paris.
Speiser, Ephraim A.
  1953   "Early Law and Civilization," *Canadian Bar Review* 31: 863–877.
  1963   "Cuneiform Law and the History of Civilization," in *Proceedings of the American Philosophical Society* 107: 536–541.
  1967   *Oriental and Biblical Studies.* Philadelphia.
Springer, Otto
  1970   "Inscriptional Evidence of Early North Germanic Legal Terminology," in Cardona, Hoenigswald and Senn, *Indo-European and Indo-Europeans.* Philadelphia 41–47.
Steele, F. R.
  1943   *Nuzi Real Estate Transactions.* New Haven.
Steible, H. and H. Behrens
  1986   *Die altsumerischen Bau- und Weihinschriften.*
Steinkeller, Piotr
  1981   "The Renting of Fields in Early Mesopotamia and the Development of the Concept of 'Interest' in Sumerian," *JESHO* 24: 113–144.
  1999   "Land-Tenure Conditions in Third-Millennium Babylonia: The Problem of Regional Variation (with Glenn R. Magid)." In M. Hudson and B. A. Levine eds., *Urbanization and Land Ownership in the Ancient Near East.* Cambridge, Mass.: Peabody Museum of Archaeology and Ethnology, Harvard Museum 289–329.
  2002   "Money Lending Practices in Ur III Babylonia: The Issue of Economic Motivation" in M. Hudson and M. Van De Mieroop, eds., *Debt and Economic Renewal in the Ancient Near East.* Bethesda, Md.: CDL Press 109–137.
Steinkeller, Piotr and Michael Hudson, eds.
  2015   *Labor in the Ancient World.* Dresden: ISLET.
Stephens, Ferris J.
  1955   "Notes on Some Economic Texts of the Time of Urukagina," *RA* 49: 132–134.
Stone, Elizabeth
  1987   *Nippur Neighborhoods.* Chicago.

Stone, Elizabeth, and Owen, David I.
    1991   *Adoption in Old Babylonian Nippur and the Archive of Mannum-meshu-lissur.* Winona Lake, Ind.

Strathern, Andrew
    1971   *The Rope of Moka.* Cambridge.

Struve, V. V.
    1969 "The Problem of the Genesis, Development and Disintegration of the Slave Societies in the Ancient Orient," in I. Diakonoff, ed., *Ancient Mesopotamia, Socio-Economic History: A Collection of Studies by Soviet Scholars.* Moskow 17–69.

Sundstrom, Lars
    1974 [1965] *The Exchange Economy of Pre-Colonial Africa.* New York.

Szlechter, Emile
    1958 "De quelques considérations sur l'origine de la propriété foncière privée dans l'ancien aroit mesopotamien," *RIDA*, 3ʳᵈ ser. 5: 121–136.

Testart, Alain
    1998 "Uncertainties of 'the Obligation to Reciprocate': A Critique of Mauss," in W. James and N. Allen, eds., *Marcel Mauss: A Centenary Tribute* (Methodology and History in Anthropology 1) New York 97–110.
    2002 "The Extent and Significance of Debt Slavery," *Revue française de sociologie* 43: 173–204.

Thureau-Dangin, François
    1905 *Les Inscriptions de Sumer et d'Akkad.* Paris.
    1921 *Rituels accadiens.* Paris.
    1936 "Textes mathématiques babyloniens," *RA* 33: 65–84.

Tigay, J.
    1996 *Deuteronomy.* Philadelphia: Jewish Publication Society.

Treadgold, Warren T.
    1997 *A History of the Byzantine State and Society.* Stanford.

Norman, Tobias
    2007 *Basil I, Founder of the Macedonian Dynasty.* Lewiston, New York.

Tosi, Maurizio
    1969 "Excavations at Shar-i Sokhta," *East and West* 19: 283–386.

Toynbee, Arnold J.
    1965 *Hannibal's Legacy.* 2 vols. London: Oxford University Press.
    1973 *Constantine Porphyrogenitus and His World.* London.

Trigger, Bruce G.
    1968 *Beyond History: The Methods of Prehistory.* New York.

Tyumanev, A. I.
    1959 "The State Economy in Ancient Sumer," in I. Diakonoff, ed., *Ancient Mesopotamia, Socio-Economic History: A Collection of Studies by Soviet Scholars.* Moskow 70–87.

Ure, Percy N.
    1922 *The Origin of Tyranny.* Cambridge.

van Buren, Elizabeth Douglas
    1949 "The Rod and the Ring," *ArOr* 17: 434–450.

Van De Mieroop, Marc
    1987 "The Archive of Balmunamḫe," *AfO* 34: 1–29.
    1995 "Old Babylonian Interest Rates: Were they Annual?" in K. Van Lerberghe and A. Schoors, eds., *Immigration and Emigration within the Near East. Festschrift E. Lipiński* (Orientalia Lovaniensia Analecta 65) Louvain: Departement Oriëntalistick 357–364.

2002 "Credit as a Facilitator of Exchange in Old Babylonian Mesopotamia," in M. Hudson and M. Van De Mieroop, eds., *Debt and Economic Renewal* 163–174.

2002b "A History of Near Eastern Debt?" in M. Hudson and M. Van De Mieroop, eds., *Debt and Economic Renewal* 59–94.

2004 *King Hammurabi of Babylon: A Biography* (Blackwell Ancient Lives). Wiley-Blackwell.

2005 "The Invention of Interest," in William N. Goetzmann and K. Geert Rouwenhorst, eds., *The Origins of Value: The Financial Innovations That Created Modern Capital Markets.* Oxford University Press 17–30.

2017 *Philosophy Before the Greeks The Pursuit of Truth in Ancient Babylonia.* Princeton: Princeton University Press.

van Driel, G.,

1985–86 "The Rise of the House Egibi: Nabû-aḫḫē-iddina," *Jaarbericht van het Voorazic̄tisch-Egyptisch Genootschap 'Ex Oriente Lux'* 29: 50–67.

1999 "Capital Formation and Investment in an Institutional Context in Ancient Mesopotamia," in J. G. Dercksen, ed., *Trade and Finance in Ancient Mesopotamia. Proceedings of the First MOS Symposium [Leiden 1997]* (MOS Studies 1) Istanbul: 25–42.

2002 *Elusive Silver: In Search of a Role for a Market in an Agrarian Environment.* Leiden: Nederlands Instituut voor het Nabije Oosten.

van Siclen, Charles Cornell III

1973 "The Accession Date of Amenhotep III and the Jubilee," *JNES* 32: 290–297.

Veblen, Thorstein

1908 "Professor Clark's Economics," *Quarterly Journal of Economics* 23 (reprinted in *The Place of Science in Modern Civilisation, and other Essays.* New York, 1919).

Veenhof, Klaas R.

1972 *Aspects of Old Assyrian Trade and its Terminology.* Leiden.

1982 "The Old Assyrian Merchants and Their Relations with the Native Population of Anatolia," in Hans-Jörg Nissen and Johannes Renger, eds., *Mesopotamien und seine Nachbarn.* Berlin.

2010 "The Interpretation of Paragraphs **t** and **u** of the Code of Hammurabi," in Yayia Hazirlayan and Sevket Dönmez, eds., *DUB.SAR É.DUB.BA.A: Studies Presented in Honour of Veysel Donbaz.* Istanbul 283–294.

Veenhof, Klaas R., ed.

1986 *Cuneiform Archives and Libraries* (CRRIA 30) Istanbul.

Verboven K. , K. Vandorpe and V. Chankowski, eds.

2008 *Pistoi dia tèn technèn. Bankers, Loans and Archives in the Ancient World. Studies in Honour of Raymond Bogaert* (Studia Hellenistica 44) Leuven.

Vernant, J.–P.

1983 *Myth and Thought Among the Greeks.* New York.

Versnel, H. S.

1970 *Triumphus: An Inquiry into the Origin, Development and Meaning of the Roman Triumph.* Leiden.

von Dassow, Eva

2013 "Piecing Together the Song of Release," *JCS* 65: 127–165.

Walters, S. D.

1970 *Water for Larsa: An Old Babylonian archive dealing with Irrigation.* New Haven.

Walther, A.

1917 *Das altbabylonische Gerichtswesen* (Leipziger Semitistische Studien 6) Leipzig: Hinrichs.

Weinfeld, Moise

1972 *Deuteronomy and the Deuteronomic School.* Oxford.

1982 "'Justice and Righteousness' in Ancient Israel against the Background of 'Social Reforms' in the Ancient Near East," in Hans-Jörg Nissen and Johannes Renger, eds., *Mesopotamien und seine Nachbarn*. Berlin 490–519.

1985 "Freedom Proclamations in Egypt and in the Ancient Near East," in Sarah Israelit-Groll, *Pharaonic Egypt, the Bible and Christianity*. Jerusalem.

Weiss, Harvey

1986 *The Origin of Cities in Dry-Farming Syria and Mesopotamia in the Third Millennium BC.* Guilford, Conn.

Wensinck, A. J.

1923 "The Semitic New Year and the Origin of Eschatology," *Acta Orientalia* 1: 158–199.

Westbrook, Raymond

1985a "Biblical and Cuneiform Law Codes," *Revue biblique* 92: 247–264.

1985b "The Price Factor in the Redemption of Land," *RIDA* 3rd sér. 32: 97–127.

1993 "Social Justice in the Ancient Near East" in K. D. Irani and M. Silver, *Social Justice in the Ancient World.*

Raymond Westbrook and Roger D. Woodard,

1990 "The Edict of Tudhaliya IV," *JAOS* 110: 641–659.

Westenholz, Aage

1975 *Literary and Lexical Texts and the Earliest Administrative Documents from Nippur.* Malibu.

Whittow, Mark

2009 "Early Medieval Byzantium and the End of the Ancient World," *Journal of Agrarian Change* 9: 134–153

Wilhelm, Gernot

2012 "Ein Konflikt zwischen König und Ältestenversammlung in Ebla," in Gernot Wilhelm ed., *Organization, Representation, and Symbols of Power in the Ancient Near East. Proceedings of the 54th Rencontre Assyriologique Internationale, Würzburg, 20–25 July 2008.* Winona Lake, Ind. 155–166.

2013 "The Dispute on Manumission at Ebla: Why Does the Stormgod Descend to the Netherworld?" *RA* 107: 187–191.

Wilson, John A.

1936 "Illuminating the Thrones at the Egyptian Jubilee," *JAOS* 56: 293–296.

Wise, Michael O., Martin G. Abegg, Jr. and Edward Cook

1996 *The Dead Sea Scrolls: A New Translation.* New York: HarperOne.

Wray, Randall

2004 *Credit and State Theories of Money: The Contributions of A. Mitchell Innes.* Edward Elgar.

Wunsch, Cornelia

2002 "Debt, Interest, Pledge and Forfeiture in the Neo-Babylonian and Early Achaemenid Period: The Evidence from Private Archives," in M. Hudson and M. Van De Mieroop, *Debt and Economic Renewal* 221–255.

Yamauchi, Edwin M.

1980 "Two Reformers Compared," in Gary Rendsburg *et al.*, eds., *The Bible World: Essays in Honor of Cyrus H. Gordon.* New York: 269–292.

Yaron, Reuven

1988 [1969] *The Laws of Eshnunna*, 2nd ed. Jerusalem–Leiden.

Yoffee, Norman

1977 *The Economic Role of the Crown in the Old Babylonian Period* . Malibu.

1979 "The Decline and Rise of Mesopotamian Civilization: An Ethno-Archaeological Perspective on the Evolution of Social Complexity," *American Antiquity* 44: 5–35.

1981 *Explaining Trade in Ancient Western Asia* (MANE 2/2) Malibu.

Young, Dwight

1977 "The Merchant at Nuzi," *Iraq* 39: 171–189.

1984 "Land Tenure and Transfer of Land at Nuzi (XV–XIV Century B.C.)," in Tarif Khalidi, ed., *Land Tenure and Social Transformation in the Middle East.* Beirut.

1987 "Aspects of Ceremonial Exchange in the Near East during the Late Second Millennium BC," in T. C. Champion, ed., *Center and Periphery* 57–65.

1988 "A Mathematical Approach to Certain Dynastic Spans in the Sumerian King List," *JNES* 47: 123–129.

1991 "The Incredible Regnal Spans of Kish I in the Sumerian King List," *JNES* 50: 23–35.

Zettler, Richard

1984 "The Ur III Inanna Temple at Nippur," PhD. dissertation, University of Chicago.

1992 *The Ur III Temple of Inanna at Nippur.* Berlin.

Illustration credits

Figure 1: Liberty Bell, opposite Independence Hall, Philadelphia, commissioned in 1752. Public domain. Figure 2: Portraits of the lawgivers in the House Chamber of the U.S. Capitol. Drawing, based on https://www.aoc.gov/sites/default/files/chamber_map_relief-portrait-plaques-lawgivers_aoc_0.png. Figure 3: Layout of the Great Isaiah scroll from Qumran. Depiction based on a Faksimile. Figure 4: 11QMelchizedeq scroll, based on faksimile. Figure 5: Autograph of Händel's *Messiah*, British Library, https://commons.wikimedia.org/wiki/File:Worthy-is-the-lamb.jpg. Figure 6: Hadrian coin, struck at Rome, 120–122 AD, depicting Hadrian himself or a lictor applying a torch to a heap of documents symbolizing the debts being cancelled. Own photograph. Figure 7: Semantic layers attached to the English verbs *shall/should*. Figure 8: Standard of Ur, War side, c. 2600 BC. British Museum. Public domain. Figure 9: Clay tablet showing a map of canals and irrigation systems to the west of the Euphrates in Southern Mesopotamia. Schøyen Collection, Old Babylonian period. https://www.schoyencollection.com/24-smaller-collections/maps/map-irrigation-ms-3196. Figure 10: Votiv plaque depicting Ur-Nanshe, énsi of Lagash. Louvre, Paris. Public domain; photo by Marie-Lan Nguyen at https://commons.wikimedia.org/w/index.php?curid=54528. Figure 11: The Ur-Nanshe dynasty of Lagash and its successors. Source: Oates 1979: 199. Figure 12: Detail from the Stele of the Vultures, c. 2450 BC. Sumerian phalanx. Limestone, Louvre, Paris. Édouard de Sarzec, *Découvertes en Chaldée*. Paris: Leroux, 1884–1912, vol. 2, pl. 48. Public domain. http://digital.library.stonybrook.edu/cdm/ref/collection/amar/id/118692. Figure 13: Detail from the Stele of the Vultures, c. 2450 BC. Vultures. See Figure 12. Figure 14: Enmetena inscription AO 24414. Louvre, Paris. Depiction based on Lambert 1972: 3. Figure 15: Enannatum, c. 2420 BC. British Museum. Public domain. Photo by Osama Shukir Muhammed Amin https://commons.wikimedia.org/wiki/File:The_name_of_Enannatum_I,_ruler_or_king_of_Lagash_is_mentioned_in_this_inscribed_cuneiform_text._Detail_of_a_stone_plaque._Circa_2420_BCE._From_Girsu,_Iraq._The_British_Museum,_London.jpg Figure 16: Clay cone of the Urukagina reform text. Louvre. Paris. Public domain. https://commons.wikimedia.org/wiki/File:Clay_Cone_-_Louvre_-_AO3149.jpg Figure 17: Head of an Akkadian ruler, probably Sargon or Naram-Sin. Public domain. https://commons.wikimedia.org/wiki/File:Sargon_of_Akkad.jpg based on Encyclopedia Britannica Online. Figure 18: Akkadian dynasty. Figure 19: Ur-Baba dynasty. Figure 20: Gudea of Lagash. Louvre, Paris. Public domain. Photograph by https://commons.wikimedia.org/wiki/File:Gudea_of_Lagash_Girsu.jpg Figure 21: Ur III dynasty. Figure 22: Specimen of the Laws of Ur-Namma, Schøyen collection. Public domain. https://www.schoyencollection.com/law/sumerian/ur-nammu-ms-2064. Figure 23: Isin dynasty. Chronology of dynastic rulers based on J. A. Brinkman, in Oppenheim 1972. Figure 24: Trade routes through Anatolia. Drawing based on Larsen 2015. Figure 25: Chronology of rulers of the Larsa dynasty. Figure 26: Chronology of rulers of the first dynasty from Babylon. Figure 27: Stele with the Laws of Hammurapi. Louvre, Paris. Public domain. https://commons.wikimedia.org/wiki/File:P1050763_Louvre_code_Hammurabi_face_rwk.jpg. Figure 28: Hammurapi before the sun god Shamash. Top of the stele. Figure 29: De-urbanization of Babylonia in the Kassite period. Figure 30: Etching by Caspar Luyken in Christoph Weigel, Regensburg 1697. Public domain. Figure 31: Jesus expels the moneylenders from the Temple, by El Greco, c. 1600. Minneapolis Institute of Art. Public domain. https://commons.wikimedia.org/wiki/File:El_Greco_Christ_Driving_the_Money_Changers_from_the_Temple.jpg. Figure 32: Leonhard Kern, *The Vision of Ezekiel*, c. 1640–1650. Berlin, Bode-Museum. Public domain, https://commons.wikimedia.org/wiki/File:The_Vision_of_Ezekiel,_by_Leonhard_Kern,_Schwäbisch_Hall,_c._1640-1650,_alabaster_-_Bode-Museum_-_DSC03416.jpg. Figure 33: Albrecht Dürer, *Geiz* (*avarice*), 1507. Vienna, Kunsthistorisches Museum. Public domain. https://commons.wikimedia.org/wiki/File:Albrecht_D%C3%BCrer_004.jpg. Figure 34: Nemesis, restorer of cosmic order. Detail of an epitaph for Johann Philipp Bethmann-Hollweg by B. Thorvaldsen. Rome, 1813–1832. Liebieghaus, Frankfurt/M. Public domain. https://commons.wikimedia.org/wiki/File:Thorvaldsen_Epitaph_Bethmann-Hollweg_Liebieghaus.jpg. Figure 35: Summa on the Codex of Iustinian. Public domain. Bodleian Library MS. Canon. Misc. 416 fol. 001r. https://iiif.bodleian.ox.ac.uk/iiif/viewer/17c212fc-ea59-4dca-b2b9-4e524cf05a86#?c=0&m=0&s=0&cv=0&r=0&xywh=-1997%2C-234%2C6781%2C4678. Figure 36: Emperor Justinian. Public domain. https://commons.wikimedia.org/wiki/File:Meister_von_San_Vitale_in_Ravenna.jpg. Figure 37: The supporters of Leo Phokas abandon him and seek clemency from Romanos Lekapenos. History of Ioannes Scylitzes. Unknown artist, 13th-century. Public domain. https://commons.wikimedia.org/wiki/File:Leo_Phokas%27_supporters_surrender_to_Romanos_Lekapenos.jpg Figure 38: Michael Psellos and his student MichaelVII Dukas. Codex 234, f. 245a. Mount Athos, Pantokrator Monastery. Public domain. https://commons.wikimedia.org/wiki/File:Michael_Psellos.jpg Figure 39: Miniature of Emperor Basil II in triumphal garb, exemplifying the Imperial Crown handed down by Angels. Psalter of Basil II (Psalter of Venice), Ms. gr. 17, fol. 3 r. Public domain. References: Paul Stephenson: https://commons.wikimedia.org/wiki/File:Basileios_II,_BNM,_MS._gr._17_Fol._3r.jpg Figure 40: Conquest of Constantinople by the Crusaders in 1204. 15th century miniature. https://commons.wikimedia.org/wiki/File:ConquestOfConstantinopleByTheCrusadersIn1204.jpg

Lightning Source UK Ltd.
Milton Keynes UK
UKHW022028100619
344168UK00004BA/28/P